Cognitive Behavioral Therapy: Techniques for Retraining Your Brain

Jason M. Satterfield, Ph.D.

THE
GREAT
COURSES®

PUBLISHED BY:

THE GREAT COURSES
Corporate Headquarters
4840 Westfields Boulevard, Suite 500
Chantilly, Virginia 20151-2299
Phone: 1-800-832-2412
Fax: 703-378-3819
www.thegreatcourses.com

Jason M. Satterfield, Ph.D.
Professor of Clinical Medicine
University of California, San Francisco

Professor Jason M. Satterfield is Professor of Clinical Medicine, Director of Social and Behavioral Sciences, and Director of Behavioral Medicine in the Division of General Internal Medicine at the University of California, San Francisco (UCSF). He received his B.S. in Brain Sciences from the Massachusetts Institute of Technology with a special minor in Psychology from Harvard University. He completed his Ph.D. in Clinical Psychology at the University of Pennsylvania (Penn), where he worked with Dr. Martin Seligman on cognitive models of bias, risk taking, depression, and aggression. Professor Satterfield was trained as a cognitive behavioral therapist at Penn's Center for Cognitive Therapy under the supervision of Drs. Aaron T. Beck, Judith Beck, and Robert DeRubeis. Professor Satterfield completed his internship and postdoctoral fellowship at UCSF at San Francisco General Hospital with Drs. Ricardo Muñoz, Jeanne Miranda, and Jacqueline Persons in the Department of Psychiatry. In 1996, Professor Satterfield accepted a position in the UCSF Division of General Internal Medicine to focus on the intersection of psychological factors and physical health.

Professor Satterfield's clinical work has included adaptations of cognitive behavioral therapy for underserved, medically ill populations and psychological interventions for patients with serious chronic illness. He currently directs the UCSF Behavioral Medicine Unit, which integrates mental and behavioral health services into adult primary care.

Professor Satterfield's research and educational interests include integrating social and behavioral science in medical education, disseminating and implementing evidence-based behavioral practices in primary care settings, and developing educational strategies to address health-care disparities. His current projects include using digital technology to facilitate behavior change, supporting interprofessional education, promoting social and emotional intelligence for physicians, developing screening and brief interventions for substance abuse, and integrating the social and behavioral sciences in medical school and medical residency curricula. Professor Satterfield is a member of the Behavioral and Social Science Consortium for Medical Education and the Council for Training in Evidence-Based Behavioral Practice, both of which are funded by the National Institutes of Health.

Professor Satterfield's book *A Cognitive-Behavioral Approach to the Beginning of the End of Life* and the accompanying patient workbook, *Minding the Body*, were recognized as Self-Help Books of Merit by the Association for Behavioral and Cognitive Therapies. He also is the associate editor of the best-selling textbook *Behavioral Medicine: A Guide for Clinical Practice* (4th edition). His special clinical publications include treatment models for cognitive behavioral therapy, treatment adaptations to improve cultural competence, and a transdisciplinary model to promote evidence-based behavioral practices in medicine, including interventions for smoking, weight management, drug abuse, and chronic disease management. Professor Satterfield is coauthor of a recent report detailing the role of behavioral science in medicine, and he served on the Behavioral and Social Science Subcommittee that revised the Medical College Admission Test (MCAT)—work that was featured in the *New England Journal of Medicine* and *The New York Times*.

Professor Satterfield currently directs the Social and Behavioral Sciences curriculum for all UCSF medical students and internal medicine residents. He has been nominated for multiple teaching awards at UCSF, including the Robert H. Crede Award for Excellence in Teaching and the Kaiser Award for Excellence in Teaching, and he received the Academy of Medical Educators Cooke Award for the Scholarship of Teaching and Learning. He is often competitively selected to teach at national conferences for a wide variety of health professionals, including physicians, nurses, social workers, and psychologists.

Professor Satterfield grew up in Middle Tennessee and was the first in his family to attend college. After living in Boston and Philadelphia for school, he moved in 1994 to San Francisco. He is an avid traveler and enjoys a large circle of friends and family. ∎

Table of Contents

Table of Contents

Table of Contents

Disclaimer

This series of lectures is intended to increase your understanding of the emotional and social lives of children and/or adults and is for educational purposes only. It is not a substitute for, nor does it replace, professional medical advice, diagnosis, or treatment of mental health conditions.

However, these lectures are not designed for use as medical references to diagnose, treat, or prevent medical or mental health illnesses or trauma, and neither The Teaching Company nor the lecturer is responsible for your use of this educational material or its consequences. Furthermore, participating in this course does not create a doctor-patient or therapist-client relationship. The information contained in these lectures is not intended to dictate what constitutes reasonable, appropriate, or best care for any given mental health issue and does not take into account the unique circumstances that define the health issues of the viewer. If you have questions about the diagnosis, treatment, or prevention of a medical condition or mental illness, you should consult your personal physician or other mental health professional. The opinions and positions provided in these lectures reflect the opinions and positions of the relevant lecturer and do not necessarily reflect the opinions or positions of The Teaching Company or its affiliates.

The Teaching Company expressly DISCLAIMS LIABILITY for any DIRECT, INDIRECT, INCIDENTAL, SPECIAL, OR CONSEQUENTIAL DAMAGES OR LOST PROFITS that result directly or indirectly from the use of these lectures. In states that do not allow some or all of the above limitations of liability, liability shall be limited to the greatest extent allowed by law.

Cognitive Behavioral Therapy:
Techniques for Retraining Your Brain

Scope:

Cognitive behavioral therapy (CBT) is a well-tested collection of practical techniques for managing moods and modifying undesirable behaviors through self-awareness, critical analysis, and taking steps toward gradual, goal-oriented change. CBT illuminates the links between thoughts, emotions, behaviors, and physical health and uses those connections to develop concrete plans for self-improvement. Built on a solid foundation of neurological and behavioral research, CBT is not simply about treating mental illness. It is an approach almost anyone can use for promoting greater mental health and improving one's quality of life.

In this course, you will learn about CBT in theory and in practice, through an in-depth discussion of techniques and therapy sessions. You will be able to take on the role of medical student, physician, psychologist, and patient as you learn about the methods used in CBT, its practical applications, and what goes on in a therapy session. You also will learn some practical tools you can use to evaluate your own needs and develop a tailored approach to reaching your goals.

We begin where therapy begins, by setting some goals. First, we will set the goals for the course: an understanding of how and why CBT works and how it might work for you. Then, we will address the importance of setting goals for yourself within the CBT framework and how to make those goals realistic and achievable. Next, we will examine how to formulate a plan to achieve those goals, based on your own individual circumstances.

From there, we will discuss a variety of common concerns that CBT can help you address. Some of these issues fall under the traditional rubric of mental health, such as anxiety, depression, and trauma. Others you might think of as everyday stressors, such as conflicts at work or the loss of a loved one. Others you might have regarded as medical issues, such as insomnia, weight management, or chronic pain. No matter how the difficulty came about, CBT can be a powerful part of better understanding the concern and enhancing the healing process. Unlike other forms of psychotherapy, CBT places the power in the hands of the patient, who learns and practices an explicit skill set that lasts long after therapy might end.

CBT comes in several varieties, and we will address which methods are most appropriate for different situations. We will discuss the roles that our families, friends, communities, and other forms of social support can play in the CBT process. We will examine some of the tools on the cutting edge of CBT— from self-help smartphone apps to social networks—that are offering new ways to engage in the therapy. We also will discuss how to assess these and other self-help tools to separate the good from the useless (or even harmful).

Finally, we will ask the most important questions: Is self-help for me, or should I seek professional help? How can I find quality materials or a quality therapist? How can I get started? How can I help someone I love get started? Knowing when you can manage on your own, when to seek professional help, how to find those resources, and how to use them effectively are primary learning goals of this course. ■

Cognitive Behavioral Foundations
Lecture 1

T he central question of this course is determining what we can change and what we can't. In either case, there are things you can do to lessen suffering and improve your quality of life. Sometimes that will mean following a program to genuinely change something about yourself, but many times it will mean learning how to accept or even value things about yourself or your world that you simply can't change. The goals of this course are to present the science of how we change—of how we can improve or even treat ourselves—and to leave you with a toolbox of practical, evidence-based strategies you can apply on your own whenever you need them.

The Science of Change

- To talk about the science of change, we first have to decide what level of analysis we want to use. We can talk about the biological (medicine and neuroscience), the psychological (emotions and cognitions), or the social (relationships in our lives, including significant others, communities, and even societies).

- We'll talk about psychotherapy research. How do we know what is evidence-based? How do we know what works for which particular problem or disorder? We want to look at what level of change we're interested in. Are we trying to change an individual? Are we trying to change a couple? Are we trying to change a family, or even a community or society?

- Whenever we talk about change, it's important that we reflect on our own personal philosophies or ideologies of change. What is your philosophy of mind? Can we change who we are fundamentally? Can we change our cognitions, emotions, and behaviors?

- Cognitive behavioral therapy (CBT) has its own ideology—its own preferences. It's grounded in Western empiricism, and it holds up the value of rationality. It holds up the power of the scientific method. It's not saying that emotions or passions are bad or wrong and that we want to push those down. It's really about striking a balance between rationality and passion or emotion.

- For our toolbox, we're going to take a CBT focus. We're going to look at the underlying foundational theories in more than 30 years of science to tell us which tools work. We're going to present specific sets of tools and skills to facilitate change when change is possible. That theory is going to help us see the complex interrelationships between cognitions, behaviors, and emotions—the CBT triangle. We're going to learn that if we change one in that complex mix, we're probably going to change them all.

- The goal is for you to become your own CBT therapist. This is a form of self-help, because any form of self-improvement is a form of self-help. But there aren't any shortcuts or magic. The CBT process can be quite difficult; it takes practice and commitment. As you will learn, one of the key ideas of CBT is that we all view the world through a subjective lens. The same will be true for how you see this course.

Mental Health and Mental Illness

- We're going to break open and examine some ideas about mental health and mental illness. What does a person with mental illness look like? What does a person who is mentally healthy look like? In both categories, there is a great range of appearances, and there is no single prototype, but there is a lot of overlap between them. In fact, it might be the same person at different points in his or her life.

- It's important to realize that mental illness is common. In fact, one in four people will have a diagnosable mental illness at some point in their lives. It's hard to watch the news without hearing about school shooters, or post-traumatic stress disorder in combat veterans, or teen suicides, or depression, or burnout, or bullying. We need more attention to mental health, and we need to reduce the stigma of reaching out for help.

- Even though a person has a mental illness, he or she can still make an important contribution to society. An example is Marsha Linehan, a psychologist and world-renowned researcher who discovered dialectical behavior therapy, probably the only effective therapy known to help individuals with borderline personality disorder or parasuicidal behavior. She discovered the therapy because she struggled with the diagnosis herself.

- This course is about a psychotherapy—CBT—but it's not psychotherapy itself. And it doesn't take the place of treatment, should treatment be needed. We're going to look at mental illness, but this is also about promoting mental health.

- As we learn about how thoughts and behaviors influence emotions and motivations, you will be having thoughts about thoughts, and you will be having feelings about feelings. This course will trigger ideas, excitement, boredom, agreement, or even outrage. Use it as a real-world CBT opportunity to dig deeper to understand your response and to possibly control or change it.

Change

- Think of three things about yourself that you believe are unchangeable. For example, you might think of your race, your height (if you're an adult), and your gender. However, these things are not so simply unchangeable.

- What if you were to undergo genetic testing to determine your racial ancestry and you discovered that you're not entirely the race that you thought you were. You are still the same person, but maybe your perception of your race has changed.

- What about your height? You're fully grown when you're an adult, barring any sort of rare diseases, but we also know that we shrink as we age. In fact, we lose one to two inches of our height as we grow older.

- What about gender? It seems unchangeable on the surface—unless you consider sexual reassignment or sexual affirmation surgeries. The line between male and female is blurred when you consider the issue in more detail.

- But what if you were to think of things that can absolutely change? Things that you know if you roll up your sleeves and just put in enough effort, you can change them. You might think of things like, well, your social skills, you can change your relationships, or maybe you can change your beliefs, but we know that things like introversion and extroversion are very difficult to change and they very much affect our capacity to learn and to use social skills. You can certainly end your relationships, but you may recreate the exact same relationship dynamics with another person.

- Change is complicated. It's not just an internal, individual process. We also want to look at external factors. And even if you can't change something, you might be able to change the way you think about it or react to it.

Therapy and the Brain
- When we talk about change, what is it that we're changing? We talk about changing our mind all the time, but what does that really mean? On a basic level, we are biological beings, so when we talk about changing ourselves, we're on some level talking about changing our brains and maybe our bodies, too. These individual changes might trigger changes in others or changes in our environment in a complex, bidirectional, iterative system.

- A helpful model to think about this is called the biopsychosocial model, which was originally developed by George Engel in the late 1970s. To understand the biopsychosocial model, imagine a Venn diagram with three circles: one for the biological, one for the social, and one for the psychological. Some factors might reside in just one circle, some might reside in two circles, and some might be right in the center, including biological, psychological, and social factors.

The Biopsychosocial Model

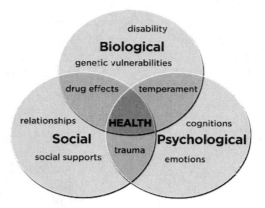

- Thinking about CBT, the psychological circle comes to mind. We've talked about cognitions and emotions, but the social circle might also come to mind as we consider relationships and social supports.

- There are a number of different pathways or mechanisms that might help change behavior, emotions, or relationships. One way is pharmacotherapy. There are a number of psychoactive agents that can reach in biologically and change an individual's mood, which will change cognition and probably behavior, too.

- In addition, there are a limited number of neurosurgeries that would influence the way an individual feels. For example, for severe obsessive-compulsive disorder, there is a brain surgery that can help those individuals.

- Another way to help change behavior is psychotherapy. CBT is a special type of psychotherapy. There's also self-help. There are some CBT tools that you can use on your own.

- Just as our brains can be exercised, or behavior-trained, to improve cognitive function, we can also train our brains to improve motivation, management of emotions, and our interpersonal skills.

- There has been research using brain scans, PET scans, and functional MRIs that analyzes whether or not there are changes in brain activation as a consequence of someone engaging in psychotherapy. The psychotherapy most commonly studied in these research studies is CBT for depression and CBT for anxiety. The research shows notable changes in the patterns of activation.

- A study conducted by Kimberly Goldapple analyzed CBT versus an antidepressant called Paxil. The patients in both groups became much less depressed after engaging in CBT or taking Paxil. In fact, they were considered remitted from their depressive episodes. But in terms of changes in brain activation, the patterns were different depending on what kind of treatment the individual received. For CBT, there was more hippocampal activation. For Paxil, there was more prefrontal activation.

- It's very interesting to think that at some point in the future, we might not just diagnosis mental illness, but we will diagnose dysfunction in patterns of brain activation. We'll be able to tailor, or maybe personalize, the kind of psychotherapy or pharmacotherapy an individual would get based on what those activation deficiencies might be. The goal is to push the field of psychiatry along so that we can get to the point of personalized psychiatry, but the field is still somewhat murky and contradictory.

- Although the brain effects are clear—the talking cure changes your brain—we don't have a consistent explanation for how that happens. This implies that our social interactions, our relationships with each other or with the therapist, have the power to change our brains. Schools, seminars, trainings, and educational videos can facilitate a sort of rewiring as we learn new skills.

- We know that therapy can cause changes, and we know how particular areas of the brain are activated and that this may cause beneficial effects in emotion, behavior, or other factors. But does any type of therapy do this? Some would say yes.

- There is a common set of nonspecific factors that make therapy beneficial. Some of these benefits include the therapeutic alliance, empathy, or a corrective emotional experience. But CBT goes above and beyond these benefits. You get the specific factors, but you also get new mood management and life skills.

- Medications can also cause changes in brain activation, but we should remember that we don't have to intervene on that level unless we choose to do so. For example, with cardiovascular disease, we can use diet, exercise, and nutrition, or we can use pharmacotherapy, such as statins for cholesterol—or you can choose to combine them. The decision is partly dependent on where you are in terms of risk or severity.

- Change of some sort is always possible, regardless of age or background, but it might not be the change you are expecting. Learning how to assess your situation and select an appropriate tool is a vital skill.

Suggested Reading

Baron and Kenny, "The Moderator-Mediator Variable Distinction in Social Psychological Research."

Frewen, Dozois, and Lanius, "Neuroimaging Studies of Psychological Interventions for Mood and Anxiety Disorders."

Goldapple, et al, "Modulation of Cortical-Limbic Pathways in Major Depression."

Goldapple, Segal, Garson, et al, "Modulation of Cortical-Limbic Pathways in Major Depression."

Kazdin, "Mediators and Mechanisms of Change in Psychotherapy Research."

1. What preexisting beliefs or assumptions do you have about psychotherapy? Where did you pick them up? What influence have they had on your efforts to maximize your mental health?

2. Traditional psychoanalysts criticize CBT as being shallow and superficial. What response do you think a cognitive therapist might have?

Cognitive Behavioral Foundations
Lecture 1—Transcript

PROFESSOR SATTERFIELD: Carol had always been shy. Even as a small child, she was the kind to always cling to her mother's leg, but now that she's 30 years old, she's sick and tired of being so anxious in social situations. She's tired of being overlooked; she's tired of being single; and she's tired of missing out on all the fun. Carol is determined to change, but can she?

At heart, Michael, a 50-year-old man, is a thoughtful old soul who genuinely cares about people; just don't make him angry. The problem is that nearly everything sets him off. He knows his fury is way out of proportion, but he can't seem to stop it from happening. He's bought a few self-help books; he's started going to the gym, but he wonders if he's just an angry person and if self-help is a big waste of time and money.

Maria, a 70-year-old woman, is tired and worried all the time. Her husband of 45 years began showing signs of Alzheimer's dementia nearly eight years ago and has gradually been slipping away from her more and more every month. She's now afraid to leave him alone and has to manage everything on her own. She's grown quite depressed and wonders if there's anything she can do to cope more effectively.

Welcome to our course on cognitive behavioral therapy. We're going to tackle many difficult questions, but perhaps none more difficult or important than what we can change and what we can't. When should we roll up our sleeves and give it another go? When is it a matter of just applying more elbow grease or a clever new technique or program? And when should we start working on our ability to accept things the way they are?

Socrates tells us, "The unexamined life is not worth living." We're admonished to know thyself. From a very young age we're told stories about the Little Engine That Could. You can do anything if you set your mind to it, right? Well, sort of. Over the next 24 lectures, we'll repeatedly come back to the question of what we can change and what we can't. But in either case, I hope to show you that there are things you can do to lessen suffering and improve your quality of life. Sometimes that means following a program to genuinely change something about yourself. But many times it will mean learning how to accept, or dare I say, even value things about yourself or your world that you simply can't change.

My goals are really twofold. First I hope to present the science of how we change, of how we can improve or even treat ourselves. Second, I want to leave you with the toolbox of practical evidence-based strategies you can apply on your own whenever you need them. So first let's talk a bit about the science of change, and to talk about the science, we first have to decide what level of analysis we want. We can talk about the biological; we could talk about the psychological; or we could talk about the social. Of course, for the biological we might talk about medicine; we might talk about neuroscience. For psychology, we might talk about emotions and cognitions. For the social, we might talk about the relationships in our lives, our significant others, our communities, or even societies.

We'll talk about psychotherapy research. How do we know what's evidence based? How do we know what works for what particular problem or disorder? We want to look at what level of change we're interested in. Are we trying to change an individual? Are we trying to change a couple? Are we trying to change a family, or even a community or a society?

Now, whenever we talk about change, it's important that we reflect on our own personal philosophies or ideologies of change. What is your philosophy of mind? Can we change who we are fundamentally? Can we change our cognitions, emotions, and behaviors? Now, CBT has its own ideology, its own preferences. It's very much grounded in Western empiricism, and it really holds up the value of rationality. It holds up the power of the scientific method. Now, it's not saying that emotions or passions are bad or wrong, and we want to push those down. It's really about finding balance. Of course this tension between rationality and passion our emotion is certainly not new. In fact, the Greek and Stoic philosophers talked about Apollonian versus Dionysian perspectives on life and their theories of mind.

Now, for our toolbox, we're going to take a CBT, a cognitive behavioral therapy, focus, and we're going to look at the underlying foundational theories in over 30 years of science to tell us what tools work. We're going to present specific sets of tools and skills to facilitate change when change is possible. Now, that theory is going to help us to see the complex inter-relationships between cognitions, behaviors, and emotions, and we're going to see if we reach into that complex mix and we change one, we're probably going to change them all.

Now, my personal goal is to give CBT away. I want to teach other people how to become their own CBT therapist. Is this a form of self-help? Well, sure it is. Any form of self-improvement is a form of self-help. But there's really no shortcuts, and there's really no magic. This can be quite difficult, and I think it takes practice, and it takes commitment.

As you'll learn, one of the key ideas of CBT is that we all view the world through a subjective lens. The same will be true for how you see this course and for how I teach it. My lens comes from clinical psychology, first starting in neuroscience at MIT, then moving to psychology at the University of Pennsylvania, where I was fortunate to learn CBT from Aaron Beck, Rob DeRubeis, and Marty Seligman. Now, from there I made my trek across the country to San Francisco, where I first worked at San Francisco General Hospital, and there I learned a great deal about serious psychopathology, about substance use disorder, and the powerful social determinants of health, especially poverty. I ended up at the University of California in the Division of General Internal Medicine, leading clinical research and educational programs, looking at integrated behavioral health and primary care. So we'll be able to bring in a number of different sciences and a number of different levels of practice.

Now, the other thing I would like us to do is to break open and examine some ideas about mental health and mental illness. I want you to picture a person with a mental illness, just in your mind's eye I want you to give them a shape, a size, give them a gender, give the person a race. What are they wearing? How well kempt are they? What does that person look like, a person with mental illness? Now I want you to picture a person who's mentally healthy, someone that has good mental health. What does that person look like? And as before, give them a shape, a height, a size, a gender, a race, an appearance. What does a mentally healthy person look like? Now, obviously in both of those categories, there is a great range of appearances, and there's no one prototype, but I hope you can hold up those two images and see that there's an awful lot of overlap between them. In fact, it might be same person at different points in their life.

So why do we want to do this? Well, I think there's a lot of stigma, and it's important that we remember that mental illness is common. In fact, one in four of us, or 25 percent of us, will have a diagnosable mental illness at some point in our lives. Just think about the recent news; it's hard to open the paper without reading about school shooters, or a post-traumatic stress disorder in combat veterans, or teen suicides, or depression, or burnout, or bullying. We need more attention to mental health, and we need to reduce the stigma of reaching out for help. It's important to remember that even though a person has a mental illness, that they can still make an important contribution to society.

A couple of examples come to mind. The first is Marsha Linehan, a psychologist and world-renowned researcher who founded a kind of therapy called dialectical behavior therapy, probably the only effective therapy known to help individuals with borderline personality disorder or parasuicidal behavior. How did she come up with the therapy? She struggled with the diagnosis herself. Or a young patient that came to me who was in the proverbial gutter using IV drugs, with HIV aids, with depression, and feeling suicidal. He's now the head of a top nursing training program, and has founded a number of clinics for homeless health care. We can look at celebrities. What about Betty Ford? What about Buzz Aldrin, Beethoven, Terry Bradshaw, Marlon Brando? And the list goes on and on.

Now I want to share a few caveats. This course is about a psychotherapy— CBT. But it's not psychotherapy itself. And it doesn't take the place of treatment, should treatment be needed. We're going to look at mental illness. But this is also about promoting mental health. Essentially you get what you put into it. I think of it as very similar; if you decide you want to be more physically fit, you get a gym membership. But you still have to go, and you still have to do those exercises.

Now, we're going to cover a lot of different topics, but I think of it as sort of a sampler platter approach. You'll get a little taste of what might interest you, and hopefully we'll be able to direct you to websites and to readings, should you want to learn more. Now, as we learn about how thoughts and behaviors influence emotions and motivations, you will be having thoughts about thoughts, and you will be having feelings about feelings. This course will trigger ideas, excitement, boredom, agreement, or even outrage. It's all *grist for the mill*. It's cognition in action. Use it as a real-world CBT opportunity to dig deeper, to understand your response, and to possibly control or change it.

Now let's get back to change. I want you to think of three things that you believe are unchangeable, any three things that you think about yourself that you can't change. You might have come up with something like, you can't change your race. If you're an adult, you can't change your height, or you can't change your sex, or your gender. Simple, right?

Well, maybe not so simple. What if you were to send off one of those genetic tests that looks at your racial ancestry, and much to your surprise, you're not entirely the race that you thought you were. Are you the same person? Well, of course, but maybe your perception of your race has changed. What about your height? Well, of course you're full grown when you're an adult, barring any sort of rare diseases, but we also know that individuals shrink as we age. In fact, we lose one to two inches of our height as we grow older. But gender and sex, definitely not changeable. Well, unless you consider sexual reassignment or sexual affirmation surgeries. That line between gender, between male and female, is much more blurred than at any time before.

But what if you were to think about things that can absolutely change, things you know that if you roll up your sleeves and just put in enough effort, you can change them. You might think of things like, well, your social skills; you can change your relationships; or maybe you can change your beliefs. But we know that things like introversion and extroversion are very difficult to change, and they very much affect our capacity to learn and to use social skills. You can certainly end your relationships, but you may recreate the exact same relationship dynamics with another person. Terms of beliefs, just look at how polarized our country is in terms of political beliefs. Are those beliefs changeable? Maybe. It's really not so easy, and it's really not so cut and dry. Change is difficult, but remember that it isn't just an internal, individual process. We also want to look at external factors. And remember that even if you can't change something, you might be able to change the way you think about it or react to it.

Now, when we talk about change, what is it that we're changing? We talk about changing our mind all the time, but what does that really mean? Now, at base we are biological beings, so when we talk about changing ourselves, we're on some level talking about changing our brains, and maybe our bodies too. These individual changes may trigger changes in others or changes in our environment in a complex, bi-directional, iterative system.

Now, a helpful model to think about this is called the biopsychosocial model, originally developed by George Engel in the late 1970s. And to understand the biopsychosocial model, you really just need to imagine a Venn diagram with three circles. We have one circle for the biological, one circle for social, and one circle for psychological. Now, some factors might reside in just one circle, some may reside in two circles, and some might be right in the center, including biological, psychological, as well as social factors. Now, if we are to think about CBT, the psychological circle obviously comes to mind; we talk about cognitions and emotions. But the social circle might also come to mind as we talk about relationships and we talk about social supports.

Now, let's go back to Carol, our young woman who has a problem with social anxiety; or Michael, who's angry; or Maria, who's stressed and depressed. They hope to change behavior and emotions, and maybe relationships, presumably by changing their minds and their brains. But how? Well, there's a number of different pathways, or mechanisms, that might help them to change. There is pharmacotherapy; there are a number of psychoactive agents that can reach in biologically and change an individual's mood, which we know will change cognition, and probably change behavior too. There's a limited number of neurosurgeries that would influence the way an individual feels. For example, for severe obsessive-compulsive disorder, there is a brain surgery to help those individuals. You might look at psychotherapy, and that's primarily where we're going to focus. And we'll look at CBT, a special type of psychotherapy. There's also self-help, and we'll talk about some CBT tools that you can use on your own, or there is a spirituality, and we'll talk about third-wave therapies that have a more spiritual component.

Now, I would posit that just as our brains can be exercised or trained to improve cognitive function, we can also train our brains to improve motivation, management of emotions, and our interpersonal skills. But what does the research show us? Now, as of 2014, I was able to find 21 studies using brain scans, PET scans, and functional MRIs that looked at whether or not there were changes in brain activation as a consequence of someone engaging in psychotherapy. The psychotherapy most commonly studied in these different research studies was CBT for depression and CBT for anxiety. There were, without question, notable changes in the patterns of activation.

I'll mention just one of the earlier studies published in 2004 and published by Gold Apple. This was a study looking at CBT versus an antidepressant called Paxil. Now, the patients in both of these groups became much less depressed. In fact, they were considered remitted from their depressive episodes. But when you looked at changes in brain activation, the patterns were different depending on what kind of treatment the individual got. For CBT, there was more hippocampal activation, and for Paxil, there was more prefrontal activation.

It's really a very interesting idea to think that at some point in the future, that we might not just diagnose mental illness, but we will diagnose dysfunction in patterns of brain activation, and we'll be able to tailor, or maybe personalize, the kind of psychotherapy or pharmacotherapy an individual would get based on what those deficiencies might be. In a 2008 review done by Frewen, trying to push the field along so we can get to that point of personalized psychiatry, she finds that the field is still somewhat murky and contradictory, although the brain effects are clear: The talking cure changes your brain; we just don't have a consistent explanation for how that happens yet,

But I want you to think about some of the implications. It tells us that our social interactions, our relationships with each other or with a therapist have the power to change our brains. Schools, seminars, trainings, educational videos can facilitate a sort of rewiring as we learn new skills. Let's follow this line of reasoning a bit and think about the implications for psychotherapy.

Now, we know that therapy can cause changes in how particular areas of the brain are activated, and this may cause beneficial effects and emotion behavior or other factors. But does any type of therapy do this? Some would say, yes, absolutely. There are a common set of what they call nonspecific factors that make therapy beneficial. So this would be things like the therapeutic alliance, empathy, or providing what's called a corrective emotional experience, but in this course, we'll suggest that CBT goes above and beyond that.

You get those specific factors, but you also get new mood management and life skills. And sure, medications can also cause changes in brain activation, but we should remember that we don't have to intervene on that level unless we choose to do so. In fact, I think of the analogy of the prevention of cardiovascular disease. Now, with a cardiovascular disease, we can use diet, exercise, and nutrition, or we can use pharmacotherapies, such as statins for cholesterol. Or you can choose to combine them. The choice is really yours, and it's partly dependent on where you are in terms of risk or in terms of severity. We believe that change of some sort is always possible regardless of our age or background. But it might not be the change you are expecting. Learning how to assess your situation and select an appropriate tool is a vital skill. As Charles Darwin tells us, "It's not the strongest of the species that survives, nor the most intelligent, but the one most responsive to change."

So, let's start laying the foundation of our tool box of change. We're going to take a look at our first therapy vignette. Here you will see Carol the 30-year-old woman with social anxiety disorder, and she's learning the basics of CBT and the CBT triangle.

[VIGNETTE START]

PROFESSOR SATTERFIELD: OK. So what I wanted to do is a little bit more of teaching the foundations of cognitive behavioral therapy. And why don't you tell me, from just the limited experience you've had so far, how is it that cognitive behavior therapy works? Or why do they even call it cognitive behavioral therapy.

CAROL: I don't know.

PROFESSOR SATTERFIELD: Fair enough. Fair enough. So it's called cognitive behavioral. Clearly, ro artistic skill in coming up with this name. Cognitive behavioral therapy, because it's about cognitions and it's about behaviors. Cognitions are just a 1 the mental activity that we have—thoughts, beliefs, values, priorities, images, memories, all the mental activity. And behaviors are really things you do by yourself. Things you do at work, things you do at home. They can be social. They can be alone. So they're both fairly big buckets.

And we believe it works because of something called the CBT Triangle. And CBT is just Cognitive Behavioral Therapy. So up at the top of the triangle, we have thoughts. So when you're in a social situation, I would guess that you have certain thoughts come to mind. And we'll get to those in just a minute. But there are also behaviors. And those behaviors might be avoidance behavior. So staying at home and just spending time with your cats is a behavior. But going out and going to work is a behavior as well. And any guess what the third corner might be on that triangle?

CAROL: Feelings? Emotions?

PROFESSOR SATTERFIELD: Exactly. So emotions or feelings are down here. And they draw it as a triangle, because all of these are really arrows. One is connected to the other. So what that means, simply, is the way you think affects the behavioral choices that you make. The way you think affects the emotions that have.

But it works the other direction, too. So if you start off feeling fairly anxious, that's an emotion. You will have more anxious thoughts. So the way you feel affects the way you think. The way you feel is going to affect your behavioral choices.

You can also flip it the other way with behaviors. If you decide that you're going to call your sister, that's a behavior that might influence your mood. You might have a great conversation, and you feel better afterwards. It might influence the thoughts. So you might be talking about something that happened a few years ago, and you start having thoughts about it. So all of these are interconnected.

19

Now, that's good news, because it's really hard to reach in and change emotions. It's less hard to reach in and capture a thought or record a behavior, and then try to make some changes. So if these emotions are getting in the way of what you want in life—and for you, it's anxiety—we have two opportunities with behaviors and with thoughts to do something about it.

So cognitive behavioral therapy, we reach in. We want to capture the thoughts first, and then decide if we can change them. Because if we change them, it's going to change emotion. If we reach in behaviors, we're going to capture them first. We're going to try to change them. If we change them, we might change emotions, as well. So it gives us two pathways, really, try to change how a person's feeling.

[VIGNETTE END]

PROFESSOR SATTERFIELD: So, as we continue through the course, we will continue looking at case vignettes. We will continue education about CBT. We've just now started at the beginning, really, at the surface, the initial teaching about CBT, but you'll see from the top, we'll proceed down towards deeper, more complex cognitive structures and more complex levels of behavioral analysis.

I think, though, as we learn about CBT, it's important to keep in mind what I see as some of the special features of CBT in comparison to other kinds of psychotherapy. First, CBT is collaborative and transparent, and by *collaborative* I mean that the patient and the therapist join together in a partnership; they roll up their sleeves together; begin collecting data on the problem from the individual's real-world situations; they create a formulation; and then they develop a treatment plan together. It's all done together as a team. It's transparent because all of those steps, and the rationale for all of those steps, is made explicit. There's no magic happening behind the screen. It's all above board; it's all on the table. Remember our goal as a CBT therapist is to teach a patient to be his or her own CBT therapist. So you need to know how it works and why we did the things that we did for your treatment plan.

The second is that CBT is empirical. And here I don't just mean psychotherapy research and evidence about whether or not it works. They have coined a term called *collaborative empiricism*. Now, we've talked about the collaborative part, but the empirical part is that we'll come up with a hypothesis, and idea, of what makes Michael angry, or what makes Maria depressed, or what makes Carol socially anxious. But it's only a hypothesis. We then have to test out that hypothesis in the real world, usually by giving homework assignments. So the patient will have their hypothesis; they'll have their homework assignment, then go out to test it out to see if it works. If it works, great. We'll go to the next step. But it if doesn't work, again, it's *grist for the mill*. We'll roll up our sleeves; we'll figure out what happened; and we'll come up with the next hypothesis or the next homework assignment.

The next feature is that CBT is time limited. There is and end point. Now, it varies depending on the individual, sometimes on the insurance company, but it usually ranges from between 12 to, say, 24 sessions, depending, again, on resources, severity, and what the treatment goals might be. It is skills focused. Again, no magic behind the curtain; we're going to teach an individual skills that they can practice in the real world, come back and talk about obstacles or challenges, they will hone those skills and continue practicing until they feel that they have mastered those skills.

It's also symptom focused. So there's oftentimes a number of different symptom measures for depression, for anxiety, for positive emotion, for whatever the issue might be. We'll want to get a baseline, but then we'll want to reassess that individual over time as they're using those skills to see if those scores, those symptoms, are improving.

CBT is also focused on the present. So we won't sit someone down and say, "Tell me about your childhood. Tell me about your relationship with your parents." We might get to that point if it's relevant to treatment, but we're going to start with where you are now, how you feel now, and what's happening in your life right now that brought you into treatment. We're going to start from the top, and we're going to work our way down. We start with the CBT triangle. We start with conceptualizations or formulations of everyday events, and then we start working our way deeper to understand the individuals' personality, and maybe their relationship dynamics.

Now, I do want to say, even though there's this focus on empiricism and on evidence and on hypothesis testing, all of this language and words used in science, it doesn't mean that we don't value the therapeutic relationship. In fact, that connection is crucial. If you're going to go through the difficult work of tackling these problems that you may have been working with for years with limited success, you're going to need a partner that you feel very safe with, that you trust, that you know is absolutely, 100 percent on your side.

So, where we'll go next with Carol is to have her start collecting data on herself, on the building blocks of behavior and cognitions by doing something called self-monitoring. Now, this can be done in a sort of diary or journal, or you can use a structured checklist that gives you examples of different activities or social contacts or cognitions. Now, if you're interested in those checklists, I would recommend three that were developed by Ricardo Muñoz, the chief psychologist at San Francisco General Hospital, and now an emeritus professor at UCSF. If you're interested in finding those instruments, I would encourage you to use our friend, Google. You just need to type in Ricardo *Muñoz*, *CBT*, and *manual*. You'll see that there are two manuals that pop up, one published by the RAND Corporation for a study he did in collaboration with them, and the other links to San Francisco General Hospital and UCSF, bot available freely for download.

So, if you wanted to give yourself some homework, you might want to review the clip about the triangle. You might want to draw your own triangle in a therapy journal. You might want to think about examples from your own life, about activating events and what were the emotions; what were the cognitions; what were the behaviors. Or you might want to use those checklists that you've downloaded from the web.

So next I wanted to introduce a new feature in this particular lecture series, something we call the FAQs, or the frequently ask questions. Now, often times when I work with patients, or when I teach CBT to learners, they are able to engage with me by asking a number of common questions that come up. You're not able to do that, but what we did in advance was to elicit questions from learners and from patients, and we're going to be sharing those questions, and I'm going to be answering those questions as we move forward.

So here's our first FAQ, frequently asked questions. It sounds as though CBT is telling me not to follow my gut. It's telling me, not to trust my feelings or my instincts. Is that right? And how can that be? Well, this is a common question, and I think a really important one, and I think it gets us back to that tension between rationality and emotion. And remember that CBT, even though it's very much grounded on rational examination of how a person is thinking, making decisions, or running their life or relationships, it's not just about rationality, it's about balance. We realize that every yin needs a yang. We need our passion and emotions, but sometimes when things are unbalanced, people start to experience a lot of emotional suffering; then it's time to raise up those rationality skills or those CBT skills.

I think as we move forward, too, you'll see that there's a number of widely different tools that fit into the CBT toolbox. Some of them are very much focused on rationality, rolling up your sleeves and wrestling with thoughts. Some of them, not so much; its more about reaching out and connecting with friends and having that emotional richness and connection that isn't so much about rationality.

FAQ number two: Why did you become a CBT therapist instead of some other kind of therapist, like a psychoanalyst or a psychiatrist? A good question, and I won't pretend that this was my master plan, and I'm exactly where thought I would be. I am surprised where I am, but happy to be here. I actually started in the neurosciences at MIT. And in the summer when I was working in a job at the Massachusetts Eye and Ear Infirmary, I was at my wet bench lab, and I was mapping the neuropathways between the auditory nerve and the superior olive in the brain stem. But in this same lab, they were developing cochlear implants. So patients and families would come in, and what really lit the fire in my belly wasn't the neuromapping, that was interesting, but it was listening to the families' stories—their beliefs, their emotions, their hopes, and their expectations. And I thought, that, that is what I want to do. So with a lot of advice and a lot of help from terrific mentors, I decided to go to the route of psychology. I ended up at the University of Pennsylvania, which is known for its training in CBT, and I was fortunate, then, to become a cognitive behavioral therapist.

The third FAQ: The CBT triangle makes sense, but it seems too simple. People and relationships are more complicated. How can something so simplistic be effective? Now, I encourage you to remember, we're just getting started. We started at the top, and the CBT Triangle is really sort of the first paragraph of the first chapter. So I ask you this, to buckle your seat belt, to join us on this journey, and follow us as we move to progressively more complex layers of analysis, helping us to understand the relationships between cognitions, emotions, and behaviors.

So in our next lecture, we're going to turn again to our clinical cases. We'll talk about how we assess these individuals, how we begin collecting and collating this data, and setting our smart goals. Thank you.

Quantified Self-Assessment for Therapy
Lecture 2

In this lecture, you will learn about the basic principles of CBT, including its history and theory, as well as what you need to know in order to understand what is in the CBT toolbox. You also will learn procedures for assessment and goal setting. In addition, you will learn how to use a battery of psychological tests to determine strengths, challenges, and opportunities for change. Furthermore, you will learn how to use self-monitoring to collect and use real-world data.

The History of CBT

- Aaron T. Beck is the father of cognitive therapy. His idea was to develop a new system that was particularly targeted for the needs of an individual and not to apply the primary paradigm at the time, in the 1960s, which was psychoanalysis.

- After this promising psychiatrist got out of Yale Medical School and finished his residency, he went to the University of Pennsylvania to start working with a cohort of depressed patients. He conducted psychoanalysis sometimes five times a week per patient over several years. He was using classic psychoanalysis, including dream analysis, but his patients weren't getting any better.

- He was frustrated by the lack of progress, but he was also frustrated by the process of therapy, where there are no objective outcome measures—no objective goals. The treatment seemed to be endless with no timeframe.

- He was frustrated that the therapist is supposed to be omniscient and that the patient should be disempowered. He was frustrated by the lack of transparency. He was frustrated by the common ways of thinking he was seeing in his depressed patients over and over again. It was his frustration with the outcomes, his frustration with the process, that led to what we call now the cognitive revolution.

- The roots of the cognitive revolution go back quite far. In fact, the roots are in Socratic traditions. One of the core skills of the CBT therapist is something called Socratic questioning. Rather than just telling the patient the answer, the therapist asks a series of questions so that the patient will find the answer himself or herself.

- While Beck is typically referred to as the father of CBT, there were a number of other very influential individuals at the time that were also taking their own part in the cognitive revolution. There was Albert Ellis and his writings and important work on rational emotive behavior therapy in the early to mid-1960s. There was an organization called the American Association of Behavior Therapy, which was founded in 1966 by 10 behaviorists that were unhappy with psychoanalysis.

- There was Michael Mahoney's book in 1974, *Cognition and Behavior Modification*, and then Donald Meichenbaum's book in 1977, *Cognitive-Behavior Modification*. But in 1979, Aaron T. Beck, A. John Rush, Brian F. Shaw, and Gary Emery wrote the classic book that opened up the field of CBT, particularly in terms of depression: *Cognitive Therapy of Depression*.

The Theory of CBT

- What are some of the things that you should be asking yourself as you learn more about the CBT model? You should be asking yourself the following questions: How would CBT explain emotions, positive or negative? How would CBT explain suffering? How does CBT explain mental illness? How would CBT be able to account for the individuality and the variation among individuals? Does the theory hold true for everyone?

- We're looking at three key variables: cognition, behavior, and emotion. Essentially, we work with all three of these variables on three different levels. First, we want to engage in detection when gathering data: We want to see what's happening in that individual's life in terms of their cognition, behavior, or emotions. Secondly, we want to look at analysis and evaluation: We know what happened, but why did it happen, and what was driving it? What were the contextual factors? Is this a one-time thing, or is this an ongoing pattern? Lastly, we want to go about challenging or even changing those cognitions, behaviors, or emotions.

- These three steps—detection, analysis, and challenge—are just the starting point. Much of the richness lies beneath the surface. An individual will come into our office and tell us about the present, including daily activities, but we want to begin drilling a little bit deeper, looking at core beliefs and potentially implicit biases.

- How might a CBT therapist respond to the charge that what they do is simply superficial? It's all a matter of perspective. You can approach psychotherapy from a top-down perspective or from a bottom-up perspective.

- Classic psychotherapy—psychodynamic psychotherapy or psychoanalysis—starts at the bottom. It involves looking at the unconscious desires, beliefs, and wishes of the individual and trying to bring them up to the top, or surface.

- Alternatively, CBT therapists start up at the top, with the everyday events that are happening, and begin sinking down further until they get to the point where the individual has achieved his or her goals.

- The difference with CBT is that we set the goals up front, and once an individual has achieved his or her goals, he or she is no longer depressed or anxious. The individual has been able to establish a new social support network, so there's really no reason to continue excavating.

Case Formulation and Assessment
- Eventually, we'll want to create what's called a case formulation, where we put together all of the data from the top, middle, and bottom, if necessary, so that we have an explanation of why the individual's life happens to be the way it is. We want to keep things

transparent, so we're going to share that formulation, and we're going to keep it open to revisions throughout the course of therapy.

- For the sake of collaboration and transparency, it's going to be important for us to set some concrete goals. What kinds of data will we be looking at? We'll be looking at questionnaires, as well as social and medical history. We'll be looking at potential symptoms of psychopathology or other medical symptoms and potential functional impairments. Is the individual having trouble operating or functioning as usual in a work setting or in a social setting?

- We want to get a sense of the timeline: When did the problem start, and how has the individual progressed over time? Of course, we want very concrete and specific examples from the individual.

- One of the advantages of assessment is that we get a clear indication of a starting point—of a baseline of where we are right now at this point in time. We can reassess that over time as a way to judge progress. It tends to be more objective, more reliable, and less biased. And it's key to getting feedback to decide whether or not our treatment interventions are working. If they're not working, we should change them.

- There are objections to measurements and to the structure that you find in a CBT approach. One of the objections is that not everything is quantifiable. This approach maybe oversimplifies an individual's difficulties, and maybe some of the survey instruments lack validity. Perhaps this method is less personal; perhaps it could hurt the therapeutic relationship. These concerns are probably ill founded.

- What are some of the types of instruments that we use? We may use surveys, questionnaires, diaries, and semi-structured interviews. These days, we also may use phone apps or websites to collect data. Even more recently, we're using wearable devices and sensors to collect information on an individual's social contacts as well as on their physical activity levels.

Keeping a diary is just one of the instruments used in a CBT approach.

- Some of the questionnaires that are commonly used include the Beck Depression Inventory (named for Aaron T. Beck), the Beck Anxiety Inventory, the PHQ-9 for depression, and the DASS-21 for depression and stress.

The Beck Depression Inventory and the Beck Anxiety Inventory can be found at the following website:

www.beckinstitute.org/beck-inventory-and-scales/

- We'll start by giving questionnaires to all patients and then begin tailoring the packet depending on what the individual's chief complaint is. For example, we might start with mostly symptom-focused questionnaires to give us a baseline. We use a guided interview to then elicit additional information that we will use in making the formulation. We use questionnaires and assessments to initiate a conversation about what the individual's goals might be.

- Other information that we might want to use is real-world data that we would collect through a process called self-monitoring. If we want to learn more about an individual's cognitions and emotions, we would give him or her a self-monitoring form to begin writing down his or her cognitions and emotions as they occur in real time throughout the week. The individual would then bring that back to us as additional data for the next session.

- All of this data gathering and interpretation is in the service of a few goals. We want to know what an individual's diagnosis is (if he or she has one), and we want to know about deficiencies. But we really want to specify some goals.

- Once we have qualitative and quantitative information from an individual, we just need to fill in more of the individual's story. We will need to learn about how everything fits together in his or her life. We need to understand what lies underneath. We need to understand what strengths he or she has, what resources he or she has, and what might get in the way.

- We need to invest a fair amount of ongoing effort to build an initial case formulation, share that formulation with the patient, and then revise it and continue to revise it over time as we get more and more information about how much progress he or she might be making.

Suggested Reading

Cipani and Schock, *Functional Behavioral Assessment, Diagnosis, and Treatment*.

Groth-Marnat, *Handbook of Psychological Assessment*.

1. Are all psychological or behavioral issues amenable to measurement? What if your goal is to have more insight or be more content with your marriage? Can everything really be measured? If not, how could you determine progress in therapy?

2. Create your own SMART goal(s) for this course. What would you like to get out of it? What do you hope will change? Be sure the goal is specific, measurable, attainable, relevant, and timely (SMART).

Quantified Self-Assessment for Therapy
Lecture 2—Transcript

PROFESSOR SATTERFIELD: I grew up in Tennessee, and we always had a garden, something I very much loved and cherished. In fact, the first real letter I ever wrote with my fat pencil and the carefully lined paper was a note to Jung Seed Company, asking them if they could please me a seed catalogue. They sent me an entire box of free seeds, and my passion was ignited. There's just something about getting another plot of land, the soil, the light, the climate, the rainfall; selecting what you think is well suited, then carefully and lovingly nourishing something to new life. There's the joy of watching it grow, bloom, or fruit, and the inevitable problem solving when something goes wrong or your plant doesn't thrive.

Now, I live in the middle of a city, so my gardening has changed, but I've managed to find a profession that I think is very much like gardening, carefully planting, nourishing, and guiding a natural process driven from within. It's psychotherapy, and particularly, cognitive behavioral therapy, a therapy where the patient cultivates, plants, and harvests their own garden.

Welcome to lecture two. In this lecture, we will look at the basic principles of CBT, the history, the theory, and what you need to know in order to understand what's in the toolbox. You'll learn procedures for assessment and goal setting. You'll learn how to use a battery of psychological tests to determine strengths, challenges, and opportunities for change. And lastly, we'll use self-monitoring to collect and to use real-world data. But first, we need to start with the history, and we'll start with the story of Aaron T. Beck, the father of cognitive therapy. Now, the T stands for Tim, and that's what he insists that everyone call him. So Tim's idea was to develop a new system that was particularly targeted for the needs of an individual, and not to apply the primary paradigm at the time, in the 1960s, which was psychoanalysis.

Now, picture this. Tim, a very smart, very promising psychiatrist, just fresh out of Yale Medical School, finished his residencies, and goes to the University of Pennsylvania. He starts working with a cohort of depressed patients, doing psychoanalysis four, sometimes five, times a week per patient over several years. He's doing classic psychoanalysis, including dream analysis, and guess what? His patients aren't getting any better.

Now, he's frustrated by the lack of progress, but he's also frustrated by the process of therapy, where there are no objective outcome measures. There are no objective goals. The treatment seems to be endless, with no time point. He's frustrated that the therapist is supposed to be omniscient, and the patient should be disempowered. He's frustrated by the lack of transparency. He's frustrated by the common ways of thinking he keeps seeing in his depressed patients over and over again. Why can't he use that?

It was his frustration with the outcomes, his frustration with the process, that led to what we call now the cognitive revolution. So, when, exactly, was the cognitive revolution? And as I said before, the roots go back quite far. In fact, the roots are in Socratic and Stoic in traditions. One of the core skills of the CBT therapist is something called Socratic Questioning; so rather than just telling the patient the answer, you ask a series of questions so that the patient will find the answer him or herself.

Or the words of the Stoic philosopher, Epictetus, "People are disturbed not by events alone, but by the views that they take of them." That's classic CBT. When, exactly was the cognitive revolution? Now, as I mentioned, Tim Beck is typically called the father of CBT, but we know there were a number of other very influential individuals at the time that were also taking their own part in the cognitive revolution. There was Albert Ellis and his writings and important work on REBT, rational emotive behavior therapy, in the early, mid-1960s. There was the organization AABT, the American Association of Behavior Therapy, founded in 1966 by 10 behaviorists that were unhappy with psychoanalysis. There was Michael Mahoney's book in 1974, Cognition and Behavior Modification, and then Don Meichenbaum's book, which followed shortly thereafter in 1977. But in 1979, that was the classic book that really opened the field of CBT, particularly looking at depression, written by Team Beck, Rush, Shaw, and Emery.

So what are some of the things that you should be asking yourself as you learn more about this particular model? You should be asking yourself how would CBT explain emotions, positive or negative emotions; how would CBT explain suffering; how does CBT explain mental illness; and yes, biology does matter; and how would CBT be able to account for the individuality and the variation among individuals? Does that theory hold true for everyone?

Remember, we're looking at three key variables. We're looking at cognition, behavior, and emotion, and essentially, we work with all three of those on three different levels. First, we want to do detection in data gathering; we want to see what's happening in that individual's life in terms of their cognition, behavior, or emotions. Secondly, we want to look at analysis and evaluation; so we know what happened, but why did it happen, and what was driving it? What were the contextual factors? Is this a one-time thing, or is this an ongoing pattern? And lastly, we want to go about challenging, or even changing, those cognitions, behaviors, or emotions—so detection, analysis, and challenge.

But this is just the starting point. Now, much of the richness lies beneath the surface, so an individual will come in and they'll tell us about the present; they'll tell us about daily activities. But we want to begin drilling a little bit deeper, looking at those core beliefs, and potentially, implicit biases. So, how might a CBT therapist respond to the charge that what they do is simply superficial? Well, think it's all a matter of perspective. Now, you can approach psychotherapy from a top-down perspective, or you can do it from a bottom-up perspective.

Now, classic psychotherapy, a psychodynamic psychotherapy, or psychoanalysis, very much starts at the bottom. So you'll look at those unconscious desires, beliefs, and wishes, and you try to bubble them up to the top, to the surface. The CBT therapists starts up at the top, the everyday events that are happening, and begin sinking down further until we get to the point where the individual has achieved his or her goals. Now, the difference there is we've set the goals up front, and once an individual has achieved their goals, they're no longer depressed, they're no longer anxious, they've been able to establish a new social support network, there's really no reason to continue excavating.

Eventually what you'll want to do, is to create what's called a case formulation, where we put together all of this data from the top, the middle, and the bottom, if necessary, so we have an idea, we have an explanation of why the individual's life happens to be the way that it is. We want to keep things transparent, so we're going to share that formulation, and we're going to keep it open to revisions throughout the course of therapy. Recall our key ideas on collaborative empiricism and on transparency, and it's going to be important for us to set some concrete goals.

So what kinds of data will we be looking at? Well, we'll be looking at our questionnaires, but we'll also be looking at social and medical history. We'll be looking at potential symptoms of psychopathology or other medical symptoms. We'll be looking at potential functional impairments, so are they having trouble operating or functioning as usual in a work setting or in a social setting? We want to get a sense of the timeline; when did the problem start and how have they progressed over time? And of course, we want very concrete and specific examples from the individual.

Now, some of the advantages of assessment is that we get a clear indication of a starting point, of a baseline of where we are right now at this point in time. We can reassess that over time as a way to judge our progress. It tends to be more objective, more reliable, and less biased, and it's key in order to getting feedback to decide whether or not our treatment interventions are working. If they're not working, we should change them.

There are objections to measurements and to the structure that you find in a CBT approach, and that not everything is quantifiable. It maybe oversimplifies an individual's difficulties, and maybe some of those survey instruments lack a validity. Perhaps it's less personal; perhaps it could hurt the therapeutic relationship. I hope through our video clips you will see that those concerns are probably ill founded.

So what are some of the types of instruments that we use? We may use surveys, we may use questionnaires, diaries, we may use semi-structured interviews, which you will see a demonstration of. We may use phone apps these days or websites to collect data. And even more recently, we're using wearable devices and sensors to collect information on an individual's social contacts, as well as their physical activity levels. Now, some of the questionnaires commonly used, we'll use things like the Beck Depression

Inventory, that name, Beck, of course comes from Tim Beck; the Beck Anxiety Inventory; the PHQ-9 for depression; or something called the DASS 21, that's the depression and stress questionnaire, and of course, it has 21 questions.

First we'll start with the broad sweep, where give questionnaires to all patients, and we'll begin tailoring that packet depending on what the individual's chief complaint is. Let's turn now to a video example from Maria, where we're going over her initial assessment packet.

[VIGNETTE START]

PROFESSOR SATTERFIELD: Hi Maria, welcome back.

MARIA: Thank you.

PROFESSOR SATTERFIELD: And I see you've brought your questionnaires today.

MARIA: I don't know if I filled it out the way you wanted, but I tried.

PROFESSOR SATTERFIELD: I'm sure they're fine. And we'll definitely go over these for today. But I did want to say that I'm sorry that you have to be here, but glad that you're willing to do something to take care of yourself.

MARIA: Ah, thank you.

PROFESSOR SATTERFIELD: OK. Well, what I'd like to do, and we'll do this in each of our subsequent visits, is as we begin we'll set an agenda. And it just helps us to make sure that we know what's on our plate for today. And we'll get to the most important things. So one thing we'll have on our agenda is to go over the questionnaires. Is there anything else that you want to make sure that we talk about today?

MARIA: Oh, I don't know. I can't think of anything. I just want to get better.

PROFESSOR SATTERFIELD: OK. And I want you to get better too. So I think one of the things we can do is to talk about goals. And we'll talk more specifically about how to get you to that point where you are feeling more like yourself and feeling better. So we'll talk about questionnaires, and we'll do some goal setting. And maybe we'll talk a little bit about how cognitive behavioral therapy works and some of the tools we might use to help you achieve those goals. Does that sound OK?

MARIA: Yeah.

PROFESSOR SATTERFIELD: All right. So first, why don't we go through some of the questionnaires here. And I know there were several. What was this like for you to fill these out?

MARIA: Well, I took time—it took me a long time to do it. I didn't know what to say exactly. You know, I did the best I could. I tried to answer the questions.

PROFESSOR SATTERFIELD: OK, OK. And just as a reminder, the reason we have these questionnaires is we want to get a sense of the severity of different symptoms that you might be experiencing. That gives us a baseline of where you're starting. We'll have you fill these out periodically, probably at least a couple more times.

So we want to see if those scores are improving or not. If they're improving, we're on the right track. If they're not improving, then we need to try something different. But it gives us that important feedback.

So the first one we have is a Depression Inventory. And it looks like you filled out all 21 items here, and you've added it up here at the bottom, and your score was a 27. That puts you just up at the top of the moderate to severe depressive range. So when you hear that, what does that mean to you?

MARIA: Well, it makes me sad. I feel just tired all the time. I feel like I just don't have the energy that I used to have.

PROFESSOR SATTERFIELD: Right. As you were sharing with me last time, sleep has been a big issue. And we're definitely going to want to talk about sleep. It's hard to cope if you're exhausted all the time.

MARIA: That's right. If I could just get some sleep, I think I could do a little better.

PROFESSOR SATTERFIELD: Yes. You see, there are other symptoms like appetite, weight, energy levels, one of them, ability to concentrate. And it looks like nearly all of those have been affected.

MARIA: Yeah, I just don't have any appetite anymore. I just don't feel like eating. I try to eat. It's hard.

PROFESSOR SATTERFIELD: All right. So we have a starting point. And we have a pretty good idea that you do meet the criteria for what we call clinical depression or sometimes people call it major depression. We consider it a chemical imbalance. It's a medical disease, often triggered by stress in a person's life.

MARIA: It's kind of scary to think about that. I mean, like I'm mentally ill or something.

PROFESSOR SATTERFIELD: Well, I know there is unfortunately a stigma that's attached to depression. But in reality, one in four people will meet criteria for a mental illness at some point in their lives, anxiety and depression being the two most common. For me, you know when I think about it, it's no different than people get diabetes; people get heart disease. It's often an accumulation of wear and tear that causes a person to have those sorts of problems, and depression's really no different.

OK. But you're here, and we have treatments that work for depression. And that will be part of the treatment plan we develop, is to how to treat that depression and get these scores down, hopefully below a 10. Everyone has a little bit of depression from time to time. That's part of life. But scores this high tell us that there's something more serious that's happening and something that we really need to take care.

OK? So the first one was your depression measure. And the second was about anxiety. And two parts of anxiety, how anxiety affects your body, so feeling keyed up or on edge, having an exaggerated startle response. And the other part was about the thoughts that often go with anxiety, so the ruminations and the worry. And it looks like for anxiety you're at a low moderate level, both for the physical and the cognitive part. How does that sound when you hear that?

MARIA: I guess. I mean, I have things to worry about now. There are things that make me anxious certainly. I mean, my husband is one thing. Worrying about money is another thing. I mean, we saved some money for retirement and everything. But we didn't expect to be spending it like this. Our medical bills are a lot. So I worry about some things. And I do think about things a lot, especially at night when I wake up. My mind is going around like a gerbil in an exercise wheel. Thinking and thinking, and I never get anywhere.

PROFESSOR SATTERFIELD: Right. OK. And what we'll do then is to make sure that treatment of anxiety is part of the plan that we put together. It's part of the goals that we'll be talking about later today. If we look just at symptom severity, it looks like depression is probably number one. Anxiety is probably number two. And then this last one that you filled out, this was a somatic symptom checklist. So it's about your physical health. And you've noted that you do have more chronic aches and pains. And you're a little worried about your physical health.

MARIA: No, I feel like I'm in pain all the time. But it's not like a headache or a bad knee or something. It's just like I hurt all over. Maybe it's not even a physical pain, but it feels that way. It's worse than a physical pain. I don't know how to say it. It's like I have an ache in my heart and it just goes all over my body.

PROFESSOR SATTERFIELD: Hard to measure and hard to quantify.

MARIA: Hard to explain.

PROFESSOR SATTERFIELD: Yeah, yeah. I'm wondering as we think about that, that ache, and I think you've described it in a very poignant way. We want to address that ache. And we might be able to reach it through treating depression, through treating anxiety. But we should keep our minds open. And if we come up with other ideas about how to treat it, through change in behaviors, through physical activity, through social contacts, those all might be treatments that could help that pain.

[VIGNETTE END]

PROFESSOR SATTERFIELD: So what did we see with Maria? We started with mostly symptom-focused questionnaires as our starting point; they gave us a baseline. We used a guided interview to then elicit additional information that we will use in making the formulation. We use those questionnaires and assessments to initiate, to open a conversation about what her goals might be.

Other information that we might want to use is real-world data that we would collect through a process called self-monitoring. So if we want to learn more about her cognitions, if we want to learn more about her emotions, we will give her a self-monitoring form to begin writing those down as they occur in real time throughout the week. She would then bring that back as additional data for our next session.

Let's move now to look at an example of self-monitoring from our case of Michael. And Michael is not looking at cognition; Michael wants help being more aware of his emotions and writing them down.

[VIGNETTE START]

PROFESSOR SATTERFIELD: That actually brings up another element when we think about emotions. There's the physical sensation, but you mentioned when you feel sad, it affects the way that you think. So you're right. Emotions affect our body, so the physical sensation. They also affect the way that our minds work. They affect our behaviors, our social relationships.

And we already talked about how cognition, sometimes it's a chicken and the egg with emotion, sometimes it fuels emotion. Sometimes the emotions affect our thoughts. So all of those are elements. And it's very rich and complicated and terrific and terrible sort of all at the same time, depending on the circumstances and emotion.

But what we want to do is to help you be aware of emotions when they happen, maybe at the beginning of that causal chain, of when you're first starting to feel sad or angry or anxious or any of those emotions. And we all feel, even though we have our habits and the emotions we gravitate to, we want you to be able to feel and to recognize the full range of emotions. And I'll tell you specifically what I'm driving at.

I think in our culture, and for men in particular, a lot of times we're told and we're raised to believe that anger's the place you're supposed to go because it's strong and it's masculine. And we use anger all the time. It's a substitute for other kinds of emotions. So we want to just sort of move that layer off and see if there are other emotions that are happening underneath.

MICHAEL: OK.

PROFESSOR SATTERFIELD: So why don't we just do sort of a quick game. And what I'd like you to do is to just start firing off emotion words, all right? So just like you're a thesaurus, an emotional thesaurus. So what kinds of words for emotions? And one would be anger. What's another one?

MICHAEL: Happiness.

PROFESSOR SATTERFIELD: So happy.

MICHAEL: Frustration or frustrated.

PROFESSOR SATTERFIELD: Frustrated. What else?

MICHAEL: Joyful.

PROFESSOR SATTERFIELD: Let's put joy.

MICHAEL: Um, sadness, sad.

PROFESSOR SATTERFIELD: Sad.

MICHAEL: Depressed.

PROFESSOR SATTERFIELD: Depressed.

MICHAEL: Anxious.

PROFESSOR SATTERFIELD: Anxious. What else?

MICHAEL: Stressed maybe.

PROFESSOR SATTERFIELD: Stress has got a lot of layers, too, huh?

MICHAEL: Yeah, I guess.

PROFESSOR SATTERFIELD: What else?

MICHAEL: Um, elated.

PROFESSOR SATTERFIELD: Uh huh.

MICHAEL: Furious. Disturbed.

PROFESSOR SATTERFIELD: Sometimes it helps to think about relationships as triggers. So think about your son or your wife, and what kinds of feelings come up with them?

MICHAEL: Love.

PROFESSOR SATTERFIELD: Yep.

MICHAEL: Um, caring.

PROFESSOR SATTERFIELD: Uh huh.

MICHAEL: Um, hopeful. Disappointed.

PROFESSOR SATTERFIELD: All right. And how about you think about work, maybe your boss or co-workers or folks you supervise.

MICHAEL: Um, puzzled.

PROFESSOR SATTERFIELD: Puzzled, all right. Oops, puzzled, that's an L.

MICHAEL: I mean, I mentioned frustrated. I guess that's something I feel a lot.

PROFESSOR SATTERFIELD: We've got frustrated here.

MICHAEL: Um, fulfilled.

PROFESSOR SATTERFIELD: Fulfilled. I guess, content, satisfied.

MICHAEL: Yeah, satisfied.

PROFESSOR SATTERFIELD: Those all kind of fit.

MICHAEL: Contentment, fulfilled.

PROFESSOR SATTERFIELD: OK, all right. Well, we can pause there. And there are actually hundreds and hundreds, as you can imagine, different emotion words in the English language. But I wanted to see first, what pops to mind for you? And if you could tell me which of these you feel most often? What's most familiar to you?

MICHAEL: Well, we all know why I'm here. So anger is pretty familiar. I'd say frustration is pretty familiar, frustrated. When we talk about my son, if I can break it down to individuals, I guess I'm hopeful but I'm probably more often disappointed. Furious, I feel furious a lot. I do feel stressed a lot. But as you say, there are a lot of layers. I don't know if we're free to use that one.

PROFESSOR SATTERFIELD: Sure, we can do whatever we want.

MICHAEL: That would probably be the top group that I feel.

PROFESSOR SATTERFIELD: OK, the top group. Do you see any commonalities?

MICHAEL: Well, yes I do.

PROFESSOR SATTERFIELD: Yeah, they're all kind of the same spice, right? They're the same flavor pretty much.

MICHAEL: Yeah.

PROFESSOR SATTERFIELD: All right. And that's kind of what we would expect. Now, another question, so if we look at this particular family of emotions, if you were to rate the range of intensity that you usually experience them, would you say you're all the way from 0, not at all, up to 100? Or do they tend to cluster in a particular level of intensity?

MICHAEL: I would say most of these are— when they happen, they're a particular level of intensity.

PROFESSOR SATTERFIELD: OK. Would you say that's above or below 50?

MICHAEL: Above.

PROFESSOR SATTERFIELD: All right. So they're fairly intense, usually above a 50. And do they come on like that? Or does it take a while to sort of build up?

MICHAEL: They tend to come on like that.

PROFESSOR SATTERFIELD: OK. So we have this family of emotions that are fairly common. They tend to be intense. They tend to come on quickly. So what I would like you to do—I mean, there's all these other emotions, right, that are happening. And I would assume that you have them. And when I prompted you to think about your family, it wasn't anger or fury or things that came up first, it was love and caring and hopeful, and those are also part of you. And I know you really care about your family. And that's part of why you're here.

MICHAEL: I do.

PROFESSOR SATTERFIELD: All right. That's part of why you're here. And we want to find those emotions, those strengths. We want to pull them out, and we want to raise them up. We want to build them up. We want to have them happen more commonly and more intensely.

OK. I would like that.

PROFESSOR SATTERFIELD: All right. And again, we're not going to truncate your range of emotions. You're going to have all of these. But we want you to start paying attention to all of them and not allow this one family to dominate.

MICHAEL: OK.

PROFESSOR SATTERFIELD: So I wanted to propose your second homework assignment for now and next time and that's to do some emotion self-monitoring. And what you do with self-monitoring is you're just collecting data on yourself. And I don't have a special form for this because you can really make whatever works for you, and I want you to have some ownership over it. But essentially what I would do—so my first thought that comes to mind, and you can totally do something different—I would do just like a calendar. So you have Sunday, Monday, Tuesday.

Wednesday and so on. You might want to have time of day, depending on when you get up in the morning, and just writing the primary emotion that you feel whether it's sadness or happiness. You don't have to do it every single hour. That'll drive you crazy. That will be frustrating, right, to have to do that.

But you know, and whenever you think about it, and then maybe at the end of the day. So what's your average emotion that you had? And we wanted intensity, too. So maybe that's 0 to 100.

So maybe you're a little angry here. Maybe you're more angry here. But maybe there's some happiness in the middle. We want you to start capturing that.

And if you want to capture other things, like what was the trigger? What was the circumstance? Were you at work? Were you home? That's fine, too, as much as you want to because again, we're gathering data. We want to help you be more aware of your emotions. And once you have that awareness, we want you to be aware of the context of what's happening around you, outside and also what's happening inside of you.

MICHAEL: OK. Let me ask you a little bit about that. Would it be better for me to take an assessment on an hourly, or you might do it every three or four hours basis, but using the time as the hook? Or whenever I feel like I'm feeling something, I note it down at that moment. Or is it a combination of the two? For example, if I suddenly realize I'm feeling quite happy and it's 11:15 in the morning, do I note that? Or is it the other way that I just note it periodically?

PROFESSOR SATTERFIELD: That's a great question. And I think both of those are important. You know, if you only write down an emotion when it grabs your attention, you're probably going to be paying only attention to the stronger emotions. So it's the others that we're going to miss. So I would say if you feel an emotion and it grabs your attention, absolutely write that one down. But you probably want a couple other times during the day, maybe just when there's a natural break in the morning, or in the afternoon, or I've had patients set an alarm on their phone just so it goes off and they know, oh, I need to write down my emotion and my intensity.

MICHAEL: I like that idea.

PROFESSOR SATTERFIELD: So we can get a little bit of both that way.

MICHAEL: OK.

[VIGNETTE END]

PROFESSOR SATTERFIELD: All right. So we're well on our way to better understanding and helping both Maria and Michael. We have interviews, we have questionnaires, and now we have self-monitoring data. All of this data-gathering and interpretation is, of course, in service of a few goals. So we'll want to know what their diagnosis is, if they have one. We'll want to know about strengths; we'll want to know about deficiencies, but we'll really want to specify some goals. Let's move to our next video clip, where we talk with Carol about creating something called SMART goals.

[VIGNETTE START]

PROFESSOR SATTERFIELD: So we've talked a little bit about the questionnaire assessments. That was our baseline. And the second thing on our agenda was goals, and you've told me about sleep and shyness and relationships. And as we dig a little bit further into goals, I want to specify what it is we mean by goals and how to set goals that maybe set us up in a way that we're more likely to see some success. And the goals I'm talking about are called SMART goals. Have you heard about SMART goals before? It's just S-M-A-R-T.

CAROL: No.

PROFESSOR SATTERFIELD: OK, and that's OK. So it stands for—you want the goals to be specific. So a goal of feeling better is not specific enough. It's hard to evaluate. You can't tell if people have made progress, so we want to be fairly specific.

We want it to be measurable. So things like the Beck Anxiety Inventory are a measure. So you might have a specific goal of to get your anxiety below a 10 on the Beck Anxiety Inventory, and our measurement then would be the Beck Anxiety Inventory.

The A stands for attainable. So we want them to be realistic. And it's OK to have big goals. You know you want that star on the horizon, something that you can shoot for. But we want more realistic goals that are closer to us so that you can have an experience of succeeding and doing those steps towards that star on the horizon. So specific, measurable, attainable.

We want it to be relevant. So we know why you're here. We know you're interested in relationships and anxiety. So our goals should be in service of those sort of bigger picture reasons that have brought you here.

And timely, so we want to know what's going on in your life. Is it work conflict, relationship conflict? We want them to be relevant to your life but also timely so it's something that matters to you now at this point in your life and maybe not something that happened five or 10 years ago or some hypothetical event that will happen in five or 10 years.

So we want the goals to be specific, measurable, attainable, relevant, and timely. So if we just walk through an example, and we'll do a quick one with sleep. And you wanted to sleep better, that's sort of the general goal. You're sleeping about five hours a night. If we wanted to set a specific goal around sleep, what do you think it would be?

CAROL: Well, I guess you mentioned sleeping seven hours a night. So I think that would be a specific goal.

PROFESSOR SATTERFIELD: All right. So we want seven hours per night. All right. And measurable, how would we measure that?

CAROL: Well, I guess I would measure it by what time I fall asleep and what time I wake up.

PROFESSOR SATTERFIELD: We could do something like a sleep diary. And I can show you what those look like. Attainable, do you think it's realistic?

CAROL: Yeah, I think it's realistic.

PROFESSOR SATTERFIELD: OK, I'm just going to put a check mark for attainable. It's definitely relevant. It's something that's going on now. And it's something that's timely. So this gives us just an idea with sleep, it's a fairly concrete specific goal. It's specific, measurable, attainable, relevant, and timely.

[VIGNETTE END]

PROFESSOR SATTERFIELD: So where does that leave us? Now, obviously, we have a lot more work to do with setting SMART goals for Carol and actually for each of our cases, but now we have qualitative and quantitative information; we just need to fill in more of their story. We still need to learn how all this fits together in each of their lives. We need to understand what lies underneath. We need to understand what strengths they have, what resources they have, and what might actually get in the way. We need to invest a fair amount of ongoing effort to build an initial case formulation, share that formulation with each of the patients, and then revise it and continue to revise it over the time as we get more and more information about how much progress they may be making.

In our next lecture, we'll be talking about how to connect those dots and how to create a case formulation. Thank you.

Setting Therapeutic Goals
Lecture 3

In this lecture, you will learn how to create a case formulation. You will learn how to use assessment data to develop a narrative that explains an individual's condition and outlines how to change it. You also will learn how to describe the links in a possible causal chain. In addition, you will learn how to develop hypotheses that explain problems and situations using cognitions, behaviors, emotions, relationships, and other social interactions. Finally, you will learn about developing a treatment plan based on a case formulation.

Case Formulation

- A case formulation is defined as an individualized theory that explains a particular patient's symptoms and problems. It serves as a basis for an individual treatment plan and guides the therapy process. This classic definition is adapted from Jacqueline Persons's 1989 classic book *Cognitive Therapy in Practice: A Case Formulation Approach.*

- When developing a case formulation, we will compile and interpret data. We will use data from self-report, surveys, observations of the patient in action, or interviews or reports. We will also use data taken from behavioral analysis. We will look at the antecedents of the behavior, the behavior itself, and the consequences that follow. Our interventions will flow from the formulation.

- It's important to remember that you can formulate a case, or a patient, as a whole. You can formulate a problem like depression or anxiety, or you can create a formulation based on a very specific situation. The word "formulation" can be misleading, but we're looking at how key ingredients combine to create an individual's current life circumstances. It's not about blame; it's about trying to understand the causes so that you can prescribe a treatment.

- We could just use a standard treatment protocol. There are fantastic treatment manuals that provide a one-size-fits-all approach. But we know that everyone is different, and we need to take into account different contextual, environmental, or family factors. We need to take into account potential comorbidities—psychiatric, medical, or otherwise—and we want to take into account an individual's specific goals.

- Formulation is always a work in progress. It is shared with the patient, who helps revise it. We'll go about hypothesis testing using the formulation, and we'll either prove or disprove particular parts of it. For the parts that prove not to be accurate, we'll change it. Our hypotheses are about psychological mechanisms and other factors that cause or maintain the disorder or the other problems that brought an individual to treatment.

- What are the key elements of a case formulation? First, we're going to start with something called the problem list or the diagnosis.

- Second, we want to develop working hypotheses. There are four important components to remember when creating a working hypothesis.
  - First, we want to look at the role of cognition and especially deeper cognitive structures, something called schemas or scripts, with a focus on Beck's cognitive model.

  - The second part of a working hypothesis looks at behaviors. We'll look at antecedents, or triggers, as well as the punishments and the rewards that a particular behavior evokes.

  - Third, we'll want to look at the origins. We're talking about early learning events or perhaps about parents or family issues.

  - Lastly, we'll tie it all together and create a summary to tell a story.

- The third key element of an overall case formulation is to focus on an individual's strengths and assets. It was probably suffering or a problem that brought the individual to therapy in the first place, but he or she also has strengths and assets that we might be able to tap into.

- Fourth, we want to create a treatment plan. Given what we know about the person—given our hypotheses and his or her strengths and assets—what are our goals? What are our measures, and what are the interventions that we're going to use?

Problem List or Diagnosis

- The first component of case formulation is a problem list or a diagnosis. In a medical setting, they would call this the chief complaint or the presenting complaint: Patient presents with pain, or patient presents with depression or anxiety. But we want to go further than that to include other domains. We want to cast a wide net in terms of other psychological issues or maybe psychiatric disorders.

- We want to look at interpersonal issues of social supports or social conflicts. We want to look at something called occupational functioning: How well are you doing at work? What are your successes? What are you failures? We'll want to include potential medical diagnoses or medical concerns or symptoms. This problem list might include finances, housing, or legal issues. It might also include basic quality of life and enjoyment.

- Once we have created a full list, it needs to be ranked. Of course, we're going to put things like suicide, violence, or any emergent-type issues at the top of our list. But we'll also want to look for something called therapy interfering behaviors. If we know that a patient has a habit of skipping their sessions, we're going to address that problem first, because if we can't get the patient in, we can't really help him or her.

Working Hypothesis

- The next step is to build a working hypothesis. We want to look for explanations as to why a particular problem exists, or we want to look at an individual's reaction to a particular situation and try to understand why they have reacted in that particular way: What caused it, or what causes it? What maintains the problem, what makes the problem worse, or what makes the problem better? We want to remember that there might be both internal factors as well as external factors.

- We're going to focus on cognitions, behaviors, and emotions. But we should remember that biology might be exerting an influence, too, so that might be on our map or in our formulation, as well.

- With the working hypothesis, there are four components: cognitions, behaviors, early origins, and a summary. The first component involves Beck's cognitive theory.

- The general assumption of cognition is that events make us think or feel a certain way: My boss makes me angry, or my significant other makes me stressed out. We might acknowledge that we have a choice in how we react, but we often see it as a direct cause-and-effect relationship.

- Beck's cognitive theory has a different model: It isn't events that trouble us, but it's how we view those events. In a cognitive model, an activating event triggers cognitions, or what are called automatic thoughts, which then cause emotional and behavioral consequences.

- Particular kinds of automatic thoughts are linked to specific reactions. For example, anger tends to be preceded by thoughts that you're being mistreated or that some sort of injustice has occurred. For depression, it's often thoughts about loss.

- Why do we have these particular automatic thoughts? Two people in exactly the same situation might have dramatically different automatic thoughts. To answer this question, we'll have to use

Anger tends to be preceded by thoughts that you're being mistreated or that some sort of injustice has occurred.

Beck's model to drill down a little bit deeper into our belief system. We'll need to better understand our rules of life, or what are called our conditional if-then assumptions. We'll need to look at what Beck calls schemas or scripts that tell us what to expect, how to react, and how to live our lives. Ultimately, we'll boil it down to our basic beliefs: our core beliefs about ourselves, about others, and about the world.

- For behavior, we cast a fairly wide net. We're talking about all sorts of activities, including mundane activities, big activities, small activities, activities we do alone, and activities we do with others. It would include activities for pleasure as well as activities for work—the things you have to do and the things you want to do. The idea is that these activities throughout the course of the day are summative in terms of how they affect an individual's mood. Many small activities can add up into a fairly profound effect.

- The roots of the behavioral part of the formulation are from behaviorism and behavioral theory, which considers how rewards and punishments from our environment subtly shift our behaviors until sometimes they create very complex functional or maybe dysfunctional behaviors. We would want to do self-monitoring for behaviors, but also for cognitions and emotions.

- Finally, we want to look at origins to formulate the hypothesis. At this point, we would start delving into the past. We want a broad picture first, and we probably won't spend substantial time going back, unless we feel that we're stuck in the present and not able to make progress. We'll weave all of this together into our hypothesis to tell a story.

- A case formulation can run between seven and ten pages and typically includes all of the assessment data, goals, and treatment plans.

Strengths and Assets and the Treatment Plan
- The last few parts of our case formulation include looking at strengths and assets. For example, strengths and assets might include insight and motivation, love for family members and value of relationships, and lack of financial stressors if the person is gainfully employed.

- The last part of our formulation is the treatment plan. We want to look at evidence-based treatments, but we also want to look at a patient's willingness to engage in those treatments as well as what the patient's preferences might be.

- We almost always share the case formulation with the patient. In fact, it's seen as a collaborative process, and if the patient tells you that the formulation is wrong, you can assume that it's wrong. You need to go back to the data and rewrite the formulation.

- A case formulation is always a work in progress, and it's always an iterative process. The formulation guides our treatment, and if we don't have the formulation right, then we might not have the treatment right.

Suggested Reading

Persons, *The Case Formulation Approach to Cognitive-Behavior Therapy*.

Questions to Consider

1. Nearly all psychotherapists create some sort of formulation about who their patient is and what he or she might need. However, CBT is one of the few that collaboratively develops and explicitly shares the formulation and treatment plan. What are the positive and negative implications of this collaboration and transparency?

2. Is a formulation (or explanation for how all the pieces fit together) really necessary for change? Can you just take a leap of faith and still get results? What benefit does the formulation give you?

Setting Therapeutic Goals
Lecture 3—Transcript

PROFESSOR SATTERFIELD: Wouldn't it be grand if people came with a user's manual, if we each had our own blueprint that mapped out how we're put together and described what it is that makes us tick? Even better, if it were to include a troubleshooting guide to assist us when things weren't going as expected.

I think we can all agree that people are too complex for that. However, CBT tries to do something along those very same lines in order to develop tailored treatment plans and promote insight. It may take weeks to pull together using multiple data sources, but each CBT therapist collaboratively creates a case formulation and constantly revises it.

Welcome to Lecture 3, where we'll build from assessment data to develop a narrative that explains an individual's condition and how to change it. We'll describe the links in a possible causal chain. We'll develop hypotheses that explain problems and situations using cognitions, behavior, emotions, relationships, and other social interactions. And we'll develop a treatment plan based on that formulation.

But what's a formulation? A case formulation is defined as an individualized theory that explains a particular patient's symptoms and problems, serves as a basis for an individual treatment plan, and guides the therapy process. This classic definition taken from Jackie Persons 1989 classic book, *Cognitive Therapy and Practice, A Case Formulation Approach*. With this case formulation, we'll be compiling and interpreting data. We'll use data from self-report, from surveys, from observations of the patient in action, or from interviews or reports from significant others. We'll also use data taken from behavioral analysis. We'll look at the antecedents of the behavior, the behavior itself, and the consequences that follow. Our interventions will flow from the formulation. It's important to remember, though, that you can formulate a case or a patient as a whole; you can formulate a problem, like depression or anxiety; or you can create a formulation based on a very specific situation.

The word *formula* can be misleading, but we're looking at how key ingredients combine to create an individual's current life circumstances. It's not really about blame; it's more about trying to understand the causes so that you can prescribe a treatment. Now, we could just use a standard treatment protocol. There are fantastic treatment manuals that are out there, a sort of one-size-fits-all approach. But we know that everyone is different. We need to take into account different contextual, or environmental, or family factors. We need to take into account potential comorbidities, either psychiatric, medical, or otherwise, and of course we want to take into account an individual's specific goals.

Now, one of the notable features of a formulation is that it's always a work in progress. It is shared with the patient, who helps to revise it. We'll go about hypothesis testing using the formulation, and we'll either prove or disprove particular parts of it. For the parts that prove not to be accurate, we'll change it. Our hypotheses are about psychological mechanisms and other factors that cause or maintain the disorder, or the other problems that brought an individual to treatment.

But what are the key elements of a case formulation? First we're going to start with something called the problem list in the diagnosis. Second we want to develop those working hypotheses, and I think there are four important components to remember when creating a working hypothesis. First you want to look at the role of cognition, and especially, deeper cognitive structures, something called schemas or scripts, and we're going to talk a little bit about Beck's Cognitive Model. The second part of a working hypothesis will look at behaviors, and here again, we'll look at those antecedents or triggers; we'll look at the punishments and the rewards that a particular behavior evokes. Third, we'll want to look at the origins, and here we're talking about early learning events, or we might be talking about your parents or family-of-origin issues. And lastly, we'll tie it all together and create a summary to tell a story.

Now, the third key element of an overall case formulation, you want to focus in on an individual's strengths and assets. Yes, it was probably suffering or a problem that brought them to therapy in the first place, but they also have strengths and assets that we might be able to tap into. And fourth, we want to create a treatment plan. So given what we know about the person, given our hypotheses, the strengths, and the assets, what are our goals? What are our measures? And what are the interventions that we're going to use?

So let's look at each of those components. The first was problem list or a diagnosis. Now, in a medical setting, they would call this the chief complaint or the presenting complaint—Patient presents with pain. Patient presents with depression or anxiety. But we want to go a little bit further than that, and we want to include other domains. So we want to cast a wide net in terms of other psychological issues, or maybe psychiatric disorders. We want to look at interpersonal issues of social supports or social conflicts. We want to look at something called occupational functioning, so how well are you doing at work? What are your successes? What are you failures? We'll want to include potential medical diagnoses or medical concerns or symptoms. It might include finances, housing, legal issues. It might also include basic equality of life and enjoyment.

Once we have a full list created, it needs to be ranked. Of course, we're going to put things like suicide, or violence, or any emergent-type issues up at the top of our list. But we'll also want to look for something called therapy interfering behaviors. So if I know that a patient has a habit of skipping their sessions, I'm going to address that problem first, because if I can't get them in, we can't really help them.

For our case of Maria, her problem list would include things like her social stressors, her husband or caregiving for her husband, her relationship with her daughters and friends and maintaining that relationship, maybe her finances. Mood and emotional problems would include depression, stress, worry, and anxiety. And she's mentioned a couple of different physical symptoms: her difficulty with sleep, her chronic pain, especially from her osteoarthritis, and she's having frequent upper respiratory tract infections. We know that her diagnosis is major or clinical depression.

Now, for Michael his problem list and diagnoses are different. His social stressors include conflict with both his son and his wife, conflict with coworkers, rejection from his friends and his neighbors. Physical and medical problems include his cardiovascular disease, his high blood pressure, his high cholesterol. We know emotionally he has a problem with rapid onset intense anger, and he sometimes has difficulty in regulating his behavioral responses to his anger. And his diagnosis? Well, he doesn't have a psychiatric diagnosis, at least not yet.

So the next step would be building that working hypothesis. And how could we go about doing that? We want to look for explanations as to why a particular problem exists, or we want to look at an individual's reaction to a particular situation and try to understand why they've reacted in that particular way. What caused it, or what causes it? What maintains the problem? What makes the problem worse? Or what makes the problem better? We want to remember that there might be both internal factors as well as external factors. I want you to recall when we talked with Carol about the CDT Triangle. We're going to focus on cognitions, and behaviors, and emotions. But we should remember that biology may be exerting an influence too, so that might be on our map or our formulation as well.

As I mentioned with the working hypothesis, there are four components. We talk about cognition, or especially schemas using Beck's model. We'll talk about behaviors. We talk about early origins. And then we tie all together to tell a summary. So let's look at the first part, Beck's Cognitive Theory. So, the general assumption is that events make us think or feel a certain way— my boss made me angry; my significant other makes me stressed out. We may acknowledge that we have a choice in how we react, but we often see it as a direct cause-and-effect relationship.

Now Beck's cognitive theory has a different model, and this really takes us back to the Greek and Stoic philosophers who tell us that it isn't events that trouble us, but it's the view we take of those events. So in a cognitive model, we have an activating event which triggers cognitions or what are called automatic thoughts, which then cause emotional and behavioral consequences. Now, particular kinds of automatic thoughts are linked to specific reactions. For example, with anger, it tends to be preceded by thoughts of, I'm being mistreated, or there's some sort of injustice that has occurred. For depression, it's often thoughts about loss.

But you might want to ask, well, why did we have those particular automatic thoughts? Two people in exactly the same situation may have dramatically different automatic thoughts. To answer that question, we'll have to use Beck's model to drill down a little bit deeper into our belief system. We'll need to better understand our rules of life or what are called our conditional if-then assumptions. And we'll need to look at what Beck called schemas or scripts that tell us what to expect, how to react, and how to live our lives. Ultimately, we'll boil it down to our basic beliefs, or core beliefs, about ourselves, about others and about the world.

Let's move to watch our first video clip, where we're talking with Michael about how to set up a formulation, and we begin to connect the dots.

[VIGNETTE START]

PROFESSOR SATTERFIELD: OK, Michael. Why don't we take a step back? And let's revisit what we had talked about a few times ago. I wanted us to talk about a case formulation. Formulation is kind of a formal term, and we can't reduce a person to a formula, obviously, but we've been gathering stories from you and you've been great in doing your homework and helping us understand what are the common thoughts, behaviors, and emotions that you have around anger. This is our opportunity to start chaining them together, to see what are some of those habits, maybe, that sort of sit inside you that we can pull out and understand and maybe change.

MICHAEL: OK.

PROFESSOR SATTERFIELD: OK? And what a formulation tends to have in it—we've talked a bit about automatic thoughts. And in the ABC, we call them beliefs. So these are the surface situational thoughts. Guy takes your parking place and thoughts pop to mind. Your wife walks out and catches you smoking out on the deck and certain thoughts pop to mind. And a lot of those thoughts were things like, this is unjust, unfair, not right. They all kind of fell into that category.

And you had lots of different kinds of events. And some of them triggered sadness, and some were happiness. But the anger ones, many of them had that sort of automatic thought.

What a formulation does is it starts drilling sort of down to get a little more deep. They call those automatic because they just pop to mind uninvited. But oftentimes, they flit in and they flit out. And they're not terribly substantial. Sometimes they are, but not always.

So a little bit deeper than that, out of all the world of possible automatic thoughts, you had this one. So it must come from somewhere. Maybe it's a prior life experience. Maybe it's the way you see the world. Maybe it's the alignment of the stars. Who knows, right? But there are reasons. There are reasons why it happens.

So in cognitive therapy, we look at the automatic thoughts. But then we also want to look at things like, I'll call this one conditional assumptions. And sometimes, they call them schemas. It's almost like having a script of the way things should be. And that would definitely relate to your perception of what's just or unjust. You have this pre-existing belief of what is right and what is wrong.

Underneath the conditional assumptions and schemas are something called core beliefs. So some would even argue that in your heart or your head or your belly or wherever you want to say, deep inside you, there are some really basic thoughts that we often learned very early on about our worth, about the world, and about what other people are like. And we want to start filling these in.

Now, this is a work in progress. It's always open to revision, and I hope it's a living document that we can keep revising. But let's see if we can come up with just a few examples. So we have lots of automatic thoughts from the ABC homework that you did before.

A conditional assumption would be like—and I've heard you make a few of them before—the guy that took your parking space at the gym, and I know that was a little while ago, but you had said something like, if I let him get away with this, then he won't be punished, or in the way of the universe, it's not fair for him to not have some sort of punishment for—so it sounds like there's a rule there. Can you put that into your words for me?

MICHAEL: People should be responsible and held responsible for their actions.

PROFESSOR SATTERFIELD: People should be held responsible. And I'll just put a dot, dot, dot. And what does that mean, held responsible?

MICHAEL: If I'm at work and one of my senior supervisors asks me to do something, I am taking on responsibility when I say yes, I'll do that. And I should then follow through. If I don't follow through, I need to be held responsible and there need to be consequences for that. So there is a contract, I guess, in the way that we all interact—that you use the example of the parking space. To my mind, the contract is if I'm there first and I've got my blinkers on, that's my spot. And he's not upholding his end of the contract, just as if I didn't do what my supervisor expected me to do, I'm breaking the rules and breaking that contract.

PROFESSOR SATTERFIELD: OK. So there's something about—and I'll just put it into words—so social contracts should not be broken. And if they are broken, then what?

MICHAEL: There should be consequences. I don't know what those consequences always should be. But I just feel that there should be consequences, whether it's, in my case, I'm reprimanded or I have to work the weekend, extra hours. I would understand that those are the consequences for breaking my social contract, as you called it here.

PROFESSOR SATTERFIELD: Now, they call these conditional assumptions, because they're often written like if then statements. So if a social contract is broken, then there must be consequences. Or earlier, when you were talking about work, you said, if I agree to a particular project, then I should be held accountable for that. And if I don't follow through with that obligation, then I should receive some sort of negative consequence.

MICHAEL: Right.

PROFESSOR SATTERFIELD: So that's a lot of rules—if-then. And the world needs rules. We have civilized society. There has to be rules. But what we want to look at is what's your set of conditional assumptions? Is there an element of flexibility or context specificity? Are they pretty hard fast regardless, applied uniformly across the board?

MICHAEL: Well, I suppose that, in the case of the driver—the jerk I've called them in the past—if I were to find out that he really was in a hurry, someone in the building that he knew, he had been called to the scene and there was an emergency, then that would be one of those kinds of circumstances that makes me not be so rigid about the consequences. If I, as an employee, am asked to do something and I become very ill and I can't deliver, that would be a circumstance.

PROFESSOR SATTERFIELD: So I'll just put if circumstances, then there needs to be some sort of flexibility.

MICHAEL: That's fair.

PROFESSOR SATTERFIELD: OK. OK. And I guess the challenge, then, is knowing when they're circumstances and knowing how much to flex.

MICHAEL: I suppose in the case of the fellow in the car, that sarcastic wave suggested to me that there were no circumstances like this. But that makes a lot of sense to me, putting it that way.

PROFESSOR SATTERFIELD: Sure. Sure. OK. Now, when we were setting goals and we were writing out your problem list, anger was definitely up at the top. And we talked about how it affects relationships, both at work and also with your wife and kid, and even extended family. But there was another element that was there too. And you had talked about work stress and there was a lot of pressure on you, and it seemed like—and we had talked a little bit, although not much—that you have a perfectionistic streak, that you have really high standards, you expect yourself to be 110%, 110% of the time pretty much. Is that fair?

MICHAEL: I think that's the way I am.

PROFESSOR SATTERFIELD: OK. Now, if we were going to put that into some sort of a conditional assumption or schema, what would that sound like? What would that look like?

MICHAEL: If I'm doing my best, people should recognize that.

PROFESSOR SATTERFIELD: OK. So if I do my best, then recognition—OK.

[VIGNETTE END]

PROFESSOR SATTERFIELD: Michael and I go on to elicit a number of additional conditional assumptions. Then we move on to discuss the deepest levels of all, schemas and core beliefs. Let's watch this next clip.

[VIGNETTE START]

PROFESSOR SATTERFIELD: So what we'll want to do as we move forward is we'll keep hearing about stories. We'll keep pulling up beliefs, automatic thoughts. But I want to start a little bit and have us think about some of the core beliefs.

Now, the core beliefs—it's really sort of a simple idea of there's really two things that sit in our core. And it's really about self-worth, and oftentimes, it's about that sense of self-worth, of who you are, the coin of which you're made. It drives our beliefs we have about the world. It drives our automatic thoughts and our relationships at home and at work. And there's two big buckets. And one is about your level of lovability, to put it simply. And the other is about your level of success. So one is really about am I a successful person, defined however you want. And the other is about relationships and connection and intimacy. Am I someone that's made of the stuff that other people will love?

For people who are depressed, they often have the thought that they're not lovable and that they're a failure. And they feel really lousy about it. But what would you guess your beliefs are in terms of lovability or success?

MICHAEL: Well, I feel that I'm successful on my own terms. And that is I expect a lot of myself. And I think that I typically deliver. So in that sense, I would expect that others would look at him, professionally say, he's successful.

Lovable—that's maybe another matter. It's hard to know what people think of you. I think that generally, my heart's in the right place, but maybe I don't express that in a way that people can really grab onto and say, that's a likable or a lovable fellow.

I guess I never really have thought about it all that much. If I had thought about it a lot and I feel I'm not lovable, than maybe it would depress me. But I don't feel that way, really. But I can see how maybe lovable isn't the word you'd naturally attach to my personality.

PROFESSOR SATTERFIELD: OK. And that's important to know and to maybe think about. And I think people's value system sometimes value success more than lovability or vice versa. There's no one right way to be. It's just different. But the other part of lovability isn't just are you lovable to other people? It's do you love yourself? Do you care about yourself? At the end of the day, when all is said and done, are you happy with who you are?

MICHAEL: I would say probably not.

PROFESSOR SATTERFIELD: OK. Tell me more about that.

MICHAEL: Well, part of it is what motivates me to talk to my wife and see what concerns her. And out of those conversations, and out of the sense of yeah, maybe my anger is getting out of control, in its physical ramifications and the way it manifested itself in the past, just in terms of my physical health, the way I feel, that's driven me here. And I guess no slam on you, but if I really were feeling that I liked myself, at the end of the day, maybe I wouldn't be here talking to you.

PROFESSOR SATTERFIELD: Right. You're right. You're right.

MICHAEL: But certainly, setting this conversation and this context aside, my anger seems to be arising out of almost a dissatisfaction. And I like to say it's a dissatisfaction with things out there, but really, maybe it's a dissatisfaction with my inability to control the things out there. And so I want to be in control. I like a guy who's in control. And if I'm not in control, maybe I don't like myself so much. Does that make any sense?

PROFESSOR SATTERFIELD: It makes a lot of sense. And it sounds like you have a working hypothesis about what's driving some of this behavior— that at core, you have this dissatisfaction with who you are or maybe the way you behave sometimes. It's not in line with your values. You tell me about your charity work. You tell me how much you love your family. And sometimes, it's not evident that that's the person that you actually are, that you have a fear of not being in control and feel like you have to control things in order to be successful, in order to be lovable, in order to protect yourself or protect your family.

So why don't we pause for now with the formulation. But I would encourage you to think a little bit in your journal and maybe even to reflect or write a little bit about this idea of lovability and control and exactly what it is that you need to do to feel comfortable in your own skin, and maybe the possibility that sometimes, all this stuff about injustice and unfairness isn't really about that. Maybe it's about your sense of self and what you think you're made of and your sense of control or power in the world.

MICHAEL: That's food for thought.

[VIGNETTE END]

PROFESSOR SATTERFIELD: So for Michael we want to formulate anger. Now, our formulation will be part cognitive theory, those kinds of thoughts that tend to precede anger, but we're also going to use real-world data from Michael's life. We want to think about those cognitive themes that precede anger, but again, we want to make it relevant and salient for him, using examples from his life.

We'll also want to look at behaviors, and for him, we'll want to look at behaviors in at least a couple of different ways. The most obvious, we will want to look at the ways that he responds to his anger. Does he act on those impulses and act out his anger with other people? And if so, how do others respond? However, we're also going to look at what are the antecedents? So what are those things that trigger his anger in the first place? And it's possible that he may be making behavioral choices that put him in high risk situations for triggering his anger.

But remember this is CBT, and thus far we've mostly focused on emotions and cognition. That leaves a fairly large area unexplored. We'll dig deeper into behavior and behavioral activation in our depression lecture, but let me for now define behavior broadly and why it would matter in terms of a formulation. So, for behavior we cast a fairly wide net, and here we're talking about all sorts of activities, mundane, big activities, small activities, activities we do alone, activities we do with others. It would include activities for pleasure, as well as activities for work, the things you have to do and the things that we want to do.

The idea is that these activities throughout the course of the day are summative in terms of how they affect our mood. A lot of little activities can add up into a fairly profound effect. Now, the roots of the behavioral part of the formulation are form behaviorism and behavioral theory, where it talks about how rewards and punishments from our environment subtly shift our behaviors until sometimes they can create very complex functional or maybe dysfunctional behaviors. Of course, we would also want to do self-monitoring with cognitions and emotions. We would want to do self-monitoring for behaviors as well.

Lastly, for our hypothesis, we want to look at origins, so here we would start delving into the past. We want a broad picture first, and we won't spend, probably, substantial time going back unless we feel that we're stuck in the present and not able to make progress. So for Michael, we might look at his history of anger at work, at home, his attempts to change, the role of anger in his family of origin. We'll weave all of these together into our hypothesis to tell a story.

Now, an actual case formulation can run between seven to ten pages, and typically includes all the assessment data, the smart goals, and treatment plans. So for Michael, I'll just share a little bit of his narrative, and it goes something like this. Michael is a 50 year old married man with one teenage son, educated and gainfully employed. He's motivated to address his anger, and sees how it will help him and others. He's uncertain if treatment can help, but he's willing to try. His anger has a quick onset and high intensity, but often a short duration. This pattern of angry arousal has been mostly life long and is similar to the pattern displayed by his own father, much to Michael's chagrin.

His anger is triggered by an number of environmental events, usually involving a perceived transgression. The combination of his perfectionism and his hyper responsibility—he must be the enforcer—further fuels his anger and his sense of self-righteousness, all in accord with a traditional cognitive model of anger.

Michael doubts his own power and influence, and often underestimates the effect he has on others. He worries that he and others won't learn or improve as human beings unless a punitive force keeps us in line. He clearly possesses some self-regulatory capacity, as he's been in a successful marriage and has been promoted and successful at work.

His anger has damaged and sometimes ended relationships, and damaged his reputation. He's currently using exercise and self-help as a means to improve his anger control. He's interested in somatic quieting, deepening his empathy, and using classic CBT.

Now, remember the last couple of parts of our case formulation include looking at strengths and assets. So, for Michael, a strength is certainly his insight and his motivation, his love and value of his relationship with his wife and his son. He is gainfully employed, so he doesn't have financial stressors, and his cardiovascular disease might actually be an asset, because it helps to raise his motivation to control his anger. The last part of our formulation would be the treatment plan, and here we want to look at evidence-based treatments, but we also want to look at a patient's willingness to engage in those treatments and what the patient's preferences might be.

Now, for Maria we're going to use the cognitive model for depression, where we'll look at a different family of cognitions and behaviors. We'll also use the model for stress and coping. And we'll want to look at her beliefs about her need to do it all and her difficulty in asking for help.

We're going to need to look at her rising and profound grief and her sense of loss, her beliefs about suffering and her personal strengths and values. And her treatment ultimately will probably be mostly focused on depression, but will include elements of stress management, as well as coping with loss.

Now, for Carol, we'll use a classic CBT model for anxiety, where it talks about the perception or misperception of threat, coupled with an estimation of having deficient coping resources. We want to help her look at her self-image, and I am curious to see if maybe there's a little bit of depression or early life events underneath that might help us to understand why she is so socially anxious. We want to know her thoughts about herself, others, and the world.

Next, I'd like to move to a frequently asked question, and a question from this individual says, "Do you always share a formulation with a patient? What if you share it, and the patient thinks you're wrong?" The short answer is yes. We almost always share a formulation with a patient. In fact, it's seen as a collaborative process, and if the patient tells me that that formulation is wrong, well, I assume that it's wrong. And we need to roll up our sleeves; we need to go back to our data; and we need to rewrite that formulation. Really, by definition, it's always a work in progress, and it's always a iterative process. That formulation guides our treatment, and if we don't have the formulation right, we might not have the treatment right.

Now, in our next lecture, we're going to talk about emerging therapies that fall into what's called CBT's Third Wave. Thank you.

Third-Wave Cognitive Behavioral Therapy
Lecture 4

In this lecture, you will learn about the therapies that preceded CBT (first-wave therapies) and therapies that have followed it (third-wave therapies). The first wave is psychodynamics. This course mostly focuses on the second wave, but there is an important third wave that seems to be qualitatively different than the other two. Third-wave therapies are not just about content; they are about the process. For each individual, it's about integrating the three waves and finding a mix of them through theory as well as trial and error that will work for that particular person.

The Three Waves of Therapy

- Although there are dozens of different types of therapies, they can be divided into three waves. Within each wave, there are of course subtypes, but each wave shares core principles. For the first wave, we have to go back to Sigmund Freud and his contemporaries. Although much of his work has been discredited today, he was incredibly influential in shaping how we think about our minds, relationships, and day-to-day functioning.

- In the first wave, our mental lives are full of deep and meaningful symbols. Dreams aren't just crazy images; they have meaning and often relate to our deep-seated desires and fears. A first-wave therapist hears what you say but is always trying to interpret what you really mean to say. In a way, it's all very mysterious and difficult to follow.

- Of course, our interest—our passion—for deep, symbolic thinking and analysis is part of our great literary and religious traditions. Both are full of hidden meanings just waiting to emerge. It's a treasure hunt, and it's a challenge.

Wave #2: Cognitive Model

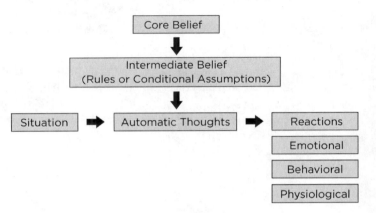

- The second wave is the cognitive model, or current CBT. In this model, an activating event triggers beliefs or thoughts, which in turn trigger particular reactions: emotional, behavioral, or maybe even physiological.

- A core assumption behind cognitive therapy is that human beings by nature aren't particularly rational. In fact, we aren't even mostly rational. We take all sorts of shortcuts in terms of how we think, how we process, and how we make decisions.

- Most second-wave CBT therapists are familiar with what are called habits of mind. An example is personalization, in which an event happens to us—and maybe in reality it was completely random— but we believe that we were individually and specifically targeted. Another example is magnification or minimization, in which we have lost perspective and made a mountain out of a molehill, or vice versa.

- We might be using a mental filter, in which we selectively attend only to the good things or to the bad things, or we might selectively recall only bad things from our past. We might engage in all-or-none thinking: You are either a complete success or you're a complete failure.

- The most common habits of mind are mind reading and fortune-telling. Mind reading often occurs in social situations. Even though we might be having a conversation with an individual, there's often a dialogue in the background where we're trying to imagine what the person is really thinking and what his or her motivations are. Fortune-telling involves trying to predict what's going to happen in the future. If you're depressed, you're probably making very negative predictions.

- Different individuals have different preferences for habits of mind. Think about this: What are your preferred or most commonly used habits of mind? What are your common conditional assumptions, or rules of life?

- Your core beliefs manifest themselves in the present by fueling particular types of automatic thoughts. What are your core beliefs or schemas about yourself, the world, and others? Can you boil it all down to lovability or achievement? Or is it more complex than that?

- In order to collect more data on yourself, consider filling out two questionnaires: the Dysfunctional Attitude Scale (a list of attitudes we commonly hold about ourselves, the world, and others) and the Automatic Thoughts Questionnaire (a list of different kinds of automatic thoughts).

- The ABCD exercise is a fairly prototypical second-wave exercise that gives us an orderly, organized, and rational framework to start dissecting potentially complex events. The ABCD exercise addresses four things: the activating event, your belief system, the consequences of your response to the activating event, and the dispute of your beliefs about the situation.

- In the second wave of therapy, as opposed to the first, it's not just about cognitions—it's also about behaviors. In the second wave, we do some self-monitoring around behaviors. We want to know which behaviors are rewarding, which are punishing, which might have been shaped over time, or which might have eroded or even disappeared over time.

- The third wave of therapy distinguishes itself from the other two waves by focusing on the process of cognition rather than on the content of cognition. It's not just about having a negative thought; it's how much attention you pay to it.

- Acceptance and commitment therapy (ACT), developed by Steven Hayes at the University of Nevada, Reno, in the late 1980s, differs from traditional CBT in that rather than trying to teach people how to better control their thoughts, feelings, sensations, memories, and private events, ACT teaches them to just notice, accept, and embrace their private events, especially previously unwanted ones.

- The core concept of ACT is that psychological suffering is caused by experiential avoidance (if we're afraid or nervous of something, we will not do it, which deprives us of the opportunity for learning and growth), cognitive entanglement (we get tangled up in our own thoughts and begin to ruminate), and the resulting psychological rigidity that leads to a failure to take needed behavioral steps in accordance with core values.

- Many of our core problems are due to FEAR: fusion with your thoughts, evaluation of experience, avoidance of your experience, and reason giving for your behavior. The healthy alternative is to ACT: accept your reactions and be present, choose a valued direction, and take action.

ACT

- ACT has six core principles that are meant to promote psychological flexibility.
    - Cognitive defusion: Learning methods to reduce the tendency to reify thoughts, images, emotions, memories.

o Acceptance: Allowing thoughts to come and go without struggling with them.

o Contact with the present moment: Awareness of the here and now, experienced with openness, interest, and receptiveness.

o Observe the self: Accessing a transcendent sense of self, a continuity of consciousness that is unchanging.

o Values: Discovering what is most important to one's true self.

o Committed action: Setting goals according to values and carrying them out responsibly.

- Research supports the use of ACT and third-wave therapies. For example, in 2013, Jessica Swain and colleagues published a systematic review of ACT and anxiety. They looked at 38 different studies that included a total of 323 different patients with a variety of anxiety disorders. They found that there was preliminary support for broad-spectrum anxiety disorders. However, these weren't particularly well-designed studies, and many of them did not yet have control groups.

- A higher-quality study, published by Vivien Hunot and colleagues in 2013, was another systematic review of third-wave therapies in comparison to both first- and second-wave therapies. Researchers found that there were only three high-quality randomized controlled trials at this point, and only about 144 people had been treated. However, they found that ACT was equal to CBT and to a subset of CBT called behavioral activation.

- In 2014, Lars-Göran Öst published an ACT systematic review and meta-analysis of behavioral research and therapy. He found 60 randomized controlled trials of about 4,200 patients and concluded that ACT is probably efficacious for chronic pain, tinnitus, depression, psychosis, obsessive-compulsive disorder, mixed anxiety, drug abuse, and work stress. For this study, there were some issues with quality, just as there were with all of these studies, but for a relatively young therapy, it's looking pretty good for ACT.

Mindfulness and MBCT

- Mindfulness is a relaxation technique that allows you to be fully present in a nonjudgmental way. There are a number of different strategies to achieve a state of mindfulness. Meditation is usually the most common. Most of them, or all of them, involve some form of concentration—often concentrating on your breath—some degree of relaxation or somatic quieting, and acceptance of the self and of others.

- Mindfulness-based cognitive therapy (MBCT), developed by Zindel Segal, John Teasdale, and others, is another third-wave therapy that combines mindfulness and cognitive therapy. The two

Meditation is one of the most common strategies to achieve a state of mindfulness.

may seem mutually exclusive at first: How can you wrestle with your thoughts in second-wave CBT, and how can you just observe your thoughts and accept them in mindfulness-based meditation?

- You can't do both at exactly the same time, but Segal, Teasdale, and others who practice MBCT suggest that it's important to have both of those tools. And depending on the situation, you might want to wrestle with your thoughts, or you might just want to sit back and practice mindfulness and acceptance.

- In a randomized controlled trial of 145 recovered but recurrently depressed participant controls versus MBCT over a 60-week period, researchers found that 66 percent of the controls had relapsed versus only 34 percent of those who were exposed to MBCT.

- In another study, a systematic review and meta-analysis by Jacob Piet and colleagues in 2011, they looked at six randomized controlled trials of nearly 600 patients. They found that MBCT significantly reduced the risk of relapse or recurrence with a risk ratio of 0.66, meaning that the relative reduction of relapse dropped by about 34 percent.

Suggested Reading

Dimeff and Koerner, *Dialectical Behavior Therapy in Clinical Practice.*

Hayes, *Get Out of Your Mind and Into Your Life.*

Hunot, Moore, Caldwell, Furukawa, Davies, Jones, Honyashiki, Chen, Lewis, and Churchill, "'Third Wave' Cognitive and Behavioural Therapies versus Other Psychological Therapies for Depression."

Layden, Newman, Freeman, and Morse, *Cognitive Therapy of Borderline Personality Disorder.*

Linehan, Armstrong, Suarez, Allmon, and Heard, "Cognitive Behavioral Treatment of Chronically Parasuicidal Borderline Patients."

Linehan, Schmidt III, Dimeff, Craft, Kanter, and Comtois, "Dialectical Behavior Therapy for Patients with Borderline Personality Disorder and Drug-Dependence."

Ost, "The Efficacy of Acceptance and Commitment Therapy."

Piet and Hougaard, "The Effect of Mindfulness-Based Cognitive Therapy for Prevention of Relapse in Recurrent Major Depressive Disorder."

Segal, Williams, and Teasdale, *Mindfulness-Based Cognitive Therapy for Depression*.

Swain, Hancock, Hainsworth, and Bowman. "Acceptance and Commitment Therapy in the Treatment of Anxiety."

Teasdale, Segal, Williams, Ridgeway, Soulsby, and Lau, "Prevention of Relapse/Recurrence in Major Depression by Mindfulness-Based Cognitive Therapy."

Williams, Teasdale, Segal, and Kabat-Zinn, *The Mindful Way through Depression*.

Questions to Consider

1. Wrestling with your thoughts and simply observing or being mindful of your thoughts without trying to change them seem diametrically opposed. How can therapies like mindfulness-based CBT and dialectical behavioral therapy work as a coherent therapeutic approach?

2. What do you imagine a fourth wave of CBT might include? What areas are left to explore or revise?

Third-Wave Cognitive Behavioral Therapy
Lecture 4—Transcript

PROFESSOR SATTERFIELD: Let's start with a quick exercise. Now, it's important that you follow my instructions in order for this to work. Whatever you do, please do not imagine a white elephant. Don't think about its shape, don't think about its size, don't think about its color. Whatever you do, don't think about its features. Do not think about a white elephant. So what happened? Well, unless you were distracted, you probably thought about a white elephant. The instructions were not to think about it, but in so doing, it made you think about it. And thus are the nature of cognitions, at least according to what's called the third wave of CBT. So what happened, and how did we get here?

Welcome to our lecture on CBT's third wave. Thus far, you've learned the basics of CBT. The CBT triangle, the basic assessment tools, how to create a formulation using the building blocks of cognition and behavior. In this lecture, we'll take a look at therapies that preceded CBT, the first wave, and therapies that have followed, the third wave.

Although there are dozens of different types of therapies, I like to divide them into these three waves. Within each wave there are, of course, subtypes, but each wave shares core principles. For wave number one, we have to go back to Sigmund Freud and his contemporaries. Although much of his work has been discredited today, he was incredibly influential in shaping how we think about our minds, our relationships, and our day-to-day functioning. In wave one, our mental lives are full of deep and meaningful symbols. Freud's cigar was not just a cigar, but a representation of something else. Dreams aren't just crazy images; they have meaning, and they often relate to our deep-seated desires and fears.

A wave-one therapist hears what you say, but is always trying to interpret what you really mean to say. In a way, it's all very mysterious and difficult to follow. But of course, our interest, our passion, really, for deep, symbolic thinking and analysis is part of our great literary and religious traditions. Both are full of hidden meanings just waiting to emerge. Seven hundred years ago Dante was telling us, "O, you possessed of sturdy intellect, observe the teaching that is hidden here beneath the veil of verses so obscure." It's a treasure hunt, and it's a challenge.

Move to wave number two, the cognitive model, or current CBT, as we know it. If you recall from our last lecture, we had talked about how often we think an activating event caused us to feel a certain way or to do a certain thing. What Beck and his contemporaries did for us is to help us to see that there's actually an important middle step, the step of cognitions, and specifically, of automatic thoughts. We have an activating situation; we have the beliefs or thoughts which are triggered; and they in turn trigger particular reactions, emotional, behavioral, or maybe even physiologic reactions.

But to dig a little bit deeper, it's important that we think about the different types of automatic thoughts that one might have and why we would care. Now, a core assumption behind cognitive therapy is that human beings, by nature, aren't particularly rational. In fact, we aren't even mostly rational. We take all sorts of shortcuts in terms of how we think, of how we process, and how we make decisions. Most second-wave CBT therapists are very familiar with what are called habits of mind.

So just to give you an idea of some of the kinds of habits of mind that we typically employ, first example would be personalization. Now, some of us do this often, all of us do this sometimes, where an event happens to us, maybe in reality it was completely random, but we believe we were individually and specifically targeted; we have over-personalized something. We may rely on magnification or minimization. Maybe we've lost perspective; we've made a mountain out of the mole hill. Or maybe someone has given us a compliment, but we have devalued it, or decreased it, or minimized the positive thing that's just happened to us.

We might be using what's called a mental filter. We may be selectively attending only to the good things or to the bad things, or we might be selectively recalling only bad things from our past. You may be engaging in all-or-none thinking; you are either a complete success, or you're a complete failure.

The last two that are most common are mind reading, often in social situations. Even though we might be having a conversation with an individual, there's often a dialogue on a back channel where we're trying to imagine what it is that they're really thinking, what their motives might actually be. Sometimes we're accurate; often we're not so accurate. And the last is something called fortune telling, where we're trying to predict what's going to happen in the future. If you're someone who's depressed, you're probably making very dire or very negative predictions.

So the first assumption is about automatic thoughts, knowing that they occur, knowing that they're not particularly rational, and knowing that we often rely on these different habits of mind; and different individuals have different preferences for some of those habits of mind. You should recall, too, another key part of Beck's model is it's not just about the automatic thoughts, but it's about the beliefs that are underneath those thoughts. In any given activating situation, different people might have very different automatic thoughts.

Why is that? It's because of those beliefs that are underneath those automatic thoughts. We have rules of life, or something called conditional assumptions. "If I don't get an A on that test, then I'm a failure." We also have core beliefs, "Am I lovable? Am I worthwhile? Am I successful? Do people care about me? Do people care about each other?" Those core beliefs, again, vary from individual to individual, and the make themselves manifest in the present by fueling particular flavors or types of automatic thoughts.

So I would suggest doing just a quick homework exercise on your own. As we begin looking at wave one, wave two, and wave three, why not apply it to your own life and see what it looks like? So ask yourself, what are your preferred or most commonly used habits of mind? Those are things like maximization and minimization, things like mind reading, fortunetelling, over-personalizing things. There's no right or wrong answer. Do you use those habits of mind, and which do you use more often than not? What are your common conditional assumptions? And these are the rules in life, the "If I'm not perfect, then I have failed," or, "If I assert myself, then people are going to reject me." It's not about being right or wrong, and remember, many times it's not even rational, but we've learned these rules growing up, we've internalized them, and they continue to influence and affect our behaviors.

What would you say are your core beliefs, or schemas, about yourself, the world, or others? And notice that I always use those three categories, and that does come from Beck, core beliefs about your value, your worth, your success, your lovability; core beliefs about the world and the way the world operates; and core beliefs about other people. Can you boil all of this down to those two core beliefs about lovability and achievement, as Beck would suggest? Or is it more complex than that?

In order to collect more data on yourself, I would also suggest that you could fill out two questionnaires on your own. The first is called the DAS, or the Dysfunctional Attitude Scale. In order to find it, you just go to our friend Google again, type in DAS, Dysfunctional Attitude Scale, and you'll find PDFs as well as scoring guides. The Dysfunctional Attitude Scale is a long list of a number of attitudes that we commonly hold about, you guessed it, ourselves, the world, and other individuals. The second questionnaire that I would recommend is something called the ATQ, or the automatic thoughts questionnaire. As you might imagine from the name, it is a list of different kinds of automatic thoughts, and you endorse whether or not you often have those particular kinds of thoughts. Again, you can find it using our friend, Google.

Let's go on to move to our first clip. This is a clip of Maria. Now, this is an example of a fairly prototypical wave-two exercise in which we're doing something called the ABCD.

[VIGNETTE START]

PROFESSOR SATTERFIELD: You've done a great job with the capturing of cognitions on the cognitive recording form. And I wanted us to take that to the next step, where you're not just capturing cognitions, but you're capturing triggers. And then we're thinking about how those cognitions affect your mood and how they affect your behavior.

What I've drawn first is something called the ABCD. They call it that just for the four boxes. The activating event is the A. The B is the beliefs, the thoughts that you have. The C IS the consequences. So that would be the emotions and behaviors that are often driven by the thoughts that you've had. And the D is the dispute box. So that's the box where if you decide the consequences aren't something that you want, you begin to wrestle to rewrite, to rethink these thoughts.

I think for us to do this, there are a couple of things we should keep in mind. One is the idea that we've talked about before that thoughts are neither true nor false. They're helpful or hurtful. They're opinions. They're interpretations. And oftentimes, we're making guesses. And any number of guesses might be accurate, I guess, if you want to use that term. But they have different consequences.

So if you're thinking about things in a certain way and it's causing negative consequences, we want to see if we can't help you to think about that same situation in an equally valid but different kind of way. So I think one assumption is we want to remember that thoughts are just thoughts. They're not facts. And they're changeable. The other assumption is that thoughts serve as an important mediator between things that happen in the world and the way that we feel as a consequence. Oftentimes, we'll talk about how work made me stressed. Or my daughter made me angry. But it's not just the external circumstance, it's also how we interpret it, how we understand it, how we think about it.

So it's the activating event—the trigger—it's how we think about it or interpret it, and those two together help us understand why you're feeling a certain way or doing a certain thing. And if we don't want that, then we go about changing it.

This exercise is all very orderly, organized, and rational, maybe deceptively so. But it does give us a framework to start dissecting potentially complex events. Now, Maria goes on to share her activating event of leaving her husband to go out to do some errands and shopping. And she was hoping to treat herself by stopping at Starbucks before going home. But she doesn't do it. She goes on to complete this exercise, and we begin to understand why in this next clip.

PROFESSOR SATTERFIELD: So you were out doing errands. And some of the beliefs you had or the feelings you mentioned, you felt guilty.

MARIA: Yes.

PROFESSOR SATTERFIELD: And you rushed through your errands. And you went home early?

MARIA: Yes, I went home early. Jack was asleep, so it didn't make any difference, but I felt so bad.

PROFESSOR SATTERFIELD: And there was no Starbucks.

MARIA: No Starbucks, alas.

PROFESSOR SATTERFIELD: OK. So those were the consequences. Those are emotions and those are behaviors. You were out doing the errands. You started having some thoughts, and you felt guilty, so you rushed, you went home early, and you didn't treat yourself.

OK. So now, we want to write down those cognitions. And this is just like that cognitive recording form that you were using. So in the moment, when you were out doing those errands, what were some of the thoughts going through your mind?

MARIA: Well, I was thinking, something could happen to Jack. I was thinking, that woman doesn't really understand him. I was thinking, I ought to be there. I'm the one that's supposed to be taking care of him. I just felt guilty about not being there and not taking care of him. I thought he might be afraid or lonely or confused, as he often is.

PROFESSOR SATTERFIELD: And I've just written down a few. And as we've mentioned before, there's always lots of cognitions. And really, the skill is to hone in on some of the more potent cognitions, more potent in the sense of they were really driving the guilt or driving the behavior changes.

So I've written down, something could happen. I can see how that would make you anxious and worried. The home health care worker, she doesn't understand him. So that's part of the guilt that's there. I should be there, and you're not there—so again, the guilt definitely seems like a driver. He's afraid and lonely and confused—and again, guilt and maybe some sadness too about that.

So all of those seem like they're pretty potent thoughts. I'm just going to draw that arrow to remind us that you have this activating event, triggers certain thoughts, gives rise to certain emotions and consequences. This brings us to the dispute box, so the D part of our ABCD.

MARIA: This is the hard part.

PROFESSOR SATTERFIELD: This is the hard part. And oftentimes, you want to come up with multiple disputes. And you probably want to pick just one of these. We can do them all, but you have to start somewhere. So which one would you like to start with?

MARIA: I don't know. What would you suggest?

PROFESSOR SATTERFIELD: Well, all of them seem to have an emotional charge. Probably one, three, or four.

MARIA: OK. Let's do one.

PROFESSOR SATTERFIELD: OK. So something could happen. OK. So what we want to do in the dispute box—and remember our goal isn't to be true or false, it's to be fair. It's to be balanced. It's to be rational. It's to think about whether a cognition is helpful or hurtful. So something could happen.

I think in the realm of possibilities, that would always be true, right? So even for a healthy person, something could happen.

MARIA: Well, that's true, yeah.

PROFESSOR SATTERFIELD: So it's really about probabilities, and the probability may be big, but it may be small. Yes, something could happen. But what would you say if you were out with Judith, your friend, and she was worried that something could happen to her daughter or her husband? What would you say to her?

MARIA: They'll be fine.

PROFESSOR SATTERFIELD: OK. And why would you say that?

MARIA: Because they can take care of themselves.

PROFESSOR SATTERFIELD: OK. But how about your husband? He can't really take care of himself.

MARIA: He can't take of himself. Well, there is that woman. She is trained. Even if she doesn't understand him and if he doesn't like her, I guess nothing terrible could happen, because she would do something.

PROFESSOR SATTERFIELD: Yes. Yes. So how about we put—so he isn't alone. A trained—just going to use a symbol that's shorter—a trained woman is there to help. And much of her training, I'm sure, is what to do in case of an emergency.

MARIA: I'm sure that's true.

PROFESSOR SATTERFIELD: So if something were to happen, if he were to fall, then she would be right there. And I'm just going to, since we're focusing on this one, I'm going to—this is the one we're disputing. But let's come up with a couple of other ways that we might dispute it.

So one is well, he isn't alone. The trained woman could be there to help. So if something does happen, it's taken care of.

MARIA: OK.

PROFESSOR SATTERFIELD: Let's come up with another dispute. What would help you take care of that anxiety? Again, imagine speaking with Judith or with a friend or just trying to find a helpful way to think about that.

PROFESSOR SATTERFIELD: Yeah. I could talk with Judith about it. But maybe I should look for a different caretaker, one that I trust a little more, one that—I don't know if he'd like another caretaker or not, but maybe that would be the thing.

PROFESSOR SATTERFIELD: And that's a good example of—in the dispute box, we usually think about cognitions. But it can also be a very specific concrete plan to do something differently. So if you are not comfortable or are not reassured by the caregiver that you have, if you're afraid she's not trained or qualified or husband doesn't like her, you can certainly find somebody else.

[VIGNETTE END]

PROFESSOR SATTERFIELD: In this exercise we go on to talk about habits of mind, finding balance, and what to do the next time she's out and she has about of anxiety or guilt. We're in a sense wrestling with her thoughts. The exercise follows three main steps we've talked about before. We first identified cognitions, we analyze or evaluate those cognitions, and then we try to rewrite or restructure them.

Now, remember in wave two it's not just about cognitions, it's also about behaviors. So we'll do some self-monitoring around behaviors. We want to know what behaviors are rewarding, which are punishing, which might have shaped over time, or which behaviors might have eroded or even disappeared over time. In our Depression lecture we'll talk a specific subset of CBT called behavioral activation, but it's still very much part of wave two.

Let's move then to talk about the emergence of wave three. And in wave three, it focuses on the process of cognition, rather than on the content of cognition. It's not just about having a negative thought; it's how much attention you pay to it. And to illustrate this, I would like to share something called the bus analogy, taken from Steve Hayes, who is the founding father of a third-wave therapy called Acceptance and Commitment Therapy.

Now, in the Bus Analogy, it goes something like this: Imagine yourself as a bus driver. You are driving your bus down the road of life, hopefully in the direction of your goals and your personal values. As you drive along, life happens, as it always does, and people get on the bus, and people might get off the bus. Some of them are very positive and very supportive. Some of them, probably most of them, are going to be fairly neutral, but some of the people that get on this bus are going to be negative. They're going to be disruptive. They're going to try to pull you in a different direction. Now, you have a choice. Are you going to stop the bus, and are you going to argue with them? Are you going to divert and go somewhere else so they don't make so much noise? Or are you going to continue driving down that true path in pursuit of your goals and in pursuit of your values?

Now, you can guess what Steve Hayes would say. You keep driving your bus. You don't give attention, or time, or credence to those disruptors that have gotten on your bus. You stay focused on your values, and you act accordingly. This is a central tenet of Acceptance and Commitment Therapy, or ACT, usually pronounced as the word act. As I mentioned, it was developed by Steve Hayes, who's at the University of Nevada in Reno, and it came out in the late 1980s.

Now, ACT differs from traditional CBT, in that, rather than trying to teach people how to better control their thoughts, feelings, sensations, memories, and private events, ACT teaches them to just notice, accept, and embrace their private events, especially previously unwanted ones. The core conception of ACT is that psychological suffering is caused by experiential avoidance. If we're afraid or we're nervous of things, we will not do it, which deprives us of the opportunity for learning and growth.

It's also caused by cognitive entanglement. This is where we get tangled up in our own thoughts and we begin to ruminate, and we often will go around in circles and circles and circles telling ourselves not to think of that white elephant, but in so doing, it makes us think about it even more. And lastly, psychological sufferings caused by the resulting psychological frigidity from avoidance and from cognitive entanglement that prevents us from driving down that road towards our values.

Now, ACT says that many of our core problems are due to fear, and it uses the word fear as an acronym, F.E.A.R, where F is fusion with your thoughts. So rather than seeing thoughts as opinions or mental activities that blow in and out of your head, you see yourself and your thoughts as the same. The E, evaluation of your experience, or maybe misevaluation of your experience, losing track of where you are. Avoidance of your experience is a. And the r, reason given for your behavior, or sometimes coming up with excuses for your behavior. And the healthy alternative is to ACT, to accept your reactions, and be present, to C, choose a value direction, and T, to take action.

Now ACT has six core principles that are meant to promote psychological flexibility. And first we've talked about a little bit, cognitive defusion, so learning methods to reduce the tendency to see thoughts in yourself as one in the same thing. Thoughts are opinions; they are just mental noise that may or may not mean anything. Acceptance: We want to allow thoughts to come and go without wrestling with them. Remember in wave two, we literally write them down and we try to rewrite those thoughts; we're actively working with them. In ACT, we don't do that. We just accept them as thoughts that have come in and thoughts that are going to go out.

We want to keep our contact with the present moment. You don't want to get tangled up in those thoughts of the past. You don't want to start fortunetelling or future tripping about what's going to happen in the future. You want to cultivate and develop a sense of mindfulness or the awareness of here and now, experience with openness, interest, and receptiveness.

You want to observe the self. You want to be able to do what Steve Hayes calls Access the Transcendent Sense of Self. And what he means by that is throughout our lives, there's a lot of things that happen, good and bad. There could be medical illnesses. There could be divorces. There could be marriages. There could be new jobs. But inside all of those events, the one thing that's common is you. The core of who you are, or some people would say, the soul of who you are. I've heard him ask patients before who were terminally ill and had a lot of physical symptoms and a lot of physical sufferings saying, how are you, the person inside that illness? How are you doing? Teaching people to observe the self. The core of who they are.

Teaching people to look at their values, now, when I mentioned driving that bus down a road towards your value, one exercise in ACT is to help people to remember what their values are. When was the last time that you sat down and created a list of your values, and did an evaluation of whether or not you're living your life in regard, or being true, to your values? And the last is committed action, so setting goals according to values and carrying them out responsibly.

So we've talked about evidence-based medicine and the importance of research. What research supports the use of ACT or third-wave therapies? And I want to share just a few studies. So the first was a systematic review published by Swain and colleagues in 2013, where they looked at 38 different studies that included a total of 323 different patients. These were with a variety of different kinds of anxiety disorders. They found that there was what they called "preliminary support for broad-spectrum anxiety disorders." The problem was, these weren't particularly well-designed studies, and many of them did not yet have control groups. So it looks good, but not particularly convincing just yet.

Next study, this was a higher quality study done by Hunot and colleagues in 2013. This was another systematic review put out by the Cochrane collaboration. If you're not familiar with Cochrane, they do a number of very high quality, and also very expensive, systematic reviews. So, a lot of scientist, researchers, teachers, and clinicians will go to Cochrane first and see if they've put out the final word on a particular treatment. So Cochrane, through Hunot, publishes this particular review of third-wave therapies in comparison to other therapies, both first and second wave. They found that there were only three high quality randomized control trials at this point, and only about 144 people had been treated. What they found, though, is that ACT was equal to CBT and to a subset of CBT called behavioral activation that we'll be talking about in our depression lecture.

The last that I'll mention is an ACT systematic review in META analysis, published by Lars-Göran Öst in behavioral research and therapy in 2014. Now, in this one he found 60 randomized control trials, about 4,200 patients and concludes that ACT is probably efficacious for chronic pain; for tinnitus, or ringing in your ears; possibly for depression; for psychosis; for obsessive-compulsive disorder; for mixed anxiety; drug abuse; and work stress. So that's a fairly long list. Again, there's some issues with quality, as there are with all of these studies. But again, for a relatively young therapy, it's looking like things are pretty good.

Let's move on to our next clip. Here, we have a clip of Michael. And in this particular clip, we are setting up what might be considered a third-way exercise. We're talking about decentering, and we're moving in the direction of defusion. Let's see how we describe this for Michael.

[VIGNETTE START]

PROFESSOR SATTERFIELD: OK, Michael. So the next thing I wanted to do is just to take a few minutes to talk about something we've been practicing a bit already, but to put a name to it and to develop the skill a little bit more. And what it's called is decentering, or sometimes called defusion.

And what I mean by that is, first of all, it's an attitude or it's an approach that we are different from our thoughts. We are different from our emotions, that our emotions, our thoughts, they're both mental activity, But they're not the sum total of who we are. We have lots of different thoughts, lots of different emotions that come and go, even if we have favorite ones we tend to gravitate to, There's still a person inside there, whatever your belief is—your personality, your soul, your whoever. There's a person in there that experiences those thoughts and emotions. And we don't have to necessarily get tangled up and pulled into those thoughts and emotions if we don't want to.

So we want to step outside of the center of the storm, if you will, to decenter yourself, or not allow yourself to be fused to those thoughts or emotions. So you defuse yourself. And part of what you've been doing with the thought records, and even with the ABCD a little bit, is that we've been stepping back and saying, thoughts are neither true nor false. They're helpful or they're hurtful.

So they're not who you are. They're not a fact out there in the world. They're an opinion. They're something that we can write down. They're something that we can think about. They're something that we can step outside of or decenter from.

So it's partly an attitude, but it's also a skill set. So I think when you are in the moment, when that storm starts to blow in those thoughts and emotions, there are things you can do, like a thought record, but there are other things that you can do that maybe work better in the moment to keep yourself from getting sort of swept up into that current.

And I know, for you, we've talked mostly about anger. A lot of different emotions, too, but anger is one that comes up. And I thought maybe we could talk about a hypothetical but likely scenario where a storm might blow in. And there are things you could say to yourself in the moment that would promote decentering. How does that sound?

MICHAEL: No, that sounds good. That sounds good. So the idea is I don't always have that thought record with me or I'm not always in a situation where I can just process it. So this is another strategy for separating out.

PROFESSOR SATTERFIELD: Exactly, and of saying and reminding yourself—and this might even be something you say to yourself in the moment—I'm different than my emotions. I'm different than my thoughts. I can choose to attend to them, to pay attention, or I can choose just to let the storm blow through.

MICHAEL: OK.

[VIGNETTE END]

PROFESSOR SATTERFIELD: So the part we weren't able to show you was the ongoing practice in mindfulness that Michael must engage in if something like diffusion is going to occur. Mindfulness is not something that can be done in one exercise, two exercises, or even ten exercises. You have to, as they say, put in your time on the cushion in order to develop those skills of being present, fully present in a nonjudgmental way. Now, there are a number of different strategies to get to mindfulness. Meditation is usually the most common. Most of them, or all of them, involve some form of concentration—often concentrating on your breath—some degree of relaxation or somatic quieting, and a hefty dose of acceptance—acceptance of the self, and acceptance of others.

Now, the last third-wave therapy I wanted to mention is something called MBCT, which stands for mindfulness-based cognitive therapy, developed by Zindel Segal and John Teasdale and others. And here, as the name implies, we're back to mindfulness, but we're melding it with cognitive therapy. In a way that Zindel has described it before, it's sort of like Buddhist meditation meets cognitive therapy.

Now, the two may seem mutually exclusive at first. How can you wrestle with your thoughts in wave two of CBT, and how can you just observe your thoughts and accept them in mindfulness-based meditation? And you're right; you can't do them both at exactly the same time, but what Zindel, and John, and others that practice MBCT would suggest is that it's important that you have both of those tools. And depending on the situation, you may want to roll up your sleeves and wrestle with those thoughts, or you may just want to sit back and practice mindfulness and acceptance; let the storm blow in, and let the storm blow out.

Again, let's turn to look at the evidence. In a randomized, controlled trial of 145 recovered but recurrently depressed patients, controls versus MBCT, over a 60-week period, they found that 66% of the controls had relapsed, versus only 34% of those who were in MBCT. In another study, a systematic review and meta-analysis by Piet in 2001, they looked at six randomized controlled trials of nearly 600 patients. They found that MBCT significantly reduced the risk of relapse or recurrence with a risk ratio of 0.66, meaning that the relative reduction of relapse dropped by about 34%. Now, we know that people who are depressed, even if treated successfully, will often relapse. So it looks like the addition of mindfulness with CBT helps to reduce the risk of relapse in those individuals.

So where does that leave us? Well, recall we have the first wave in psychodynamics. This course is mostly focusing on second waves, but there is this important third wave that seems to be qualitatively different, where it's not just about content, it's about process. Now, there are a number of case implications for Carol, who is tormented by anxiety-provoking thoughts with clear experiential avoidance. For Michael, who may need to review his values and is he behaving in a way that's in accordance with his values? Or for Maria, her primary stressor, her husband's death, is beyond her control. What would acceptance bring for her?

Now, in the end it's about integration of the different waves, and it's about finding a recipe, a mix through theory and trial and error that will work for each individual. People can learn seemingly contradictory skills and switch between them if one turns out not to work so well.

Please join me for our next lecture, where we'll talk about stress. We'll talk about the what, the how, the why. We'll talk about assessment, and most importantly, we'll talk about interventions.

Stress and Coping
Lecture 5

In this lecture, you will learn about the phenomenon known as stress. Stress is normal, but if it's chronic or severe, or if a person has selected maladaptive coping strategies, it can become detrimental to your health and well-being. As you will learn in this lecture, stress can be managed in a number of ways, including by looking at appraisals, using somatic quieting, and reaching out to people in social supports. Specifically, you will learn about stress in relation to cognition and behaviors.

Stress

- We've all experienced stress before. We all know roughly what it entails. But it's officially defined as a highly orchestrated response to a perceived threat or challenge that includes biological, behavioral, cognitive, and emotional elements. The stressor is the real or imagined thing—the event—that sets the whole process off. Humans are unique in this respect: We can stress ourselves out with hypothetical events, things that never happen or might never happen.

- There are a few other features of stress to keep in mind as we're thinking about how to help people cope more effectively with stress. First, is it a chronic or an acute condition? Acute stress is usually short term. Sometimes that elevated level of stressful arousal can give us the energy, the tunnel vision, and the focus to face whatever stressor or challenge lies directly ahead of us. But with chronic stress, we develop a chronic wear and tear on our bodies, often from things that won't change or can't change.

- From a CBT perspective, we are going to look at the cognitive viewpoint of stress, and we're going to look at a very specific kind of cognitions called appraisals, but we also want to look at the behavioral viewpoint of stress.

- Behaviors are important in two different ways when it comes to the stress process. First, we might be engaging in behaviors that make us more or less likely to experience stressors. Second, on the other end of the process, we might be engaging in behaviors as a way of coping that could either be adaptive or maladaptive.

- A basic stress assessment includes the following common questions.
    - How often have you felt nervous or stressed out in the past month?

    - What has been causing you to feel stressed out? Of course, the answer is the stressors. But is there anything else? Multiple stressors can occur at the same time.

    - How long has this been going on? We want to know whether it's acute or chronic. If it is chronic, we want to know what the duration has been?

    - How has this stress been affecting you? How has it affected your relationships or your performance at work? Have there been any other effects?

    - What have you been doing to cope with this stressful situation? The answer is your coping behaviors. How well has that been working for you? How can others help you? How can you illicit helping behaviors from people in your social support network?

- When thinking about stress assessment, it's important to know where you are starting, which is the purpose of these five questions about frequency, cause, duration, impact, and coping.

The Relaxation Response

- Somatic quieting is a relaxation strategy in which we are essentially creating what is called a relaxation response, or the opposite of a stress response. We are battling two primary physiological stress pathways: the hypothalamic-pituitary-adrenal

(HPA) axis, which is responsible for secreting a stress hormone called cortisol, and the sympathetic-adrenal medullary system, which is responsible for secreting epinephrine or adrenaline and causes the fight-or-flight response.

- The "relaxation response" is a term that was coined by Herbert Benson in his book *The Relaxation Response* in 1976. Essentially, it is the opposite of the stress response. As opposed to the stress response, in the relaxation response, we get a decrease in respiration, heart rate, blood pressure, and stress hormones.

- How do we get to the relaxation response? Fortunately, there are a number of different ways we can accomplish this goal. We usually need some form of focused concentration—maybe on your breath or on a guided image—a quiet environment, and a passive attitude of allowing yourself to slowly sink into the process of relaxation.

- Both stress and relaxation are mediated by the autonomic nervous system. Throughout the day, think about events that trigger your autonomic nervous system that either push you up or push you down—maybe getting an obnoxious e-mail from a coworker, arguing with the bank about refinancing your mortgage, getting an extra-long hug from a grandchild, or unwinding in a bubble bath with soft jazz playing in the background. It's all about the outside events getting inside through our autonomic nervous system, and it behooves us to be aware of it and potentially to change it.

The Basic Cognitive Behavioral Model of Stress

- Stress affects cognitions, emotions, and behaviors, but it is also affected by—or maybe even caused by—cognitions and behaviors. On the cognitive side, there is the special kind of cognition called appraisals.

- Appraisals come in two different forms. The first kind is primary appraisals, which are our thoughts about the nature of a stressor. Is it big? Is it small? Is it threatening? Does it matter? How is it going

The relaxation response—mediated by the autonomic nervous system—involves decreases in respiration, heart rate, blood pressure, and stress hormones.

to influence you? How likely is it that it will actually happen? The second kind of appraisals is called secondary appraisals, which have to do with our estimations of our coping skills and coping resources.

- If you have a very high or strong primary appraisal—it's a very big stressor that's likely to happen—and you have very low secondary appraisals—you don't know what to do and you don't have any coping resources—then your experience of stress is likely to be quite high.

- From a cognitive behavioral perspective, what might go wrong is that an individual's appraisals might be out of sync with reality, or they might be out of touch with their actual coping skills or coping abilities.

- What about the selection of coping strategies? Coping behaviors can be classified into two different categories. Emotion-focused coping focuses on changing your emotional state to help you feel better. Somatic quieting falls in that category. Problem-focused coping focuses on the problem. For example, you might get to work studying for a test that is causing you to be stressed.

- One coping behavior is not necessarily better than the other. It depends on what needs to be done at the time, and you need a balance between the two kinds of coping. CBT data helps by allowing you to analyze your preferred coping styles and determine whether or not you're selecting the most adaptive strategies.

- You want to select behaviors. You might select behaviors that evoke a relaxation response, which would fall into the category of emotion-focused coping. You might decide to reach out and ask your social supports for help. That could be emotion-focused coping, but it might also be problem-focused coping.

- You could have task-oriented behaviors. If you're really stressed about the state of your home, you might decide to do some home improvements, which would be problem-focused coping. You could also just decide to schedule pleasant activities, things that bring you a sense of joy or that at least allow you to escape an unchangeable stressor for a short period of time.

- Most of the high-quality research in the realm of cognitive therapy for stress management is done by Michael Antoni at the University of Miami. He essentially wrote the book on what's called cognitive behavioral stress management (CBSM). He has conducted a number of studies on "regular" people but also on people who have chronic medical stressors, such as HIV, cancer, or chronic fatigue.

- The most common outcomes Antoni is analyzing are depression, anxiety, and quality of life. For people with medical conditions, he is sometimes looking at adherence to treatment or the progression or slowing of their particular illness.

- Antoni has found fairly strong support for a mix of cognitive restructuring (wrestling with those thoughts), relaxation, coping skills, assertiveness, and being able to—and feeling entitled to—ask for the support that you need.

- In an interesting study of CBSM in 2014, Antoni and his colleagues studied women with breast cancer. They did a five-year follow-up using CBSM and found that women with breast cancer who underwent this particular mixed treatment had less depression and a higher quality of life.

Mindfulness-Based Stress Reduction

- Mindfulness-based stress reduction (MBSR) is a third-wave type of stress-reduction intervention. It is a modern variant of meditation and yoga that has been applied to stress reduction. Like meditation, it builds concentration, present focus, acceptance, and somatic quieting. It was developed by Jon Kabat-Zinn at the University of Massachusetts and has since been applied to a wide range of medical problems, but it all started with chronic pain.

- Most MBSR programs last about eight to 10 weeks. They consist of two-and-a-half-hour daily classes and often will have a single-day or maybe weekend retreat at the end. It's not particularly spiritually based, but there is certainly a Buddhist element, and there are Buddhist roots to the mindfulness that these individuals are learning.

- MBSR has been shown to improve chronic pain, low back pain, pain in general, stress, and mood. An interesting study even showed improvements in immune function.

- In 2004, Paul Grossman and his colleagues published a meta-analysis in the *Journal of Psychosomatic Research*. They analyzed 20 high-quality MBSR studies that covered a wide spectrum of patients—including individuals with cancer, pain, cardiovascular disease, depression, and anxiety—and they looked at the standardized measures of physical and mental well-being. Across the board, they found moderate to strong effect sizes.

Suggested Reading

Antoni, Ironson, and Schneiderman, *Cognitive-Behavioral Stress Management*.

Benson and Klipper, *The Relaxation Response*.

Davis, Eshelman, and McKay, *The Relaxation & Stress Reduction Workbook*.

Gawaine, *Creative Visualisation*.

Grossman, Niemann, Schmidt, and Walach, "Mindfulness-Based Stress Reduction and Health Benefits."

Kabat-Zinn, *Full Catastrophe Living*.

Lazarus and Folkman, *Stress, Appraisal and Coping*.

Lehrer, Woolfolk, and Sime, *Principles and Practice of Stress Management*.

Sapolsky, *Why Zebras Don't Get Ulcers*.

Snyder, *Coping*.

Stagl, Antoni, Lechner, Bouchard, Blomberg, Glück, Derhagopian, and Carver, "Randomized Controlled Trial of Cognitive Behavioral Stress Management in Breast Cancer."

Measure your personal stress with the following web-based inventory.

Hassles Scale:

http://www.possibilitiesamplified.com/downloads/Health-Hassle-Scale.pdf.

Assess your personal coping style with the following web-based inventory.

Brief COPE:

http://www.psy.miami.edu/faculty/ccarver/sclBrCOPE.html.

Stress and Coping
Lecture 5—Transcript

PROFESSOR SATTERFIELD: The kids are sick again and need to stay home from school, but work is really busy and your boss has already chewed you out for not being a team player. Your bank account is almost overdrawn, you still haven't paid the electric bill, and your elderly mom still needs you to cover her dental bills. Your adult brother still thinks he's a kid, and he's off on one of his adventures, no doubt assuming he can call you when he needs something. Your house is a mess. Your refrigerator is empty, and the dog just peed on the carpet again. Your spouse, well, that marriage ended several years ago, and now you're on your own.

Welcome to Life 101 and to our lecture, where we'll talk about the phenomenon we call stress. We will define our constructs, relate them to cognition and behaviors, and demonstrate both a stress assessment and a somatic quieting exercise with our cases.

So what is stress? We've all experienced it before. We all know, roughly, what it entails. But it's officially defined as a highly orchestrated response to a perceived threat or challenge that includes biological, behavioral, cognitive, and emotional elements. Now, the stressor is the real or imagined thing, the event, that sets the whole process off. It's important to remember that humans are unique in one respect. We can stress ourselves out with hypothetical events, things that never happen or might never happen.

We need to keep in mind a couple of other features of stress when we're thinking about how to help people cope more effectively. First, is it a chronic or is it an acute condition? Acute stress is usually short term; it's time limited, and sometimes that level of stressful arousal can give us the energy, the tunnel vision, and the focus to face whatever stressor or challenge lies ahead of us. Chronic stress is a very different story. We get that chronic burn, that chronic wear and tear, on our bodies oftentimes from things that won't change or can't change.

From a CBT perspective, we are, of course, going to look at the cognitive viewpoint of stress, and we're going to look at a very specific kind of cognition called appraisals, but we also wanted to look at the behavioral viewpoint of stress. And behaviors are important in sort of two different points on the stress process. First of all, we might be engaging in behaviors that make us more or less likely to experience stressors. On the other end of the process, we may be engaging in behaviors as a way of coping that could either be adaptive or maladaptive. Let's move now to look at our first clip where we do a much more in-depth assessment of stress with Maria.

[VIGNETTE START]

PROFESSOR SATTERFIELD: So I think the next thing we should probably do is talk in a little more detail about your experience of stress. And you had mentioned that you've been stressed for quite some time. It's mostly related to care giving. You're worried it's affecting your health, and we know that it's affected your mood. So I just wanted to get a little more information on both the quantity and quality of stress that you're experiencing so we know a better idea of what we're trying to tackle.

MARIA: OK.

PROFESSOR SATTERFIELD: So if you were going to rate, on a scale of one to 10, how your average stress level, say the past couple of weeks, what would you say you are, where 10 is the highest level of stress?

MARIA: Well, maybe a seven. I feel stressed most of the time.

PROFESSOR SATTERFIELD: OK, so you're a seven. And on any given day, do you ever get up to a 10?

MARIA: Oh, yeah. Oh, yeah. I do that easy.

PROFESSOR SATTERFIELD: OK, up to a 10. What's the lowest level you can get to, usually?

MARIA: You mean to relax down to?

PROFESSOR SATTERFIELD: Mhm.

MARIA: I don't know. Maybe a 4, maybe a 5.

PROFESSOR SATTERFIELD: OK, so you range between 10 and 4, and it sounds like you're more often closer to 10.

MARIA: Yeah, I feel like that. It's a rare thing when I really feel anywhere near good.

PROFESSOR SATTERFIELD: All right. And how much of, say, the past several months have you felt stressed? Is it present all the time, 75%, 50%, 25%?

MARIA: It feels like it's all the time. Sometimes it's a little less, sometimes it's a little more. But it's all the time.

PROFESSOR SATTERFIELD: So it's pretty much chronic.

MARIA: Yeah.

PROFESSOR SATTERFIELD: And how long has this been going on—six months, a year, two years?

MARIA: Really the last two years, I just haven't been myself.

PROFESSOR SATTERFIELD: OK. So for about two years, pretty chronic and non-remitting stress. And at least recently, it's been up near 10. But sounds like more than just recently, it's been pretty high for quite some time.

MARIA: Yeah.

PROFESSOR SATTERFIELD: So it's not surprising that your body and your mood have had a lot of wear and tear.

MARIA: Yeah.

PROFESSOR SATTERFIELD: Now, I wanted to talk a little bit about the sources of stress. And I know that care giving and your husband's illness is the primary thing. And you've talked a little bit about finances, too. You've put money away, but there's still, of course, stress and concern.

MARIA: A lot of expenses with—

PROFESSOR SATTERFIELD: Right. Other than caring for your husband and the financial stressors, are there any other things that you think contribute to your stress levels?

MARIA: I worry what's going to happen after he goes. I mean, if I were 50, I could imagine making a life for myself. I mean, it's something I can't even really think about because it means him dying. And I feel so bad about that, that I'm going to be here and he's not. But I don't know what kind of life—I'm 70, you know, how am I going to make a life for myself at 70? I worry about that. That's the stress for me.

PROFESSOR SATTERFIELD: Right. When you're caring for someone with a chronic disease, and especially something like a progressive dementia, the grieving starts right away, really. Because you can see the trajectory, even if you don't know the endpoints—

MARIA: Yeah. You know what's coming.

PROFESSOR SATTERFIELD: —of progression, you know that it's coming. And to me, it sounds, at least in part, you're grieving. And you're worrying about the loss—

MARIA: I am.

PROFESSOR SATTERFIELD: —that you will experience.

MARIA: I mean, he doesn't even know our children anymore. And a lot of days, he doesn't know me. And you know, to tell you the truth, some of the time, I don't even know him anymore. It's almost like we're two strangers and we're trapped in this nightmare or something. He's not the man I married or that I spent 40 years raising kids and wrestling through a life with, you know? He's just not there anymore. It's like his spirit already went. Except once in a while, you know, it kind of peeks through again.

PROFESSOR SATTERFIELD: Savor those moments.

MARIA: Yeah.

PROFESSOR SATTERFIELD: Maria, I want you to know that you're not alone in this. And I know you're coming here and working on things.

MARIA: Oh, and I do appreciate it. I really do. It means so much to me to be able to come and talk with you. At first, I thought it would just be one more awful thing I'd have to fit into a day. But it just means so much to me to be able to say what I'm feeling.

PROFESSOR SATTERFIELD: Good. And I want to just plant a seed, if I may, about another possible source of support for you. You are not the only person going through the loss of a spouse, or care giving of a spouse. And I hear it from so many different patients, of how isolated and alone they feel, and they will join a caregiver support group and they'll realize that they're not alone, that there are other kind, caring, compassionate, stressed-out, maybe depressed people who are also caring for their spouses. And it becomes a wonderful source of support to know that it's not just you. Other people have those same worries and those same fears.

MARIA: I'm sure that's true.

PROFESSOR SATTERFIELD: Have you ever gone to a support group, or thought about it?

MARIA: No, I haven't thought about it at all. It seemed like it'd just be depressing to see somebody as depressed as I was.

PROFESSOR SATTERFIELD: OK. All right. Well, I'll just leave it as a seed for right now, but hope that you'll think about it.

MARIA: I will.

PROFESSOR SATTERFIELD: I can personally recommend a couple of caregiver support groups. In fact, we run just around the corner here.

MARIA: OK.

PROFESSOR SATTERFIELD: But think about it, and we'll revisit it a bit down the road.

MARIA: OK. Thank you.

PROFESSOR SATTERFIELD: I want to just wrap up our assessment about stress. You were sharing the sources of stress, and had talked about your worries about losing your husband and what comes next. I wanted to ask if there's any other sources of stress.

MARIA: Seems like enough. I feel, I don't know. I feel guilty a lot of the time. Maybe that's a source of stress.

PROFESSOR SATTERFIELD: What is that related to?

MARIA: I feel guilty about everything. I mean, I feel guilty about feeling so tired. I feel guilty about not being able to help my husband more than I do. I feel guilty about being the one that's going to be alive, and he's dying. Sometimes I just wish it were over, you know? And wish he could die and be out of it. And then that way lies madness. I mean, I just feel really guilty about even having those thoughts. So I don't know. Are those stressors, too?

PROFESSOR SATTERFIELD: Yeah. And it's all part of the picture for sure. And again, you're not alone in that. Those thoughts are common.

MARIA: I feel guilty about being here because he's not with me.

PROFESSOR SATTERFIELD: Well, my next question is not about the sources of stress, but the consequences of stress. And you've mentioned the trouble with sleeping. And of course, we've talked about depression and anxiety. What other ways does stress affect you, or your relationships, or your behaviors?

MARIA: Well, I think I'm not as outgoing as I used to be. I'm so focused on him, and us, and getting everything done. You know, I used to spend more time with my grandchildren and call my son who's out in San Francisco, and I just don't have the energy for it. I just don't want to cope with it. So I think that might be one.

PROFESSOR SATTERFIELD: OK. Any other changes in behavior, or other consequences of stress you've noticed?

MARIA: I don't know. Some irritability sometimes, I guess.

PROFESSOR SATTERFIELD: OK, again, a common symptom.

MARIA: Yeah. I'm just so frustrated when everything—you know, you try so hard to make it all right. And then just isn't. And it can't be.

PROFESSOR SATTERFIELD: So how do you cope with stress? What sorts of things do you do to feel better?

MARIA: Just try to keep going, I guess. I like music. Sometimes I put jazz on or something, listen to that, some Edith Piaf when I'm really down. I don't know. Music sometimes helps. It used to help more. But that can help.

PROFESSOR SATTERFIELD: And do you ever reach out to others as a way of coping?

MARIA: I used to, more. I mean, my daughter, yeah, sometimes. She's so kind. She's so busy with her own life. And the kids are at a very busy age where she's always driving to soccer practice and this and that. So I don't like to lean on her too much. But we do talk sometimes. Maybe I should call her more, but it's hard.

PROFESSOR SATTERFIELD: And what could another person do to help you with your stress? What would you like others to do?

MARIA: Just talk, I guess. Just have someone else to talk to. I guess it would help to have more help around the house, maybe. I mean, we can afford it.

Money is scary, you know, that it goes so fast. But we can afford that. Maybe I should get some more help. I keep thinking like I ought to do it all myself. But you're right. I can't.

PROFESSOR SATTERFIELD: And are there any groups, communities, neighborhood groups, spiritual communities that you're part of, that might be a source of support for you?

MARIA: We used to go to church. But I don't know. That doesn't seem to—it's another thing that we did together. I don't like to go alone without him.

PROFESSOR SATTERFIELD: OK. If we were just creating a list—I'm just going to write down the things that you used to do. And you can decide if you want to revisit those or not. And we want you to have a menu of options available. So when you feel like you need support, you have some choices that have already been written down for you.

MARIA: Well, maybe my friend that I told you about earlier, Judith. She means the world to me. And we haven't been talking much lately. It's kind of like I've shut her out.

You know, it's so embarrassing when somebody that's known you the way you were comes over, and then Jack is all weird. I just don't feel like having him remembered that way. He was such a fine man.

PROFESSOR SATTERFIELD: But I think we have a much better picture of your stress—the causes, the contributors, the duration, things you do to cope, the way that it affects you. We're going to add that into our formulation for you, and into our treatment plan. We want to make sure you feel supported. We want to make sure that you have plenty of healthy ways to cope with your stress.

As you mentioned before, some things are out of your control, your husband's illness. So some of those sources of stress, we can't change. But maybe we can change the backup, or the support that you have, that you need in order to address those challenges.

MARIA: Thank you.

[VIGNETTE END]

PROFESSOR SATTERFIELD: So let's break down what we've just seen in this extended clip. On the surface, we've done a basic stress assessment. Let's review those common assessment questions that you could use yourself. Step one, first question, how often have you felt nervous or stressed out in the past month? Question two, what's been causing you to feel stressed out? The stressors. Always remembering to ask yourself, "Is there anything else?" Since multiple stressors can occur at the same time.

Step three, how long has this been going on? We want to know if it's acute, and if it's chronic, and if it is chronic, what has the duration been? Step number four, how has this stress been affecting you? How has it affected your relationships or your performance at work? Any other effects? And the last question, what have you been doing to cope with this stressful situation? Your coping behaviors. How well has that been working for you? And the important question, how can others help you? How can you illicit those helping behaviors from people in your social support network? So when thinking about stress assessments, it's important to know where it is that you're starting. Those five questions about frequency, cause, duration, impact, and how you're coping.

But what else did you notice in the extended clip from Maria? I hope you noted that grief and loss is very much entangled in her experience of stress. She is anxious about her future as she imagines a future without her husband. She also talks about the importance of social support, and how oftentimes in her life now, it's missing. But there are two other nonspecific factors that I wanted to point out.

First, notice that the therapeutic relationship matters very much. Some criticisms of CBT say it's too data driven at the expense of interpersonal connection. I couldn't disagree more. I will not hesitate to push aside all of the questionnaires and all of the data if someone needs support and someone needs that sense of connection. Secondly, I want to point out that just by coming to therapy, by giving herself that degree of love and attention, by investing in herself, she has already started the coping and the healing experience. It takes a lot for people to make that first step and have that first appointment, and I always try to remember that.

So what, then, is our plan with Maria? She's already said that she's not interested in medications at this point in time. We know that she has both changeable and unchangeable stressors; many of them are chronic. She also has untapped coping resources, both financial resources, as we as social support resources. She has a number of complex emotions that need to be sorted out; they need to be normalized, and we need to help her to work through them. She has become cognitively and behaviorally unbalanced over time, so we want to take a step back and help her with those thoughts and help her with those behaviors.

We will, of course, want to treat her depression and give her help around the practical challenges of caregiving, but we will also want to help her with some somatic quieting exercises, some relaxation strategies, and help her with some cognitive work to address her hopelessness and her feeling of being overwhelmed. For somatic quieting, we are essentially creating what's called a relaxation response, or the opposite of a stress response; we are battling two primary physiologic stress pathways. We are battling the HPA axis, the hypothalamic-pituitary-adrenal axis, responsible for secreting a stress hormone called cortisol. We are also battling the sympathetic-adrenal medullary system, our fight-or-flight response, responsible for secreting epinephrine or adrenaline.

So what is the relaxation response? A term coined by Herb Benson in 1976. Well, essentially, it's the opposite of the stress response, a sort of yin to the yang, but in the relaxation response, we get a decrease in respiration, decrease in heart rate, decrease in blood pressure, and a decrease in those stress hormones. So how do we get to a relaxation response? And fortunately, there are a number of different ways you can accomplish this goal. You usually need some form of focused concentration, maybe on your breath, maybe on a guided image. You need a quiet environment, and you need a passive attitude of allowing yourself to slowly sink into the process of relaxation. Let's move to our next clip of Carol, where she is learning a very basic somatic quieting exercise.

[VIGNETTE START]

PROFESSOR SATTERFIELD: So why don't we do diaphragmatic breathing. And again, it's a very forgiving method. So there's no absolute way that you have to do it. But in general, most folks will do it while they are seated. You want your feet flat on the floor just so there's no constriction with your legs and you feel relatively comfortable. You want your posture to be fairly good—not uncomfortable, but fairly straight. And that's just because we want your lungs to be able to fully inflate. And if you're hunched over, it's harder to take a deep breath.

So what we want to do is use the diaphragm. And they call it diaphragmatic breathing because you're using the diaphragm. The diaphragm is a flat sheet of muscles that's right below your lungs. And when you breathe in, it helps to expand your lungs and pushes your stomach down. Think of it like a bellows, and it fills air up into your lungs. And then when you exhale, it contracts and pushes that air out.

So if you're doing diaphragmatic breathing properly, your belly should move a little bit. And the way you can tell that is if you feel your sternum—and that's where your ribs come together. If you want to just put a couple of— right below your sternum, a couple of fingers there. And you can press just a little bit. You're going to breathe in through your nose.

And you breathe through your nose just because it slows your rate of breathing. Your nostrils are just a smaller opening than your mouth. So it just takes you a little longer to get a breath in. So you want to breathe through your nose. And if you're breathing from your belly, then your hand should be pushed out a little bit by your belly. So why don't we take just a breath, and we'll breathe in through our nose. And then when you exhale, you can even push a little bit. You can exhale through your mouth.

Try another one through your nose. And then through your mouth.

So it looks like you're doing pretty good. And I want to tell you what I'm looking for, because you might want to, when you get home, look in the mirror, and make sure that you're doing this, OK? So one thing I'm looking for is your shoulders. If you are anxious in your breathing, people tend to take more shallow, rapid breaths. So they'll go—

[SHALLOW, RAPID BREATHS]

And you can actually see my shoulders going up. And a lot of times, people aren't even aware they're doing that. It may be triggered by a situation that's made them anxious. And they just start—

[SHALLOW, RAPID BREATHS]

—panicking a little bit. And their shoulders are going up. So we don't want to see your shoulders moving. And I didn't really see them moving. And I saw the diaphragm working a little bit.

So why don't we do that just a couple more times. Again, find your sternum. You breathe in through your nose. Out your mouth. Again. Again.

Do you notice you feeling a little bit different after just a couple breaths?

CAROL: Little bit. A little light headed.

PROFESSOR SATTERFIELD: Yeah, yeah, so just a little bit. And you can alternate the rate, how many breaths you're taking per minute. Usually in only five breaths or so you'll notice that there's a little bit of a difference. And we want you to do this when you're in bed so you'll be lying flat.

And again, you can put your finger here just to feel it. But if you feel like you understand how to do it, and you're doing it right, you can also just look down. If you see your belly breathing a little bit, then you know you're doing it right.

We'll only want you to do it for five to seven minutes or so. So that's not very long at all. So tell me how you would do this, what you think might get in the way, any things you're worried about.

CAROL: I think it would be fine, especially lying in bed, like you said. I'm there, anyway. As long as that's OK. You mentioned that most people do it in a chair or sitting. So bed would work, if I'm there, anyway.

I don't know how I feel about doing it in a meeting, or a holiday party, or something. I feel like that would look weird if I was just sitting there with my fingers on my sternum. But in bed, I think it would be fine.

PROFESSOR SATTERFIELD: And I think after practice, you'll get to be a pro at this, and you don't need to use the fingers. That's just to make sure that you're doing it right. And what we're hoping it will generate eventually is that you're a little more aware of how you're breathing throughout the day.

And I wouldn't want you in a social situation to disengage, and focus on your breathing, and just forget all the people around you. Because the point is we want you to be able to interact. But it's OK for you to be aware of tension in your body, or how you're breathing throughout the day.

And even if you're waiting for the elevator, or you're on your walk home, if you can say, breathe. And you know then to take some belly breaths, to slow your breathing down, not to breathe with your shoulders, those anxious breaths. And that's OK. You don't have to do the whole five minutes. Just an awareness to slow things down, and again, to turn down the volume. That's what we're after.

CAROL: OK.

PROFESSOR SATTERFIELD: All right.

[VIGNETTE END]

PROFESSOR SATTERFIELD: So we've learned a little bit about the yin and yang of stress and relaxation, both mediated by your autonomic nervous system. What I would encourage you to do is, throughout the day, to think about events that trigger your autonomic nervous system that either push you up or push you down, maybe getting an obnoxious e-mail from a coworker, arguing with the bank about refinancing your mortgage, getting an extra-long hug from a grandchild, or unwinding in a bubble bath with soft jazz playing in the background. It's all about the outside, those outside events, getting inside through our autonomic nervous system, and it behooves us to be aware of it, and potentially, to change it.

But let's tie the experience of stress back to CBT. How does stress relate to thoughts, feelings, and behaviors? Remember that stress affects cognitions, emotions, and behaviors, but it is also affected by, or maybe even caused by, cognitions and behaviors. So let's take a look at the basic cognitive behavioral model of stress. On the cognitive side I mentioned the special kind of cognition called appraisals. Appraisals come in two different forms, primary appraisals, which are our thoughts about the nature of a stressor; is it big, is it small, is it threatening, does it matter, how is it going to influence you, how likely is it that it will actually happen?

The second kind of behaviors, or appraisals, are called secondary appraisals, and these have to do with our estimations of our own coping skills and our coping resources. If you have a very high or strong primary appraisals, it's a very big stressor that's likely to happen, and you have very low secondary appraisals, you don't know what to do and you don't have any coping resources, your experience of stress is likely to be quite high.

From a cognitive behavioral perspective, what might go wrong is that an individual's appraisals may be out of sync with reality, or may be out of touch with their actual coping skills or coping abilities. If you're interested in how to uncover those appraisals and to begin restructuring or wrestling with those appraisals, I would encourage you to Google "Satterfield, Minding the Body tools." A website will pop up; click on companion website and downloadable tools, and you will see a worksheet to guide you through working with and changing primary and secondary appraisals.

So what about the selection of coping strategies? And here we're talking about those behaviors again. So a stressor happens, you have your appraisals, you have a stress response, then you do something, maybe helpful, maybe not helpful. But we think of those coping behaviors in two different categories. One focuses on changing your emotional state, so helping you to feel better; somatic quieting falls in that category. Or, the other category is problem-focused; so you may roll up your sleeves and get to work studying for that test that's causing you to be stressed, so emotion focused and problem-focused coping.

One is not necessarily better than the other. It depends on what needs to be done at the time, and you need really a balance between those two particular kinds of coping. What CBT data does is it looks at your preferred coping styles and sees whether or not you're selecting the most adaptive strategies.

So you want to select behaviors. You may select behaviors that evoke a relaxation response, emotion-focused coping. You may decide to reach out and ask your social supports for help. That could be emotion-focused coping, but might also be problem-focused coping. You could have task-oriented behaviors. If you're really stressed about the state of your home, you decide to roll up your sleeves and do some home improvements. That would certainly be a problem-focused coping. You could also just decide to schedule pleasant activities, things that bring you a sense of joy, or at least allow you to escape an unchangeable stressor for a short period of time. But does it work? What does the data show us? Most of the high-quality research in the stress management, cognitive therapy realm is done by Mike Antoni, who's at the University of Miami. He essentially wrote the book on what's called cognitive behavioral stress management, or CBSM. He's done a number of studies of regular folks, but also individuals that have chronic medical stressors, such as HIV, cancer, or chronic fatigue.

The most common outcomes he's looking at are depression, anxiety, quality of life, and for folks with medical conditions, he's sometimes looking at adherence to treatment or the progression or slowing of their particular illness. What he has found is fairly strong support for a mix of cognitive restructuring, wrestling with those thoughts, of relaxation, coping skills, and also assertiveness, and particularly, being able to and feeling entitled to ask for the support that you need.

In a recent interesting study of CBSM, he looked at women with breast cancer with Stagl and other colleagues in 2014. They did a nice, long five-year follow up using CBSM and found that in these women with breast cancer who underwent this particular treatment, they had less depression and a higher quality of life.

I wanted to end by talking about a different form of—I guess we would call it a third-wave type of stress reduction intervention. It's something you might have heard of; it's called MBSR, or mindfulness-based stress reduction. Mindfulness-based stress reduction is a modern variant of meditation and yoga that has been applied to stress reduction. Like meditation, it builds concentration, present focus, acceptance, and somatic quieting, all probably familiar at this point. It was developed by Jon Kabat-Zinn at the University of Massachusetts, and has since been applied to a wide array of different medical problems, but it all started with chronic pain.

Most MBSR programs last about eight to ten weeks. They consist of two-and-a-half-hour weekly classes, and oftentimes will have a single-day or maybe a weekend retreat at the end. It's not particularly spiritually based, but there's certainly a Buddhist element and Buddhist roots to the mindfulness that these individuals are learning. Now, MBSR has been shown to improve chronic pain, low back pain, coping with pain in general, stress, mood, and even an interesting study looking at improvements in immune function.

I wanted to share just one meta-analysis published in 2004 by Paul Grossman and his colleagues in the *Journal of Psychosomatic Research*. What they did was to look at 20 high-quality MBSR studies that covered a wide spectrum of patients—cancer, pain cardiovascular disease, depression, anxiety. And they looked at the standardized measures of physical and mental well-being. And across the board, they found moderate to strong effect sizes. So it looks like there's really something there to MBSR. And I would encourage you, if you're interested, just to Google online "mindfulness-based stress reduction tools," and a number of tools, videos, and workbooks will pop up.

So let's wrap up just by talking about one of our frequently asked questions, and this is a question that I often get. Is resilience to stress an enduring characteristic, or is it something that comes and goes? How can I make it stay? Well, I think it's a little bit both. I think it's partly dispositional, and maybe that has to do with our genetics. Maybe it has to do with early life experiences. But I do think that resilience and certainly cognitive based stress management are skills that we can learn. We can, in essence, build up our strength. We can build up our stamina. We can build up our endurance, especially if we know that very stressful times are to come.

Now, one other important point that I want to make is just because an individual is sensitive, it doesn't mean that they're fragile. For some reason some individuals, again, it might be dispositional, it might be life experiences, they simply feel stress, or in general, emotions, much more intensely than others. That means they have a higher burden in terms of learning emotion-regulation skills, but it doesn't mean they're going to break. In fact, some of those sensitive folks might be the strongest people that you'll ever meet.

So, in summary, we know that stress is normal, but we worry if it's chronic, we worry if it's severe, and we worry if a person has selected maladaptive coping strategies. We want to manage it by looking at appraisals; we want to use somatic quieting; and we certainly want to help people reach out to their social supports.

In our next lecture, we'll talk about anxiety and take a much closer look at the social anxiety that Carol has. Thank you.

Anxiety and Fear

Lecture 6

I n this lecture, you will learn about fear and anxiety, which are adaptive functional features within the human emotional repertoire that only sometimes misfire and cause impairment. However, when they are excessive—when they do misfire—they can cause a great deal of pain and suffering. Although CBT was originally developed as a treatment for depression, the developed tools have proven effective in managing anxiety and a number of other disorders. The classic milieus of CBT tools are about the same, but in this case, we focus on the misperception of threat at excessive physiological arousal and the avoidant behaviors that often come with anxiety.

Fear and Anxiety

- The family of anxiety disorders includes phobias, obsessive-compulsive disorder, post-traumatic stress disorder, social anxiety, panic, and generalized anxiety disorder. Fear and anxiety are psychological and physiological responses to danger.

- In general, fear is conceptualized as an emotional and physiological response to a definite threat. Think about your fight-or-flight reactions, the sympathetic nervous system. Fear is basic, primal, and gripping. Its purpose is to keep us alive.

- Anxiety is different. Anxiety is a diffuse, unpleasant, vague sense of apprehension. It is influenced by culture, cognition, personality, and a number of other internal factors. Anxiety can trigger fear, and fear can result in lingering anxiety.

- Fear and anxiety are protective emotional reactions in response to real or anticipated threats. They can be healthy, and they can be central to our essential harm-avoidance systems. An anxiety disorder, however, refers to a heterogeneous group of syndromes characterized by abnormally increased sensitivity to fearful stimuli, inappropriately intense experience of fear and anxiety, or inappropriately extreme action based on fear or anxiety.

- There is a wide range of what is considered normal in the population, and there are large cultural differences in what is considered normal, as well. But, in general, the diagnosis of an anxiety disorder is based primarily on the degree of interference with normal function at work and in your social or personal life.

- A little anxiety is actually a good thing. In fact, it might even improve performance. The Yerkes-Dodson curve, which is an inverted-U function, reminds us that low levels of arousal equal low levels of performance. We just don't care; we haven't risen to the occasion. Moderate levels of stress, anxiety, or arousal increase our level of performance: We are energized to face whatever challenge is ahead of us. Higher levels of arousal lower our performance because now we're overwhelmed with our stress or anxiety.

- For anxiety disorders though, the anxiety has gotten so extreme that it has taken on a life of its own. In a way, the disorder becomes the stressor. It becomes a mental illness.

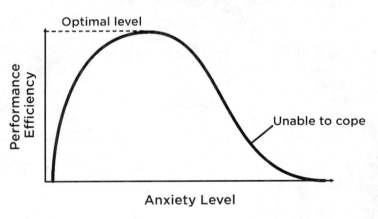

Yerkes-Dodson Curve

- A person who is impaired and often frozen by anxiety would meet the diagnostic criteria for social anxiety disorder, or what used to be called social phobia. In addition to social anxiety disorder, there are a number of other anxiety disorders.

- Generalized anxiety is mostly about worrying. With a panic disorder, an individual has a panic attack and is worried about when the next attack might happen. Additional anxiety disorders include obsessive-compulsive disorder, specific phobias (such as fear of heights or fear of spiders), and post-traumatic stress disorder.

- As with any patient in CBT, you would first want to do a semi-structured diagnostic interview. Then, you might send the patient home with a packet of questionnaires and some self-monitoring homework regarding his or her social contacts.

Measuring and Treating Anxiety
- Some of the questionnaires that are good for measuring anxiety include the Beck Anxiety Inventory, which is the classic questionnaire named for Aaron T. Beck. In addition, the Anxiety Sensitivity Index, developed in 1992, is a 16-item questionnaire that is especially predictive of panic attacks and panic disorder. The Anxious Self-Statements Questionnaire, developed by Steven Kendall and Philip Hollon, is a 32-item questionnaire that focuses on cognitions. The GAD-7, a seven-item questionnaire about worry and anxiety, is commonly used in primary care settings. The DASS 21 measures depression, anxiety, and stress at the same time.

- There are medications that can be helpful for anxiety. They tend to fall into two categories. The first category is antidepressants. Even though they were initially developed for depression, antidepressants work for many anxiety disorders as well. The second category of drugs is the benzodiazepines. These are antianxiety drugs, such as Xanax, Ativan, and Klonopin. All medications tend to have side effects and pros and cons to taking them, and it's a personal decision whether someone wants to go that route.

- The other route available is CBT, with its cognitive and behavioral interventions. Recall that the CBT triangle involves emotions, thoughts, and behaviors. The components for anxiety disorders would include behavioral interventions, such as exposures to a feared stimulus. When an individual is anxious, he or she often avoids the things that make him or her anxious, so we want to diminish those avoidant behaviors. Cognitively, we want to challenge those thoughts about threats in the environment, or about not being able to cope with something, or about not having adequate coping resources.

- We also would want to teach a mix of cognitive behavioral exercises, including reality testing, helping the individual build a sense of confidence or mastery, and relaxation, or somatic quieting.

Exposure Therapy
- Avoidance behaviors, or safety behaviors, are very natural. When an individual is afraid, he or she avoids the thing that makes him or her fearful. For example, if an individual has social anxiety and is afraid of connecting with people, he or she might engineer his or her life and situations so that he or she has as little contact as possible with other people. The problem is that this prevents the individual from connecting with others.

- In this case, we want to do some exposure therapy. In particular, we want to do a kind of therapy called systematic desensitization, which involves systematically desensitizing the individual to the things that cause him or her anxiety. We'll start by having the individual construct something called an anxiety hierarchy using subjective units of distress (SUDS) ratings. This involves creating a list of sources of anxiety and rating them on a scale from 0 (no anxiety) to 100 (unbearable anxiety).

- Once all the levels of the patient's SUDS hierarchy have been fleshed out, we would then tell him or her to start at the bottom of the scale—something that causes him or her very little to no anxiety—and between this appointment and the next, we would want him or her to experience that event as often as he or she could until it loses its charge.

- Once the patient was successful in doing that, he or she would climb to the next rung on the ladder, and then the next rung, and so on. What's important is that the patient is in charge, because this is the hierarchy that he or she created for himself or herself, and he or she can go as quickly or as slowly as he or she wants to. Eventually, the patient should develop a sense of mastery at overcoming his or her anxiety.

- But does exposure therapy work? In 2006, a comprehensive review of studies was conducted by Yujuan Choy, Abby Fyer, and Josh Lipsitz that looked at systematic desensitization and in vivo, or live, exposure. They found that the live, intense exposure all at once was most effective, but people didn't like it and tended to drop out of it, so it was a little too intense. What seemed to work better, and people stuck with it more consistently, was systematic desensitization, creating a hierarchy and slowly working their way up the hierarchy.

Subjective Units of Distress (SUDS)

100	• giving a wedding toast (100)
75	• making a presentation at work (80)
	• going to a party (70)
50	• conducting a performance review (60)
25	• interacting with an acquaintance (30)
	• making a phone call (20)
0	• reading a book (0)

- On the cognitive side, we might also want to teach the patient to do a thought record as a way to wrestle with his or her cognitions. In fact, the patient might do some of this while working up the ladder of the SUDS hierarchy.

- After the patient has gone out into the world and tried to tackle the sources of anxiety one by one, he or she is going to come back and tell us how it went. If it seems like this exercise was a success, we would want to repeat the symptom measures to ensure that his or her anxiety scores were indeed dropping.

- In addition, we would want to make sure that we're working in service of the patient's goals, with a special focus on increasing the quantity and quality of social contacts, for example. We also would move to give him or her more control in developing assignments. As the therapy progresses, we want the therapist to step back and the patient to step up—so that the patient becomes not just a partner but potentially the leader, the driver, in his or her own therapy.

Suggested Reading

Allen, "Cognitive-Behavior Therapy and Other Psychosocial Interventions in the Treatment of Obsessive-Compulsive Disorder."

Bandelow, Seidler-Brandler, Becker, Wedekind, and Rüther, "Meta-Analysis of Randomized Controlled Comparisons of Psychopharmacological and Psychological Treatments for Anxiety Disorders."

Beck and Emery, with Greenberg, *Anxiety Disorders and Phobias*.

Bourne, *The Anxiety and Phobia Workbook*.

Butler, *Overcoming Social Anxiety and Shyness*, p. 226–233.

Choy, Fyer, and Lipsitz, "Treatment of Specific Phobia in Adults."

Frewen, Dozois, and Lanius, "Neuroimaging Studies of Psychological Interventions for Mood and Anxiety Disorders."

Hunot, Churchill, Teixeira, and Silva de Lima, "Psychological Therapies for Generalised Anxiety Disorder."

Mitte, "A Meta-Analysis of the Efficacy of Psycho- and Pharmacotherapy in Panic Disorder with and without Agoraphobia."

Questions to Consider

1. If anxiety is often based on a misperception (exaggeration, for example) of external threats, then why doesn't reality provide a corrective experience over time? For example, why don't people just get over phobias of spiders or dogs or heights, assuming that bad things don't keep reinforcing those fears?

2. What's the distinction between introversion, shyness, and social anxiety? Is there a risk of overpathologizing people who aren't outgoing or popular?

Anxiety and Fear
Lecture 6—Transcript

PROFESSOR SATTERFIELD: Anxiety and fear are adaptive functional features within the human emotional repertoire that only sometimes misfire and cause impairment. However, when they are excessive, when they do misfire, they can cause a great deal of pain and suffering, as in the case of Carol with her social anxiety. Let's look at an early CBT exercise helping Carol apply the CBT model to a recent event.

[VIGNETTE START]

PROFESSOR SATTERFIELD: I want you to think about a time just this past week, so relatively recent, when you felt anxious. So we're going for an emotion. So can you recall a time, maybe even just the past few days when you felt anxious?

CAROL: We were in a meeting at work and in the meeting my boss who was talking, called on me and asked me to directly answer a question. And I got really anxious because there were a lot of other people in the room and I didn't know if I would get the answer right. And so I got really nervous about being called out in front of everybody.

PROFESSOR SATTERFIELD: OK, perfect example. So relevant, timely, absolutely you were in a meeting and your boss called you out, put on spot, more or less. And you felt anxious. So we have the emotion. So what we want to do is we want to fill in these two as well. So the triggering event was your boss calling on you in a meeting and expecting an answer and you felt anxious. That was the emotion. Now, what were the thoughts you had when your boss call on you?

CAROL: Oh, it was something along the lines of, please don't call on me, please don't call on me. And then you know he did and I guess my next thought was—I guess, panic is more of a feeling. But I was just trying to find the right answer and I couldn't. And it took me a lot longer to find it than

I think it probably would've taken someone else who is normal and didn't have anxiety about something like that.

PROFESSOR SATTERFIELD: OK, so there's a lot that's there. And that's fantastic. What we're doing is we're taking a real world event and we're sorting it's element into different buckets. And we have three different buckets. You've mentioned anxiety. You mentioned panic. And you're right, that is more of a feeling.

Some of the thoughts were oh, please don't call on me. Uh oh, I just got called on. I can't do this. Wait I have to think of the right answer. Probably, your mind was going a mile a minute. And what we want to do as you get more practice with this is figuring out first, post hoc how to slow it down and actually write down, literally write down those thoughts so we can capture them again to work with them.

The part we have less of it is the behavior. And it sounds like you were called on and there was a pause. What did you do? What were your behaviors? Did you start fidgeting or did you look down at the ground? Or did you speak up? Or did you turn red? Or like what happened?

CAROL: I don't know if I turn red. I'm sure I did. But yeah, I started fidgeting. I started looking through my papers to find the answer, even though I knew it wasn't there. Eventually, I tried to make something up. And it was one of those questions that could have had a million different answers, and mine wasn't necessarily the one that she was looking for. That was I guess the big thing.

PROFESSOR SATTERFIELD: And when you spoke up, do you think you had good posture, it was bold, it was confident, it was loud, people heard you, or was it a different way?

CAROL: I doubt it was like that. I didn't feel like that, anyway. I think I was nervous and my voice was probably shaking because I didn't want to answer to begin with.

PROFESSOR SATTERFIELD: So I'm hearing there was some paper shuffling, maybe a little bit of stalling, some nervousness, may be visible nervousness. When you spoke up, you may have sounded audibly nervous or uncertain or definitely lacking in confidence. So we have the panic and anxiety tied to the thoughts, tied to the behaviors and they're all related to one another.

[VIGNETTE END]

PROFESSOR SATTERFIELD: So what did we see? We saw a relatively minor work event where Carol's anxiety was impairing her performance. We want her through working through these examples to see the relevance of the CBT model in explaining and hopefully intervening with her anxiety.

Now, CBT was originally developed as a treatment for depression, but the developed tools have proven effective in managing anxiety and a number of other disorders. The classic menus of CBT tools are about the same, but in this case, we look more at the misperception of threat, at excessive physiologic arousal, and the avoidant behaviors that often come with anxiety. Let's move now to our second clip with Carol, where we help her understand why it's important to journal her behaviors, and we start stitching all this data together.

[VIGNETTE START]

PROFESSOR SATTERFIELD: And what we'll want you to do before we start reaching in and trying to reconfigure thoughts and behaviors, we just want you to do some self-monitoring. On the next week, I would say pick a couple of negative emotions and a couple positive ones. Write down what the triggering event was. What were the emotions? What were the thoughts? What were the behaviors? Put those in your journal and we'll start to stitch those together.

And what you'll find is after we do a number of these, we'll be able to find that there are common threads. So even though the circumstances are different, some are at work, some are at home, some are with strangers, some are with friends, the same kind of thoughts pop out. And we have habits of mind and certain thoughts will pop out because that's part of your history. That's part of what you bring to the table. Certain behavioral habits will pop out, maybe even emotional habits. And once we have a better idea of how that works for you, we'll have a better sense of what will the most effective interventions be to change thoughts or to change behaviors.

[VIGNETTE END]

PROFESSOR SATTERFIELD: So at this point, we've partnered with Carol and hopefully empowered and interested her in collecting more information on cognition and behavior. As she brings in this data, we'll start to flesh out the CBT model of anxiety, what causes it, what maintains it, and how it's treated. But before we go there, we need to look at what fear and anxiety are and the functions they might serve. We will define the family of anxiety disorders that includes things like phobias, obsessive-compulsive disorder, post-traumatic stress disorder, social anxiety, panic, and generalized anxiety disorder. First, some definitions. Fear and anxiety are psychological and physiologic responses to danger. In general, fear is conceptualized as an emotional and physiologic response to a definite threat.

Think about your fight-or-flight reactions, the sympathetic nervous system. Fear is basic, primal, and gripping. Its purpose is to keep us alive. Now, anxiety is different. Anxiety is a diffuse, unpleasant, vague sense of apprehension. It's influenced by culture, by cognition, personality, and a number of other internal factors. Anxiety can trigger fear, and fear can result in lingering anxiety.

Now, fear and anxiety are protective emotional reactions in response to real or anticipated threats. They can be healthy, and they can be central to our essential harm avoidance systems. An anxiety disorder, however, refers to a heterogeneous group of syndromes characterized by abnormally increased sensitivity to fearful stimuli, inappropriately intense experience of fear and anxiety, or inappropriately extreme action based on fear or anxiety.

Now, there's a wide range of normal in the population and large cultural differences in what's considered normal. But in general, the diagnosis of an anxiety disorder is based primarily on the degree of interference with normal function at work and in your social or personal life. So how can you decide if there's interference? Remember that a little anxiety is actually a good thing. In fact, it might even improve performance. If you look at the Yerkes-Dodson curve, which is an inverted U, it reminds us that low levels of arousal equal low levels of performance. We just don't care; we haven't risen to the occasion. Moderate levels of stress, anxiety, or arousal actually increase our level of performance. We are energized to face whatever challenge is ahead of us. Higher levels of arousal, again, lower our performance, because now we're overwhelmed with our stress or our anxiety.

For anxiety disorders, though, the anxiety has gotten so extreme that it's taken on a life of its own. In a way, the disorder becomes the stressor. It becomes a mental illness. Now, for Carol, she isn't just shy, she's impaired, and she's often frozen by her anxiety. She's a lovely, kind, hardworking person, but she's often terrified, and consequently, she's alone. She does meet diagnostic criteria for social anxiety disorder, or what used to be called social phobia. There are, of course, a number of other anxiety disorders—generalized anxiety, which is mostly about worrying; panic disorder, an individual has a panic attack and they're worried about when the next attack might happen; obsessive-compulsive disorder; specific phobias, like fear of heights or fear of spiders; and of course, post-traumatic stress disorder, which we'll talk about in a later lecture.

As with any patient in CBT, you would first want to do a semi-structured diagnostic interview. We did this with Carol. Then we sent her home with a packet of questionnaires and some self-monitoring homework regarding her social contacts. So what sorts of questionnaires are good for measuring anxiety? Well, we have the classic Beck Anxiety Inventory. We also have the Anxiety Sensitivity Index, developed in 1992; it's a 16-item questionnaire that's especially predictive of panic attacks and panic disorder. We have the Anxious Self-Statement Questionnaire focusing on cognitions, 32 items developed by Kendall & Hollon. Commonly used in primary-care settings is something called the GAD-7, seven questions about worry and anxiety, and also the DASS 21, which looks at depression, anxiety, and stress, all at the same time. Now, Carol scored in the top of the moderate range for anxiety on our questionnaires, but she also showed mild symptoms of depression and shared that she occasionally drinks just a little too much before bed as a way to help her with her anxiety and to help her get to sleep.

Now, there are medications, which can be helpful for anxiety. They tend to fall into two categories. There are the antidepressants. Even though initially developed for depression, they work for many anxiety disorders as well. Then there are a category of drugs called the benzodiazepines; these are the anti-anxiety drugs, such as Xanax, Ativan, or Klonopin. Of course, all medications tend to have side effects and their pros and cons, and it's a personal decision if someone wants to go that route or not. The other route available is, of course, CBT, with its cognitive and its behavioral interventions.

So what would CBT for anxiety disorders look like? And first I want you to recall the CBT triangle with its emotions, thoughts, and its behaviors. The components, of course, would include behavioral interventions, such as exposures to a feared stimulus. Remember, when an individual is anxious, they often avoid the things that make them anxious, so we want to diminish those avoidant behaviors. Cognitively, we want to challenge those thoughts about threats in the environment or challenge those thoughts about not being able to cope with something, or the beliefs that they don't have adequate coping resources. We would also want to teach sort of a mix of cognitive behavioral exercises, something called reality testing, helping them build a sense of confidence or a sense of mastery, and of course, relaxation or somatic quieting.

Now, I wanted to say a word about avoidance, or something called safety behaviors. And I think that it's something, these sorts of behaviors are very natural. When an individual is afraid, you avoid the thing that makes you fearful. In Carol's case, she is afraid of people. She is afraid of connecting with people and embarrassing herself, and really, underneath all of that, she is really afraid that maybe she is not that lovable and people won't want to be around her. So what she's done is to engineer her life and situations so that she has as little contact as possible with other people. In her social life, well, it means she doesn't really have one. She doesn't return phone calls; she doesn't reach out to others; she doesn't respond to conversation opening comments from potential friends. At work, she is in and out as quickly as she can. She keeps her headphones on, and again, she is creating this bubble of safety around her, so it doesn't raise up her social anxiety. The problem is, it prevents her from connecting with others, and it prevents her from testing out those beliefs that she actually is competent socially and people might actually like her.

So we want to do some exposure therapy with her, and in particular, we want to do a kind of therapy called systematic desensitization. And as the name implies, we will systematically desensitize her to things which cause her anxiety. What we'll do is we'll have her construct something called an anxiety hierarchy using SUDS ratings, and SUDS stands for subjective units of distress. We'll have here create a list from 0, no anxiety at all, all the way up to 100 of different things that, eventually, she will need to go out and experience so that she can develop that sense of mastery and overcoming her anxiety. So let's move now to watch Carol creating her SUDS hierarchy.

[VIGNETTE START]

PROFESSOR SATTERFIELD: OK, Carol why don't we take a moment to learn about something called the Subjective Units of Distress. Now, it's kind of a funny term. We just call it a SUDS hierarchy. It's a hierarchy because it ranges from 0, doesn't cause you any distress, all the way up to 100. And I want to take a step back to talk about why we would need something like this. If you recall the hallmark of anxiety is avoidance, that's the most common behavior because it's instinctive. If something makes you feel anxious, you avoid it.

The problem is if you avoid things that would build your social muscles, you never get any stronger. But we don't want to put you in a situation that's so overwhelming that it becomes traumatizing. We want to put you in a situation that is just the right level, where it's challenging you, but it's not too much. We can have some success then you move to the next level and the next level and the next level. So you start somewhere near the bottom and slowly work your way up.

We know though that people are different. What might be a 50 for you is different than my 50, or a 0 for you is different than my 0. So we want to create a personally tailored SUDS hierarchy so we can get a sense of what's OK, what's overwhelming—right now, it's at 100—and we can think about the steps in between. So if we're thinking about social interactions, and this could be work or this could be home, interactions with another person, what would be a 0, something that you feel totally comfortable about? You don't get those anxious thoughts, those anxious feelings. What would that be?

CAROL: I guess reading a book with my cats at home or watching TV with them.

PROFESSOR SATTERFIELD: OK, so the social interaction is really just with characters on a page. So that's pretty non-threatening. I'll put you down at a zero, so reading a book. Where would talking on the phone with your mom be?

CAROL: I guess it depends, but—

PROFESSOR SATTERFIELD: Or your sister.

CAROL: Yeah, so my sister would probably be like, I don't know, a 20 or 30, probably 20.

PROFESSOR SATTERFIELD: This is a midpoint the 25, so we'll put your phone call sister. And is mom higher or lower than that?

CAROL: She's higher.

PROFESSOR SATTERFIELD: OK. Is she above or below a 50?

CAROL: She's, I'd say probably right at a 50.

PROFESSOR SATTERFIELD: And what would be absolute most embarrassing, difficult, anxiety provoking social situation you can imagine? And for a lot of people, just to give you an example, is standing up in front of a crowd of people and giving a public speech. That's like 100 for some people.

CAROL: That would be 100 for me.

PROFESSOR SATTERFIELD: OK, so, all right.

[VIGNETTE END]

PROFESSOR SATTERFIELD: With Carol we would continue this exercise, and we would flesh out all of the levels of her SUDS hierarchy. We would then tell her to start at the bottom, something that causes her no to very little anxiety, and between this appointment and the next, we would want her to go out and to experience that event as often as she could until it lost its charge. Once she was successful in doing that, she would climb to the next rung on the ladder, and again the next rung, and the next rung.

What's important, though, is that she is in charge; she has the power. This is her hierarchy she has created herself, and she can go as fast or as slow as she wants to. But does exposure therapy work? And I'll just mention one study, actually, a comprehensive review of studies done by Choy, Fyer, and Lipsitz in 2006. What they did is they looked at systematic desensitization and something called in vivo, or live, exposures. They found that the live, intense exposures, sort of all at once, were most effective, but people didn't like it, and they tend to drop out; it's a little too intense. What seemed to work better, and people stuck with it more consistently, was systematic desensitization, as we used with Carol, creating that hierarchy and slowly working their way up the hierarchy.

Now, on the cognitive side, we might also want to teach Carol to do her ABCD, or a thought record, as a way to wrestle with her cognitions. In fact, she might actually do some of this while she is working her way up that ladder up her SUDS hierarchy. I'd also like to illustrate, though, one other behavioral strategy that we used with her to challenge her cognitions, and that strategy was called a behavioral experiment.

[VIGNETTE START]

PROFESSOR SATTERFIELD: So we've talked about the importance of testing out thought, that thoughts are opinions. Sometimes they're helpful. Sometimes they're hurtful. And we did an exercise called the ABCD where we drew the four squares and talked about activating events and beliefs. It was all out of the moment and it was all on paper. And those can be really helpful.

But I wanted to talk about a different kind of way to test out thoughts that's not in writing. It's in action. And it's something that's called a behavioral experiment. By experiment it just means we're testing out a thought. And you had a thought that you shared recently in one of your homework assignments that you feel very awkward and uncomfortable in public. And the first thing that happens in the morning after you get up and go through your routine, you walk to work and you pass by people and you feel uncomfortable. It's not hugely intense, but you feel uncomfortable and you imagine people just aren't particularly interested in seeing you. So it's a sort of a bad way to start off every day feeling sort of anxious an unwanted. I was hoping we could explore the possibility of doing a behavioral experiment while you're walking to work.

CAROL: So what exactly would I have to do?

PROFESSOR SATTERFIELD: Good question, because we want to be specific and we want to make sure that it's helpful and realistic. So what you would do, the same morning routine, walk to work exactly the same way. If you see someone walking towards you, you make eye contact. That's important. And you say good morning or hello or how are you or just a simple social greeting and smile and continue walking.

CAROL: OK.

PROFESSOR SATTERFIELD: Does that seem doable? I can tell you're a little apprehensive about that, but what do you think?

CAROL: I don't know. I'll try it.

PROFESSOR SATTERFIELD: OK.

CAROL: Yeah.

PROFESSOR SATTERFIELD: All right, so what is that you're going to do? So let's say tomorrow morning, you're walking to work and there's a mom with a stroller sort of walking toward you. What are you going to do?

CAROL: I will make eye contact, and I'll smile at her and maybe say hi or good morning, and see how she reacts and how that makes me feel.

[VIGNETTE END]

PROFESSOR SATTERFIELD: So now you see how a behavioral experiment works and how you might set it up. What I'd like us to do is to fast forward to the next session after Carol has gone out into the world; she's done her homework; and now she's going to come back and tell us how it went.

[VIGNETTE START]

PROFESSOR SATTERFIELD: Carol, I believe you have a behavioral experiment as part of your homework. Is that right?

CAROL: I did.

PROFESSOR SATTERFIELD: OK. Well, why don't you talk about first what the experiment was and then let me know how it went. So what was the experiment you were doing?

CAROL: So you said that I should walk down the street on my way to work, because I had told you that it was a big source of anxiety for me that always felt like people didn't want to talk to me or that I was taking up too much space or in their way. So my homework was to instead of ignore them or try to get out of their way, to actually say hi and make eye contact and smile and see what they did.

PROFESSOR SATTERFIELD: So that's tough, and I remember you were a little nervous about doing that and you were worried you might chicken out.

CAROL: I was.

PROFESSOR SATTERFIELD: So what happened?

CAROL: I was nervous at first and I chickened out a couple of times when I started. But after I did it once or twice, it wasn't so bad. The first person that I successfully said hi to was actually just like a little kid. I don't know. He was probably 10 or 11. And he was just walking his dog and I smiled and said hi. And he said hi back. And then after that, I tried a little lady walking down the street and she looked fairly nonthreatening. So I tried that with her next. And she was really sweet and said hi, how are you. I said good, good morning. And then we continued on our way.

PROFESSOR SATTERFIELD: Did you feel connected in that moment in that second with her?

CAROL: A little bit yeah.

PROFESSOR SATTERFIELD: And did it feel pleasant or unpleasant?

CAROL: It felt pleasant. It was definitely unexpected, but it felt good. I mean there are a couple of people who didn't say hi back. But I'm not sure if they heard me or saw me. I don't know.

PROFESSOR SATTERFIELD: Now, you had mentioned before the you're especially anxious around men, especially men that would be in your dating range. So did you pass any guys in that range, and did you say hello to any of them?

CAROL: I didn't. I mean I didn't say hello to any of them per se. But I did, I tried to make eye contact with them.

PROFESSOR SATTERFIELD: And a smile?

CAROL: And smile.

PROFESSOR SATTERFIELD: OK, and what did you get back?

CAROL: I got a smile back if they were looking.

PROFESSOR SATTERFIELD: And would you say that was positive, negative, neutral?

CAROL: I'd say it was a neutral because it was nice that they smiled back, but I was still really nervous to do that.

PROFESSOR SATTERFIELD: Going back to those beliefs, and it was the beliefs that you were testing out, that people would reject you and people don't want you around and people won't acknowledge you, and it would be unpleasant. Do you think those beliefs were supported or they were proven not to be so accurate?

CAROL: I think they're proven not be so accurate.

PROFESSOR SATTERFIELD: Yeah.

[VIGNETTE END]

PROFESSOR SATTERFIELD: So it sounds like this was a success for Carol. But where would we go from here? Well, we'd want to repeat symptom measures to assure that her anxiety scores were, indeed, dropping. We would want to make sure that we're working in service of her smart goals with a special focus on increasing the quantity and quality of her social contacts. We would also move to give her more control in developing assignments. As the therapy progresses, we want the therapist to step back and the patient to step up, so that they become not just a partner, but potentially the leader, the driver, in their own therapy.

Let's move now to our frequently asked questions section, and we often get a number of questions about anxiety and about stress, and particularly, about medications. Here is our first frequently asked question. Sometimes emotions are so fast, it doesn't seem like thoughts could have come first, like the CBT model suggests. Could thoughts maybe come after emotions? Maybe thoughts are just a way to put a nonverbal emotional sensation into words.

Well, it's a good question, and we do have this very simple, linear cognitive model given to us by Aaron Beck that says we have an activating event, it triggers particular thoughts or beliefs. Those thoughts or beliefs then cause different behavioral or emotional reactions. That's in its most simplest, and

I think, surface form. But I think you're right, that often, many of those pathways are so well worn, it seems to happen almost instantaneously.

For Carol, she has a lot of very deep-seated beliefs about social situations and how threatening they might be, so when she walks into a cocktail party, it's not a slow progression through a linear process; it feels like it all happens at once. But if we were to somehow be able to push slo-mo, we could see that Carol was actually going through these processes; they're just happening on a subconscious, very fast level.

Now, is it possible that it happens the other way around? Of course it's possible, but I think, either way, whether cognitions come first or whether cognitions are the explanations for emotions and behaviors, they give us a substance that we can capture, that we can write down, and that we can begin to work with.

Second question, are there medications that can help with stress? I know they won't solve the problem, but maybe they can quiet the storm enough so that I can do what I need to do. And as I mentioned earlier, I think this is a personal decision, but there's a number of different pros and cons to weigh. To my knowledge, there is no medication that cures stress. There are medications which can dampen the physiologic sensations of stress. There are medications that can help us to feel less distressed, to have more energy, to be more motivated. Again, there aren't necessarily medications that can reach in and solve those problems in our environment that might need our attention.

For me, and in my conversations I have with patients, I often think it's more a matter of degree. Are they able to roll up their sleeves and do the work that needs to be done? Or are their physiologic symptoms so overwhelming that we first need to bring those down to a level where they can begin to do the work that they have to do? That varies by person to person. So, again, a personal decision.

Now, in the next lecture, what we're going to do is to switch gears, and we're going to look at CBT for depression, and we'll return to the case of Maria, our caregiver. Thank you.

Treating Depression

Lecture 7

Depression is a common condition. At the far end of the spectrum of depression, it is considered a medical disease that has medical treatments. In this lecture, you will learn about depression. Specifically, you will explore the epidemiology (how the disease spreads and can be controlled) and etiology (the causes of the disease) of this medical disorder. In addition, you will learn about the leading treatments for depression and emerging treatments on the horizon.

Depression

- There is a continuum of depression, with a medical disorder—a serious chemical imbalance—on one end and everyday sadness on the other end. Many of us have been somewhere on that continuum, often after we've had a particular loss of some sort. Many of us have experienced grief or the loss of a loved one. Many times, that sadness, or depression, is considered nonpsychiatric, even though it might be helpful for an individual to talk to someone.

- However, some individuals go beyond the level of everyday sadness and develop a full-blown major depressive episode. In a major depressive episode, an individual has a depressed mood most of the day nearly every day and/or a loss of interest in his or her normal, everyday activities for at least two weeks or longer.

- In total, the individual has to have a total of five symptoms from a list of nine hallmark symptoms of depression. There must be significant impairment or distress at work, at home, or both.
  - A sad or low mood. Sometimes it manifests as an irritable mood, particularly in men.

  - Anhedonia. This is where an individual is unable to enjoy things that he or she normally enjoys.

- o Changes in appetite or weight. This is a dysregulation, so it could go in either direction; you could have increases or decreases in weight.

- o Changes in sleep. You could have hypersomnia or insomnia. You'll see differences in the way a patient moves or in his or her energy levels.

- o Psychomotor agitation or psychomotor retardation. Psychomotor agitation is where the patient is shaky and jittery; psychomotor retardation is often described by patients as feeling like they are moving underwater or moving through molasses.

- o Poor concentration or memory. This might manifest as difficulty following conversations, difficulty reading, or difficulty remembering particular events.

- o Fatigue and low energy.

- o Feelings of worthlessness or guilt.

- o Suicidal ideation.

- There are a number of different instruments and questionnaires that are available online for assessing the full continuum of depression. The first is the classic Beck Depression Inventory. Beck also created the Hopelessness Scale, which is a 20-item scale that was found to be particularly useful in predicting suicidal behaviors. The Patient Health Questionnaire-9 (PHQ-9) focuses on depression and is commonly being used in primary care settings.

The Beck Depression Inventory and the Beck Hopelessness Scale, along with other tools for assessing depression, can be found at the following website:

www.beckinstitute.org/beck-inventory-and-scales/

- Other questionnaires are measures of cognitive styles, such as the Dysfunctional Attitude Scale, the Automatic Thoughts Questionnaire, and the Attributional Style Questionnaire.

The Epidemiology of Depression

- Major depressive disorder affects about 15 million adults—about seven percent of the population that are 18 years old and over. The lifetime prevalence is about 17 percent, and the rates are double in women when compared to men. The average age of onset is about 32 years, but major depression, the disease, can strike at any particular age, from children to adolescents to older adults. Major depressive disorder is the leading cause of disability in the United States for people of ages 15 to 44.

- Fortunately, a major depressive episode usually remits within 12 to 24 months, even if untreated. However, once you've had one episode of major depression, you have about a 50 percent chance of having a second episode. If you've had two episodes, you have a 70 percent chance of having a third episode. If you've had three episodes, you have a 90 percent chance of having a fourth episode. The more episodes you have, the more likely you are to have the next episode.

- In terms of prognosis for depression, the thing that we worry most about is suicide. In the United States, suicide is the eighth leading cause of death, accounting for about 32,000 deaths per year.

- Fortunately, there are quite a few treatments that are effective in treating a number of different kinds of depression in many different populations and age ranges. There is behavior therapy—not looking at cognition, just the behavioral component. There is the combined cognitive and behavioral therapy (CBT).

- In addition, there is interpersonal therapy, which looks at transitions in an individual's life. It looks at the core areas of work and home as well as core contributors to an individual's sense of self and well-being and how those might have been broken or somehow become disconnected. It's also short term and fairly standardized, much like CBT.

- Furthermore, there is pharmacotherapy, or a number of different kinds of antidepressants. In fact, it seems that more and more antidepressants are developed each decade.

CBT Perspectives on Depression

- We're going to look at the CBT triangle: emotions, thoughts, and behaviors. With depression, the emotion that we're talking about is sadness. It might have an element of stress, of feeling overwhelmed, or of feeling worthless or hopeless.

- According to Beck's cognitive model, the thoughts are about the self, about others, and about the world. For a depressed individual, all of those are quite pessimistic and negative. For the behaviors, there's a special relationship between behaviors and depression: When an individual becomes depressed, he or she tends to become behaviorally inactivated.

- CBT for depression can be divided into four stages. Of course, these stages can be adapted depending on where an individual is starting and depending on what his or her particular interests or abilities might be.
  - In general, for stage one, you start with education about the disorder and about CBT. We want to start the process of data collection—collecting information maybe on behaviors, maybe on cognition, maybe on both. We will teach them about the three downward spirals.

  - Stage two is called behavioral activation and mood monitoring. If a patient has become deactivated because of his or her depression, we want to turn that around. If the patient has been spiraling downward, we want to help reverse that spiral and start spiraling up.

- For stage three, we address cognition by having the patient engage in thought records, cognitive challenges, and exercises.

- In the fourth and final stage, we might have to make social and environmental changes. A lot of depression might reside within an individual, but it also might be driven by things that are in his or her environment that probably need to change.

The Four Stages of CBT for Depression
- Cognitions, behaviors, and social contacts are three depressive spirals that a patient might find himself or herself in. Depressive spirals are explained to patients in the first stage of treatment for depression with CBT as part of the education phase.

- We tell patients that cognitions and depression are very much related. A depressed mood causes an individual to think more negatively and have more negative biases. But when a person thinks more negatively, that causes him or her to become more depressed, which causes him or her to think more negatively, and so on. The individual is spiraling downward because of the relationship between cognition and depression.

A depressed mood causes an individual to think more negatively, which causes that individual to become more depressed, which triggers a depressive spiral.

- For behavior, it's a similar story. A depressed mood causes inactivity, which lowers mood, which further lowers activity. Social contacts are the same: When an individual is depressed, it lowers the number of social contacts he or she has; the person doesn't enjoy his or her contacts as much as before and might be more sensitive to rejection than before. The individual pulls away from others, but that makes him or her more depressed, which makes him or her pull away more.

- In addition to education, the first stage of CBT for depression involves data collection. To elicit data, we would most likely start with an exercise called activity monitoring. We would ask the patient to start recording all of his or her activities, or at least the highlights, throughout any given day and throughout the week in an activity log. We would also ask him or her to rate his or her mood on a 1-to-10 scale at the end of each day. We would ask him or her to note potential relationships between the activities he or she has chosen to do in a day and his or her mood at the end of that day.

- As part of the second stage, behavioral activation, we could also use this same activity record to do something called activity scheduling. It could be used as a sort of diary to document what the patient has done, or it could be used to prospectively look into the next week and determine when there is time to make plans with another individual or to do something that might have a positive impact on the patient's mood.

- Both before and after the activity is completed, the patient should rate the level of pleasure that he or she expected to experience and actually experienced. Often, patients find that the activity was much more pleasurable than their depression had predicted it would be.

- In the third stage of CBT for depression, cognitive restructuring, we want to look at the constellation of cognitions that tend to cluster around negative thoughts about the self, about others, and about the world.

- There are different ways to measure these cognitions. You can do a thought record or interview the patient, but you can also use questionnaires, such as the Dysfunctional Attitude Scale (DAS). The DAS used to be quite long—about 100 items—but it has been reduced to only 40 items. It's particularly good at measuring self-critical thoughts and unrealistic expectations about the self, including things like perfectionism. It's also useful in helping to predict who is going to do well in terms of being able to treat or remit their own depression.

- We also want to teach patients about the common habits of mind. Often, we make particular shortcuts that aren't very rational in terms of how we understand or explain the events happening in our world. We may use personalization, magnification, or minimization. We may selectively attend to all of our failures or things that just didn't go well. We may use all-or-none thinking. We may imagine or tell ourselves what we believe that other people are thinking. We may use fortune-telling. When someone is depressed, he or she has very dire and pessimistic predictions about the future.

- The fourth and final stage of CBT treatment involves social and/or environmental changes. This might include having the patient reach out to any friends that he or she might have lost touch with. We might also encourage the patient to join a support group, because it is often helpful to talk to other people who have had similar experiences.

- In addition, there are quite a few effective medications for depression. Research has shown that medications and CBT are equally effective for mild to moderate depression at the end of treatment and at a six-month follow-up. But if you go further out, it looks like CBT is superior to medications, unless a person wants to be medicated for the remainder of his or her life. In more severe cases, a combination of medications and CBT might be necessary, but it depends on the patient's preferences.

Suggested Reading

Beck, et al, *Cognitive Therapy of Depression*.

Brown, Beck, Steer, and Grisham, "Risk Factors for Suicide in Psychiatric Outpatients."

DeRubeis, Hollon, Amsterdam, Shelton, Young, Salomon, O'Reardon, Lovett, Gladis, Brown, and Gallop, "Cognitive Therapy vs. Medications in the Treatment of Moderate to Severe Depression."

Frewen, Dozois, and Lanius, "Neuroimaging Studies of Psychological Interventions for Mood and Anxiety Disorders."

Segal, Vincent, and Levitt, "Efficacy of Combined, Sequential and Crossover Psychotherapy and Pharmacotherapy in Improving Outcomes in Depression."

Williams, Teasdale, Segal, and Kabat-Zinn, *The Mindful Way through Depression*.

Questions to Consider

1. Complete your own depression inventory. What was your score, and what does it mean? Be sure to discuss with a health professional if needed.

   PHQ-9:

   http://www.patient.co.uk/doctor/patient-health-questionnaire-phq-9.

2. Recent epidemiological research has shown that the rates of depression in developed countries have been escalating for the past 50 years, despite impressive advances in diagnosis and treatment options. What explanation might account for this finding? What remedy might best address this problem?

Treating Depression
Lecture 7—Transcript

PROFESSOR SATTERFIELD: Maria is a 70-year-old retired schoolteacher, caring for her husband of 45 years. She has a great deal of chronic stress and more recently, she has slipped into a depression. Her goal is to be the best caregiver possible, to feel less depressed, to have more energy, to sleep better, to prepare herself to cope with the loss of her husband, reconnect with friends and family, and to find a source of meaning. Let's move to look at our first clip of Maria, where we teach her about the CBT basics and get her started with behaviors.

[VIGNETTE START]

PROFESSOR SATTERFIELD: Maria, now that we have a pretty good idea of your baseline symptoms, we've had, I think, a good initial discussion about your goals and your SMART goals, your specific goals. We should probably take a step back and talk a little bit about how we plan to get to those goals, the tools that might be in our toolbox. And we should talk about cognitive behavioral therapy, and sort of how it works. This is only session number two for you, so it's the perfect time for us both to do a little bit of board work, and to talk about how we think CBT works. So let me ask you first, what do you know about cognitive behavioral therapy?

MARIA: Well, after the first time, I went and looked it up online. And it's about thoughts that you have and feelings and stuff, and making that come together. It's supposed to be helpful for depression. So I thought, I'm the right place.

PROFESSOR SATTERFIELD: Sure, sure. And I think you are. And you're right. It was originally developed for the treatment of depression, and the strongest evidence is in treatment for depression. But we know it helps for a number of different things, like anxiety and sleep as well. It's been around—

MARIA: I'm in the right place.

PROFESSOR SATTERFIELD: Good. It's been around long enough that there are a lot of subtypes that are specifically targeted for those different symptoms that are on your list of goals. Just to explain a little more about how we think this works, if our goal is to change emotions—and that might be depression; it might be anxiety, both of which are relevant to you—you can reach in biologically with medications and change moods that way.

But that's not your only choice. There are a couple of different possibilities. We can look at behaviors or activities. We can also look at thoughts or—they're called cognitions, and that's why they call it cognitive behavioral therapy. Because the two pathways or the two categories of tools that we'll use fall into cognitions and into behaviors or activities. And I've drawn this as a triangle, with these bi-directional arrows, because we believe that each of these are connected. So your emotions—let's say you're depressed—it will affect the behaviors that you are able to engage in. So if you don't have energy, you don't enjoy things, you're going to be doing a lot less.

MARIA: I know that.

PROFESSOR SATTERFIELD: It works both ways. So if you do something you really enjoy or spend time with a friend, that's going to affect your emotions. If you have a conflict or a fight or are withdrawn, that's also going to affect your emotions. The same is true for cognitions or thoughts. We have thoughts all the time, often times out of our awareness. Some are very sort of superficial and fleeting, and some are really in your heart, and they really have a much deeper and longer lasting effect. But the way you think affects the way you feel. The way you feel affects the way you think. And your behaviors are also going to affect your thoughts. So they're all related.

The good news about that is that if we want to change emotions, then we can change behaviors and/or change the way that you're thinking. Let me ask, what questions do you have about this particular triangle?

MARIA: Where do you start? They're all going every way.

PROFESSOR SATTERFIELD: Good question—so where do you start? And there's no one right place to start. I will say that most people start here, in behaviors. The reason for that is oftentimes, if you come in with a substantial level of depressive symptoms, it's harder to concentrate and to focus.

On one of your questionnaires you mentioned that that was one of the symptoms and the challenges that you were having if you were doing a thought exercise that requires a bit more concentration and focus. So we want to start with behaviors.

We want to give you some immediate relief. And then we'll move on to doing some of the thoughts. And eventually, we'll try out a number of different tools in both categories, and you can pick which ones you think are going to work best for you.

[VIGNETTE END]

PROFESSOR SATTERFIELD: Welcome to our lecture on depression. In this lecture, we'll define this medical disorder, take a quick look at depression epidemiology, and explore what we know about etiology, or what causes it. We'll then move to look at leading treatments for depression and emerging treatments on the horizon. But first let's look at the full continuum of depression, where on one end we have a medical disorder; we have a serious chemical imbalance, such as the case with Maria.

On the other hand, we have every-day sadness. Many of us have been somewhere on that particular continuum, often happening after we've had a particular loss of some sort. Many of us have experienced grief or the loss of a loved one, also on that same continuum. Many times, that sadness, that depression, we consider non-psychiatric, even though it might be helpful to talk to an individual.

In Maria's case, however, she's gone beyond the level of everyday sadness. She's gone beyond the level of what we might expect with anticipatory grief, and she has developed what's called a full-blown major depressive episode. In a major depressive episode, an individual has a depressed mood most of the day, nearly every day, and/or a loss of interest in their normal everyday activities for at least two weeks or longer. In sum total, they have to have a total of five symptoms from a list of nine hallmark symptoms from depression. There has to be significant impairment or distress, and again, this can be at work, or home, or both.

So what are those nine hallmark symptoms of a major depressive episode? Well, I've mentioned the first already. So you have to have a sad or low mood, or sometimes it manifests as an irritable mood, particularly in men. There has to be a symptom called anhedonia. This is where an individual is unable to enjoy things that they normally enjoy. There's often changes in appetite or weight. And this is a dysregulation, so it could go in either direction. You could have increases in weight, or you could have decreases in weight.

The same is true for sleep. You could have hypersomnia, or you could have insomnia (difficulty sleeping). You'll see differences in the way a patient moves or in their energy levels. You'll see something, potentially, called psychomotor agitation, where they are shaky and jittery, or you might see psychomotor retardation, which is often described by patients as they feel like they're moving underwater or moving through molasses. We often see poor concentration or memory, difficulty following conversations, difficulty reading, difficulty remembering particular events. We see fatigue and low energy, feelings of worthlessness or guilt, and sometimes we even see suicidal ideation, or a patient becoming convinced that the world would be a better place if they weren't in it.

So how do we go about assessing depression? And here, I'm really talking about that full continuum of depression. There are a number of different instruments and questionnaires that are available online. The first is the classic Beck Depression Inventory. He also created something called the Hopelessness Scale. It's a 20-item scale which was found to be particularly useful in predicting suicidal behaviors. There is the PHQ-9; that's the Patient Health Questionnaire-9, which focuses on depression and is more and more commonly being used in primary care settings. Other questionnaires that you might want to consider are process measures of cognitive styles, such as the Dysfunctional Attitude Scale, the Automatic Thoughts Questionnaire, or the Attributional Style Questionnaire.

I want to just spend a little bit talking about the epidemiology of depression so we have a sense of how incredibly common it is and what some of the consequences might be. We know that Major Depressive Disorder affects around 15 million adults; that's around 7% of the population that are 18 years and over. The overall lifetime prevalence is around 17%, and the rates are double in women when compared to men. The average age of onset is around 32 years, but it's important to remember that major depression, the disease, can strike at any particular age, from young kids to adolescents to older adults. We know that major depressive disorder is the leading cause of disability in the U.S. for ages 15 to 44.

What about the prognosis? What's the outlook? Now, fortunately, a major depressive episode usually remits within 12 to 24 months, even if untreated. However, once you've had one episode, you have about a 50% chance of having a second episode. If you've had two episodes, you have a 70% chance of having a third episode. And if you've had three episodes of major depression, you have a 90% chance of having a fourth episode. It's almost as if, probably because of neural circuitry, that disorder is gaining momentum, and the more episodes you have, the more likely you are to have the next episode. Of course, in terms of prognosis, the thing that we worry most about is suicide, suicide related to depression. In the U.S., suicide is the eighth leading cause of death, accounting for about 32,000 deaths per year.

So, what are the treatments? And fortunately, we do have treatments, quite a few of them, that are effective in treating a number of different kinds of depression in many different populations and age ranges. We, of course, have straight behavior therapy, not looking at cognition at all, just the behavioral component. We have the combined cognitive and the behavioral therapy that we'll talk about in the context of helping Maria.

We have something called interpersonal therapy. Now, in interpersonal therapy, it really looks at transitions in an individual's life. It looks at those core areas in work and home. It looks at core contributors to an individual's sense of self and wellbeing and how those may have been broken or somehow become disconnected. It's also short term, and it's fairly standardized, much like CBT. And lastly, we have pharmacotherapy, or a number of different kinds of antidepressants, and it seems that more and more come out each decade.

But let's move specifically to talk about Maria's depression, and let's talk about CBT perspectives on Maria's depression. At this point, you probably know the place where we're going to start. We're going to look at the CBT triangle. Remember the triangle has emotions, thoughts, and behaviors as its three corners. With depression, of course, the emotion that we're talking about is sadness, depression. It may have an element of stress, of feeling overwhelmed, of feeling worthless, or hopeless.

The thoughts, if you go back to Beck's original model, are thoughts about the self, thoughts about others, and thoughts about the world. And for a depressed individual, all of those are quite pessimistic and quite negative. For the behaviors, there's a special relationship between behaviors and depression, where when an individual becomes depressed, they tend to become behavioral inactivated.

So what would see CVT for depression look like? And I'd like to divide it into four different stages. Now, this is essentially the prototype of what CVT for depression would look like. Of course, you're going to adopt this depending on where an individual is starting and depending on what their particular interests or abilities might be. But, in general, for stage one, you start with education about the disorder; you start with education about CVT, and you've seen us do that with Maria already. ,

We want to start the process of data collection. So, collecting information, maybe on behaviors, maybe on cognition, maybe on both. We have our theory, but we want to see if it actually works in an individual's life. We'll teach them about something called the Three Downward Spirals, which I'll explain in just a moment. Stage two is called behavioral activation and mood monitoring. So here we move to that behavioral corner of the CVT triangle. If a patient has become deactivated because of their depression, we want to turn that around. If they've been spiraling downward, we want to help and to reverse that spiral and start spiraling up. And we'll show you some video clips and exercises on how to do that.

Now, for stage three, we move over to the cognitive corner of that triangle, and we talk about thought records, cognitive challenges, and exercises, such as the ABCD. And in the fourth and final stage, we may have to make a social and environmental changes. Of course, a lot of depression may reside within an individual, but it also may reside or be driven by things that are in their environment that probably need to change.

So what did I mean by depressive spirals? This is something we teach patients about in the very first stage of treatment for depression with CBT. So first we tell them that cognitions and depression are very much related; we know on that one side of the triangle between emotions and between cognitions. We know that a depressed mood causes an individual to think more negatively and have more negative biases. But when a person thinks more negatively, that causes them to become more depressed, which causes them to think more negatively, which causes them to be more depressed, and they're spiraling downward because of that relationship between cognition and depression.

For behavior, it's a similar story. A depressed mood causes inactivity, which lowers mood, which further lowers activity. Social contacts are the same. When an individual is depressed, it lowers their amount of social contacts. They don't enjoy them as much as before. They may be more sensitive rejection than before. They pull away from others, but that makes them more depressed, which makes them pull away more. So, cognitions, behaviors, social contacts, three depressive spirals that a patient may find themselves in. Let's turn now to look at our second clip from Maria, where we talk about the basics of behavior and depression and how that spiral might be operating in her life.

[VIGNETTE START]

PROFESSOR SATTERFIELD: The way that depression and behaviors are often related—and you've sort of hit on a couple of important points—it doesn't mean if you're depressed that you're inactive or you're not doing anything or you're not working hard.

MARIA: I'm still trying.

PROFESSOR SATTERFIELD: You are. You absolutely are. But it often feels like you're spinning in place—

MARIA: —or swimming through molasses or something.

PROFESSOR SATTERFIELD: And it's not just the energy or your sense of what you can accomplish. It's also the kinds of things that you spend your time doing. And I know just 10 years ago, or less than that really, you were a schoolteacher.

MARIE: That's right.

PROFESSOR SATTERFIELD: And [that] brought you a lot of joy.

MARIE: I retired when he got sick. I wanted to be with him.

PROFESSOR SATTERFIELD: So one big source of behaviors and pleasure and enjoyment and meaning—teaching—that was no longer part of the picture. And that's going to affect you mood.

MARIA: That's right. I still get letters sometimes or e-mails from my old students.

PROFESSOR SATTERFIELD: And if I were you, I would savor those.

MARIA: I do. I do. I loved being with the students.

PROFESSOR SATTERFIELD: But behaviors are—our job, our profession's a big category. But there are a lot of other behaviors that happen throughout the day, many of them small. But when you add them all up, they can have a fairly substantial effect on your mood.

And by behaviors, I'll just give you an example. So taking a shower in the morning's a behavior. What you eat for breakfast is a behavior. If you read the newspaper, if you go for a walk, if you call a friend on the telephone, if you turn the TV—all those are—

MARIA: I used to do all those things.

PROFESSOR SATTERFIELD: And what happens with depression is a lot of those things go away.

MARIA: Yeah.

PROFESSOR SATTERFIELD: People just stop. And again, it's a gradual, insidious sort of process that you slowly pull away from those things that you enjoy, the things that gave you meaning, the social contacts, the sources of reward, of pleasure, of positive reinforcement. And eventually, you're spiraling down to a place where—kind of where you are now.

MARIA: Sometimes those things pull away from you too, though. When somebody's sick the way my husband is sick, it almost seems like people are afraid of you. They want to be helpful, but then they—my husband, he acts kind of strange.

He'll ask the same question. He'll say, how's Ed, in this very kind way that he has. But he's asked it, like, seven times and Ed has been dead for five years. And people just don't know what to say and they're afraid to come by. And so your world gets so tiny.

PROFESSOR SATTERFIELD: You're right.

MARIA: It's just us.

PROFESSOR SATTERFIELD: And you've brought up a really good point, that behaviors—the full gamut of behaviors—are quite different. Some are very simple and are absolutely within your control. If you choose to read the newspaper or not, that's pretty much in your control. What your friends are willing to do or your social supports, how they behave, isn't entirely in your control.

I think where we want to start—so we want to start with things that are within your control, maybe things that used to be part of your day that have somehow slipped away. And if we can start adding those back in and seeing if they have an influence on mood.

So what the theory tells us is that when a person's depressed, they do less, which makes them more depressed, which makes them do less, which makes them more depressed.

MARIA: That sounds like the story of my life lately.

So we want to reverse that spiral and have you add some things in to lift your mood, which makes it easier to add things in, which lifts your mood.

[VIGNETTE END]

PROFESSOR SATTERFIELD: So what we need next from Maria is data, and specifically, we need data about her behaviors. So how would we go about pulling out or eliciting that data? Well we would most likely start with an exercise called activity monitoring. We would ask her to start recording all of the activities, or at least the highlights of her activities, throughout any given day and throughout the week. We would also ask her to rate her mood on a simple 1 to 10 scale at the end of each day. We would ask her to note potential relationships between the activities she's chosen to do in a day and her mood at the end of that day. If you're curious about what a standard activity monitoring form might look like, again, I encourage you to Google "Satterfield, Minding the Body tools" and clicking on the companion website and downloading the tools from that website.

In general, what an activity log would look like is very similar to a calendar. Across the top of that calendar, you would just have the days of the week—Monday, Tuesday, Wednesday, Thursday, Friday, Saturday. On the left-hand column, you would have the hours of the day. Essentially, you've created a grid, where the individual simply has to write in maybe hour by hour, maybe not that granular, the major activities that they did during that day. We want to know when they got up. We want to know when they went to bed. We want to know if they were social contacts, if there was work, if there were play, if there were good events, if there were bad events. And again, at the end of the day, they would rate their mood on a 1 to 10 scale. Sounds very simple.

We could also use this same activity record to do something called activity scheduling. So, you could just use it as a way, a sort of diary to write down what you've done, or you could prospectively look into the next week and say, "OK, where are my open windows of time, and can I make plans to do something with the social support, or with another individual, or maybe just something that I think will have a positive impact on my mood?"

One thing that often happens with folks who are depressed is they've lost the ability to enjoy things. So when you tell them, "You should schedule something that you would enjoy," it's a little bit confusing for them. Sometimes they need to be reminded of things that they used to enjoy. Sometimes they literally need a list of things that might be enjoyable, and they can select from that list. What I often ask them to do is to suspend disbelief. Right now, their cognitions are telling them, "I shouldn't do this because it's going to be terrible and I'm not going to enjoy it." OK, let's push pause on that cognition and let's test it out. Go ahead and schedule it, do the activity, and once you've finished, rerate the level of pleasure that you've experienced. Often, in fact, nearly all the time, they find the activity was much more pleasurable than their depression had predicted it would be.

Let's move on to our third clip of Maria. In this particular clip, we see her begin to work with an activity schedule, and we see how it might be used in a therapeutic session to highlight the relationship between activities and mood on any given day.

[VIGNETTE START]

PROFESSOR SATTERFIELD: So why don't we start, then by looking at your activity schedule. Looks like you were able to fill that this past month.

MARIA: Tried to.

PROFESSOR SATTERFIELD: What was this like for you to record your activities and your mood?

MARIA: Well, at first it seemed like I just didn't have anything to write down. There was just hardly anything. So I started doing some things so I'd have something to write down.

PROFESSOR SATTERFIELD: And that's not a bad thing, because we want to raise your activity levels and we hope that that helps to improve your mood. Looks like you were successful. So you have quite a few things on here. And I can see too that a lot of those activities are caregiving-related.

MARIA: It takes most of my time.

PROFESSOR SATTERFIELD: And down here at the bottom, so your mood—you have a two, a three, a two, a one, a three, a three, and a five. So pretty low mood for most of the week. But then looks like at the end there, you had a good day. Well, why don't we—again we're looking to see how activities and mood are related for you and in your life.

And I usually like to look at one of the lowest days and the highest day and see if we can see any differences between what might have caused those differences in mood. So why don't we look, say, it looks like on a Wednesday there, you had a mood of one. And what do you see about the activities there?

MARIA: Well, I got up in the morning and Jack had wet the bed. So we were starting off kind of on the wrong foot. And he was in a bad mood. And I got him breakfast and got him cleaned up and everything. And I just didn't have any energy. I just didn't feel like doing anything.

I don't know. I got through lunch and everything, and he fell asleep and I just kind of sat at the kitchen table, looked out the window. That was kind of the whole day. Had TV on in the background sort of for company.

PROFESSOR SATTERFIELD: Sure, sure. And your mood that day was a one, so that was a pretty rough day.

MARIA: It was a terrible day.

PROFESSOR SATTERFIELD: Let's jump ahead a few days. And it looks like your mood—that was your five, your mood of five on the other day, which is—

MARIA: That was the day I decided to start writing some things in, do some things so I could write something in.

PROFESSOR SATTERFIELD: And tell me about these activities you have here.

MARIA: Well, I had breakfast. And Jack was in a pretty good mood, and I called my daughter, just to touch base and everything. She said she she'd come over for a little bit.

So she came over and I got to go out of the house for the first time in maybe 10 days and get some errands done, which I needed to do. I also took a little guilty moment for myself and had a Starbucks cappuccino. And then I got some takeout for dinner, and I didn't have to cook for one night. So that was nice too.

PROFESSOR SATTERFIELD: So there were a number of things. You called your daughter. And you took the initiative to do that. And she came over and you were able to go and do some practical things. Sounds like errands are things you have to do, but then there were things you wanted to do.

You treated yourself and got some takeout. And your mood at the end of that day was a five. And if we were to contrast the activities in that day versus the activities in the low mood day, so what differences do you see?

MARIA: There were a lot more activities on the day when I felt better. I don't know if it was because I felt better that I could do more, or that I did more and it just lifted me a little.

PROFESSOR SATTERFIELD: Right and it is sort of chicken and the egg. So you feel better, you do more. And we had talked about those spirals with depression. When you feel bad, you do less, but that makes you feel worse. It works the opposite way, too.

MARIA: Spiral going in the other direction.

PROFESSOR SATTERFIELD: So looks like on the low mood day, there was that downward spiral. And on the high mood day, it was more of an upward spiral.

Now what I want to point out are these activities on the positive mood day, the higher mood day. Those were under your control, that you made a decision whether intentionally or not, to call your daughter, have her come over, and give yourself the space to do some other things that you needed to do.

Now, what if you did that more than just one day a week? What if it were two days or three days a week?

MARIA: I wonder if there'd be time. But I could try. I would be willing to try.

PROFESSOR SATTERFIELD: So one of the challenges we have is there's the very real and important need of caring for your husband and a need to find support for you, respite for you, of having the home health worker or your daughter or whomever pick up some of the—

MARIA: My daughter really has her own life. She's got her own kids to worry about. The home health person, I don't know. My husband doesn't really like her very well. I hate to leave him with her for very long.

PROFESSOR SATTERFIELD: OK. So it sounds like that's, on a practical level, that's something we can talk about. And the home health worker stirs up some feelings and thoughts for your husband, but stirs up some feelings and thoughts for you too.

MARIA: I sort of feel like it's my job. I should really be doing it.

PROFESSOR SATTERFIELD: And I know it's easy as a caregiver to feel that you should be on 24 hours a day, seven days a week. But in reality, it's not possible.

MARIA: It doesn't seem to be. You're right.

PROFESSOR SATTERFIELD: Even if you're Superwoman, it's just not possible to happen. And maybe the best gift you can give your husband is to take care of yourself, so that when you are there, you're fully there.

[VIGNETTE END]

PROFESSOR SATTERFIELD: So from here, we would probably have her continue adding in new activities and assessing their effect on her mood. We want to look for both quantity and quality, and we want her to have a balance between the things she has to do and the things she wants to do. Recall, though, that this relatively simple exercise isn't just about activities, and it isn't just about creating those tiny little bumps in mood. It's helping to break through a depressed person's sense of helplessness. An individual who's depressed, they've tried all sorts of things and nothing seems to work. So, in essence, they've given up, but by giving them this relatively simple exercise, by doing something very small that bumps up their mood ever so slightly, it shows them that change is possible. It shows them that they can make a decision that will have a positive consequence in terms of lifting their mood. If they can make one decision to do one little thing that helps a little bit, what if they did two? What if they did three? What if they did four? What if they filled their entire week with those sorts of activities? What you do matters.

Now, recall the four stages of CBT for depression. So first was education and data collection, followed by the second stage of behavioral activation. So, we're now in the cognitive restructuring or the third stage of CBT for depression. Remember, we want to look at these constellation of cognitions, which tend to cluster around negative thoughts about the self: "I'm unlovable; I'm unworthy; I'm a failure." Negative thoughts about others: "No one cares about you; people will hurt you and exploit you." Negative thoughts about the world: "It's a very cold, uncaring, dangerous, or even violent place." There are different to measure those cognitions. Of course, you can do a thought record. You can interview the patient.

But you can also use questionnaires, such as the Dysfunctional Attitude Scale, or the DAS. Now, the DAS used to be quite a long questionnaire, about 100 items. It's been recently reduced to only 40 items. And it's particularly good at measuring self-critical thoughts and unrealistic expectations about the self, including things like perfectionism. It's also useful in helping to predict who's going to do well in terms of being able to treat or to remit their own depression.

What are some sample items from the DAS? There are items such as, "My value as a person depends greatly on what others think of me." If other people know what you are really like, they'll think less of you." "My happiness depends more on other people than it does on me." "If you cannot do something well, there's little point in doing it at all."

Of course, we also want to remind people or teach patients about the common habits of mind we talked about earlier. Often, we make particular shortcuts that aren't very rational in terms of how we understand or explain the events happening in our world. We may use personalization, magnification, minimization; we may selectively attend to all of our failures or things that just didn't go so well. We may use all-or-none thinking. We may imagine what, or tell ourselves what we believe other people are thinking. And we may use fortune-telling. And when someone is depressed, they have very dire and pessimistic predictions about the future.

So, for our cognitive interventions with Maria, we'll use self-monitoring or cognitive checklists first. We'll use exercises, such as the ABCD, or we'll do something called the 7-Column DTR. DTR is dysfunctional thought record, sometimes called daily thought record. And why would this be helpful? Remember, it's partly about the skills of identifying cognition and wrestling with that cognition, but it's also about empowering a disempowered, helpless, hopeless individual to show them that they can do something to help themselves to feel better. As they begin wrestling with more balanced and more helpful cognitions, in the process they learn to show more loving kindness to themselves. They give themself more compassionate explanations than they might have done before.

Now, stage four, or the last stage of CBT treatment, involves social and/or environmental changes. So for Maria this might be reaching out to her friends that she's lost touch with. I'm also going to encourage her to join a caregiver support group, given how common these kinds of stressors are that she's going through. It's often helpful to talk to other people who have been there too. Another change we might encourage her to make is to use some of her financial resources to hire more in-home support so that she can have more time off and not expert herself to be a caregiver 24 hours a day, seven days a week.

Now, what about medications for depression? As I mentioned, there are quite a few that are effective. For Maria, she has decided to try CBT first, and if she needs to add in medications later, she would do that. Folks often ask which is better, medications or CBT. It's partly a personal choice, but the bottom line is that medications and CBT are equally effective for mild to moderate depression at the end of treatment and at a six-month follow up. But if you go further out, it looks like CBT is superior to medications, unless a person wants to be medicated for the remainder of their lives. And why might that be? If you think about CBT, remember my goal is to help you to be your own CBT therapist, to give you a toolbox of interventions that you can pull out and use anytime you want. So when you finish CBT for depression, you've ended your connection with me, but you still have that toolkit, and you can keep dosing yourself, essentially, with those interventions.

In a study done by Rob DeRubeis and Steve Holland in 2005, they did a randomized control trial of cognitive therapy versus pharmacotherapy in moderate to severe depression. They had 24 sessions delivered by experienced therapists, and they found that cognitive therapy was as efficacious as pharmacotherapy. Now, this is notable in that it used to be the assumption that if someone was severely depressed, you had to break out pharmacotherapy and you couldn't do cognitive therapy, and that just doesn't seem to be the case. In a similar study be Siegel, Vincent, and Levitt in 2002, they looked at combination therapy, and they found that combination therapy of medications and cognitive therapy was probably superior to either alone. End of the story is, you could use either. In more severe cases, I would probably recommend a combination, but again, depending on patient preferences.

So, in summary we see that depression is a common condition. At the far end of the spectrum we do consider it a medical disease that does have medical treatments. There are clear elements of cognition and behavior. We start with the basic behavioral tools, such as activity scheduling, and then we move on to do the more advanced cognitive work.

Now, in our next lecture we'll be talking about anger. Thank you.

Anger and Rage
Lecture 8

A aron T. Beck's cognitive model involves beliefs about the self, the world, and others. With anger, the typical family of cognitions has to do with the perception of being unjustly treated, wronged, or cheated in some way. There's also a biological component to anger. Often, it is driven by our amygdalas—located deep in the center of our more primitive animal brains—which give us a quick surge of adrenaline and/or energy. In this lecture, you will learn about anger and how to deal with it.

Anger and Anger Management

- Anger is regulated by culture and potentially by rules about how a particular sex or gender might be able to act. Many more men go to therapy for anger issues than women, and often those men aren't necessarily angry, but they're depressed. Society tells them that it's not okay for a man to be vulnerable or depressed, but it is more acceptable for him to be angry. Hence, he becomes angry.

- If we're using the cognitive model of anger, we're going to want to look at the triggering event. This varies from individual to individual, because it's not so much about the activating event— it's about the way we interpret the event through the activating or automatic thoughts we have.

- We want to first work on the patient's level of general arousal, or pre-anger state. If someone's reserves are on empty at a particular point in time, his or her trigger is going to be much more sensitive in terms of responding to a negative event. We want to look at the appraisals of those events, the automatic thoughts.

- Two cognitive errors are overpersonalization and magnification. We might want to see if we can change the patient's autonomic nervous system. This would include targeting the relaxation response. It is nearly impossible to be extremely angry but to be relaxed at the same time; the two are mutually exclusive. So, if we teach someone to have more reserve—to be closer to a state of relaxation—he or she is less likely to get angry.

- Anger management is used to change cognition and behavior. There are many different kinds of anger management programs, but they include some common elements. One of these elements involves first improving the early detection of how an individual is feeling. Anger picks up steam over time, so if you catch it very early in the process, you have a much better chance of being able to regulate how you're feeling and to not act out behaviorally on a particular impulse. The longer you wait, and the angrier you get, the less likely you're going to be able to control your angry reaction.

- The next common element has to do with identifying the cause of the anger. There was something in the environment, something you remembered, or something you think might happen in the future that caused you to be angry. Emotions, including anger, are important because they often tell us information about our environment and are often what we notice first. So, if you suddenly feel anger, you need to pause and reflect on whatever triggered your anger.

- The next component of many anger management programs is an assessment of whether or not it's worth the investment of energy and resources to get angry. There are small triggering events as well as large triggering events. Anger, whether it is in response to something small or large, takes a toll on our bodies, particularly on our relationships. So, is it worth the investment?

- The final common component of anger management programs has to do with problem solving. Is this event that happened, or this wrong that occurred, a problem? Is it something that can be changed or rectified? From a CBT perspective, we would look at automatic thoughts and, specifically, habits of mind, such as personalization and magnification. We will work to hopefully decrease hostile fantasies, or when an individual is triggered for anger and then starts to imagine all sorts of things he or she is going to say or do. Anger management strategy teaches you to capture the process early and take your mind elsewhere.

- Third-wave therapies teach us that it's not necessarily effective just to tell yourself not to think angry thoughts—sometimes that actually makes you think angry thoughts. Instead, they teach us to use distraction and relaxation. Preoccupy yourself with something else to take your mind out of those angry ruminations. There are a number of different somatic quieting modalities that an individual could try, from meditation to deep breathing.

- Another intervention that we might try for individuals who are unable to think clearly and communicate constructively— particularly if we're talking about couples therapy or family therapy—is calling a time-out, in which we ask individuals to step out to do some somatic quieting and to cool off.

- We also want to look for other things that might be impairing an individual's judgment. For example, if someone is drinking too much, it lowers his or her inhibitions, makes his or her anger more readily available, and makes it more difficult to regulate his or her emotions.

- Sometimes anger is simply the surface manifestation of something else. The individual may be very stressed, may have a lot of physical or psychic pain, or may be fatigued. If there is an underlying cause, we want to make sure that we address that underlying cause.

- A potential cause of poor anger regulation is a failure to remember the humanness of the object of your anger or the impact that your rage might have on them. For example, when angry, many people might say something in a particular way in an e-mail that they would never say to another person if they were face to face.

- One of the things you want to determine up front is whether or not an individual feels remorse or guilt as a consequence of his or her anger. If the individual does, then you have something that you can build upon.

- If we want to build empathy, then we can use a seven-column dysfunctional thought record (DTR), sometimes called a daily thought record. It takes more time to do this particular exercise than an ABCD exercise, for example, but it provides more information. The critical part, as with the ABCD exercise, is in reconstructing or restructuring the cognitions.

The Seven-Column DTR
- The seven-column DTR includes prompts to think about, such as evidence for and evidence against a particular thought. Essentially, it prompts a rational analysis of a situation. It reminds us that thoughts aren't facts; instead, thoughts are opinions, and we should always weigh, consider, and potentially change those opinions. This approach is preferred for particular personality types, especially for those with legal backgrounds.

> The dysfunctional thought record can be found at the following website:
>
> http://psychology.tools/dysfunctional-thought-record.html

- There is also a set of prompts that you can use to help yourself soften up an emotionally charged thought and to start rewriting it. Some of those prompts might include the following.
  - If my best friend had this thought and I wanted to help him or her see things differently, what might I say?

  - Am I using a habit of mind? Am I using all-or-none thinking? Am I maximizing or minimizing? Am I doing mind reading?

  - Have there been times or situations when this thought doesn't or hasn't seemed true?

o   If I were to pretend to do a U-turn in my beliefs, what might I say or think instead?

o   When I've felt or thought this way in the past, what helped me?

o   Is this thought balanced? Is it fair?

o   What's the worst-case scenario? Can I live with that?

o   Will I care about this five years from now? Is it really worth the investment right now?

o   Are there any positives, maybe a silver lining that I'm not seeing?

- In the final column of the DTR, the patient rerates the intensity of his or her emotion to assess whether or not the cognitive restructuring has lessened the intensity of the emotion. If it hasn't, then there's probably more work to do.

- The seven-column DTR can help with anger, but it is a tool that we can use with nearly any scenario. As always, the patient has a role in helping to select the tools that resonate with him or her.

CBT and Anger

- Does CBT work for anger? A study by Margaret-Anne Mackintosh and colleagues in 2014 involved a group anger management programs in a sample of 109 veterans who had post-traumatic stress disorder. They looked at potential mechanisms that helped the veterans get control of their anger.

- They found that the veterans were able to better regulate their anger at the end of group therapy, but there were two skill sets in particular that seemed to be most helpful: calming skills (somatic quieting skills) and cognitive restructuring. When they compared the power of those two, they found that the strategy of calming skills was slightly more powerful than cognitive restructuring, but both were helpful.

- In 1998, Richard Beck and Ephrem Fernandez did a meta-analysis of 50 studies of CBT for anger. They found that the CBT patients did about 76 percent better than untreated patients for their reduction of anger. In 2005, Nana Landenberger and Mark Lipsey looked at 58 studies of CBT for violent offenders. They found that those individuals also responded positively in being able to regulate their anger, and recidivism, or bouncing back to jail once they got out, dropped by as much as 25 percent.

Consequences of Anger
- Anger does not just have consequences on social or professional relationships; it also has consequences for the individual. Type A personality is a behavioral and emotional style marked by an aggressive, angry, hostile struggle to achieve more and more in less time, often in competition with others. Studies have shown that the key element that causes issues for individuals is the hostility.

Research has shown that cynical hostility in men is associated with having a first heart attack.

- Research on hostility and cardiovascular events has shown that hostility in a sample of young students predicted the calcification of arteries 10 years later. In addition, studies have shown that the health hazard ratio was increased by about 25 percent if an individual has high scores in hostility. Furthermore, hostility, especially cynical hostility in men, is associated with having a first heart attack. The damage hostility causes begins early and usually takes decades to matter.

- One of the first studies to show that we can manage our emotions and improve our cardiovascular health was published by Meyer Friedman, the individual who coined the term "Type A personality." In the study, published in 1986, men who had just had their first heart attack were placed in a Type A intervention group. Some of them had supportive group therapy; some of them had interventions that were specifically targeting hostility. In the Type A intervention group, there was a recurrence of cardiac events only 13 percent of the time, compared to the usual care group, which had a recurrence of 28.2 percent of the time.

Suggested Reading

Beck, *Prisoners of Hate.*

Beck and Fernandez, "Cognitive-Behavioral Therapy in the Treatment of Anger."

Chida and Steptoe, "The Association of Anger and Hostility with Future Coronary Heart Disease."

Friedman, Thoresen, Gill, Ulmer, Powell, Price, Brown, Thompson, Rabin, Breall, et al, "Alteration of Type A Behavior and Its Effect on Cardiac Recurrences in Post Myocardial Infarction Patients."

Iribarren, Sidney, Bild, Liu, Markovitz, Roseman, and Matthews, "Association of Hostility with Coronary Artery Calcification in Young Adults."

Landenberger and Lipsey, "The Positive Effects of Cognitive-Behavioral Programs for Offenders."

Lipsey, Landenberger, and Wilson, "Effects of Cognitive-Behavioral Programs for Criminal Offenders."

Mackintosh, Morland, Frueh, Greene, and Rosen, "Peeking into the Black Box."

Salzberg, *Loving-Kindness*.

Questions to Consider

1. How was anger expressed in your family, and who was "allowed" to express it? Did you adopt a similar style? Have you worked to change your style of anger?

2. How can you differentiate between "true" anger and anger that is used to cover up shame, embarrassment, or insecurity? How often do you think that people use anger as a cover? What can you do about it?

Anger and Rage
Lecture 8—Transcript

PROFESSOR SATTERFIELD: In our third lecture, we discussed how to create a case formulation and used an extended video clip of me teaching Michael about the layers of cognition that go into a formulation: the automatic thoughts, the conditional assumptions or rules of life, the schemas, and the core beliefs. We populated those categories with real examples from Michael's life, giving the formulation salience and hopefully improving its accuracy.

In this lecture on anger, we'll go back to those real-world examples and explore how we selected and analyzed them to better understand his anger and what to do about it. Let's move to our first clip about Michael, where he shares an everyday event that triggered his anger and how he responded to it.

[VIGNETTE START]

PROFESSOR SATTERFIELD: I think what we want to do is to start hearing stories, and I think of stories as—they're data. They're grist for the mill, and they help us to begin to see patterns in the way you think, the way you feel, and the things that you do. And it's not right or wrong, or good or bad. It's just these are things that have happened recently, or maybe in the distant past, that we will start to chain together and see if we can see any common themes that are emerging for you.

Now, you mentioned the fight with your wife. And usually, fights with significant others have all kinds of dimensions to them. You mentioned it wasn't a new one, the issue about conflict over smoking, so I would guess there's a whole lot of layers.

MICHAEL: There's a history.

PROFESSOR SATTERFIELD: There's a history, for sure. So I would suggest we start with maybe another example that's a little more recent, maybe with a stranger or something that wasn't really that big of a deal, but it was a time when you felt pretty angry. What we'll do is we'll start with that. We will start looking at the elements of that event, putting it into different buckets—into triggering events, into emotions, into cognitions, things that you're thinking—and we'll eventually work our way to the argument with your wife.

MICHAEL: OK.

PROFESSOR SATTERFIELD: All right? And I think probably the best way to keep all that organized is to do a little bit of board work, so why don't we do that?

MICHAEL: OK.

PROFESSOR SATTERFIELD: OK, Michael. Why don't we start digging in with some of those stories? And you mentioned that you had in mind a recent event where you had felt angry. Do you want to tell me about that? And we'll start putting this into different buckets.

MICHAEL: Sure. It's a little embarrassing, but I guess it's a good example. Start on the good side—actually, we talked about maybe getting some exercise, and I did get a gym membership, and I'm trying to make good use of it. And so that's where the story actually begins. I was going to the club, and the parking lot there is really small. I don't know why. You figure you'd have a big parking lot because you want a lot of folks coming to your gym, but it's a really small lot.

Well, anyway, I'm getting there in my car, and I'm going to park, and I'm waiting for someone to pull out. I've even got my blinker on so anybody else can see I'm claiming that spot, right? So there I am. The person pulls out. And just as I'm about to pull into the parking spot, this guy in a white Prius cuts in front of me, goes right into the spot instead of me. I had the blinkers on, right? Anybody would have seen. That means he's claimed this spot.

Well, I was really, really pissed off, I have to say. It just—this seems to be outside the bounds of common courtesy. So I gestured at the guy, said a few things inside the comfort of my car that maybe he wouldn't have been happy to have heard. He gets out of his car. He gives me one of those sarcastic waves, like how you doing, pal? Look who got the spot, huh? And so he gives me one of those waves, and that doesn't make the situation worse, if you can imagine.

So I'm very hot. I find another space, and I'm thinking what I'd like to do is key this guy's car. I'm just really, really mad. But I figure, OK, well, that's not the thing I should do. So what I decided I would do, just to vent a little bit, to show this guy that he really shouldn't be able to get away with this in a just universe, right?

I had a can of Coke that was open, and so I went over to the car, and I guess I drunk about half of it, so I poured the other half on his car. OK, well, figure at least he's going to get the message that somebody was displeased. It leaves a little bit of stickiness and no big deal. So that's that.

I'm going inside, and I begin to feel, hey, that was kind of childish and a little silly, plus I guess there's a possibility that that could do some damage to the paint job in the long run. I don't know. So I'm feeling that was a stupid thing to do, so I actually went inside and filled a bottle up with water, and I went back and kind of rinsed off the spot.

So again, kind of embarrassing, a little bit childish, but I must say, the fella kind of deserved something, and I kind of still feel that. I don't really know how to handle it when people think they can get away with this kind of thing.

PROFESSOR SATTERFIELD: Great example.

[VIGNETTE END]

PROFESSOR SATTERFIELD: So you can see here, we're using the basic ABC model, the activating event, the beliefs, and the consequences, in order to start fleshing out and teaching Michael the cognitive model of anger. So Michael and I are in the phase of collecting data, and in this case, stories relevant to anger. We're going to use these stories as a way to educate him more about the cognitive model, and again, increase salience. But also to continue assessing him and to work on his case formulation.

We go on to use this story to illuminate what you know as the ABCs, the activating event, the parking issue in this case; the beliefs or thoughts that he was unjustly treated; and the consequences. His pouring the Coke on the car, and later going back to wash it off, his emotions and his behaviors. I do want to point out, though, that the richness of the event he shared isn't just captured in the ABC. After he acted on his anger, poured the Coke on the guy's car, he left, but he started to feel guilty. Now, why would that be? According to CBT, a new set of a thoughts must have emerged that generated this new emotion of guilt instead of anger. There wasn't really a new event, but there was a shifting chain of cognitions that caused a shift in his emotional state. It tells us that he does have a moral code, that he does have a conscience, and that he can self-regulate. We just want to help him work on his impulse control.

So, what is anger about? Of course, we're going to look at cognitions, and we've talked before about Beck's Cognitive Model—beliefs about the self, the world, and others. And in anger, the typical family of cognitions have to do with the perception of being unjustly treated, wronged, or cheated in some way. We know that there's a biology to anger, often driven by our amygdalas deep in the center of our more primitive animal brains that give us this quick surge of adrenaline or of energy. Michael often calls it his blip of anger that he then tries to grab and pull back down before he starts to act on it.

We also know, though, that anger is regulated by both culture and potentially rules about how a particular sex or gender might be able to act. I see many more men that come in with anger issues than women, and often, those men aren't necessarily angry, but they're depressed. And society tells them it's not OK for a guy to be vulnerable or depressed, but is more acceptable for him to be angry; hence he becomes the angry guy.

Now, if we look at the cognitive model of anger, were going to want to look at the triggering event, and this varies from individual to individual. Because remember, it's not so much about the activating event, it's about the way we interpret the event; it is the activating or the automatic thoughts that we have. So we want to first work on his level of general arousal, or I think of it as sort of his pre-anger state. If someone's reserves are on empty at a particular point in time, their trigger is going to be much more sensitive, in terms of responding to a negative event.

We want to look at the appraisals of those events, those automatic thoughts. And two cognitive errors that we often see are over personalization, and we see magnification. We might want to reach in and see if we can do something in terms of changing his autonomic nervous system. And here I'm thinking about a relaxation response. It is nearly impossible to be extremely angry, but to be relaxed at the same time; the two are mutually exclusive. So if we teach someone to have more reserve, to be closer to a state of relaxation, they're less likely to get angry. We want those changes in cognition. We want those changes in behavior.

So how does anger management work? And of course, these days, it's definitely out in the popular press, and there's even a TV show about it, but there is a longstanding tradition of research looking at how individuals can manage their anger. There's a lot of different flavors to different anger-management programs, but they include some of the following common elements. So one of those elements involves, first, the improving the early detection of how you're feeling.

Now, I think of anger as something that picks up steam over time. If you catch it very early in the process, you have a much better chance of grabbing it and being able to pull it down, to regulate how you're feeling, and to not act out behaviorally on a particular impulse. The longer you wait, and the more angry you get, the less likely you're going to be able to control your angry reaction.

The next common element has to do with identifying the cause of the anger. So there was something out in the environment, or there's something that you've remembered, or something you think might happen in the future, that caused you to be angry. Now, remember that emotions, including anger, are important. They often tell us information about our environment, and they're often what we notice first. So if you find yourself at home, maybe alone, maybe in the office, and suddenly you feel anger, that's a signal that you need to pause and reflect and to pull out those cognitions about whatever event you were just imagining that triggered your anger.

The next component of many anger-management programs is an assessment of whether or not it's worth the investment of energy and resources to get angry. There are small triggering events, and there are very large triggering events. We know that anger, whether it is in response to something small or large, takes a toll on our bodies, particularly, takes a toll on our relationships. So, is it worth the investment? The final common component of anger-management programs has to do with problem solving. Is this a problem, this event that happened, this wrong that occurred, is this something that can be changed? Is this something that can be rectified?

From a CBT perspective, we would do, of course, cognitive restructuring, and here we're going to look at those automatic thoughts, and we're specifically going to look at habits of mind, such as personalization and magnification. We will work to hopefully decrease what are called hostile fantasies, or when an individual is triggered for anger, then they start to imagine all sorts of things they're going to say or they're going to do. How many of us have had arguments with our significant others when the significant other isn't even there? And anger-management strategy teaches you to capture that process early and to take your mind elsewhere. Remember what we've learned from third-wave therapies is it's not necessarily effective just to tell yourself not to think angry thoughts. Sometimes that actually makes you think angry thoughts. But use distraction; use relaxation. Get yourself preoccupied with something else to take your mind out of those angry ruminations. The last piece we would want to teach Michael is somatic quieting. There's a number of different modalities that he could try from meditation to deep breathing.

Other interventions that we might try, particularly if we're talking about a couples therapy or a family therapy, if individuals are getting a little bit too hot, if they're unable to think clearly and to communicate constructively, we'll often call a timeout, where we'll ask individuals to step out to do some somatic quieting and to cool off.

We also, of course, want to look for other things that might be impairing an individual's judgment. So if someone is drinking too much, it lowers their inhibitions and makes their anger more readily available, makes it more difficult to regulate their emotions. And as I mentioned before, sometimes anger is simply the surface manifestation of something else. The individual may be very stressed. He or she may have a lot of physical or psychic pain, or they may be fatigued. If there is an underlying cause, we want to make sure we get to that underlying cause.

Now, one potential cause of poor anger regulation is a failure to remember the humanness of the object of your anger or the impact that your rage might have on them. E-mail flames, a relatively recent phenomenon, are a classic example, where the human being has been removed from the equation so that anger is no longer well-regulated. Many people, when angry, will say something in a particular way in an e-mail that they would never say to another person if they were face-to-face.

Of course, one of the things you want to determine up front is whether or not an individual feels remorse or guilt as a consequence of their anger. If they do, you're in luck. You have something that you can build upon. So if we want to build empathy, then what can we do? Let's watch this next clip of Michael working through another event.

[VIGNETTE START]

PROFESSOR SATTERFIELD: You have one more thought record. Shall we do the third one?

MICHAEL: Yeah, let's talk about the third one. And this is actually, I must say, of the three, the one where I felt most embarrassed about. But it's a very simple one. Everybody goes through this. I was at home. I guess it had been kind of a long day, so I'm at home, and the cell phone rings, and I answer it, and—not a number I recognize, but I answered it. Maybe that was a silly thing to do, but I did, and it's a telemarketer who somehow got my number. It's a telemarketer. So OK, yeah, I blew up. I blew up and got very angry, and in fact ripped into this telemarketer.

PROFESSOR SATTERFIELD: OK. So trigger—unwelcome telemarketing call—

MICHAEL: Very unwelcome.

PROFESSOR SATTERFIELD: —at home. The emotion was—

MICHAEL: It was irritation. Annoyance.

PROFESSOR SATTERFIELD: Any sort of fury, hostility?

MICHAEL: There's hostility there, yeah. There's definitely a hostility there.

PROFESSOR SATTERFIELD: And if you were rating on a 0 to 100 intensity scale?

MICHAEL: At that moment, I would say probably 70%.

PROFESSOR SATTERFIELD: 70%, OK. And the behavior, then, was to yell and to lash out. What were some of the thoughts? So you got the call. You sort of feel your blood pressure rising, and that anger or hostility's building up. What was going through your mind? What thoughts did you catch?

MICHAEL: Well, a couple of thoughts that I captured here on the thought record was don't you—telemarketer person—have anything better to do with your time? And the other big thought that I wrote down is this is my time that you are invading. So those were the two big ones that I wrote down.

PROFESSOR SATTERFIELD: It almost has a how dare you—sort of that violation again of—for someone to come into my home or take my time, they should be invited or be welcomed, and you're not.

MICHAEL: I did not ask for this call.

PROFESSOR SATTERFIELD: Right.

MICHAEL: There was, though—and I don't know how to weave this into the story—but it wasn't immediate, but really in the process of really tearing into this telemarketer person, I began to realize that that person is just doing their job, right? So why am I ripping into somebody who, after all, is just doing a job, probably doesn't get paid all that well anyway?

So I did begin to realize, hey, this is kind of stupid. I didn't apologize to the telemarketer, but I kind of backed off, got off the phone, and I really actually felt a little bit embarrassed after the call. And there was a little bit of twinge that said, you know, maybe you should find out how to get back in touch with that telemarketer and apologize. I didn't take that step, but those were some of the thoughts and the emotions that were also playing out after that initial outburst.

PROFESSOR SATTERFIELD: So it sounds like you were almost a little surprised by the intensity that got evoked so quickly by a call. But calls are annoying, I think most people would say, and not welcome. But it really flipped that switch for you. But in the moment, you started having empathy. You started having empathy for the other person and started imagining what it would be like if your job was as a telemarketer. You're in a minimum wage job. You're calling people that don't want to be called, and I bet they have a lot of people yell at them all day long. It would kind of stink to be a telemarketer.

MICHAEL: It would kind of stink.

PROFESSOR SATTERFIELD: For sure. So even in the moment, with empathy, without even needing to wrestle with thoughts, the empathy diffused your anger.

MICHAEL: It did.

PROFESSOR SATTERFIELD: OK. So if you were to rate the anger now or maybe after the call, what did it go down to?

MICHAEL: I don't—the anger about the call is probably way down to the 0% to 5%. It just seems an overreaction as I look back on it.

PROFESSOR SATTERFIELD: And you mentioned a new emotion came out, and that was embarrassment or remorse or something. So that's, again, that's one of those chains of events or event inside of an event. So there were, I'm sure, thoughts that triggered that embarrassment. And what kind of thought—

MICHAEL: One of the thoughts that I had was that people are just doing their job. And I understand what it's like to do a job and not necessarily to like every minute of it. That person probably doesn't like every minute of it either, and so I guess you used the word empathy. That thought, for me, connects back—if we're all just trying to get by, we're all just trying to do what we can, you don't need somebody chewing you out just because you're doing what you're asked to do.

PROFESSOR SATTERFIELD: And that's a very sort of kind and compassionate way of looking at the world and something definitely to strive for, and we can all aim to be kind and compassionate and do the best that we can. And sometimes, we're not. But then again, it's that opportunity to learn and to grow and to turn it into something constructive.

MICHAEL: Yeah, I would hope so. And I must say that I still feel a little bit of embarrassment. But one of the things that I wrote down about a more objective thought I might have had was if next time—I don't say if—next time a telemarketer calls, to front-load these thoughts that we're talking about and to be prepared when that happens to say things to yourself in your own head. It's just a telemarketer. That doesn't mean I have to spend my evening talking to this person. I can end the call, but there's no reason to inflict my anger on someone else.

[VIGNETTE END]

PROFESSOR SATTERFIELD: So what did we just see? Notice that we've moved from the simpler ABCD exercise to a more detailed seven-column thought record, or DTR (dysfunctional thought record), sometimes called a daily thought record. It takes more time to do this particular exercise than an ABCD, but it does provide more information. The critical part, as with the ABCD exercise, is in reconstructing or restructuring the cognitions.

I'll describe the seven-column DTR in greater detail, but I don't want us to lose the point of how we build empathy. Notice that with Michael, being out of the situation with the telemarketer, and having time to reflect, was essential. He mentions feeling embarrassed and ashamed of losing his temper. The DTR exercise itself, in some of its prompts, asks him to see the events through the eyes of someone else, in order words, to develop empathy. After repeat exercises, like this one, Michael will become quicker to see the point of view of others, and hopefully, he will remember his lessons learned.

So now let's take a moment to unpack the seven-column DTR a little bit. We'll explore this more in the next lecture, but I think it's worth going over now, as it can be quite challenging to work with. In the seven-column DTR, it includes prompts to think about, evidence for, and evidence against a particular thought. It prompts, essentially, for a rational analysis of a situation. It reminds us that thoughts aren't facts. Thoughts are opinions, and we should always weigh and consider, and potentially change those opinions.

For particular personality types, they love this approach, especially those with legal backgrounds used to looking at evidence for or evidence against. There are also, though, a set of prompts that you can use to help yourself to soften up an emotionally charged thought and start to rewrite it. So, some of those prompts might be, if my best friend had this thought and I wanted to help him or her see things differently, what might I say? Or you could ask yourself, "Am I using a habit of mind? All-or-none thinking? Am I maximizing or minimizing? Am I doing mind reading right now? Have there been times or situations when this thought doesn't or hasn't seemed true? What's the other side of the coin? If I were to pretend to do a U-turn in my beliefs, what might I say or think instead? When I've felt or thought this way in the past, what helped me? Is this thought balanced? Is it fair? What's the worst case scenario? Can I live with that? Will I care about this five years from now? Is it really worth the investment right now? Are there any positives, maybe a silver lining, that I'm not seeing?

In the seventh and final column of the DTR, the patient rerates the intensity of their emotion to assess whether or not the cognitive restructuring has lessened the intensity of their emotion. If it hasn't lessened the intensity, then there's probably more work to do. If you are interested in what a seven-column DTR might look like, I would encourage you again to go to our friend Google. Just type in "seven-column dysfunctional thought record," and you will see many, many very similar versions of this particular exercise.

In the last clip, we used the seven-column DTR with Michael to help him with his anger, but it's a tool that we can use with nearly any scenario. And remember that the patient always has a role in helping to select the tools that resonate with them. Sometimes we move from the ABCD to the DTR. Some patients prefer just to stick with the ABCD. Some patients prefer to start with the DTR. It's really up to you.

But let's go back to anger. Does CBT work for anger? I wanted to share just a couple of studies, one of the more recent from Macintosh and colleagues in 2014, where they did a group anger-management program in a sample of veterans who had post-traumatic stress disorder. So again, it's not just about anger, but there's also something, namely, exposure to trauma, that's underneath. In the sample of 109 veterans, they looked at potential mechanisms that helped them to get control of their anger. In all of their veterans, they found that they were able to better regulate their anger at the end of group therapy, but there were two things in particular, two skill sets that seemed to be most helpful. The first was calming skills, or what we call somatic quieting skills. So again, you're turning down the flame, that sort of physiologic arousal that often accompanies anger. The other was cognitive restructuring; that's back to the ABCD, and that's back to the DTR. When they compared the relative power of those two, they found that calming skills was slightly more powerful than cognitive restructuring, but both were actually helpful.

In an older study done by Beck and Fernandez in 1998, they did a meta-analysis of 50 studies of CBT for anger. They found that the CBT patients did about 76% better than untreated patients for the reduction of anger. In a study by Landenberger and Lipsey in 2005, they looked at 58 studies of CBT for violent offenders. So here we're not talking about everyday anger; we're actually also talking about folks with a history of violence.

They found that those individuals also responded positively in being able to regulate their anger, and in fact, recidivism, or bouncing back to jail once they got out, dropped by as much as 25%.

Now, the last piece I wanted to move to was to talk not just about the consequence of anger on relationships or on social or professional functioning;

I wanted to look at the consequences of anger on the individual. There is this idea that a prototypical type A, aggressive, angry, hostile, usually business-type guy would have a heart attack, or maybe he would have a stroke. Is it true that anger, or specifically something called type-A personality, might predispose an individual to have a serious medical event like that?

Type-A personality style wasn't discovered in a laboratory, or by a scientist, even. It was by a practicing cardiologist who had a rather posh practice in the Pacific Heights neighborhood of San Francisco. He noticed that his furniture was getting a little bit worn, so he called in a furniture upholsterer. The furniture upholsterer took the measurements, but noticed, and said to the doc, "Hey, Dr. Friedman, it looks like you must see some really interesting patients, because they're always fidgeting with the arms of the chairs, and they're always bouncing their legs up and down, rubbing the front of the chair. What kind of patients do you see?"

The light bulb went off for Meyer Friedman, and he realized that these mostly 40-, 50ish-year-old men that he saw with her first heart attack were very time pressured, very aggressive, and very competitive. He called it a type-A behavior pattern, defined as a behavioral and emotional style, marked by an aggressive, unceasing struggle to achieve more and more in less time, often in competition with others. Through a number of different studies over several decades, he found that, really, the key element wasn't the time urgency, or even the competitiveness, it was the hostility.

So, if we look at hostility and cardiovascular disease, what does the evidence show us? And there are actually a well over 100 studies at this point, so I'll just give you a couple of highlights. In one classic study by Iribarren, published in the Journal American Medical Association in 2000, we see that hostility in a sample of 374 young 18- to 30-year-old students predicted calcification of coronary arteries 10 years later. So what this particular study showed us, is not just guys in their forties or their fifties that might be having this harm caused by hostility. It actually starts much earlier in life and builds, potentially, over decades. In the next study by Chida and Steptoe from 2009, they did a meta-analysis of 44 studies of hostility and cardiovascular events. They found that the health hazard ratio was increased by about 25% if an individual has high scores in hostility.

So when I say "high scores in hostility," what does that mean, exactly, and what sorts of scales do we use? Well, as you can imagine there's a number of different ones, but many of these studies have used something called the Cook-Medley Hostility Scale. It lists a number of different beliefs, and it is a true-false scale. Some sample items would be: True or False? "No one cares much what happens to me." "Some of my family have habits that annoy me very much." "People often disappoint me" Or, "It's safer to trust nobody." Now if we're honest, all of us are going to get a few points on the Cook-Medley Hostility Scale, but we're really most interested in the top 20 to 25 percent of folks on that particular scale in terms of being worried about their cardiovascular health.

Now, it's well known that hostility, and especially cynical hostility in men, is associated with having a first heart attack. We know the damage hostility causes begins early and usually takes decades to really matter. But is there anything that we can do about it? If you or your loved one might be on that top 20 percent of people who are hostile, is there hope? And the answer is yes. Personalities don't necessarily change, but we can learn to better manage our emotions. One of the first studies published to show us that we can manage our emotions and improve our cardiovascular health was published by Meyer Friedman, the individual who coined the term type-A personality. This was published in 1986 and was a four-and-a-half year randomized control trial, where he about 1,000 guys who had just had their first heart attack and put them in a type-A intervention group. Some of them had supportive group therapy; some of them had interventions that were specifically targeting that hostility. Fortunately, for folks who are hostile and for the ones who love them, he had positive results. In the type-A intervention group, there was a recurrence of cardiac events only 13% of the time, compared to the usual care group, which was 28.2% of the time. So there's hope.

But honestly, we don't have a lot of hope just yet. There haven't been a lot of studies since the Meyer Friedman study that show that we can decrease anger, and there are going to be consequences in terms of improving cardiovascular health. There are a lot of studies that are ongoing, there are meta-analyses that show that CBT can work to reduce anger, but they haven't connected all of the links in that particular chain. CBT reduces anger, and reducing anger improves cardiovascular health.

So what does this mean for Michael? Well, we're going to add behavioral interventions, social interventions, and somatic quieting. I think we can definitely reduce his anger. We hope to improve his relationship with his wife and his son, and his relationships with coworkers. But it's unclear if this would improve his cardiovascular health.

So in our next lecture, we're going to continue talking about these seven-column daily thought record, and we're going to talk about some common challenges that come up when treating anxiety, treating depression, or treating anger, all grist for the mill. Thank you.

Advanced Cognitive Behavioral Therapy
Lecture 9

This lecture moves from a basic cognitive restructuring to a more in-depth look at the seven-column dysfunctional thought record (DTR) with regard to treating anxiety, depression, or anger. In addition, you will learn how to fill out a core beliefs worksheet. You also will learn about what happens when an exercise fails. But even when things go wrong, it's all useful work. As the patient does his or her homework, he or she is learning and growing.

The Seven-Column DTR in Practice

- If a patient tends to have thoughts that devalue him or her in terms of how likable, lovable, or interesting he or she might be and thoughts that amplify or magnify potential dangers that are in the environment or possible negative reactions that other individuals might have toward him or her, we want to help the patient see those recurring thoughts, or recurring themes, and help build up his or her muscles in having common helpful responses that come quickly.

- The advantage of acknowledging the patterns is that when the patient is out of the moment—when things aren't going so well—then he or she can write detailed responses that are convincing and meaningful for him or her and then call them to mind much more quickly than if the patient hadn't gone through this exercise.

- There might be certain well-rehearsed negative thoughts that will pop into a patient's mind in social situations, but once he or she is prepared, his or her negative thoughts will pop back out of the mind almost as quickly.

- We're going to discuss how to fill out each of the seven columns of the DTR, specifically focusing on places where individuals tend to get stuck. This is a core skill, and it is one of the more complex skills that you'll do in cognitive therapy.

- First, we need to address how to identify an event. This is the first column on the seven-column DTR. There are all sorts of events that you could choose from.

- If you're early in the process of learning how to do this, it is recommended that you pick one that has a mild to moderate level of emotional intensity. You don't want something so charged that it's difficult to finish the exercise. If you're more advanced, move from moderate to something that's more severe.

- When you describe the event in the first column, you want to keep it fairly neutral. There's no interpretation. It's just the facts. It's just the context. It's just the circumstance.

- In the next column, you want to describe the emotion. You want to rate it in intensity from zero to 100, with 100 being the most intense. If necessary, if you're having trouble coming up with the right words to describe the emotion you had, consider creating a sort of emotional thesaurus that can help you whenever you need to be able to put a word to a feeling that you are having.

- Many people struggle with the next column, in which you actually capture the automatic thoughts portion, but here are a few tips that might help you. You might ask yourself the following questions: At this moment, what was going through my mind? What images or memories did this particular activating event evoke for me? What meaning did I assign to it? What does it say about me or my future? If I were to put words to the feelings I had, how would I describe them?

- You might want to use a technique called the downward arrow to try to dig a little bit deeper. For example, some common automatic thoughts might be about anger and some sort of injustice. The patient might tell us that someone is disrespecting him or her. Then, we would ask the patient, what does it mean if you let someone get away with disrespecting you? The patient might respond, "It means that I'm weak and I'm asking to be abused again." We might say, what does it mean if you're weak? The patient might say, "It means that I'm a loser and that no one likes me."

- The purpose of this technique is to drill down to get to the heart of the matter—to get at the underlying belief. If you're able to work with that underlying belief, you'll probably be more effective in changing your mood.

- The next two columns involve finding evidence for and against the automatic thought. Sometimes this comes very easily to people, and others might struggle with it. You might ask yourself the following questions: What are the facts, and what are the opinions? What are the assumptions or guesses that I might be making? What has happened in the past in similar situations or with other people? Are my automatic thoughts using habits of mine? Am I using all-or-none language? Am I saying things like "always" and "never"? Are there other habits of mine, such as overpersonalization or magnification, that I might begin to shrink down a bit?

- You should think of yourself as an investigative team of sorts. If you're completely stuck, you can also run the thought record by a loved one or friend, or you can do a behavioral experiment. For example, if you have the belief that you're socially invisible—that even if you try, no one wants to interact with you—then you would design a behavioral experiment where you go into a social situation and test out whether or not people interact with you and whether or not you're truly socially invisible.

- The next column involves how you arrived at the new thought. This is one of the more challenging parts. You can use a strategy called "yes, but," which acknowledges some of the truth in what you originally thought but that there is another side. For example: Yes, I at times seem invisible in social situations, but I can change my behavior to reach out more to others.

- You want to go for balance or at least softening and qualifying those automatic thoughts. You might try for perspective. What's the worst-case scenario? Will this matter in five years? Is there a silver lining? Is there a bigger picture? What we want to do is help you find a more compassionate, caring, and forgiving way to think about the situation, and then rewrite it.

- The final step is to rerate the intensity of the emotion. Did the intensity decrease? If not, go back and try to figure out why. Did you pick the right automatic thought? Do you need to dig a little bit deeper, using something like the downward arrow? Was the new thought believable? Is this an unchangeable fact that you should probably work on accepting and coping with?

- Remember that all of this work is useful; nothing is a waste of time as long as the patient is learning and growing. Patients sometimes learn the most when they have tried to do a thought record on their own, get stuck, and bring it back, and we work on it together and figure out what adaptations they can make for next time.

The Core Beliefs Worksheet
- Another exercise that can be used in CBT is called the core beliefs worksheet. The cognitive model addresses the automatic thoughts on the surface, but we have these core beliefs underneath. Often, they're developed early in life, and they might not be particularly rational, but they have a strong, emotional charge attached to them and are fairly resistant to change.

- To use a core beliefs worksheet, start with a blank sheet of paper. The patient writes the core belief at the top of the page. For example, it might be "I'm an unlovable person." The patient would then rate the percent strength that he or she currently has in that belief. The patient would create two columns on that piece of paper: evidence for and evidence against. He or she would look for all of the prompts that you might use on a DTR but would use them on the core beliefs worksheet. The patient might talk to significant others. At the bottom of the core beliefs worksheet, the patient would write a new tentative belief at the bottom, along with his or her percent agreement.

- A one-page exercise that takes the patient 15 or 20 minutes certainly isn't going to change a core belief, but if we think of the core belief as a boulder that is weighing heavily on the patient, each time he or she does this exercise, he or she chips away a piece of that core belief. And with enough practice, over time, we hope that the patient can make shifts in how he or she feels about himself or herself.

When Things Go Wrong

- What do we do when things go wrong? We want individuals to practice their skills. We want them to make adaptations over time. It should be an evolving process, but sometimes the homework just doesn't work out. Sometimes it doesn't have the desired effect.

- The important part is to remember that nothing works all the time. You often don't get it right the first time. It's the partnership—the collaborative problem solving—in CBT that creates the flexibility and creativity to finally find something that works for a particular person, given his or her life circumstances.

Suggested Reading

Areán, Raue, Mackin, Kanellopoulos, McCulloch, and Alexopoulos, "Problem-Solving Therapy and Supportive Therapy in Older Adults with Major Depression and Executive Dysfunction."

Cuijpers, van Straten, and Warmerda, "Problem Solving Therapies for Depression."

Unützer, Powers, Katon, and Langston, "From Establishing an Evidence-Based Practice to Implementation in Real-World Settings."

1. If core beliefs are, by definition, deeply held from a very early age, then how can CBT hope to change them? Does CBT change core beliefs, or does it teach compensatory strategies to work with what you have?

2. Complete your own daily thought record. First, select a triggering event, and then see if you can fill out the columns for emotions, automatic thoughts, evidence for and against, the new thought, and the new emotion ratings (see DTR form). Did you get stuck? Where? Be sure to try the tips mentioned in the lecture to help you move forward.

Advanced Cognitive Behavioral Therapy
Lecture 9—Transcript

PROFESSOR SATTERFIELD: There's a concept sweeping the smartphone-app industry in Silicon Valley. It's called adaptive difficulty, and the idea is to first quickly assess the skill and knowledge level of your new user, then set your game or learning app at the appropriate level of difficulty, usually just one short stretch for the user. It feels a little challenging, but it gives rewards right away, and the customer feels motivated to continue. As the user gets better and better, the game gets harder and harder, always pushing the user to improve and to grow stronger.

Now, CBT isn't a game, but it does involve knowledge and skill, and I've often thought that CBT therapists use something like adaptive difficulty. You start with the assessments to gather data on baseline knowledge and skills, but you also use specific interviewing techniques, like Socratic questioning, or Ask-Teach-Ask, as a way to set the initial bar for the level of difficulty. Tell me what you know about depression and cognition. Depending on the answer you get from the patient, you know what to teach and you know where to start. As the patient does their homework, and they learn, and they grow, you adjust the level of difficulty upwards. In this lecture, we'll adjust upwards from basic cognitive restructuring to a more in-depth look at the Seven-Column DTR. We'll also look at what happens when an exercise fails. There is a way to almost always have a win-win scenario. Remember, it's all grist for the mill, even when things go wrong.

So let's review what skills we've gone over so far, starting with the behavioral category. We started with self-monitoring, and we'd had an activity record. We moved from the activity record to prospectively scheduling activities with an activity schedule. We wanted to look at the relationship between activities and mood. We talked about a variant where we could add in something called pleasure predicting, where an individual, usually a depressed individual, makes a prediction in advance of how much they will enjoy an event. They do the event, and then they re-rate their level of pleasure, often finding that their initial predictions were too negative.

Another behavioral strategy we used is something called the Behavioral Experiment. This is when Carol decided that she would walk down the street and say hello to strangers. She had a particular prediction about what would happen, and it turned out to be wrong. The last category of behavioral interventions we've discussed thus far falls into the realm of Somatic quieting, things like breathing, meditation, or progressive muscle relaxation.

So in our other bucket of skills, the cognitive bucket, we've done things like self-monitoring, and here we're monitoring cognitions. We want to do detection; we want to do analysis; and we want to do restructuring of those cognitions. We've done things like the ABCD exercise, and we talked a little in the last lecture about the Seven-Column DTR, or dysfunctional thought record. We're going to do another one. And, if you want to follow along with your own DTR form, again, you can Google "Seven-Column dysfunctional thought record." Let's move now to our second example of how a Seven-Column DTR might work with a clip from Carol.

[VIGNETTE START]

CAROL: So, I brought my homework in, and I think that it would be good to talk about that first, the thought record.

PROFESSOR SATTERFIELD: Sure, sure, absolutely. So you have a thought record.

CAROL: Yes.

PROFESSOR SATTERFIELD: And did you do the ABCD or the seven-column one?

CAROL: I did the seven-column on.

PROFESSOR SATTERFIELD: Perfect, perfect. All right, so why don't we start with that then? So what was your activating event?

CAROL: Well, I went to the movies by myself, just because there was a movie out—

PROFESSOR SATTERFIELD: Sure, sure.

CAROL: —that I thought was good. And I noticed that I was the only one there by myself. Everyone else who was there was in a group, or they had a boyfriend or a girlfriend with them. And it was kind of frustrating, and I don't know. I was a little embarrassed to be there alone, and I almost—I mean, I thought about leaving the movie for a short period of time.

PROFESSOR SATTERFIELD: All right, so if we look in this first column, the situation or trigger, you went to the movies alone and looked around and saw that other people weren't alone.

CAROL: Yeah.

PROFESSOR SATTERFIELD: And the emotions I see here, you have embarrassed, ashamed, lonely, and sad. OK, and looks like you've circled sad, so that was the primary emotion, the one you wanted to focus on.

CAROL: Yeah.

PROFESSOR SATTERFIELD: OK. And the intensity ratings go from 0 to 100, and it looks like you've rated sad and lonely both at a 70. So that was a pretty strong feeling, not as strong as possible, but that's pretty strong.

CAROL: Yeah.

PROFESSOR SATTERFIELD: OK. All right. And tell me about these thoughts. So, you have three different thoughts that you put down. These are the automatic thoughts that popped to mind. So what were they?

CAROL: Sure, well, I think that the one that made me feel that sad and that lonely, which I circled there too, was that I'm 30. And most of my friends are married, but here I am, 30 years old, still going to the movies by myself. So that was sad. It just made me feel, I don't know, kind of down. But the other ones were—I feel like everyone else I know, they're not as lonely as I am, so that makes me feel even more like a failure.

PROFESSOR SATTERFIELD: Sure.

CAROL: And then the last one I kind of already mentioned is that I should have stayed at home or I should have just left.

PROFESSOR SATTERFIELD: OK. All right. And I'm glad you captured multiple thoughts. And as we've talked before, every situation usually brings up a lot of different thoughts. And the challenge is to be aware of them. Looks like you're aware of them and you caught them, even though they were evoking negative emotions and sort of prompting you to leave or to escape the situation. And you've gone ahead and you've circled the hot thought or the one that you really wanted us to work on today. So that's all perfectly done.

So, the one you circled was, I'm 30 and I still go to the movies alone. And those are one of those thoughts, it's an automatic thought, so it pops to mind. It's on the surface. And I always suspect that there's a lot of thoughts underneath it. Because different people could have that exact same thought— I'm 30 and I go to the movies alone—and they might not feel sad.

They might feel relieved or they've given themselves a treat. But for you there's more that's underneath, right? That contributes to the feeling. So, when you have the thought, I'm 30 and I go to the movies alone, what does that mean to you? What does it say about you?

CAROL: Well, I don't really know. I mean, I feel like for me, I just—it feels like I'm always going to go to the movies alone, like I'm never going to have anyone to go to the movies with. And I didn't really think a whole lot of it when I went to the movies. And then I go and I see everybody there, and I realize, OK, this isn't how it's supposed to be.

PROFESSOR SATTERFIELD: Right. And the fact that you're there alone means there's something wrong.

CAROL: Missing.

PROFESSOR SATTERFIELD: Something missing. And the fact that you're 30 means this—well, what does that mean, the fact that you're 30? You should have been coupled by now? Is that the idea?

CAROL: Yeah, I guess so. I feel like most people who are 30 or even 20s have someone—a friend or a boyfriend or a girlfriend—that they can share those experiences with. And I don't feel like I do.

PROFESSOR SATTERFIELD: If someone's 30 and they don't have someone, what does that say about them? What would that mean?

CAROL: That they're unlovable I guess, and nobody really likes them, that nobody really wants to be with them.

PROFESSOR SATTERFIELD: Right. So now we're sort of getting down to the core stuff. And it sounds like there's some doubts about lovability and some worries that maybe no one will want to be with you.

CAROL: Yeah. That's pretty accurate.

PROFESSOR SATTERFIELD: Yeah, and no wonder it's a 70 for feeling sad and lonely. It's really sad to think that way. Well, remember that thoughts aren't true or false or good or bad. They're helpful or hurtful. That one seems like it's more on the hurtful side. And the thing to do is to roll up our sleeves and see if we can do something about that thought to see if it's fair, see if it's evenhanded.

And these next two columns ask you to find evidence or facts that support or argue against the thought. And if we were to say the thought is, I'm unlovable and I'll always be alone, what would be evidence that supports that belief?

CAROL: Well, I'm 30. That's fact. I'm at the movies alone with no one else. And—

PROFESSOR SATTERFIELD: OK, so again, the thought we're looking for evidence for and against is that you're always going to be alone or that you're unlovable. So you're 30. You're right. That's fact. You were at the movies alone that time. Have there been times when you went to the movies with someone else, your sister or a friend or someone?

CAROL: Sure.

PROFESSOR SATTERFIELD: OK, and have there have been events, holidays, dinners where you had other people's company?

CAROL: Yeah.

PROFESSOR SATTERFIELD: OK. And how about, have you been on dates before?

CAROL: A couple.

PROFESSOR SATTERFIELD: OK, so you've been on those before too. So what would those serve as evidence for? Do you think they might be in the proof that you're going to be alone or maybe evidence against that?

CAROL: Probably evidence against that.

PROFESSOR SATTERFIELD: OK. All right. And if you had a friend, say a best friend, sister, or someone, that thought, "I'm always going to be alone. I'm 30, and that proves it," what would you say to her?

CAROL: Well, if she was my friend, then I would say, you're clearly not alone, because we're friends.

PROFESSOR SATTERFIELD: Right, right, right. And how about in the case for you? Is there anyone in your life that you would consider a friend or a social support?

CAROL: Yeah, I guess. I mean, I talk to my sister a little bit.

PROFESSOR SATTERFIELD: And you had mentioned some good friends from college too, like a roommate from college.

CAROL: Yeah, yeah, who I still talk to. And we don't talk often, but when we do—

PROFESSOR SATTERFIELD: Sure, sure. And just to remind you, a few sessions ago we talked about habits of mind and how it's very easy to slip into black or white and all or none. So I'm either alone, or I'm completely connected and have a huge army of friends. And for most of us, we're somewhere in the middle.

So it sounds like you're somewhere in the middle. You would like to always have someone to go to the movies with, or you would like to have a significant other. You're not there yet, but you're also not at zero, never having any social contacts or any friends. Does that feel believable and balanced? Is that fair enough to say?

CAROL: I think so, yeah.

PROFESSOR SATTERFIELD: OK. So if we were going to try to rewrite that thought, you we're always going to be alone and you're not lovable, we want to rewrite it in a way that maybe takes some of the sting out of that original automatic thought. But it's still believable. It's still fair. So what would be a way to rewrite that thought? What do you think?

CAROL: Well, it's OK to be alone sometimes.

PROFESSOR SATTERFIELD: OK. All right, so it's OK to be alone sometimes.

CAROL: Mm-hmm. There's still time. I know that I had mentioned, yeah, I'm 30, and so I should be doing all these things. But I guess there are people who are older than 30, and they don't meet all of those expectations. So there's still plenty of time for me to do all those things and to make friends and go on dates. So I guess life isn't over. I still have plenty of time. And it's OK to be alone sometimes. I shouldn't feel sad about that.

PROFESSOR SATTERFIELD: Sure, sure. And in fact some of those couples you saw at the movie, who knows? Maybe next week one of them will go on their own, or maybe the week before they did. We saw a particular snapshot. And yes, you were at the movies alone that particular time. But maybe next week you can invite a friend or your sister. But it doesn't mean that in the future that will always be the case.

OK, Carol, so now that we've rewritten the alternate thought and it feels less all or none, a little more balanced, and to me sounds a little more hopeful, why don't we do the last step and have you re-rate the intensity of emotions? And you had sadness and loneliness were both at a 70. So where would you be now if you were going to re-rate those?

CAROL: I feel a little better. So I guess if I had to re-rate the sadness, I think I could go down to about a 40.

PROFESSOR SATTERFIELD: OK. All right.

CAROL: And I guess for loneliness, loneliness maybe a 45.

PROFESSOR SATTERFIELD: OK. All right, so you went from a 70 to a 40 for sadness and a 70 to about a 45.

CAROL: Yeah.

PROFESSOR SATTERFIELD: So a decent drop, but it's still—and I think it feels realistic. It's not magic; you still feel some sadness and some loneliness. There's some things you want to change. That's why you're here. You're working on changing them. But I hope this is a good example of how an exercise that you're going to get better and better at doing the more you practice it can drop maybe by as much as half the intensity of a negative emotion you're feeling. And if you're not spending that energy feeling that negative emotion, hopefully it frees you up to do other things that you want to do and definitely helps you feel better. OK?

So, the next step from here, I think it would be helpful to keep practicing with the daily thought records, in particular honing in on that hot thought and drilling down a little bit deeper, looking for evidence for and against. And I'll give you another copy of—we had a little cheat sheet of questions to ask yourself. And we went through some of them together. What would you say to a best friend? What would you say to someone else that's in a similar situation that needed a little bit of encouragement? So we'll give you that. It's totally fair and fine to use it as you're filling this out. And bring it back next time and we'll go over it, work through it again.

CAROL: OK.

PROFESSOR SATTERFIELD: All right, thank you.

[VIGNETTE END]

PROFESSOR SATTERFIELD: So by now we've seen several exercises with Carol, and I hope that you're starting to see variations on a theme for her. She tends to have thoughts that devalue herself, devalue how likable, how lovable, or how interesting she might be. She also tends to have thoughts that amplify or magnify potential dangers that are out in the environment or possible negative reactions that other individuals might have to her. What we want to do is to help her see those recurring thoughts, those recurring themes, and to really sort of build up her muscles in quickly building common helpful responses.

The advantage of seeing those variations on a theme is, when she's out of the moment, when things aren't so hot, she can write those detailed responses that are convincing and meaningful for her. When she's in the moment, she can then call them to mind much more quickly. I have a patient that calls them his mantras, because he knows that there are certain well-rehearsed negative thoughts that will pop to mind in social situations, but now he's prepared, and his mantras will pop back almost as quickly.

We're going to talk about how to fill out each of those columns of the DTR, and I specifically want to focus on places where individuals tend to get stuck. This is really a core skill and one of the more complex skills that you'll do in cognitive therapy. So first let's talk about how to identify an event, and this is just the first column on that Seven-Column DTR. Now, there's all sorts of events that you could choose from; and I usually recommend, if you're early in the process of learning how to do this, you pick one that has a mild-to-moderate level of emotional intensity. You don't want something so charged or so difficult that it's hard to finish the exercise. If you're more advanced, go ahead and move from moderate to something that's more severe.

When you describe the event in that column, you want to keep it fairly neutral. There's no interpretation. It's just the facts. It's just the context. It's just the circumstance. In the next column you want to describe the emotion, and you want to rate it in intensity from 0 to 100, with 100 being the most intense. If necessary, if you're having trouble coming up with the right words to describe the emotion you had, think back to the exercise we did with Michael, where he created sort of emotional thesaurus that helped him whenever he need to be able to put a word to a feeling that he was having.

Now, many folks struggle with the next column where you actually capture the automatic thoughts portion, but here are a few tips that might help you. So, you might ask yourself: At this moment, what was going through my mind? What images or memories did this particular activating event evoke for me? What meaning did I assign to it? What does it say about me or my future? If I were to put words to the feelings I had, how would I describe it?

And you might want to use a technique called the downward arrow to try to go a little bit deeper. Now here's the downward arrow works. If you remember some of the common automatic thoughts from Michael, they were about anger, and they were about some sort of injustice. So Michael tells us, I can't let that guy get away with disrespecting me. I would ask him, but what does it mean if you do let him get away with it? He might respond, it means I'm weak and I'm asking to be abused again. And what does it mean if you're weak? Well, it means I'm a loser and that no one likes me. We're drilling down; we're using that downward arrow to really get to the heart, to get at that underlying belief. And if you're able to work with that underlying belief, you'll probably be more effective in changing your mood.

Now, the next two columns are finding evidence for and against the automatic thought. And as I mentioned before, sometimes this comes very easily to people, and others might struggle with it. You might ask yourself, what are the facts, and what are the opinions? What are the assumptions or guesses that I might be making? What has happened in the past in similar situations or with other people? Are my automatic thoughts using habits of mind? Is my language all or none? Am I saying things like always and never? Are there other habits of mind, such as over-personalization or magnification, which I might begin to shrink down a bit? You should think of yourself off as an investigative team of sorts, the Sherlock Holmes of automatic thoughts.

Now if you're totally stuck, you can also run the thought record by a loved one or a friend, or you can do a behavioral experiment. So if you have the belief, I'm socially invisible, even if I try, no one wants to interact with me, what you would do, then, is design a behavioral experiment where you go into a social situation and you test out whether or not folks interact with you and whether or not you're truly socially invisible.

Next column, how do you arrive at that new thought? Again, this is one of the more challenging parts on the ABCD; this is the D box or the dispute box. You can use a strategy called *Yes, But*, which acknowledges some of the truth in what you originally thought, but that there is another side. Yes, I at times seem invisible in social situations, but, I can change my behavior to reach out more to others. You want to go for balance, or at least softening and qualifying those automatic thoughts. You might try for perspective. What's the worst case scenario? Will this matter in five years? Is there a silver lining? Is there a bigger picture? What we want to do is to help you find a more compassionate, caring, and forgiving way to think about the situation, and then rewrite it.

Now, the final step is to rerate the intensity of the emotion. Did the intensity go down? If not, go back and try to figure out why. Did you pick the right automatic thought? Do you need to dig a little bit deeper using something like the Downward Arrow? Was the new thought believable? Is this an unchangeable fact where you should probably work on acceptance and coping? But remember, it's all grist for the mill. In fact, I think my patients learn most when they've tried to do a thought record on their own, they get stuck, they bring it back, and we work on it together and figure out what adaptations they can make for next time.

Now there's a new exercise I wanted to describe just briefly, called the Core Beliefs Worksheet. Now, if you remember the cognitive model talks about the automatic thoughts on the surface, but we have these core beliefs underneath. Often, they're developed earlier in life, and they may not be particularly rational, but they have a strong, emotional charge attached to them, and they're fairly resistant to change. The way you would do a core beliefs worksheet, you can take a blank piece of paper. You write that core belief up at the top.

So, for Carol, it might be, I'm an unlovable person. She would then rate the percent strength that she currently has in that belief. She would create two columns on that piece of paper, evidence for, evidence against, probably sounding familiar now. She would look for all of those prompts that you might use on a DTR, but using them on the core beliefs worksheet. She might talk to significant others. At the bottom of that core beliefs worksheet, she will write a new tentative belief at the bottom and her percent agreement.

Now, a one-page exercise that takes her 15 or 20 minutes certainly isn't going to change a core belief. But if we think of that core belief as a boulder that's weighing heavily on her, each time she does this, she chips away a piece and chips away a piece. And with enough practice, over time, we hope that she can really make shifts in how she feels about herself. If you are interested in these or other CBT tools, I do encourage you to go online to psychology. tools. There is a veritable treasure trove of free handouts for CBT and other kinds of therapy that are available for free downloads on that website.

Now, what do we do, though, when things go wrong? We really want individuals to practice their skills. We want them to make adaptations over time. It should be an iterative process, but sometimes the homework just doesn't work out. Sometimes it doesn't have the desired effect. Let's go to a clip of a new patient, Scott, who does a meditation exercise that just doesn't work

[VIGNETTE START]

PROFESSOR SATTERFIELD: But I see this. As we talked before, this is all grist for the mill. So something works. Something doesn't work. There's a positive emotion, negative emotion. We can always use that as an opportunity to learn more about what makes you tick and what sorts of interventions we might be able to develop to help you, especially with your anger.

So why don't we use this as an activating event for the ABCD. And the A is the activating event, and so I'm just going to put meditation practice. And it sounds like one of the consequences you felt, it was awkward feeling.

SCOTT: Yes, definitely.

PROFESSOR SATTERFIELD: And what, was it weird, or what was the word you used?

SCOTT: It just didn't make any sense. I don't know how you could word that.

PROFESSOR SATTERFIELD: All right, so, remember the consequences are for the emotions and behaviors, and the thoughts go here. So one thought is, this doesn't make any sense. Remember, thoughts are thoughts. They're opinions. They're not right or wrong or good or bad.

SCOTT: Right.

PROFESSOR SATTERFIELD: That they have consequences, so they often contribute to the way you're feeling or the things you're doing.

SCOTT: So the consequences might be that there were times where I thought, well, this isn't going to work, and I'm just going to quit.

PROFESSOR SATTERFIELD: OK, so you wanted to quit. But did you quit, or did you—

SCOTT: No, because I'm trying to help myself here.

PROFESSOR SATTERFIELD: Right. So I'm going to put your behaviors. You didn't quit. You stuck with it. All right, you didn't quit. What were some of the other thoughts that you had?

SCOTT: Well, just the words just didn't have—I mean, what is Zen? I mean, I don't know what—so it's just maybe that part of the same doesn't make any sense. And just repeating things, three phrases, over and over again, maybe it's just because it wasn't the way I would have worded it.

PROFESSOR SATTERFIELD: OK.

SCOTT: But usually with things, when I word them my way they make more sense.

PROFESSOR SATTERFIELD: Sure.

SCOTT: But when you recite a script, it's kind of—I don't know. I tried.

PROFESSOR SATTERFIELD: And I appreciate your honesty. So it put having you write your own mantra might make more sense for you.

SCOTT: Yeah.

PROFESSOR SATTERFIELD: Any other thoughts or consequences we should capture? You did mention that you felt somewhat relaxed.

SCOTT: Yeah. Well, after about the third or fourth try, yeah.

PROFESSOR SATTERFIELD: I'll put a bit. And that's after some practice, third or fourth try.

SCOTT: Yeah. So, I mean, that's probably the reason why I didn't quit was because I thought, well, maybe this is starting to work. Let's see what happens.

PROFESSOR SATTERFIELD: All right.

SCOTT: And this guy does know what he's doing.

PROFESSOR SATTERFIELD: OK. Maybe this is starting to work. All right, so, just as a reminder, when we look at this horizontal line, these are usually the things we notice. They're above ground, so to speak, your feelings, your behaviors, the triggering event. All of the stuff below the horizontal line is below ground. We've got to dig a little bit to get to them. And these are the beliefs or the automatic thoughts, things that pop to mind.

We got some positive. We have some negative. The consequences, awkward but relaxed after you practiced a bit, and you didn't quit. Now, this is the dispute box. And remember, these two are directly related. So if you believe that some of these thoughts are unhelpful or unfair or unbalanced or you want to think about it in a different way, then you rewrite those thoughts in the dispute box.

So why don't we start with the very first one? This doesn't make any sense. And let's use some of those strategies that we had talked about. And just as a reminder, one of them was, so, if your friend was trying out something new and said, man, this doesn't make sense. And you wanted to encourage him, so what would you say to him?

SCOTT: Well, what I would say to them is, it doesn't make any sense at first. But nothing new does, so you have to give it a chance.

PROFESSOR SATTERFIELD: So, nothing new makes sense at first. You have to give it a chance. And it seems like you did that.

SCOTT: Yeah.

PROFESSOR SATTERFIELD: It didn't make sense, but you stuck with it.

SCOTT: Well, I trust the professionals. When a professional says, do this. This is going to work, then you—

PROFESSOR SATTERFIELD: OK. All right, so I'm going to put another thought you had or you just shared was to trust the professionals, suspend your disbelief. Get in there and try it.

SCOTT: Yeah. I'm trying to get help. And so if I trust a professional, if I practice with the professional, there's obviously a reason why. I'm not the first person that this has been done on.

PROFESSOR SATTERFIELD: Right. And I think your experience really matches what a lot of other folks have shared as well. We didn't—most of us—didn't grow up learning about meditation, or Buddhism, or Zen, or what have you.

SCOTT: That's right. I certainly didn't.

PROFESSOR SATTERFIELD: Some folks did. So if you try something different, it feels a little maybe awkward in the beginning.

SCOTT: Yes.

PROFESSOR SATTERFIELD: But you stuck with it. You felt a little relaxed. We have a choice point here. So you can either go ahead and continue practicing this, or you can try a different relaxation strategy. Remember, the goal was to turn down the flame a bit so that you had a little more reserve when you're in stressful situations and you're not as close to erupting as has happened in the past.

Yes.

[VIGNETTE END]

PROFESSOR SATTERFIELD: The important part is to remember that nothing works all the time, and you often don't get it right the first time. It's the partnership, the collaborative problem solving in CBT that creates a flexibility and the creativity to finally find something that works for that particular person, given his or her life circumstances.

Now, in our next lecture, we're going to try something different. We have the same toolbox, but we're going to see if we can use those tools to evoke positive emotions. Thank you.

Positive Psychology
Lecture 10

Although CBT was developed for the treatment of psychopathology and negative mood states, it has more recently been used as a way to encourage or induce positive emotion. In this lecture, you will be exposed to the other side of the emotional spectrum—positive emotions—starting with gratitude and what we know about it. In addition, you will learn that research in the field of positive psychology has offered theories regarding why positive emotion might matter from a survival standpoint, as well as some data on the adaptive power of positive emotion in coping with stress as a sort of replenishment.

Gratitude

- Recently, there has been a great deal of research on gratitude, or what has been called an "attitude of gratitude." Gratitude has been linked to better health, sounder sleep, less anxiety and depression, higher long-term satisfaction with life, and kinder behavior toward others, including romantic partners. Another study shows that feeling grateful makes people less likely to turn aggressive when provoked.

- A good example of some of the seminal work that was conducted on gratitude was done by Robert Emmons at the University of California, Davis. He started with a program that he called "gratitude lite." In this program, individuals were asked to complete a gratitude journal, in which they listed five things, once per week, and only were allowed one sentence per item. After two months, the results began to show that subjects were more optimistic, were happier, worked out more, and had fewer physical complaints.

- We're not just talking about gratitude when we talk about positive emotions. We're including happiness, joy, love, and excitement. We know that all emotions, including positive emotions, have a physiological impact as well as social consequences. But what are the functions of the positive emotional family?

- We know that anger helps us face or correct injustice and that anxiety helps us see and recognize threats that might be in our environment. But why do we need happiness, joy, or love? Do they really help us survive? And if so, how?

- This was the question that Barbara Fredrickson asked as she developed her broaden-and-build model: What is the evolutionary purpose of positive emotions? She reminds us that when we are in a negative emotional state, it gives us a sort of cognitive tunnel vision. It narrows our cognitive repertoire. We're focused on a particular problem. When we're in a positive mood state, that repertoire is broadened. We're able to think more broadly and more creatively.

- We also know that when we are in a negative mood state, we circle our social wagons. We are more closed to outside social contacts or to building new relationships. The opposite is true for positive emotions. When we're in a positive emotional state, we're more likely to reach out to others, meet new people, or deepen existing relationships.

When we're in a positive emotional state, we're more likely to reach out to others, meet new people, or deepen existing relationships.

- So, Fredrickson believed that positive emotions are there to broaden our cognitive repertoire and to build important social relationships that will sustain us in the negative times of the future.

- In 2008, Fredrickson published an interesting study in the *Journal of Personality and Social Psychology* on loving-kindness meditation. She studied 139 adults, half of whom meditated and half of whom were in a control condition. She found that meditation increased the daily experience of positive emotions and produced increases in a wide range of personal resources—including mindfulness, purpose in life, and social support—and decreased illness symptoms. These increased resources predicted increased life satisfaction and reduced depressive symptoms.

- A similar study was conducted by Judith Moskowitz. Published in 2012, the study analyzed whether or not the idea of positive emotion sustaining us through difficult times would be true in different groups of subjects.

- The first group of subjects was college students. The second group was caregivers of ill children (obviously experiencing a lot of chronic stress), and the third group was individuals recently diagnosed with HIV.

- Moskowitz found that positive emotion was correlated with better self-regulation performance, independent of the effects of negative emotion. The effects were not as strong longitudinally. However, she found that her studies of all three populations did provide modest support for the broaden-and-build model.

Positive Psychology

- Positive psychology became popular in the early 21st century, through the guidance of Martin Seligman, who is most known for his work with depression and negative mood states, especially learned helplessness and pessimism. He decided that he wanted to look at life with regard to things like happiness, gratitude, creativity, enthusiasm, wisdom, and insight.

- Much of the early work in the field of positive psychology was sort of an epidemiology of positive psychology, and it specifically involved looking at happiness. Many surveys found that approximately only one-third of Americans would describe themselves as happy. In addition, we learned that happiness is not necessarily predicted by income, age, or gender; instead, it is correlated with extroversion and spirituality, and relationships and friendships are key. Interestingly, there seems to be a bimodal distribution in happiness, in which we are happiest in our 20s and in our 60s, on average.

- An interesting study—a survey done by Columbia University—looked at what might be the happiest spots on Earth and, specifically, what might be the happiest countries on Earth. Then, the researchers wanted to deduce whether there was something about those cultures that supported those happy mood states.

- Researchers discovered that the top three happiest countries were clustered closely with one another: Denmark, Finland, and Norway, with Denmark being the happiest, Finland the second happiest, and Norway the third happiest.

- They found that even though Qatar is the richest country in the world, it is number 31 in happiness. The United States is the sixth wealthiest but is number 11 on the list. Japan has the longest life expectancy, but it is number 44 on the happiness list. Hong Kong has the lowest murder rate of anywhere in the world, but it is number 67 in happiness.

- Clearly, happiness is not just about safety, life expectancy, or income—it's something much richer and more meaningful than that. Ultimately, the promise of positive psychology isn't necessarily to make us happy, but it might have quite a bit to offer in terms of coping and even in terms of improving our physical health.

- The classic study that opened up the relationship between longevity and positive mood states was the Nun Study, which was published in the early 21st century. In this study, nuns kept a diary in their 20s, and their diaries were analyzed for positive emotional words. The nuns who were most positive were most likely to live into their 80s and 90s, compared with their more negative, or pessimistic, counterparts.

- The question remains, though: Is there a way that we could generate positive emotions if we believe it has positive physiological effects over the long term and might even have effects on our longevity?

- Judith Moskowitz conducted a series of studies in which she created a toolbox of different strategies to promote positive emotions. Some of those strategies included things like intentionally helping a person notice or selectively attend to positive events, something that she called capitalizing or savoring. Often when something negative happens, we ruminate about it over and over again. Could we also cause a sort of rumination about positive events, called savoring?

- Moskowitz also addresses gratitude and mindfulness, positive reappraisals of situations, focusing on personal strengths, setting attainable goals and noticing when you've reached them, and acts of kindness toward others.

- An established study published by Moskowitz in 2011 looked at health-related stress. Moskowitz wanted to see if it was possible for her toolbox to increase positive emotions even in individuals who were very stressed. So, she analyzed people who were newly diagnosed with HIV. She found that the toolbox was effective in terms of increasing positive affect, or emotions, and decreasing negative affect in these individuals.

- In 2014, a pilot study was conducted by Glenna Dowling that analyzed caregivers. Dowling used a randomized controlled trial of 24 caregivers, and half of them had five one-on-one positive-affect interventions. These caregivers were caring for a loved one who had frontotemporal dementia.

- Researchers analyzed measures of emotions—such as caregiver mood, stress, distress, and caregiver burden—at the baseline, at the end of the five-week intervention, and then at a one-month-post follow-up. They found that positive affect increased, negative affect decreased, and stress improved all around at the end of the intervention and also one month after the intervention.

- It is not wise to be preoccupied with positive emotion and happiness. We have positive emotions and negative emotions for a reason. We need a balance between the two, and each of them might tell us something important about ourselves, about our world, or about our relationships.

Suggested Reading

Danner, Snowdon, and Friesen, "Positive Emotions in Early Life and Longevity."

Dowling, Merrilees, Mastick, Chang, Hubbard, and Moskowitz, "Life Enhancing Activities for Family Caregivers of People with Frontotemporal Dementia."

Emmons and McCullough, "Counting Blessings versus Burdens."

Fredrickson, Cohn, Coffey, Pek, and Finkel, "Open Hearts Build Lives."

Moskowitz, Shmueli-Blumberg, Acree, and Folkman, "Positive Affect in the Midst of Distress."

Moskowitz, Hult, Duncan, Cohn, Maurer, Bussolari, and Acree. "A Positive Affect Intervention for People Experiencing Health-Related Stress."

Seligman, *Authentic Happiness*.

———, *Flourish*.

Smyth, et al, "Effects of Writing about Stressful Experiences on Symptom Reduction in Patients with Asthma or Rheumatoid Arthritis."

1. For the next week, write down an answer to the following three questions before bedtime. Be sure to note any effect this has on your mood.

    What surprised me today?

    What moved me today?

    What inspired me today?

2. Gratitude and a focus on the positive have been shown to have health and mood benefits. Is this just the classic "power of positive thinking"? How can we take material in this area as more than Pollyannaism?

Positive Psychology
Lecture 10—Transcript

PROFESSOR SATTERFIELD: Although CBT was developed for the treatment of psychopathology and negative mood states, it has more recently been used as a way to encourage or induce positive emotion. Let's look at a short clip of Maria trying a positive CBT exercise.

[VIGNETTE START]

PROFESSOR SATTERFIELD: So Maria, we've talked a lot about management of depression and anxiety negative emotions, but I want to see if we can do something a little bit different and talk about the other end of the spectrum. So instead of life from 0 to −5, maybe life from 0 to +5. Would that be all right?

MARIA: Sounds good.

PROFESSOR SATTERFIELD: So what I'd like to talk about first is about positive emotions. And positive emotions—love, enthusiasm, excitement, curiosity, contentment—all those sort of fit in that category. And as you're learning to better manage the negative side, we would like to help you to cultivate the positive side as well. And there is a type of psychology called positive psychology, which focuses exactly on that life from 0 to plus 5. And there's a growing body of research where they're testing out different interventions to see what is the most potent generator of positive emotion. And one of the things that seems to have some of the strongest research support is called a gratitude journal. Have you heard of that?

MARIA: Yeah, actually, I have. I have a girlfriend who—she and her husband have a boat, and they named it Gratitude. I think she probably does a gratitude journal.

PROFESSOR SATTERFIELD: Sure. Sure. And it's been in the popular press and I think people sort of do this public declaration of things that they're grateful for. But it doesn't have to be public. It can be private. It can be in a journal. But it's really writing down things, big and small, that you've noticed. That you appreciate. And that you are grateful for.

So the way this assignment typically goes is people will pick a time of the day. Morning, noon, or night, doesn't really matter. But it's a dedicated time, could be 5 or 10 minutes, where you will begin to write things you're grateful for. And what happens, just like with when you're recording activities or cognitions, if you know that time is coming up when you're going to be writing things down, you start looking for them in the day. And you start making these mental notes.

MARIA: Can they be really little things?

PROFESSOR SATTERFIELD: They can be really little things. The sun came out. We are grateful for that. It was a beautiful day. Your roses started blooming. Those are all things to be grateful for. So why don't we have you start it today. So if you could go ahead and just open up your journal, and I'll let you borrow my pen. And you can start just with today's date. And what is something today that you've noticed that you're grateful for?

MARIA: Actually, something happened that I am grateful for.

PROFESSOR SATTERFIELD: And what was that?

MARIA: Well, it was in the middle of the night and I was lying awake, as I often am in the middle of the night. And Jack was awake too. He didn't say anything, but you know how you can kind of tell from a person's breathing whether they're awake or not. So I said, are you all right Jack? Are you hurting? And he said, no, just wakeful.

And so I got up, and I went into the kitchen and I made some cocoa. And I brought it back to bedroom and it was snowing out. And so I turned on the outside light and we sat side by side in the bed with our mugs of cocoa and watched the snow come down. It was so pretty against the trees.

And Jack was telling this story about when the kids were little and he and they built a snowman. I'll spare you the snowman story, but it always made him laugh. And so he was chuckling, and he got me to laughing. And I think, just for one minute, I completely forgot that he was dying. And I'm very grateful for that. And I think I'm also grateful for the 40-plus years that we had together when we really were partners and really knew how to love each other. So I am grateful for a lot of things.

PROFESSOR SATTERFIELD: That's wonderful. And I would encourage you to actually record those things. To write them down. And in times when you are feeling down or low, there the record is there. And if your mental energy isn't there, you don't need it. You just have to open up the book and remind yourself of the things that you're grateful for. Why don't you go ahead and write that one down as the first entry for today. It's a wonderful first entry. And if you could then think about a time that you could do this each and every day, do that for the next week. And when you come back, we'll look at what you have in your gratitude journal.

MARIA: OK.

PROFESSOR SATTERFIELD: I think of it as another tool in the toolbox. And you may choose to keep doing it, or you may just decide a week was enough and you have a good enough record. But it's entirely up to you.

MARIA: Good.

[VIGNETTE END]

PROFESSOR SATTERFIELD: In this lecture, we'll continue looking at the other side of the emotional spectrum—positive emotions. But let's start with gratitude and what we know about it. Now recently, there's been a great deal of research on gratitude, or what has been called an "attitude of gratitude." Now, gratitude has been linked to better health, sounder sleep, less anxiety and depression, higher long-term satisfaction with life, and kinder behavior toward others, including romantic partners. Another study shows that feeling grateful makes people less likely to turn aggressive when provoked.

A good example of some of the seminal work was done by Robert Emmons at the University of California and Davis. He started with a program that he called

Gratitude Light. And in this program, individuals were asked to complete a journal, a gratitude journal, where they list five things, once per week, and only allowed one sentence per item. After two months, the results began to show in intervention subjects. Those subjects were more optimistic; they were happier; they worked out more; and they had fewer physical complaints.

Of course, we're not just talking about gratitude when we talk about positive emotions. We're including happiness, joy, love, and excitement. We know that all emotions, including positive emotions, have a physiologic impact, as well as social consequences. But what are the functions of the positive emotional family? We know that anger helps us to face or to correct injustice. We know that anxiety helps us to see and to recognize threats that might be in our environment. But why do we need happiness, joy, or love? Do they really help us to survive? And if so, how?

This was exactly the question that Barbara Fredrickson asked as she developed her Broaden-and-Build Model. What is the evolutionary purpose of positive emotions? She reminds us that when we're in a negative emotional state, it gives us a sort of cognitive tunnel vision. It narrows our cognitive repertoire. We're focused on a particular problem. When you're in a positive mood state, that repertoire is broadened; you're able to think more broadly and more creatively.

We also know that when an individual is in a negative mood state, they circle their social wagons. They're more closed to outside social contacts or to building new relationships. The opposite is true for positive emotions. When we're in a positive emotional state, we're more likely to reach out to others, to meet new people, or to deepen existing relationships. So positive emotion, she believed, are there to broaden our cognitive repertoire and to build important social relationships that will sustain us in the negative times ahead.

She went on to do an interesting study in 2008, published in the Journal of Personality and Social Psychology, on loving-kindness meditation. There, she took 139 adults, half of them meditated, half of them were in a controlled condition. She found that meditation increased the daily experience of positive emotions and produced increases in a wide range of personal resources, including mindfulness, purpose in life, social support, and decreased illness symptoms. These increased resources predicted increased life satisfaction and reduced depressive symptoms.

In a similar study done by Judy Moskowitz and published in 2012, she looked at whether or not this idea of positive emotions sustaining us through difficult times would be true in different groups of subjects. Our first group of subjects were college students; the second group, caregivers of ill children, obviously experiencing a lot of chronic stress; and the third group, individuals recently diagnosed with HIV. She found that positive emotion was correlated with better self-regulation performance, independent of the effects of negative emotion. The effects were not as strong longitudinally. However, she found that her studies in all three populations did provide modest support for the Broaden-and-Build model.

So, we have a theory that tells us why positive emotion might matter from a survival standpoint, and Judy Moskowitz has given us some preliminary data on the adaptive power of positive emotion in coping with stress as a sort of replenishment. But let's take a step back and look at the broader field of positive psychology. Now, positive psychology became popular around 10 to 15 years ago through the guidance of Marty Seligman. Now, Marty is most known for his work with depression and negative mood states, especially learned helplessness and pessimism. He decided that instead of looking at life from −5 to 0, he wanted to look at life from 0 to +5 to look at things like happiness, like gratitude, creativity, enthusiasm, wisdom, or insight.

Much of the early work in positive psychology was sort of an epidemiology of positive psychology, and specifically looking at happiness. Many of these surveys found that approximately only one third of Americans would describe themselves as happy. We learned that happiness is not necessarily predicted by income, by age, or by gender. It is correlated with extroversion and spirituality, and relationships and friendships are key. Interestingly, there seems to be a bimodal distribution in happiness, where we are happiest in our 20s and happiest in our 60s, on average.

An interesting study, a survey done by Columbia University, looked at what might be the happiest spots on Earth, and specifically, what would be the happiest countries on Earth. They then wanted to deduce if there was something about those cultures that really supported those happy-mood states. They found the top three were clustered close to one another. Number 1 was Denmark; number 2 was Finland; number 3 was Norway; and the United States came in at number 11.

They found that even though Qatar is the richest country in the world, they're number 31 in happiness. U.S. is sixth most wealthy, but again, number 11 on the list. Japan has the longest life expectancy, but they're number 44 on the happiness list. And Hong Kong has the lowest murder rate of anywhere in the world, but they're number 67 in happiness. So clearly, it's not just about safety, life expectancy, or income, it's something much more rich and meaningful than that.

Ultimately, I don't think the promise of positive psychology lies in making us happy, but it may have quite a bit to offer in terms of coping, and even in terms of improving our physical health. The classic study that opened up the relationship between longevity and positive mood states was the Nun Study. Now, this study was published approximately 15 years ago, and what this particular study showed us is that nuns who kept a diary in their 20s, they had their diaries analyzed for positive emotional words. The nuns who were most positive were most likely to live into their 80s and 90s, compared with their more negative, or pessimistic counterparts.

The question then remains, though, is there a way that we could generate positive emotions if we believe it has positive physiologic effects, and over the long term, may even have effects on our longevity. I wanted to mention a couple, a series of studies done, again, by Judy Moskowitz, the IRIS Project Study, and her Chi Study, where she created a sort of tool box of different strategies to promote positive emotions. Some of those strategies included things such as intentionally helping a person to notice or selectively attend to positive events. Something that she called Capitalizing or Savoring—often when something negative happens, we ruminate about it over and over again. Could we cause a sort of rumination about positive events called savoring? She also mentions gratitude and mindfulness, which we've heard about. Positive reappraisals of situations, focusing on personal strengths, setting and noticing when you've reached attainable goals and acts of kindness towards others.

An established study published by Judy in 2011 looking at health-related stress, she wanted to see if it was possible for this toolbox to increase positive emotions, even in individuals who were very stressed, so she looked at people newly diagnosed with HIV. She found that the toolbox was effective in terms of increasing positive affect and decreasing negative affect or negative emotions in these individuals.

I wanted to mention just one more study, and this was a pilot study done looking at caregivers by Dowling in 2014. Now, Dowling used a randomized controlled trial of 24 caregivers, and half of them had five one-on-one positive affect interventions. Now, these caregivers were caring for a loved one that had frontotemporal dementia. They looked at measures of emotions, caregiver mood, stress, distress, caregiver burden at baseline; at the end of the five-week intervention; and then at one month post follow up. They found that positive affect increased, negative affect decreased, and stress improved all around at post and also one month following the intervention.

Let's move now to look at a different sort of positive affect intervention: the clip of Carol.

[VIGNETTE START]

PROFESSOR SATTERFIELD: So Carol, I believe you had some slightly different homework you were going to do this past week. Do you want to tell me about it?

CAROL: Sure. So to kind of help me wind down my day before I went to bed, I was supposed to keep a journal and answer three questions. What moved me? What surprised me? What inspired me? Not necessarily in that order.

PROFESSOR SATTERFIELD: Sure. What surprised, moved, and inspired you. And is that your journal?

CAROL: Yes.

PROFESSOR SATTERFIELD: OK, perfect. And were you able to answer those three questions before bed?

CAROL: Yeah, most nights.

PROFESSOR SATTERFIELD: OK. Well, show me what you've got. So what did you write down?

CAROL: OK. On Tuesday, surprised me, was I actually dropped something out of my purse when I was scrambling in it to find something, I guess. And I dropped it, and instead of just walking by, one of my coworkers picked it up and handed it back to me.

PROFESSOR SATTERFIELD: So someone paused and did you a favor, and that surprised you. OK. And what moved you on Tuesday?

CAROL: We were really busy at work, and one of my coworkers, I was clearly very stressed out about it, and she offered to help me and take a little bit of my workload. So that was kind of nice of her.

PROFESSOR SATTERFIELD: The kindness and generosity moved you.

CAROL: Yeah.

PROFESSOR SATTERFIELD: OK. And inspired. So what inspired you on Tuesday?

CAROL: Well, I don't know. It was just something kind of little. But it was a stressful day. And so I went home and I looked at a picture of my dad, who was also an accountant, and the reason why I became an accountant. And I just remembered that he worked day after day after day, and he never complained about it. And I'm sure that he had really stressful days too. And so that just kind of inspired me to keep going.

PROFESSOR SATTERFIELD: So your dad's an inspiration for you, and that picture reminded you, it sounds like.

CAROL: Yeah.

PROFESSOR SATTERFIELD: Great. Now, what was the effect of answering these questions? Did it have any effect on your mood at all?

CAROL: It did, actually. I guess it kind of put the day into perspective. And so it was, you know, the day was really stressful. Kind of force me to look at some of the positive things that happened that day. So it was kind of de-stressing.

PROFESSOR SATTERFIELD: Yeah. And as we talked about last time, it's a way to intentionally shift your focus, cognitively, on to something that was positive. Because most of us—and I think this is just the way we are wired through evolution—we are trained to notice the bad things or the threatening things, the things that might get us in trouble or cause danger. We're trained to remember those, and that's sort of what we carry around with us. And especially if you're anxious or depressed, those things are sort of like in bold relief. And it takes a little bit of effort to push those to the side and to realize that every day has a mix of positive and negative. We just sometimes have to search a little more to find the positive.

Now this was an exercise. It only takes a few minutes, but it is a special exercise. And what we eventually want you to do is to develop the facility of being able to notice and to appreciate, in a way to savor, those positives during the day and throughout the day. So I thought maybe just off-the-cuff here—I know we're only halfway through the day today, but if you were to answer those three questions right now. What surprised you? What moved you? And what has inspired you so far today? It can be small. But what, since you have this morning, so what has surprised you?

CAROL: Well, when I got up, I guess—I don't know, this is really—

PROFESSOR SATTERFIELD: It's a tough one, yeah.

CAROL: —little.

PROFESSOR SATTERFIELD: Yeah. But go ahead.

CAROL: I got ready a lot faster than normal. So that surprised me. I didn't do anything particularly special.

PROFESSOR SATTERFIELD: So you were in the groove, and you were efficient, and you got it together quick today. All right. And what moved you today?

CAROL: Well, when I, like, right before I went to work and I was kind of eating my breakfast and watching TV, and one of my cats came up and they just snuggled right in to me. And I don't know, I just—it was—again, I feel like that's kind of silly, but I just thought it was really sweet. And kind of moved me a little bit.

PROFESSOR SATTERFIELD: And when you were walking here, did anything inspire you or anyone inspire you?

CAROL: Yeah, I guess I saw—I walked past this couple who were older, and they'd clearly been together for 50 or 60 years. Then it was just—I don't know, it's just inspiring that people can do that. That they can be together for that long, I guess.

PROFESSOR SATTERFIELD: Right. Right. That's great. And I would encourage you—again, it doesn't have to be formal—but whenever you can pause and you can think, or when something like that's happening, of going, I'm being moved. I'm being inspired. I'm being surprised. And that's something to appreciate.

[VIGNETTE END]

PROFESSOR SATTERFIELD: So, as you were watching the clip, I hope you were thinking about the Judy Moskowitz Positive Emotion Toolbox. What tools were being used? Well, we had asked Carol, through having her answer those three questions, to shift her attention to things that were positive that had happened during the day. But we were also having her do some subtle reframing or reappraising of those events that had happened, and having her recall them to write them down, we were encouraging some savoring or some rumination, if you will, about those positive events that had occurred.

Now, is it wise to be preoccupied with positive emotion and with happiness? And I think the answer is no. We have positive emotions and we have negative emotions for a reason. We need a balance between the two, and each of them might tell us something important about ourselves, about our world, or about our relationships.

Now, for our last clip, I'd like to demonstrate a different sort of positive psychology exercise. This is one that shifts the attention, but it isn't about simply generating positive emotions. It's an exercise called My Best Self, or Signature Strengths.

[VIGNETTE START]

PROFESSOR SATTERFIELD: So I have a new positive psychology exercise for you that I thought we could try out. I know that we have tried the gratitude journal before, and this is along those lines. It's shifting our focus, again, away from things that are broken or negative to things that are more positive. And I think within each of us we have stories of failure and loss, but we have stories of success and achievement. And often times, when we are depressed or stressed, we think about the negative. So we want an exercise to help you to think about positive.

But in this particular exercise, it's not just your perspective. Your perspective matters. We're going to be collecting data from other people about you. So you're going to be looking at yourself through the eyes of another person. How does that sound?

MARIA: I don't know.

PROFESSOR SATTERFIELD: OK. I appreciate your being willing just to try it out and see what happens. We have done what we call behavioral experiments, so if you have a thought or a worry or an anxiety, that's OK. But the important part is to go and still test it out and see if it holds true. Or maybe things are a little bit different than you thought they might be.

So this is called "At my best" exercise. It's sometimes called a "Signature strengths" exercise. Again, the idea is to see yourself and your strengths at least through three lenses. One from yourself, and then two other people. So the prompts that you have—and usually it's written in about a page, a page and a half or so—the prompts are as follows.

"I am at my best when" blank. And there's no one particular right answer. The next one is "When I'm at my best I am" you fill it in. And then "When I'm at my best I do."

So the first one is really asking for, sort of, character or personality, what you send. And then the next one's asking about behavior, the things you do. Then it asks you to share an example that illustrates you at your best. And it could be current or it could be somewhere in the distant past, but it's just an example.

So we won't take time to fully flesh this out, but I thought maybe we could get you started. Why don't we go back up to the top and just tell me, again, what it is that pops to mind. We're looking at you when you're at your best. When your strengths are really being showcased. So you are at your best when—

MARIA: Well, I guess one of the best times of my life was when I was teaching. I loved teaching and I loved being in the classroom and I was good at it.

PROFESSOR SATTERFIELD: OK. So you're at your best when you're teaching.

MARIA: When I was teaching. Yeah.

PROFESSOR SATTERFIELD: All right. And when I'm at my best I am—

MARIA: Enthusiastic. Curious. Excited.

PROFESSOR SATTERFIELD: And when I'm at my best I do—

MARIA: I do—

PROFESSOR SATTERFIELD: Or we could change the verb, I—it's about behaviors.

MARIA: OK. What do I do? I help people. I learn things. I try to look into things. I'm trying to figure things out. I guess those are things that I do when I'm at my best.

PROFESSOR SATTERFIELD: Sure. Sure. So how about, now, an example of you at your best? And I know this is off the top of your head, and you can totally change your mind later. But when we think about those strengths, those signature strengths that you just mentioned, what's a story that illustrates you at your best?

MARIA: Well, there was this one kid that I had in class. I taught high school English. And I had this one kid who just didn't get it and didn't get it. And I kept trying and trying and I'd work with him after school, and so forth. And he didn't care all that much. And I tried to find books that would interest him, that would get him going. And he got into some detective fiction that he sort of liked and everything. He got maybe a C in the class at the end of the year. And I thought, well, that's that. Then he came back about 10 years later, and he'd gone to college, and he was successful at what he was doing. And he came back and he said, I owe this all to you, Maria. And I just felt—I mean, I know that wasn't true. But I just felt so good about it. It just made it all worthwhile.

PROFESSOR SATTERFIELD: Knowing you had a part, at least.

MARIA: That I was a little teeny part of that. That was wonderful.

PROFESSOR SATTERFIELD: Yeah. How rewarding. And what a wonderful memory to recall and to savor. OK. Well, I'm going to give you this form. And like I said, you can totally change later, if you want. But I'm going to ask you to fill this out. A page is totally fine. And then what we want is to have two other people do this exercise. And we want them to answer these same questions, but it would be, "Maria's at her best when— When Maria's at her best she is— When she's at her best she does—" so same sorts of questions. And then we want them to share an example of you at your best.

And they'll probably have some questions. And they might feel like, "Oh no, I want to make sure I do it right." There's no right or wrong way. It's about them sharing their perspective about you. And I want to you to those and to bring all three in, so we have yours and then from two other people. And let's go ahead and designate who those two people would be. So who would you like to have to do this exercise?

MARIA: Judith.

PROFESSOR SATTERFIELD: So your friend Judith, OK.

MARIA: Maybe my daughter.

PROFESSOR SATTERFIELD: Your daughter. OK.

MARIA: Yeah.

PROFESSOR SATTERFIELD: All right. So give them a call, or e-mail, or whatever. And ask them about this exercise. Tell them you have a deadline to do your homework. And you want to bring it back for next time. And of course you'll read them before you bring them back. And just note what people say, and the emotions that you have when you read it. OK?

MARIA: OK. Thank you.

[VIGNETTE END]

PROFESSOR SATTERFIELD: So what did Maria get back from her daughter and her friend? Well, she was surprised by how both saw her as a very strong person, as a role model, and as a loving, kind, and selfless person. She was a bit embarrassed, but really couldn't dismiss the direct, positive feedback regarding her strengths. She's going to re-read those write-ups whenever she needs to be reminded of that positive feedback.

So thus far, we've seen some exercises to address, and hopefully grow, the positive. Next up, we'll talk about CBT and trauma.

Healing Traumatic Injuries
Lecture 11

The focus of this lecture is on trauma and CBT. In this lecture, the diagnosis of post-traumatic stress disorder (PTSD) will be defined, and you will learn how CBT can be used to treat stress-response syndromes like PTSD. Essentially, we want CBT to "unstick" the brain and begin the process of repairing damage. Traumatic events can arise from a number of different sources, including combat-related PTSD, random violence, car accidents, sexual abuse, or even intensely powerful losses. This lecture will highlight common features and solutions.

Trauma

- The Substance Abuse and Mental Health Services Administration (SAMHSA) tells us that individual trauma results from an event, a series of events, or a set of circumstances that is experienced by an individual as physically or emotionally harmful or threatening and that it has lasting adverse events on the individual's functioning and physical, social, emotional, or spiritual well-being.

- Traumatic events overwhelm the usual methods of coping that give people a sense of control, connection, and meaning. This might include sexual assault, combat, car accidents, or even vicarious traumatic experiences.

- With the exception of sexual molestation or sexual assault, trauma is much more likely to happen to a man than to a woman. A man has a 35 percent chance in his lifetime to witness violence, while a woman has a 15 percent chance. Men have a 25 percent chance of being involved in an accident, while women have a 15 percent chance. This is mostly accounted for in motor vehicle accidents, which are more likely to be caused by men than by women. Men have a 20 percent chance of being threatened with a weapon, while women have a 6 percent chance.

- The opposite is true when it comes to rape or sexual assault: Men have a 3 percent chance, while women have a 20 percent chance of being raped or sexually assaulted.

- On the severity spectrum of responses to trauma, it ranges from the expected stress-response syndromes to adjustment disorder, to acute stress reaction, to the most severe and lasting reaction of post-traumatic stress disorder (PTSD).

PTSD

- The Diagnostic and Statistical Manual of Mental Disorders (DSM-5), published in 2013, gives criteria A, B, and C for PTSD. Criteria A: There has to be some sort of trauma that has happened. An individual has to be exposed to death, threatened death, serious injury or threat of serious injury, or actual or threatened sexual violence. You can be directly exposed, you can witness it in person, you can be indirectly affected by it (as in a vicarious trauma of hearing about a close friend or family member), or it could be repeated or extreme indirect exposure (something that a police officer or firefighter might experience).

- For criteria B, there has to be something called intrusive symptoms that are persistently reexperienced. It might be recurrent and intrusive memories, traumatic nightmares, or flashbacks or other dissociative reactions.

- As part of criteria C, there is a persistent or effortful avoidance of distressing trauma-related stimuli. There might be trauma-related thoughts or feelings or trauma-related external reminders, such as triggers in your environment that bring back a flood of emotions and reactions.

- Other criteria might include changes in cognition and emotion and changes in arousal and reactivity, and the duration has to be greater than one month. Like many different mental illnesses, there needs to be some level of functional impairment.

Diagnosing PTSD

- The gold standard for assessing an individual who suspects that he or she might have PTSD is a clinician interview. Clinicians do a semistructured interview using questions derived from the DSM-5 criteria A, B, and C. Other measures include the PTSD Symptom Scale–Self-Report (PSS-SR), the PTSD Checklist (PCL), or the classic Impact of Event Scale (IES) developed by Mardi Horowitz and later revised in the 1990s.

- It is estimated that there is a lifetime risk of PTSD of about 8 percent for adults in the United States. PTSD is more common in women than in men, but men are more likely to be exposed to trauma. Often, it's the type of trauma that lays the groundwork for PTSD. For example, women who have been exposed to sexual violence or rape have a much higher risk for developing PTSD than for some other kinds of trauma.

- Not everyone who is traumatized goes on to develop PTSD. The most powerful risk factor has to do with the severity of the trauma. Other factors might include whether the individual has had prior

Trauma can result from a number of different events, including combat, random violence, car accidents, and sexual abuse.

traumas or prior traumatization. Gender is also a factor; PTSD is more common in women than in men. If an individual has had prior mood disorders, depression, or anxiety disorders, or a family history of those disorders, then those factors make the risk for PTSD higher.

- Keep in mind that PTSD might not be the only issue. People might be coping with their disorder by self-medicating with things like alcohol or drugs. They might be reacting to the surge of feelings they have by becoming aggressive or violent. There might be suicidal ideation or maybe even suicidal attempts. They might distance themselves or break away from loved ones. There might be problems at work, problems in relationships, or even homelessness and joblessness.

CBT for PTSD

- CBT for PTSD has been around for quite some time. In fact, most of the founding fathers of CBT, such as Aaron T. Beck or Albert Ellis, all had versions of CBT for PTSD.

- With behavioral strategies, we want to push against avoidance, so CBT might help an individual face fearful situations. But clinicians need to give the individual skills to be able to deal with the effects of arousal. They want to teach them somatic quieting and cognitive restructuring. They want to teach them how to tell their story but not become overwhelmed with emotions.

- A number of different variants of CBT for PTSD have subsequently emerged, including stress inoculation training by Donald Meichenbaum, prolonged exposure and cognitive processing by Edna Foa, and, more recently, eye movement desensitization and reprocessing (EMDR).

- In Edna Foa's prolonged exposure and emotional reprocessing, patients are encouraged to repeatedly recount the event and confront feared situations in people. They are taught relaxation or other emotional-mastery skills so that they convey a sense of control and safety while they are exposing themselves to these potential triggers.

- This kind of therapy proceeds through a number of different stages. In the first stage, therapists do basic relationship building, establish safety, educate the patient about the disorder and about the treatment, conduct assessments, and look for comorbidities. This is CBT, and it still has the common features of collaboration, because the relationship matters, but you have a partnership with the patient in developing a treatment plan and setting some goals.

- In the second stage, therapists teach emotion-regulation skills, self-soothing, and somatic quieting, and they begin talking about the event. A sample early homework assignment that a patient might do is as follows.
  - Please write at least one page on what it means to you that you were traumatized. Please consider the effects the trauma has had on your beliefs about yourself, your beliefs about others, and your beliefs about the world. Also consider the following topics while writing your answer: safety, trust, power, esteem, and intimacy. Bring this with you to the next session.

- This assignment might sound a little abstract, and it is—on purpose. You need to have the individual do an exercise that is challenging but not overwhelming before you move on to the third stage.

- In the third stage, the individual starts reprocessing the memory while being exposed to the triggers, and many strong emotions are brought up. A sample midpoint, or more advanced, third-stage assignment for the patient is as follows.
  - Write a detailed account of the trauma. Include as many sensory details as possible, including your thoughts and feelings during the trauma. The patient reads his or her assignment in the next meeting, might redo this assignment in between meetings, and also will listen to tape recordings of his or her therapy session in between meetings to continue exposing himself or herself to this particular story and practicing emotional-mastery skills.

- Approximately 80 percent of PTSD patients show significant reduction in symptoms and improvement in functioning after 12 weeks of CBT treatment. In a paper published by the *Journal of the American Medical Association* in 2007, research showed that more than 40 percent of women with combat-related PTSD no longer met criteria for the disorder after only 10 sessions.

- A meta-analysis conducted by Bradley Watts and colleagues in 2013 that looked at 112 studies found that the effective treatments were CBT, exposure treatment, and EMDR. They found that effective medications and drugs included Paxil, Zoloft, Prozac, Risperidone, Topiramate, and Venlafaxine. This study showed that there is a menu of different treatments—both psychotherapies and pharmacotherapies—that work.

- In a study done by Jonathan Bisson and colleagues in 2007, published in the *British Journal of Psychiatry*, a systematic review of 38 studies found that trauma-focused CBT was helpful along with EMDR. In a similar study, more recently done by Bisson in 2013, researchers found that individual trauma-focused CBT and EMDR did better than typical treatment.

- In 2013, Anette Kersting and colleagues studied a group of women who had miscarriages, which can be very traumatic for families, particularly when people won't talk about it or if the mother blames herself. In this randomized controlled trial, they looked at Internet-based CBT versus waitlist controls for 228 women during a five-week CBT intervention, and their primary outcome measure was the IES.

- The treatment group for the Internet-based CBT showed significantly reduced symptoms of post-traumatic stress, prolonged grief, depression, and anxiety relative to the waitlist control. They found that further significant improvement in all symptoms of PTSD and prolonged grief was found from the post-treatment evaluation to the 12-month follow-up. The attrition rate was relatively low, at 14 percent.

- There has been a recent move to more types of trauma-focused CBT online, and there are many programs that are not just for miscarriages. For example, there is a program on the Medical University of South Carolina's website that analyzes trauma-focused CBT online for children and adolescents.

Suggested Reading

Bisson, Ehlers, Matthews, Pilling, Richards, and Turner. "Psychological Treatments for Chronic Post-Traumatic Stress Disorder."

Bisson, Roberts, Andrew, Cooper, and Lewis. "Psychological Therapies for Chronic Post-Traumatic Stress Disorder (PTSD) in Adults."

Kersting, et al, "Brief Internet-Based Intervention Reduces Posttraumatic Stress and Prolonged Grief in Parents after the Loss of a Child during Pregnancy."

Layden, Newman, Freeman, and Morse, *Cognitive Therapy of Borderline Personality Disorder*.

Rothbaum, Foa, and Hembree, *Reclaiming Your Life from a Traumatic Experience*.

Rye, Pargament, Pan, Yingling, Shogren, and Ito, "Can Group Interventions Facilitate Forgiveness of an Ex-Spouse?"

Schnurr, Friedman, Engel, Foa, Shea, Chow, Resick, Thurston, Orsillo, Haug, Turner, and Bernardy, "Cognitive Behavioral Therapy for Posttraumatic Stress Disorder in Women."

Shapiro, *Eye Movement Desensitization and Reprocessing (EMDR)*.

Watts, Schnurr, Mayo, Young-Xu, Weeks, and Friedman, "Meta-Analysis of the Efficacy of Treatments for Posttraumatic Stress Disorder."

1. Trauma at any age can be devastating and can have lasting effects. However, it seems that childhood trauma/abuse often predisposes a person to serious struggles with mental illness and substance abuse. Is it possible to intervene with these children to prevent the harmful aftereffects? Is it possible to intervene with adults who were abused as children to help alleviate negative effects that have already emerged?

2. What does it mean to be cured after a trauma? How might a trauma positively alter someone's life at a later time? Should we expect that? Can we facilitate it?

Healing Traumatic Injuries
Lecture 11—Transcript

PROFESSOR SATTERFIELD: Over the past 20 years, I've worked with many wounded warriors and those who have endured other traumas. They each have incredible stories, but those stories are often too painful or terrifying for them to share, at least at first. They can't explain it to their families. They may not even be able to explain it to themselves. They just feel they're broken, damaged, ripped apart somehow from the inside. When I recently asked a young veteran how he felt, he handed me his sketch pad that he had entitled, The Silent Scream. And on the cover he had pasted a picture of the famous painting, *The Scream*, by Edvard Munch. He handed it to me, then burst into tears, and that's where we started.

In this lecture, we'll review what we mean by trauma. We'll define the diagnosis of post-traumatic stress disorder and, most importantly, discuss how CBT can be used to treat stress response syndromes like PTSD. Essentially, we want CBT to unstick the brain and begin the process of repairing damage.

Although combat-related PTSD is very much in the popular press, as it should be, I want to make sure we remember that traumatic events can arise from a number of different sources—random violence, car accidents, sexual abuse, or even intensely powerful losses. I hope we can highlight common features and common solutions.

Now SAMSA, the substance abuse and mental health services administration, tells us that individual trauma results from an event, a series of events, or a set of circumstances that is experienced by an individual as physically or emotionally harmful or threatening, and that it has lasting adverse effects on the individual's functioning and physical, social, emotional, or spiritual well-being. Traumatic events overwhelm the usual methods of coping that give people a sense of control, connection, and meaning. This might include sexual assault, combat, car accidents, or even vicarious traumatic experiences.

So how common is trauma? With the exception of sexual molestation or sexual assault, trauma is much more likely to happen to a man than to a woman. A man has a 35% chance in their lifetime to witness violence, a woman 15%. For an accident, men have a 25% chance, women 15. And here, this is mostly accounted for in motor vehicle accidents, more likely to be caused by men than by women. Threat with a weapon, 20% men, 6% women, and the opposite is true when we're talking about sexual assault.

Now, on the severity spectrum of responses to trauma it ranges from the expected stress response syndromes to adjustment disorder to something called acute stress reactions, all the way up to the most severe and lasting reaction of post-traumatic stress disorder. And that's where we're really going to focus.

Now, if we look at the DSM-5, they give us criteria A, B, and C for post-traumatic stress disorder. Criteria A, obviously, there has to be some sort of trauma that's happened. An individual has to be exposed to death, threatened death, serious injury or threat of serious injury, and actual or threatened sexual violence. You can either be directly exposed; you can witness it in person; you can be indirectly affected by, as in a vicarious trauma of hearing about a close friend or family member; or it could be repeated or extreme indirect exposure, something that a police officer or a fireman might experience.

For criteria B, there has to be something called intrusive symptoms that are persistently re-experienced. So it might be recurrent and intrusive memories. It might be traumatic nightmares. It might be flashbacks or other dissociative reactions. There's a persistent or effortful avoidance of distressing trauma-related stimuli as part of criteria C. There may be trauma-related thoughts or feelings, or trauma-related external reminders, such as triggers in your environment that bring back those flood of emotions and reactions. Criteria C for avoidance. Other criteria might include changes in cognition and emotion, changes in arousal and re-activity, and the duration has to be greater than one month. And of course, like all of the different mental illnesses that we've talked about, there needs to be some level of functional impairment.

So how would you go about assessing an individual if they suspect they may or may not have post-traumatic stress disorder? Of course the gold standard is a clinician interview, and they do a semi-structured interview using questions derived from the DSM-5, criteria A, B, and C. Other measures that they might use, and measures that you yourself could find online, include the PTSD symptom scale, or the PSS-SR. They may use the PTSD checklist or PCL, or the classic IES, or impact of event scale, developed by Mardi Horowitz, and lately revised in the 1990s.

So how common is post-traumatic stress disorder? Well they estimate that there's a lifetime risk of about 8% for adults in the U.S. PTSD is more common in women than men, but remember that men are more likely to be exposed to trauma. Often, it's the type of trauma that lays the ground work for the PTSD, where we know that attacks, such as sexual violence or rape in women, have a much higher risk for developing PTSD than for some other kinds of trauma.

So, what are some of the risk factors? We know that not everyone traumatized goes on to develop post-traumatic stress disorder. And of course the most powerful has to do with the severity of the trauma. But other factors might include whether the individual has had prior traumas or prior traumatization. Gender, remember that PTSD is more likely in women than men. If an individual has a prior for mood disorder, depression, or anxiety disorders, or a family history of those disorders, then all of those make the risk for PTSD higher.

But remember we may not just be talking about post-traumatic stress disorder; people may be coping with their disorder by self-medicating with things like alcohol or drugs. They may be reacting to the surge of feelings they have by becoming aggressive or violent. There may be suicidal ideation, or maybe even suicidal attempts. There may be distancing or breaking away from loved ones. There may be problems at work, and of course, problems in relationships, or even homelessness and joblessness.

Now, cognitive behavioral therapy for post-traumatic stress disorder has been around for quite some time, in fact, most of the founding fathers, such as Beck or Albert Ellis, all had versions of CBT for post-traumatic stress disorder. Many started in the '70s working with veterans from Vietnam, and they drew heavily on learning theories, but remember this was also when the cognitive revolution was just emerging, and so they began to fold in, not just behavioral strategies, but cognitive strategies as well.

Now some of the things they wanted to help an individual with, remember with behavioral strategies, we want to push against avoidance, so they might help an individual to face those fearful situations, but they learn that they need to give the individual skills to be able to deal with that affect of arousal. They wanted to teach them somatic quieting. They wanted to teach them cognitive restructuring. They wanted to teach them how to tell their story, but not become overwhelmed with emotions.

Now, there is a number of different variants of CBT for post-traumatic stress disorder, which have subsequently emerged. There's stress inoculation training by Meichenbaum. There's prolonged exposure and cognitive processing by Edna Foa. And more recently there's EMDR, or eye movement desensitization and reprocessing. Let's focus on some of Edna Foa's work on prolonged exposure and emotional reprocessing.

Now, in this particular kind of therapy, patients are encouraged to repeatedly recount the event and to confront feared situations in people. They're taught relaxation or other emotional mastery skills so that they convey a sense of control and safety while they are exposing themselves to these potential triggers. It proceeds through a number of different stages. So in stage one of this kind of therapy, they do basic relationship building, establishing safety, education about the disorder, about the treatment, assessments, and looking for comorbidities. So remember this is CBT, and it still has those common features of collaboration, the relationship matters, but you have a partnership with the patient in developing a treatment plan and setting some goals.

In stage two, they teach emotion regulation skills, self-soothing, somatic quieting, and they begin talking about the event. Let me give you a sample early homework assignment that a patient might do. It goes as follows: Please write at least one page on what it means to you that you were traumatized. Please consider the effects the trauma has had on your beliefs about yourself, your beliefs about others, and your beliefs about the world. That should sound very familiar. Also consider the following topics while writing your answer: safety, trust, power, esteem, and intimacy. Bring this with you to the next session. Now, you might be thinking that that sounds a little bit abstract, and it is, on purpose. You need to have the individual to have an exercise that's challenging, but not overwhelming, before you move into stage three.

And stage three is where the individual starts reprocessing the memory while being exposed to the triggers, and a lot of strong emotions are brought up.

So this is a sample midpoint or more advanced stage three exercise assignment: Write a detailed account of the trauma. Include as many sensory details as possible, including your thoughts and feelings during the trauma. The patient reads his assignment in the next meeting; they may redo this assignment in between meetings; and they also will listen to tape recordings of their therapy session in between meetings to continue exposing themselves to this particular story and practicing those emotional mastery skills.

So does it work? Well, approximately 80% of patients show significant reduction in symptoms and improvement in functioning after 12 weeks of treatment. In a paper published by the Journal of the American Medical Association in 2007, it showed that greater than 40% of women with combat-related PTSD no longer met criteria for the disorder after only ten sessions.

I wanted to show a few broader systematic reviews and meta-analyses, the first done by Watts in 2013, where they looked at 112 studies. They found that the effect of treatments were cognitive behavioral therapy, exposure treatment, and EMDR. They found that effective medications included Paxil, Zoloft, Prozac, and drugs Risperidone, Topiramate, and Venlafaxine. And I think the bottom line for this particular study, it showed that there is a menu of different treatments, both psychotherapies and pharmacotherapies that work. There's hope.

In a study done by Bisson in 2007, published in the British Journal of Psychiatry, they did a systematic review of 38 studies, and again found that trauma-focused cognitive behavioral therapy was helpful, along with EMDR. In a similar study, more recently done by Bisson in 2013 as part of a Cochran review, they found that individual trauma-focused CBT, and again, EMDR, did better than treatment as usual. There are choices. There's data that supports that these types of treatment happen to work.

So what are some new directions that we might go in? Now, we hear a lot about technology. We hear about Internet therapy. We hear about smart phone applications. And I wanted to share just one example where they're looking at a different sort of trauma, and here they're using Internet or web-based trauma-focused cognitive therapy. So with this Internet CBT, Cursting and colleagues in 2013 looked at a group of women that had had miscarriages, sometimes called spontaneous abortions. Now this can be very traumatic for families, in particularly, when folks won't talk about it, or if the mother blames herself.

In this randomized controlled trial they looked at Internet CBT versus waitlist controls. They looked at 228 women doing a five week CBT intervention, and their primary outcome measure, they use the IES, the Impact of Events Scale. So what was the outcome? So the treatment group for this internet CBT showed significantly reduced symptoms of post-traumatic stress, prolonged grief, depression, and anxiety, relative to the waitlist control. They found that further significant improvement in all symptoms of PTSD and prolonged grief was found from the post treatment evaluation to the 12 month follow up. The attrition rate, as you can imagine, was relatively low— it's only at 14%.

Now, there's a recent move to move more types of trauma-focused CBT online, and not so specialized just on miscarriages. There's a program on the Medical University of South Carolina, looking at TF, or Trauma-Focused CBT online, for children and adolescents. If you are interested, I would encourage you to look at tfcbt.musc.edu, where they have the full program available online.

Let's next move to a core exercise that could be part of trauma-focused CBT, or nearly any other type of CBT that calls for somatic quieting as stress reduction. You'll see Maria with her first experience of progressive muscle relaxation and guided imagery. I would encourage you to first watch or listen to the exercise, and then try it on your own.

[VIGNETTE START]

PROFESSOR SATTERFIELD: All right, so let me give you this, and why don't we move on then to our next agenda item. And it falls in the category of behavior, but it's really a behavioral skill. It's a tool that we can take out of our toolbox to help you to feel less stressed.

It can take 2 minutes; it can take 20 minutes just depending on how much space and time you have to give it. It falls into a category of interventions called relaxation strategies or sometimes they call it somatic quieting, and there are lots of different things to try. And I just wanted to demonstrate one today and maybe have you practice it a few times.

It is a behavior, but what we'll do is we'll start with behavior of relaxation and then we'll do a little bit of guided imagery, which moves us back into cognition. So it sort of links behavior and cognition. The goal of both is to help you relax. So it's just to turn down that anxiety and that stress and that tension a little bit.

MARIA: OK.

PROFESSOR SATTERFIELD: So what I would recommend we do—we can just sit our things here. And if I could get you to put your feet flat on the floor and we will try a strategy called progressive muscle relaxation. Have you done that before or heard about that before?

MARIA: No.

PROFESSOR SATTERFIELD: OK, all right. So it's fairly simple to do. I'll walk you through it this time. You can try it on your own. If you find that you get stuck, next time we can make an audio recording for you and you can just listen to me guiding you through it as much as you want.

They call it progressive muscle relaxation because you progress from your toes all the way up through your body and you are progressively relaxing your muscles. It's based on a couple of premises. One is that we're often stressed throughout the course of the day and we hold the tension in our body. But we're not often aware of the stress, so we may have tightness in our shoulders, our neck, in our lower back that happens a lot for folks.

So what we want to do is to in a sense control or even manipulate the tension that's in our muscles. So we'll first tense them up, and then we'll relax them and we'll tense them and relax them. And by contrasting those two states, it helps you to develop more of an awareness of when you're tense and when you're relaxed. And we want to do—

MARIA: I'm a little tense right now.

PROFESSOR SATTERFIELD: OK, and hopefully we could take care of tension. What we'll do is we'll just start your toes, we'll move to your calves, we'll then move to your thighs, and then we'll move up to your shoulders and have you make a fist, and we'll probably stop at that point. All right.

So just go ahead and get comfortable. Looks like you're sitting up straight. It usually helps to close your eyes, and that's just to minimize distractions. Nearly all of the relaxation strategies start by first focusing on your breath. We want you to breathe through your nose because it slows down the rate of breathing, and we want you to breathe from your belly—so those nice, deep breaths.

So just give yourself a couple of nice slow breaths and just let yourself relax into that chair. Feel it supporting you, holding you. And just let your shoulders hang loose, and just let yourself relax.

I'm going to ask you to direct your attention to your toes. Just think about your toes. Notice how your shoes feel on your toes. What I'm going to ask you to do is to scrunch up and tighten your toes. So just scrunch them up. Feel the tightness. Feel a little bit of that tension in your toes, how they're pushing against your shoes, and then just relax. And relax. And relax. Just imagine this warm wave of relaxation is now washing over your toes. And we're going to tense them up one more time. So tense up those toes. Push out that relaxation. Squeeze them tight and feel that tension. And then relax. Relax. And just imagine that wave is, again, lapping at your feet, relaxing your feet and your toes.

Next we're going to move up to your calves. And to tighten your calves, you just raise your heels up off the ground. So tighten your calves. Tighten them. Feel that large muscle getting a little bit warmer. Feel that tension, feel that squeeze, feel the burn. And relax. Lower your heels back down. And relax. Feel that nourishing blood rushing back to the calves. Feel that wave of relaxation washing over your calves and over your feet.

Next we're going to move up to the thighs. So I want you just to squeeze your legs, squeeze your thighs, tighten those thigh muscles. Hold it. Feel the tension. These are your largest muscles. Feel the tension, and then release. And release. And release some more. Just feel the chair holding those relaxed leg muscles. Feel that warm wave of relaxation is now washing all the way up to your waist. With each successive wave, it pulls out more tension. And you feel your legs completely relaxed.

Next we're going to go to your hands and your arms, and I just want you to make a tight fist. So make a really tight fist. You can feel it in your forearms. You can feel it in your hand. You feel that tension. Just feel that squeeze. And then relax. Let your hands drop back to your lap. Let your fingers relax. Imagine now that wave of relaxation is watching over your arms, your legs. It's nourishing. It's relaxing. It's pulling out all the tension.

And last, we'll go up to your shoulders. And I want you to raise your shoulders up to your ears and just raise them all the way up. You feel the tension across your back. You feel it in your neck. You feel it in your shoulders. Feel the tension. And release. Release. Let your shoulders relax. Just imagine that wave, again, of relaxation is washing all the way up to your neck now. It's pulling out all the toxins, all the tension. Relaxed all the way up to your neck.

The last thing I want you to do, I just want you to tense your face by pressing your lips together and scrunching up your nose. Just press it together. Feel that tension. Feel the tension in those facial muscles, and then relax. And relax.

Imagine you're in that warm bath now, completely covered and completely relaxed. All that tension is gone. Direct your attention back to your breath. Those nice belly breaths, breathing through your nose.

And just do a quick scan of your body starting at your toes working all the way up. If there's any spots of tension, just imagine that wave is coming— that wave is massaging away any tension.

Now we're going to try a little bit of guided imagery. Just continue to breathe deeply, but we're going to help you take your mind somewhere—somewhere that brings you peace or brings you joy. I want you to imagine your picture of paradise, a place where you would love to go. Maybe it's on a beach, in the mountains, the forest, maybe it's in the city. Wherever brings you peace and happiness.

I want you to look around this place that you've created, this place that's completely under your control. I want you to notice what's there. I want you to notice if there are other people around, or maybe you're by yourself.

Notice the light. Notice the temperature. Pay attention to whatever sounds you might be hearing. Notice any smells that might be there.

Allow yourself to enjoy the full sensory experience. This is a place that belongs to you. Allow that place to feed you, to nourish your soul, to take away your stress and your pain. Remind yourself that you can go back here any time you want. It's your place.

I want you to take a last look around. You're going to say goodbye for now, but you're going to make a promise to come back sometime soon. Again, notice the sights, the sounds, the smells, and make that promise to come back.

Draw your attention back to your breath and back to where you are.

MARIA: Well, that was lovely.

PROFESSOR SATTERFIELD: So where did you go?

MARIA: I was on our sailboat and we were off the coast of Maine, and the water is sparkling and the wind is blowing through our hair. Jack is at the helm, this big shock of white hair blowing in the breeze. You could hear the whisper of the water under the boat and the flap of the sails and the breeze, and that occasional gull that's always chasing you, cawing up above. Just the sparkle of the sun on the water—that was what was so beautiful.

PROFESSOR SATTERFIELD: And I see you smiling, so I guess the effect on your mood was a positive one.

MARIA: Oh, absolutely.

PROFESSOR SATTERFIELD: How about on your tension and your stress?

MARIA: I feel so relaxed. I almost felt when you started that like I was going to collapse or something, like lose all of my support. But it just feels really good, like euphoria or something.

PROFESSOR SATTERFIELD: You tried progressive muscle relaxation, more of a physical experience, and then we tried the guided imagery, more of a cognitive experience. Any differences you noted or want to try—

MARIA: They were both helpful. Really, I don't think I would have been able to imagine what you were having me imagine if I hadn't been more relaxed. I'm always still thinking about what I should be doing and what I'm not doing that I ought to be doing. It just helps to be relaxed.

PROFESSOR SATTERFIELD: Do you think this is something that you want to do on your own?

MARIA: Oh, I would love to, yes. Yes.

PROFESSOR SATTERFIELD: And do you see any obstacles that might prevent you from doing that?

MARIA: It's just the time, or if someone interrupts or something, but it doesn't take that long. What was it, five minutes that we spent doing it?

PROFESSOR SATTERFIELD: No, it wasn't a long time. Now, there are if it helps to have an external voice guiding you, I can give you a couple of websites and resources. And if those don't work, we can do it again next time and we'll just record it and we'll give you that audio recording.

MARIA: I liked hearing your voice. It's nice to have that with me.

PROFESSOR SATTERFIELD: So let's plan do that, then.

MARIA: Yeah, thank you.

[VIGNETTE END]

PROFESSOR SATTERFIELD: So what did you just see? I hope you noticed it's brief, simple, but effective, and you can see the implications for those dealing with the stressful fallout of a trauma. But remember that CBT for trauma isn't just about somatic quieting; that might help you with emotional mastery, but you still need exposures, and you still need the reconstructing, the telling, and the reconstructing of the story; those are truly key.

Let's close by going to our next frequently asked question. A patient asked: Traumas are often random, meaningless events that happen, like a car accident, or a flood, or a mugging. How can we rationally and cognitively approach something that by its very nature just doesn't make sense? Terrific question, and I think it's important to remember that even though CBT is very much grounded in Western empiricism and rationality, the goal of trauma-focused CBT isn't to give a rational explanation for why bad events occur. Instead, it really resides more in the behavioral realm, where we're looking at behavioral avoidance, and how particular triggers now have the power to cause extreme physiologic arousal in an individual.

What we want to do is to create a sense of safety, then behaviorally we want to expose that person to those triggers and those situations. We've given them cognitive tools not to promote rationality, but we've given them cognitive tools to be able to do self-soothing and somatic quieting. So we hope that the cognitive therapy part can help them do the behavioral therapy part so that they can begin to face those triggers and to become a master over those particular fears.

So, I hope you'll join us next time for our lectures on forgiveness and meaning.

Forgiveness and Letting Go
Lecture 12

Forgiveness, and its associated health benefits, begins with a cognitive decision and can be promoted with both cognitive and behavioral strategies. This lecture summarizes the research on forgiveness and illustrates exercises that help individuals let go and move forward toward forgiveness goals, including the forgiveness of another person or of oneself. Research has shown that short-term CBT—usually in groups, but it can be in individual settings as well—can be effective in promoting forgiveness and that behavioral activation can be helpful in treating pathological grief.

Research on Forgiveness

- For the most part, when we think of forgiveness, we think about forgiving another person, and it usually starts with a transgression. The emotional reaction might include the initial shock, the guilt, the anger, the thoughts of betrayal, the disbelief, the chagrin, the judgment, and the what-ifs. The behavior might include avoidance, rumination, different social interactions, and the physiological effects. It might affect our sleep or appetite. We might become depressed or angry. It might even affect our level of cardiovascular arousal and blood pressure.

- In research published in 2000, Robert Enright and Richard Fitzgibbons tell us that people, upon rationally determining that they had been unfairly treated, forgive when they willfully abandon resentment and related responses to which they have a right and endeavor to respond to the wrong doer based on the moral principles of beneficence, which may include compassion, unconditional worth, generosity, and moral love.

- They tell us that forgiveness is not forgetting. Forgiveness is not surrender, resignation, or passivity. Forgiveness is not necessarily reconciliation, and it's not excusing or condoning. It's not letting time heal or somehow balancing the scales. Forgiveness is an active, ongoing process that may take years to evolve. But it typically starts with a decision—a desire to forgive or at least to begin that process. The primary beneficiary of forgiveness is the person who is doing the forgiving.

- In the Stanford Forgiveness Project, published in 2006, Alex Harris and colleagues recruited individuals who had recently been wronged or transgressed. They took a wide range of different individuals with different types of transgressions experienced. They designed six 90-minute groups, and half of the subjects got the intervention and half were controls out of a total sample of 259 individuals.

- In the forgiveness classes, they started with somatic quieting or stress reduction and relaxation. Then, they moved on to some anger-management exercises. The individuals learned to depersonalize, or take less offense. They also taught the individuals to be aware of the personal health consequences of holding a grudge and to choose to redirect their attention elsewhere. They helped them build empathy skills—to see the situation from different perspectives—and develop something they called grace, or accepting that other individuals make mistakes and do things that may hurt others. Then, they encouraged the individuals to take small steps and do easy forgiveness first before tackling a big transgression.

- The intervention reduced negative thoughts and feelings about the target transgression two to three times more effectively than the control condition, and it produced significantly greater increases in positive thoughts and feelings toward the transgressor. Significant treatment effects were also found for forgiveness self-efficacy, forgiveness generalized in new situations, perceived stress, and trait anger.

- In an interesting adaptation to this study published by Mathias Allemand, et al, in 2013, researchers did a randomized controlled trial in which they looked at an intervention group versus the waitlist control group. However, in this study, they were focused on older adults, whose average age was 70 years old. They essentially used the Stanford Forgiveness Project curriculum, but they adapted it for issues that might be more salient for older adults. They found that the intervention reduced the levels of perceived actual transgression painfulness, transgression-related emotions and cognitions, and negative affect.

- In 2005, Mark Rye and colleagues conducted a randomized controlled trial that analyzed 192 individuals. They had an eight-session forgiveness group, but they had three different conditions: a secular forgiveness group, a religious forgiveness group, and a waitlist control. They looked at forgiveness outcomes and mental health right after the class ended and six weeks after. They found that participants increased significantly more than comparisons on self-reported forgiveness of an ex-spouse and understanding of forgiveness. Participants in the secular condition, though, showed a greater decrease in depressive symptoms than comparison participants. Intrinsic religiousness didn't seem to help, but it didn't seem to hurt.

- Developed by Loren Toussaint in 2014, the Restore curriculum was framed as a self-forgiveness curriculum. It was a randomized controlled trial of 83 cancer patients and their caregivers who were analyzed versus waitlist controls. Researchers found that the project Restore encouraged self-acceptance, self-improvement, and commitment using prayer, meditation, reflection, and expressive writing. After looking at before and after outcomes, they found that patients and their caregivers scored higher than controls on self-forgiveness, self-acceptance, and self-improvement, and they scored lower on pessimism.

Predictors of Forgiveness

- Ryan Fehr and colleagues conducted a meta-analysis of 175 different studies that analyzed more than 26,000 subjects. They found some key features that were predictors of forgiveness: the intent to forgive, the receiving of an apology, the capacity for empathy, and the capacity to manage or control their own angry reaction.

- A study by Tila Pronk also analyzed predictors of forgiveness, but this study looked more at executive functioning, or cognitive functioning or skills. In particular, three were important for promoting forgiveness: inhibition (involves reducing ruminations about the transgression), task switching (if memories of an event are triggered), and flexibility (the ability to rewrite or revise their story).

- The process of forgiveness starts with the decision to forgive. We need to stop ourselves from going down a rabbit hole of rumination that amplifies our negative emotions and makes it difficult to let go. We need to think about task switching, engaging in distractions, and inducing positive emotions. We might want to rewrite the story or build empathy through new attributes or explanations about why an event occurred. Most importantly, we need to remember that forgiveness is for you—not someone else.

Pathological Grief

- Sometimes there isn't a person, or anything exterior to us, to blame. Something tragic happens—such as a loss or a death—and you're just not able to move on. Maybe you're stuck because of self-forgiveness, because you feel like moving on is a betrayal of the person you've lost, or because of unresolved grief.

- There's no one right way to grieve, nor is there a right intensity or duration for grief, but pathological grief is when an individual seems to have a number of mental health difficulties after bereavement and doesn't seem to be recovering by connecting with their usual activities or social contacts.

- There are treatments that have been validated for pathological grief. In a study conducted by Anthony Papa, Rodd Sewell, and colleagues in 2013, they analyzed pathological grief. They used a randomized controlled trial of immediate treatment versus a waitlist control, and they looked at these individuals at 12, 24, and 36 weeks after their treatment. This particular treatment was called behavioral activation, and it focuses on activating certain behaviors. Compared to no treatment, behavioral activation was associated with large reductions in prolonged, complicated, or traumatic grief; PTSD; and depressive symptoms.

- Behavior activation is a highly tailored approach to the ongoing assessment and formulations about why a person does or does not engage in particular behaviors. Much of it is based on the seminal work of Peter Lewinsohn at Oregon Health & Science University.

- Behavioral activation looks at contingent if-then beliefs: What are the drivers, or the inhibitors, of behaviors? The goal is to increase rewards and problem resolution and to decrease avoidance and rumination. Behavior slowly evolves, or in some cases devolves, over time. According to seminal work by Neil Jacobson in the mid-1990s, evidence shows that behavioral activation might be equal to the hybrid model of CBT for depression.

- With behavioral activation, there is an orientation to treatment and education, just like in hybrid CBT. We want to develop our treatment goals. We want to individualize the activation plans and engagement targets by doing functional analysis, or a formulation of situations and behaviors. We want to have individuals try to increase their activation. Individuals are going to encounter obstacles, but they will do some troubleshooting about why they had trouble increasing their behaviors or connecting with new people or activities. We also want to review and consolidate gains.

- With behavioral activation, we not only want to increase activities, but we also want to look for examples of maladaptive behaviors that an individual has learned as a way of coping. Many times, people will use maladaptive behaviors because these types of behaviors have an immediate reward, and it's not entirely obvious that they might have a negative consequence later.

- An example of a maladaptive coping behavior would be taking long naps in the middle of the day. When you're feeling depressed, there is a natural tendency to want to escape. A long nap can be reinforcing. It helps you escape, but it prevents you from going out to do things that might be more reinforcing or from connecting with your social supports.

- Another example of a maladaptive behavior would be drinking alcohol when you're stressed. It is a depressant, and it turns down the stress response, but it doesn't help you solve any of the issues that might be causing you to have that stress response.

Drinking alcohol while stressed is a maladaptive behavior. Alcohol turns down the stress response without solving the issues that caused the stress response.

- With behavioral activation, we increase positive behaviors and decrease negative, or maladaptive, behaviors. An acronym is used to remind us about the steps that an individual would need to take: ACTION, where A stands for assess, C stands for choose a new behavior, T stands for try the chosen behavior, I stands for integrate it into your new routine, O stands for observe the results, and N stands for never give up.

Suggested Reading

Allemand, Steiner, and Hill, "Effects of a Forgiveness Intervention for Older Adults."

Enright, *Forgiveness Is a Choice.*

Goldman and Wade, "Comparison of Forgiveness and Anger-Reduction Group Treatments."

Harris, Luskin, Norman, Standard, Bruning, Evans, and Thoresen, "Effects of a Group Forgiveness Intervention on Forgiveness, Perceived Stress, and Trait-Anger."

Jacobson and Hollon, "Cognitive-Behavior Therapy versus Pharmacotherapy."

Koenig, King, and Carson, *Handbook of Religion and Health.*

Luskin, *Forgive for Good.*

Papa, Sewell, Garrison-Diehn, and Rummel, "A Randomized Open Trial Assessing the Feasibility of Behavioral Activation for Pathological Grief Responding."

Pronk, Karremans, Overbeek, Vermulst, and Wigboldus, "What It Takes to Forgive."

Toussaint, Barry, Bornfriend, and Markman, "Restore."

Questions to Consider

1. How do the different major world religions conceptualize forgiveness? Consider Christian, Muslim, Buddhist, and Jewish traditions. How do these different traditions shed light on this complex and important psychological process? Does forgiveness need to have a religious or spiritual element in order to work?

2. Would Stanford's forgiveness program work if the person you are trying to forgive is yourself? How does the process of forgiving someone else differ from self-forgiveness?

Forgiveness and Letting Go
Lecture 12—Transcript

PROFESSOR SATTERFIELD: Julie, a patient of mine, is in her mid-50s and used to be very close to her slightly older brother. When her father became terminally ill, she had to shoulder the burden and got very little help from him. In fact, her brother didn't really show up until the very end and was mostly present when they were figuring out their dad's will, and there was a lot of money on the table.

Julie was furious, disappointed, and very hurt. She ended up going years without talking to her brother. She missed him, but she could still feel the burning resentment and had this image of him looking at her smugly at the reading of the will. He got most of the money. She wanted to let go and move on but felt very, very stuck. That's when we begin working on forgiveness using a CBT approach.

Forgiveness and its associated health benefits begins with a cognitive decision and can be promoted with both cognitive and behavioral strategies. This lecture summarizes the research on forgiveness and illustrates exercises that help us let go and move forward towards those goals.

Remember that this can be forgiveness of another, or, it can be forgiveness of ourselves. An example might be having a car accident, losing a job, losing your temper and blaming yourself for it. It may have affected another person, or it might just be something that affects you. You may feel guilty for getting sick. You may feel guilty for being a burden on your family.

For the most part, when we think of forgiveness, we think about forgiving another person, and it usually starts with a transgression. There is the emotional reaction, maybe the initial shock, the guilt, the anger, the thoughts of betrayal, the disbelief, the chagrin, the judgment, the what ifs? The behavior that might include avoidance, rumination, different social interactions, and of course, the physiologic effects. It might affect our sleep. It might affect our appetite. We may become depressed, angry. It may even affect our level of cardiovascular arousal and blood pressure, but how does this play out with our cases?

Now, we know that Michael often loses his temper, and then he feels guilty or ashamed later. He might need to work on self-forgiveness, but others in his life may need to work on forgiving him. Maria feels guilt for not being a perfect caregiver. She really needs to focus on forgiving herself. Although each are quite different, we'll want to go through the same process of formulating the situation using our cognitive ABCs. Let's turn to our first clip of Michael, who describes an event that happened with his wife.

[VIGNETTE START]

PROFESSOR SATTERFIELD: So this is just an example of one event. Why don't we just do one more event? And you had mentioned the fight with your wife. So why don't we go ahead and jump to that one? So what was the activating event for that?

MICHAEL: Well, that would have been the fact that I'm not supposed to be smoking. And I actually needed some nicotine, so I went out. I didn't think that she was around, so I went out on the deck. It was dark. I figured I could get away with having one cigarette.

PROFESSOR SATTERFIELD: All right. So you were smoking on the deck at home, and your wife—

MICHAEL: And she obviously was around, and she came out and caught me smoking.

PROFESSOR SATTERFIELD: All right. So it sounds like you guys have an agreement that you're not smoking, or—

MICHAEL: That is our agreement, and it ties into some of the health issues we've discussed. But I was not—I admit, I was not supposed to be smoking, and I did have a sense, even when I went out there, that I was sneaking a smoke.

PROFESSOR SATTERFIELD: Right. OK, so you knew that for your health and for your own good, that's not something you want to do, but she came out and was unhappy when she saw it.

MICHAEL: She was unhappy, to say the least.

PROFESSOR SATTERFIELD: OK. And what were the consequences of that event? What were the feelings or behaviors?

MICHAEL: Well, the consequence, again, was anger on my part. And the reason for that is although intellectually, I can understand that it's not a good thing to be doing, it's just one cigarette, and I think the way that she responded to it by lecturing me, which is really what happened, was on her part insensitive. So I guess I was kind of reacting to that, the fact that she can't see that sometimes, it's just one cigarette, and I might need one.

PROFESSOR SATTERFIELD: OK. I'm just going to put she's insensitive. I need a cigarette. Other emotions? Embarrassment, indignation, resignation?

MICHAEL: I guess there's a little bit of embarrassment there because it's like you're the kid, and you got caught with your hand in the cookie jar. So there was embarrassment there.

PROFESSOR SATTERFIELD: OK. All right. Anything else?

MICHAEL: Well, I don't know how far you want me to go into the event, but as she lowered the boom on me about the rules and the rules that I was breaking, my response was to talk about the needs that I have. And one of those needs at the moment was obviously the need to unwind with a cigarette because it had been a really, really difficult day, and that's when I'm talking about the sense of that she was insensitive.

She wasn't appreciating that, and so one of my ways of responding was— and I know this was completely inappropriate, but my way of responding was she's been staying at home for years, has not been working herself, and so I kind of threw that back in her face that you really don't understand. It must be really nice to have a day when you can stay at home all day, a week when you can do that all day. And yeah, I guess in that case, maybe I wouldn't need a cigarette, either.

PROFESSOR SATTERFIELD: OK. And remember, in consequences, we're going for emotions and behavior, so it sounds like the behaviors was a counterattack?

MICHAEL: Counterattack would be a good way of putting it.

PROFESSOR SATTERFIELD: So a counterattack.

MICHAEL: And maybe that has something to do with being embarrassed, and that's also a way of responding to that.

PROFESSOR SATTERFIELD: Sure. And sometimes with these kind of—when people fall off the wagon, there's disappointment, and sort of disappointed in yourself, but knowing that you had to do it. There might be some defensiveness that's there too sometimes, when people are telling you something that you know, but you feel like you have to defend yourself about it.

We forgot to put the consequences up here, and we know this was the Coke on the car incident, right? But then there was the washing the car off. OK. There was also the key words that you said and the gestures that you were making, and so that all sort of fits in the picture. All right. Any words or gestures with your wife?

MICHAEL: Well, I guess there's a sort of—I didn't call her any names, but there's the accusation that I'm throwing at her of being—I didn't call her lazy, but I guess that's what I was trying to get at, or at least the she's unappreciative.

PROFESSOR SATTERFIELD: Yeah, and I—

MICHAEL: So that's kind of the language that—

PROFESSOR SATTERFIELD: I think often in long-standing relationships, you know really where people's buttons are, and you can zing them pretty easily with very few words because you've been down that path before.

MICHAEL: Exactly.

PROFESSOR SATTERFIELD: Well, this gives you an idea. So we have just two events here, very different events, but it looks like the consequences are kind of similar. I mean, this one has more fury. This has sort of an embarrassed, defensive aspect to it. But in each case, there were thoughts which fueled these emotions. What I want to follow up on a little bit—so here, she's insensitive. She's not supportive. Is there any element of, you were owed support and she didn't give it to you? Or you should have been supported?

MICHAEL: Well, yeah. I guess that's part of reacting that way when somebody calls you out for something that, as you say, you both know. I feel that we have a lot of time invested, many years invested in each other, and that she should have been sensitive enough in that situation maybe not to have gone right to the accusation, but perhaps to have talked me through that. I see you're smoking. Whatever—kind of the way that you and I talk, right?

PROFESSOR SATTERFIELD: Yeah. Well, and I'm—sort of what I'm after with that is, again, to understand how beliefs or cognitions are related to emotions. And oftentimes, the feelings behind anger are the perception that something that was rightfully yours was taken away, or violated, or damaged. It sounds like you really want the support of your wife and the positive regard, and when you don't get that, it makes you angry.

MICHAEL: I think that's fair to say.

PROFESSOR SATTERFIELD: OK. Yeah.

[VIGNETTE END]

PROFESSOR SATTERFIELD: So in the realm of transgressions, this one is fairly minor, at least on the surface. It carries a bit more of an emotional charge because of their shared history and what the event means or symbolizes to each of them. In this case, there may be an issue of forgiveness and acceptance on both sides. Michael can forgive his wife for being angry and trying to control his behavior. His wife, who we'll meet later in other lectures, could forgive him for breaking a promise and doing something that he agrees is unhealthy.

Enright and Fitzgibbons in 2000 tell us, people upon rationally determining what they had been unfairly treated, forgive when they willfully abandon resentment and related responses to which they have a right and endeavor to respond to the wrong doer based on the moral principle of beneficence, which may include compassion, unconditional worth, generosity, and moral love. They tell us that forgiveness is not forgetting. Forgiveness is not surrender, resignation, or passivity. Forgiveness is not necessarily reconciliation. It's not excusing or condoning. It's not letting time heal or somehow balancing the scales. Forgiveness is an active, ongoing process that may take years to evolve. But it typically starts with a decision, a desire to forgive, or at least to begin that process.

The primary beneficiary of forgiveness is the person who is doing the forgiving. But let's look at the research and see what the research tells us? And I want to talk just briefly about something called the Stanford Forgiveness Project in a paper published by Harris and his colleagues in 2006. Now, in this particular project, they recruited individuals who had recently been wronged or transgressed. They took a wide range of different individuals with different types of transgressions they had experienced. They designed six 90-minute groups, and half of the subjects got the intervention and half were controls out of a total sample of 259 individuals.

So what do they teach in these forgiveness classes? Well, they started with somatic quieting or stress reduction and relaxation. Then they moved into some of the anger-management exercises, which we've also talked about. The individuals learned to de-personalize, or to take less offense, and that term, personalization, should pop to mind as one of those common habits of mind that we often tackle when we're doing cognitive therapy.

They taught the individuals to also be aware of the personal health consequences of holding a grudge and to choose to redirect their attention elsewhere. They helped them to build empathy skills, to see the situation from different perspectives, and to develop something that they called grace, or accepting that other individuals are infallible and make mistakes and do things that may hurt others. They then encouraged them to take small steps and do easy forgiveness first, so don't start with the big transgression; start with something a little bit easier until you build up your skills with forgiveness, and then tackle that big transgression.

So what was some of the results? The intervention reduced negative thoughts and feelings about the target transgression two to three times more effectively than the control condition, and it produced significantly greater increases in positive thoughts and feeling towards the transgressor. Significant treatment effects were also found for forgiveness self-efficacy, forgiveness, generalized in new situations, perceived stress, and decreased trait anger.

An interesting adaptation to this study published by Allemand in 2013, they did a randomized control trial where they looked at an intervention group versus the wait list group, but here they were focused on older adults, where the average age was 70 years old. Here they took the Stanford Forgiveness Project curriculum, essentially, but they adapted it for issues that might be more salient for older adults. What they found is that the intervention reduced the levels of perceived actual transgression painfulness, transgression-related emotions and cognitions, and also, decreased negative emotions.

The next study I wanted to mention was interesting way of breaking things apart done by Ryan, 2005, again, a randomized control trial, looking at 192 individuals. They had an eight-session forgiveness group. But here they had three different conditions. So they had a secular forgiveness group, they had a religious forgiveness group, and then they had a wait list control. They looked at forgiveness outcomes, they looked at mental health, and they looked at outcomes right after the class ended, and six weeks follow up. They found that participants increase significantly more than comparisons on self-reported forgiveness of an ex-spouse and understanding of forgiveness. Participants in the secular condition, though, showed a greater decrease in depressive symptoms than comparison participants. Intrinsic religiousness didn't seem to help, but it didn't seem to hurt.

The last study I wanted to mention is something called the Restore Curriculum, and this was framed as a self-forgiveness curriculum, developed by Toussaint in 2014. Again, a randomized control trial, where they're looking at waitlist controls. They have 83 cancer patients and their caregivers. They found that the project Restore would encourage self-acceptance, self-improvement, and commitment, and they used prayer, meditation, reflection, and expressive writing, and again, they looked at pre and post outcomes. They found that patients and their caregivers scored higher than controls on self-forgiveness, self-acceptance, self-improvement, and they were lower on pessimism.

So, what are some of the predictors of forgiveness? If we're looking for ways to promote it, we want to know, what might predict it? A study by Fehr, actually, a meta-analysis of 175 different studies, where they looked at over 26,000 subjects. And they found that there were some key features, which will probably sound a little bit familiar. One of the predictors of forgiveness was first having the intent to forgive. As we said, forgiveness, or the process of forgiveness, starts with a cognitive decision.

Second was receiving an apology. Now, that may seem somewhat simplistic but having another individual, particularly the transgressor, acknowledge that a wrong occurred, and acknowledge regret that the wrong occurred can actually go quite a long way in terms of promoting healing and forgiveness. Next predictor was the capacity for empathy and the capacity to manage or to control their own angry reaction.

In a study by Pronk, they were also looking at predictors of forgiveness, but Pronk was looking more at what he called executive functioning, or we would call it cognitive functioning or cognitive skills, and he found that there were three that were particularly important. The first had to do with inhibition. Remember, often times when we're angry, or if we have been harmed or hurt in some way, we will ruminate about that transgression. The more we ruminate, the more it raises up our anger and the more entangled we get with our own cognitions. So an individual that's able to inhibit or step outside of those ruminations is more likely to be able to forgive.

The second cognitive skill had to do with task switching, and I think it's related somewhat to inhibitions, but they're able to switch tracks completely if they find that somehow they've been triggered into memories about a particular event; they're quickly able to move themselves on to something else. And the last cognitive skill has to do with flexibility, an ability to step back, to be able to rewrite or to revise their story.

So how can we move more towards forgiveness? Well, remember that it first starts with the decision to forgive. We need to stop ourselves from going down that rabbit hole, from going into those ruminative spaces that really amplify our negative emotions and make it difficult to let go. We need to think about task switching. We need to think about distractions. We need to think about possibly that toolbox of positive-emotion strategies that can pull us away from the harm that was done by the transgression. We might want to use our skills that we learned in our trauma lecture about rewriting the story or building empathy via new attributions or explanations about why an event occurred. And most importantly is to remember that forgiveness is for you, and it's not necessarily for someone else.

So, let's return to our story about Julie. This is the woman who was desperately wanting to forgive her brother for not helping out with the death of her father, then showing up for his inheritance. Note that she had already made the decision that she wanted to move on. It had been years; she missed her brother; she couldn't excuse what had happened, but she had spent a lot of time worrying and ruminating about what had happened. She wanted to forgive, but she felt stuck, and just couldn't do it. So what did we do?

Well, first, of course, we did a CBT formulation. We started collecting stories, particularly triggers around the event, but also stories about her relationship with her brother. We started looking at beliefs and consequences. We started using those cognitive ABCs. We then wanted to look at core beliefs, or rules of living, that were tapped for her. What is her sense of justice or injustice in the world? And when injustice occurs, from her worldview, what is it that needs to happen?

We started working on empathy by first having her recall positive times with her brother, then recalling times when he needed her and her support, then ask her to imagine how or why people act as they do when someone is dying, and why greed may come up, and why it comes up so often, and how society or culture might play a role in telling us what we should do when we're care giving and whose responsibility it might be.

From there, we moved to writing. She wrote several letters to her brother, with each one taking more time to try to understand and graciously explain his behavior. We kept remembering the bigger picture. This was about her health. This was about her relationships. This was about her moving on in pursuit of her values and her goals. The event was long gone, and we can't change the past. And she actually felt grateful that she was able to share those last few years with her father. In the end, she mailed her brother a letter. It briefly shared her feelings, including how much she missed him. She didn't give in, but she did let him know that she was going to let it go, and she hoped that they could see where it went from there.

Now, when we think about Michael, it would be fair to wonder if we should be talking about forgiveness or anger management. The two are certainly related, given what we know about the cognitive basis of anger, but the approach might be somewhat different. An interesting study done by Goldman and Wade in a 2012, randomized controlled trial of about 112 students. They had an anger group, versus a forgiveness group, versus a control group. They had six 90-minute sessions that took place over three weeks. So what happened? Well, in the forgiveness group, they had better outcomes for decreasing hostility, for managing their psychological symptoms, and they had more empathy for the offender when compared to the anger group or the wait-list control. Both the treatment conditions, the forgiveness as well as the anger management, reported greater reductions in desires for revenge than those in the wait list condition. So it looks like a little bit different, but maybe better outcomes, at least in this one particular study for forgiveness.

So let's go ahead and shift gears a bit and remember that sometimes there isn't a person or anything else exterior to us to blame. Something tragic happens. There's maybe a loss, or a death, or a random occurrence, and you're just not able to move on. You very much feel stuck. Maybe it's self-forgiveness. Maybe it's feeling like moving on is a betrayal of the person that you've lost. Maybe it's unresolved grief. We know that letting go is something that Maria is really struggling with. Her husband is still very much around, but his mind, and really, his identity and all of their history they've shared together are rapidly disappearing. She's devastated and she needs help. Let's watch this next clip of her sharing her perspective early in the course of treatment.

[VIGNETTE START]

MARIA: In a marriage as long as I've been in a marriage—this is 45 years now—you go through a lot of different things, and you say, well, things will be better later. Kids sleep through the night, or when they're all in school, or you get the mortgage paid off, but this is really different from that. This is—he can't get better, you know? What can I wish for at this point? I wish that he was dead. I can't wish that. What's my life going to be like after that? I just can't even imagine. It just seems hopeless.

PROFESSOR SATTERFIELD: Right. And it is a really painful place that you're in right now, and I can see why you would feel helpless and hopeless about it. And my hope is that we can help you to connect to a source of meaning, to something that gives you life, that gives you hope, to other friends, to other family. Things won't be the same with your husband again, as far as we know.

MARIA: I know. I know that.

PROFESSOR SATTERFIELD: But I hope to help you find reasons to—

MARIA: You know, it helps me already to be able to say these things to you because I can't say them to him, and there's really nobody else that I can talk to like that. He was always my best friend. But it's nice to be able to just say how much it hurts.

[VIGNETTE END]

PROFESSOR SATTERFIELD: So in that very brief but poignant clip, I hope you were able to see the situation that Maria's in and the pain that she might be feeling. As a psychotherapist, one thing I worry about is something called pathological grief. There's no one right way to grieve or no one right intensity or duration, but we do worry when an individual seems that they're having a number of mental health difficulties after bereavement, and they don't seem to be recovering, they don't seem to be connecting to their usual activities or to their social contacts.

We know that Maria's not there yet, but fortunately, there are treatments that have been validated for the treatment of pathological grief. And I want to share just one study done by Papa, Sewell, and colleagues in 2013, where they looked at pathological grief. In this particular study, they used a randomized controlled trial of immediate treatment versus a waitlist control. And they looked at these individuals at 12, 24, and 36 weeks after their treatment. This particular treatment was something called behavioral activation. If you think back to our basic behavior lectures, we did activity recording; we did activity scheduling; and we're trying to activate Maria because she was more depressed. In behavioral activation, it really just focuses on activating those behaviors. What did they find?

So compared with no treatment, behavioral activation was associated with large reductions in prolonged, complicated, or traumatic grief, decreases in PTSD, and decreases in depressive symptoms; 70% at post and 75% at follow up responded to treatment, with 45% at post and 40% at follow up being classified as high-end stake functioning at 12 weeks. Looks like it worked.

Now, for behavioral activation, recall the activity-monitoring forms, the activity schedules we did with Maria. And in her case, it was really about reconnecting her with sources of positive reinforcement and with her social contacts. But note that she's also grieving. She's losing a little bit of her husband day by day as his mind slips away. The study by Papa put together a full behavior activation program, and we did more of a combined hybrid program with Maria.

So if we were doing a full behavior-activation program, what might that look like? Well, it's not as simple as it sounds; people can't just snap out of it, because if they could, they would. It's a highly tailored approach to the ongoing assessment in formulations about why a person does or does not engage in particular behaviors, and much of it is based on the seminal work of Pete Lewinsohn in Oregon Health Sciences University.

So, what are some of the goals and ideas in behavioral activation? Well first we want to look at those contingent if-then beliefs. But we're really looking at what are the drivers, or what are the inhibitors of behaviors. And we're talking about small behaviors, medium behaviors, large behaviors, behaviors by yourself, or with others. The goal is to increase rewards and problem resolution, and to decrease avoidance and rumination. We want to recall and remember that behavior slowly evolves, or in some cases, devolves over time. Often when an individual comes to treatment, their life has devolved to a particular point where they've become disconnected from the things that used to really give them enjoyment or support or love. We found that behavioral activation, in terms of the evidence, shows that it may be equal to the hybrid model of CBT in treatment for depression, and this is some of the seminal work by Neil Jacobson, published as early as the mid-1990s.

So what are some of the components, then, of behavioral activation? So we have an orientation to treatment and education, just like in hybrid CBT. We want to develop our treatment goals, again, not very different. We want to individualize the activation plans and engagement targets, so we're doing our functional analysis, sort of our formulation of situations and of behaviors. We want to have the individual go out and try increasing their activation. They're going to encounter obstacles. It's all grist for the mill. They'll come back, and we'll do some troubleshooting about why they had trouble increasing their behaviors or connecting with those new people or activities. We want to review and we want to consolidate gains.

Now, the other important part that I really like about behavioral activation, and I often borrow these ideas, is we not only want to increase activities, but we want to look for examples of maladaptive behaviors that an individual has learned as a way of coping. And a lot of times, people will use these maladaptive behaviors because they have an immediate reward, and it's not entirely obvious that they might have a negative consequence later down the line. So an example of a maladaptive coping behavior would be taking long naps in the middle of the day when they you're not feeling very good. Now, I don't mean when you're feeling physically sick. When you're feeling depressed, there's a natural tendency just to want to escape. A long nap can be reinforcing. It helps you to escape, but it prevents you from going out to do things that might be more reinforcing or connecting with your social supports. Another example of maladaptive behavior would be drinking alcohol when you're stressed. It is a depressant; it certainly turns down the stress response, but we know that it doesn't help you solve any of the things that might be causing you to have that stress response.

The last example I'll give has to do with the telephone. Telephones are ubiquitous, but oftentimes an individual, when they're feeling anxious, like Carol, depressed, like Maria, they just won't answer their phone. Over time, what happens is you train those people who call you to stop calling you because you never answer, and then you feel more isolated. So, in behavioral activation, we increase those positive behaviors and we decrease those negative or maladaptive behaviors.

They use an acronym to remind us about the steps that an individual would need to take. It's called ACTION, where the A stands for the assessment. C stands for choose a new behavior. T, try the chosen behavior. I, integrate it into your new routine; we want to create new habits that are long lasting even after the therapy ends. O, we want to observe the results: What was the effect on mood, on energy, other symptoms that might be of interest? And N, it's never give up. Even if it doesn't work the first, second, or third time, it's all grist for the mill, and we'll be able to change it later. So in summary, we've seen that short-term CBT, usually in groups, but it can be in individual settings as well, can be effective in promoting forgiveness of others or in promoting forgiveness of the self. We know that behavioral activation, and presumably its link to depression, can be helpful in pathological grief.

Let's end by addressing one of our frequently asked questions. How well do CBT and religion mix? CBT is all about rationality, and religion is often about faith. The two seem kind of opposite. Great question. And it's true that CBT is a secular approach, grounded in Western empiricism and rationality, and faith is something that's very much different. But remember that the CBT approach is based on things like Socratic questioning. It's based on a scholarly look at life and at things that need to be examined. It specifically focuses on how we oftentimes jump to conclusions; we use habits of mind in ways that hurt ourselves or hurt others. If our religion, if our religious beliefs or our faith are helpful to ourselves, are helpful to others, you probably wouldn't turn that CBT lens on it in the first place.

So in our next lecture, we'll continue along these lines and talk about CBT and finding perspective and finding meaning. Thank you.

Digging Deep and Finding Meaning
Lecture 13

This lecture moves past finding explanations for why events have happened and begins to consider what those events mean in our broader perspective and how our reactions can be intentionally shaped depending on our personal values. Shifts in mood states are beneficial to a healthy relationship. Sometimes larger changes to perspectives or attitudes are necessary to meaningfully change our quality of life. In this lecture, you will learn how CBT can provide tools to support those shifts in perspective and meaning.

Finding and Maintaining Perspective

- We've all been knocked to our knees, and we've all had trouble standing back up. We need to find perspective, we need to be present, and we need to connect to meaning. Meaning is constructed—it is actively built—and we can be its architect.

- How can we adopt or maintain a constructive and balanced perspective? The very nature of loss or trauma is that we develop tunnel vision. We become focused on the event. We want to understand it for a variety of reasons—to prevent it, to solve it, to absolve ourselves from blame—but finding perspective means broadening our vision.

- Finding perspective means considering our life course, our families, and our communities and recalling events both tragic and triumphant that we have survived or even grown from. It's not about discounting; it's about adopting a bigger picture and remembering that sometimes today's low point sets us up for tomorrow's high.

- At first, this might seem like the ultimate exercise in cold rationality or maybe even sophistry. The timing is critical, because we all need time to experience our loss and grieve, but then we need to find perspective and construct meaning. Eventually, the calculus has to be done: What does this mean? How bad is it? Can I survive this? The event has to be put into perspective.

- To put an event into perspective, we need to place it on a personal timeline. Is it the worst or best event we've ever experienced? Where does it occur in our life course? Is the outcome of the event likely to remain the same? Is our perspective likely to stay the same? What are other things that are going on that might balance what happened, or things that might happen in the near future? Have there been times in the past when all seemed hopeless but things changed? Have there been times when you thought you wouldn't make it but you did? Place the event in the greater context of family and community.

Systems of Belief and Meaning

- In part, we evolve systems of belief to help us find the answer to "why" questions and to provide instructions on how we should live our lives. Essentially, we tap into our own system of belief. We all have different systems of belief,

Belief systems help us find answers and provide us with instructions on how we should live our lives.

and there is no single right system. You might believe in karma or in God's plan; you might believe in the physical or scientific laws of nature. Often, these systems of belief, although they've been with us our whole lives, are activated following a tragedy or with a medical illness.

- Meaning is something that we construct. We get to choose how and where we find our meaning. Take a moment and just think about what matters to you the most. Is there a larger picture? Is there a grand scheme? There may or may not be, but we can all agree that we have values and priorities that bring us satisfaction, and sometimes we lose sight of these.

- To address this issue, try the acceptance and commitment therapy (ACT) values clarification, or meaning, exercise. The following are the core categories that are used in this exercise: intimate relationships, parenting, family, friendships/social, education/personal growth, career, recreation, spirituality/religion, physical health, and helping others.

- For each of the core categories, you rate how important it is on a scale of one to five (five being the most intense and one being the least intense) for you personally, and then you rate how you currently spend your time and resources. Do your values match where you're spending your resources?

- Karen Wyatt, a family physician and spiritual writer, tells us that there are five key components that we need to consider as we're thinking about meaning—particularly meaning in our lives following a trauma or negative event.
  ○ Perspective: Life is limited and precious. We have to acknowledge the fact that we're mortal and that life will end.

  ○ Prioritization: There is no room for squandering our precious moments of life. But identifying what does matter requires some thought, because our values change as life progresses.

  ○ Preparation: There is no substitute for planning ahead for some of the changes that will come, especially changes that come later in life.

  ○ Practice: Finding meaning in life requires effort, and that effort is best devoted to some sort of daily practice, such as mediation. By choosing to carry out a specific activity at a regular time every day, you can create mental discipline and focus, which are necessary skills in the search for meaning.

- Presence: Living in the present moment has become a common catchphrase, but it's important to be able to appreciate where you are and what's around you in the moment in order to hold on to the meaning of life in the present.

- Loving-kindness meditation, or compassion mediation, is a form of meditation that isn't just about mindfulness or presence, although it includes those elements. It's also about reminding us of our shared connection with others. For many people, it helps to reconnect them with an important source of meaning.

- Most simply, loving-kindness meditation gives people some somatic quieting and, hopefully, a compassionate way of thinking about others. But this practice also employs presence, focus, and, in some respects, mindfulness, all of which we believe are related to perspective and meaning making.

Belonging and Meaning

- An interesting study done by Nathaniel Lambert and colleagues in 2013 tested the idea of whether or not a sense of belonging was linked to an individual's having meaning in life. This study, which was actually four linked studies, analyzed 644 individuals.

- The first study was a simple survey study in which researchers wanted to see if there was a correlation between feeling like you belong and having a sense of meaning—meaningfulness. They found that there was a very strong, positive correlation. The more you felt like you belonged, the more meaning you felt you had found in life.

- In the second study, researchers wanted to look at this relationship between belongingness and meaning longitudinally. So, at the first time point, they looked at an individual sense of belonging and wanted to see if it predicted meaning at some point down the road—specifically, about three weeks down the road. Again, they found that there was a relationship.

- In the third and fourth studies, researchers wanted to manipulate an individual sense of belongingness. They primed participants with feelings of belongingness. They read stories, talked about social supports, and talked about social values. They essentially increased the participants' sense of feeling like they were connected and like they belonged to other individuals. They found, as anticipated, that by increasing the sense of belonging, they were able to subsequently increase a sense of meaning.

CBT and Meaning

- Belongingness and meaning might be different, but they do seem to be closely related to one another. But what if someone feels like they don't belong? What if they're isolated or alone? This is the situation in which you would break out your core CBT skills and begin working on both cognitive and behavioral levels for the individual.

- Consider some of the core CBT skills. Core cognitive skills might include journaling (starting to write stories), self-monitoring, and cognitive restructuring. We would want the individual to recall habits of mind, and we would want him or her to do exercises like the ABCD exercise or the dysfunctional thought record.

- There are also core behavioral skills. What activities help you feel a sense of connection? We want to do the behavioral analysis of why an individual is or isn't doing particular activities. We might want to do some behavioral activation to increase the prevalence of when and how the individual does those activities. We want to do activity scheduling. We might want to do behavioral experiments in order to test out particularly strong negative cognitions that cause the individual to feel disconnected from others. Of course, we will want to increase social contacts, hopefully along with intimacy. We might even want to add somatic quieting, prayer, or mediation.

Suggested Reading

Bath, Bohin, Jone, and Scarle, *Cardiac Rehabilitation.*

Frankl, *Man's Search for Meaning.*

Fredrickson, Grewen, Coffey, Algoe, Firestine, Arevalo, Ma, and Cole, "A Functional Genomic Perspective on Human Well-Being."

Hayes, *Get Out of Your Mind and Into Your Life.*

Lambert, Stillman, Hicks, Kamble, Baumeister, and Fincham, "To Belong Is to Matter."

Seligman, *Flourish.*

Questions to Consider

1. How has your personal sense of meaning evolved over time? Were those changes dramatic or minor? What caused the source of your meaning to change?

2. Try the ACT values clarification exercise. How do you rate in each category? Are you living your life in accordance with your values?

Digging Deep and Finding Meaning
Lecture 13—Transcript

PROFESSOR SATTERFIELD: Viktor Frankl tells us, "Life has a meaning to the last breath. The possibility of realizing values by the very attitude with which we face our destined suffering exists to the very last moment. He who has a *why* to live can bear with almost any *how*." In 1942, Viktor Frankl, a prominent Jewish psychiatrist in Vienna was arrested and sent to a Nazi concentration camp. His pregnant wife, parents, and extended family were also arrested and sent to other camps. He immediately noticed that some prisoners gave up right away, while others continued to struggle and survived even long after they should have rightfully died given their injuries and malnourishment.

Ever the psychiatrist, he couldn't help but ask why. He quickly understood that it was about meaning. "He who has a *why* to live can bear with almost any *how*." Frankl's meaning was his family, reuniting with his wife, imagining her as a light in the darkness. He looked for small joys—a sunrise, a bird singing, a farmhouse in the distance.

When the war ended and the camps were liberated, he learned that all of his family, with the exception of his sister, had been killed. His wife and his unborn child were dead. His meaning was gone. But he did something extraordinary. His meaning became sharing the importance of *meaning* with the world, of founding a new field of therapy called Logotherapy, and writing, according to the Library of Congress, one of the 10 most influential books of all time, *Man's Search for Meaning*.

In this lecture, we'll move past finding explanations for why events have happened and begin to think about what those events mean in our broader perspective and how our reactions can be intentionally shaped depending on our personal values. Shifts and mood states are beneficial to a healthy relationship. Sometimes larger changes to perspectives or attitudes are necessary to meaningfully change our quality of life. I hope to show you that CBT can provide tools to support those shifts and perspective in meaning.

As John Gardner puts it,

> Meaning is not something you stumble across, like the answer to a riddle or the prize in a treasure hunt. Meaning is something you build into your life. You build it out of your own past, out of your affections and loyalties, out of your own talent and understanding, out of things you believe in, out of the things and people you love, out of the values for which you're willing to sacrifice something.

So how can we adopt or maintain a constructive and balanced perspective? The very nature of loss or trauma is that we develop tunnel vision. We become focused on the event. We want to understand it for a variety of reasons—to prevent it, to solve it, to absolve ourselves from blame. But finding perspective means broadening our vision; it means considering our life course, our families, our communities, and recalling events both tragic and triumphant that we have survived or even grown from. It's not about discounting. It's about adopting a bigger picture and remembering that sometimes today's low point sets us up for tomorrow's high.

At first, it may seem like the ultimate exercise in cold rationality or maybe even sophistry. The timing is critical, as we all need time to experience our loss and grieve. But then we need to find perspective; then we need to construct meaning. Eventually, the calculus has to be done. What does this mean? How bad is it? Can I survive this? The event has to be put into perspective. So, how do we do that?

We need to place the event on a personal timeline. Is it the worst or best event we've experienced ever? Where does it occur in our life course? Is the outcome of the event likely to stay the same way? Is our perspective likely to stay the same? What are other things going on that might balance what happened or things that might happen in the near future? Have there been times in the past when all seemed hopeless, but things changed. Have there been times when you thought you wouldn't make it, but you did?

Place it in the greater context of family; place it in the greater context of community. In part, we evolve systems of belief to help us find the answer to *why* questions and to provide instructions on how we should live our lives. Essentially, we tap into our own system of belief. Now, we all have our different systems of belief, and there's no one right system. You might believe in karma. You might believe in God's plan. You may believe in the physical or scientific laws of nature, and often, these systems of belief, although they've been with us our whole lives, they're activated following a tragedy or with a medical illness.

Remember that meaning is something that we construct. We get to choose how and where we find our meaning. I would encourage you to take a moment and just think about what matters to you the most. Is there a larger picture? Is there a grand scheme? There may or may not be, but I think we can all agree that we have values; we have priorities, things that bring joy and satisfaction, and sometimes we lose sight of these. This next clip shows how Maria addressed this very issue.

[VIGNETTE START]

PROFESSOR SATTERFIELD: So Maria, I think next I would like us to try a different kind of activity. We've been capturing behaviors and even scheduling behaviors and activities. We've been capturing cognitions. We've been wrestling with cognitions with ABCDs and thought records and so on. This is a little bit different, and it asks us to take a step back and to think about values. And values are things that are important to you: beliefs, areas of life, relationships that you feel are of value and are important and deserve time, attention, and resources.

They call this the values clarification exercise because it asks you to step back and just think about your own value system in these different categories, how important they are to you. And then it asks you to think about how you currently spend your time, energy, and resources, and whether or not your time and energy is going to things you value the most, all right?

MARIA: OK.

PROFESSOR SATTERFIELD: The way the rating system goes, it's usually a zero to five. So zero, it, if it's in this, it's not important at all; and five, it's very important. In this column, a zero would be it gets no time, energy, or resources, and a five is it is maxed out in terms of getting everything it could possibly get.

MARIA: OK.

PROFESSOR SATTERFIELD: So why don't we just start up at the top? And we'll go through importance first. So for you, and there's no right or wrong answer. It's just what's important to you, and what do you value. Your marriage: so a zero to five.

MARIA: It's a five, absolutely a five.

PROFESSOR SATTERFIELD: OK. And parenting? So I know your kids are adults, and you have grandkids.

MARIA: It was very important to me when my children were young, but it's less important now, maybe a three.

PROFESSOR SATTERFIELD: Maybe a three, right. And once a mom, always a mom. Grandkids, sure, and family. And family really means the broader unit. So that would be brothers, sisters, cousins, nephews, nieces.

MARIA: I don't have a lot that are living near us, so I would put that a little lower, maybe a two.

PROFESSOR SATTERFIELD: A two, OK. So it's really about the marriage and your kids and your grandkids. That's a unit. The social category includes friendships, social relationships.

MARIA: Friendships have always been very important to me, and I think that's one of the things that I'm missing the most now. So I would give that at least a four.

PROFESSOR SATTERFIELD: OK, so that's a four. The next one is about career or employment, a job.

MARIA: My career as a teacher was very important to me. I loved doing that, but I don't do it anymore, so I guess at this point it must be a zero. I don't plan to go back.

PROFESSOR SATTERFIELD: So not important at this point. The next one is about education or maybe personal growth, learning things.

MARIA: That's always been really important to me. And again, that's something I haven't done much lately, but I'd rate that a five.

PROFESSOR SATTERFIELD: That's a five. All right. And recreation.

MARIA: Well, as I say, we used to sail. We used to dance together. We used to hike in woods and mountains. We don't do any of that now. I don't know what to say, really. I guess it's less important than it used to be.

PROFESSOR SATTERFIELD: OK. And I want you not necessarily to think about the actual column yet, but if with resources and time and stressors aside, how much do you value those activities?

MARIA: Well, let's say a three.

PROFESSOR SATTERFIELD: A three, OK. Next category is spirituality.

MARIA: What do you mean by spirituality?

PROFESSOR SATTERFIELD: Well, it's sort of a broad category. It doesn't have to mean organized religion, but it can. So a belief in a higher power and a higher organizing principle, a connection to something larger than yourself that gives you a source of meaning.

MARIA: That's hard to say. I'm not sure about that. I think in the grand scheme of things, we humans don't matter all that much, except perhaps to each other. I don't know. Make it a two.

PROFESSOR SATTERFIELD: A two, OK. And citizenship.

MARIA: Well, I vote, and I pay my taxes, try to drive sort of near the speed limit, but it's not very important to me. Give it a one.

PROFESSOR SATTERFIELD: And your physical health, and this is your health.

MARIA: My health.

PROFESSOR SATTERFIELD: Yeah, your health.

MARIA: Well, that's something else that I think is really important because if you don't have your health, you don't have anything. All of the rest of it is gone if you don't have that, so let's give that a five too.

PROFESSOR SATTERFIELD: This is a five. OK. So if we look at the things you value the most, we have your marriage. We have education and personal growth. We have your physical health, and your friendships are pretty high up there as well. So let's do the second column then. And again, you're rating not how important it is to you, but how much of your current time, energy, and resources go towards that category. So for your marriage, zero to five?

MARIA: It's about a six.

PROFESSOR SATTERFIELD: It's about six. OK, well, we'll give it a six. That is where it's all going. How about, we'll jump to the social. How about the social?

MARIA: That's gone practically to zero, I think. I just haven't had time, and I haven't been able to keep up relationships.

PROFESSOR SATTERFIELD: And education, personal growth?

MARIA: That's a zero too. I do a little bit of reading, but it's so hard to concentrate, I just can't think long enough to really learn anything new.

PROFESSOR SATTERFIELD: And how about your physical health?

MARIA: I'm not sick. I can still do things, but I don't feel as good as I once did. I don't have the energy. I feel many times like I'm in pain.

PROFESSOR SATTERFIELD: Sure. So again, it's the amount of time, energy, and resources you're spending in that particular category. So how much time, energy, and resources are you spending to improve your personal health?

MARIA: Well, lately, since I've been coming here, I've been trying to do a little more, taking a walk when I can take a walk, maybe two or three times a week, a short walk. Maybe a two.

PROFESSOR SATTERFIELD: Sure, a two. All right.

MARIA: Just coming here maybe gives me a two. I'm trying to get better.

PROFESSOR SATTERFIELD: And we'll just hit these others threes here because those are still pretty important. Parenting, how much time and energy goes to that?

MARIA: You know, I don't spend—I used to e-mail and text with my grandchildren all the time, and I really haven't done that very much lately. Maybe a one for that.

PROFESSOR SATTERFIELD: All right. And recreation?

MARIA: It's just about zero.

PROFESSOR SATTERFIELD: That's about a zero. OK. All right. We won't do these others, but you get the gist of how this goes.

MARIA: Yes, I see.

PROFESSOR SATTERFIELD: We're looking for the difference, so where the largest discrepancies are. So we have a difference of two here, four here, five here, and three here. There's only so many hours, and it's only so much energy in a day, as you well know. But I think in each of us, when we're not devoting or dedicating sufficient time to the things that matter to us, to our values, we feel that something important is missing, and you feel guilty.

MARIA: Yes.

PROFESSOR SATTERFIELD: And you not just feel guilty, but you're losing sources of meaning. You're losing sources of positive reinforcement or of pleasure and energy.

MARIA: That's true.

PROFESSOR SATTERFIELD: So if we're looking for the highest-yield places to direct some of your time and your energy, it looks like it's your friendships, education and personal growth are probably the first two places to go. When you see this, though, what's your reaction or thought about this?

MARIA: Well, my feeling is that I know I've been trying to do a few more things in the day, and I find that I can do a few more things because just doing them gives me enough energy to do them. I could call my friends. I could start being more social. I think that's a place that I could really start. I don't know about the education and growth. As I say, it's very hard for me to concentrate now, and I have so many interruptions and things that I can't control, so I don't know if I can do much there. But certainly, I could try to contact my friends.

PROFESSOR SATTERFIELD: OK. So I'm going to just put a star by this one. This is the place you're going to start. I think as you've mentioned before, energy is an issue. Motivation is sometimes an issue. And as we learned with the activity scheduling, sometimes action precedes motivation. So even if you don't really feel like calling a friend, sometimes it takes that leap of faith. Pick up the phone. Make a call. And once you've activated yourself to do that, you might find that you're actually enjoying it, and you're feeling more motivated once you've already begun the activity.

MARIA: I'll certainly give it a try.

PROFESSOR SATTERFIELD: All right. I'll hold onto this, and I'll sort of keep it in our notes. And we'll come back and revisit it. What we want to do is have you begin to sort of reshape and redirect resources. Obviously, your marriage is important, and caregiving is going to be a big part of what you do. But we also want to help you share that responsibility with other family members and with caregivers so you can take care of some of these other categories as well.

MARIA: OK.

PROFESSOR SATTERFIELD: OK?

MARIA: Thank you.

[VIGNETTE END]

PROFESSOR SATTERFIELD: I would encourage you to try the Act, Values, Clarification, or Meaning exercise on your own, and I think it's worth reviewing those core categories. And remember, for each of those categories, you rate how important they are on a scale of 1 to 5 for you personally; then you rate how you currently spend your time and resources—five, most intense; one, least intense. Do your values match where you're spending your resources? So those categories—your intimate relationships, parenting, family, friendships and social relationships, education or lifelong personal growth and learning, your career, recreation, spirituality or religion, your physical health, or helping others.

Karen Wyatt, a family physician and spiritual writer, tells us that there are five key components that we need to consider as we're thinking about meaning, and particularly, meaning in our lives following a trauma or a negative event. She tells us that first we need to have perspective. We need to remember that life is limited and precious. We have to acknowledge the fact that we're mortal and life will end someday. Two is prioritization. There is no room for squandering or throwing away our precious moments of life, but we have to identify what does matter, and it requires us to think, to dig, because our values change as life progresses.

The third element is preparation. There's no substitute for planning ahead and being ready for some of the changes that will come, especially changes later in life. And last, or fourth, is practice. Finding meaning in life requires effort, and that effort is best devoted to some sort of daily practice, such as mediation. But whatever activity can help you remember those sources of meaning and those values that requires the discipline and the skills you'll develop to find and hold on to that meaning. And last has to do with presence, of living in the present moment. It's become a common catchphrase, but if you'll recall our lectures on mindfulness, it's important that you're able to appreciate where you are in the moment, and what's around you in the moment, in order to hold on to that meaning of life in the present.

Now in this next clip we see an example of loving-kindness meditation, or compassion mediation. Now, in this form of meditation, it isn't just about mindfulness or presence, although it includes those elements. It's also reminding us of our shared connection with others. For many, it helps to reconnect them with an important source of meaning.

[VIGNETTE START]

PROFESSOR SATTERFIELD: And now what I'm going to ask you to do is just to close your eyes and start taking some deep breaths. And I just want you to focus on your breathing, just the sensation of pulling air in, maybe the sensation of breathing air out. Your mind's going to wander because that's what minds do. Legs walk. Minds wander. That's what happens. Just bring yourself back to your breath. If there's any tension in your body, just imagine yourself letting the breath blow it right away as you sink down into your chair, relax your shoulders, relax your back. That's it.

And continuing to focus on that breath and bringing your attention back, now what I would like you to do is to pick an image of a person, just a mental image. It could be your wife. It could be your son, whoever you'd like. And just imagine you're looking at that person. Continue breathing in. And now, you're focusing on that image. Now we're going to say a simple mantra, and I want you to imagine we're saying it to that person. May you be free. May you find peace. May you find grace and courage. May you be free.

MICHAEL: May you be free.

PROFESSOR SATTERFIELD: May you find peace.

MICHAEL: May you find peace.

PROFESSOR SATTERFIELD: May you have grace and courage.

MICHAEL: May you have grace and courage.

PROFESSOR SATTERFIELD: Now, I want you just to keep saying that over and over to that one image. May you be free.

MICHAEL: May you be free.

PROFESSOR SATTERFIELD: May you find peace.

MICHAEL: May you find peace.

PROFESSOR SATTERFIELD: May you have grace and courage.

MICHAEL: May you have grace and courage. May you be free. May you find peace. May you have grace and courage. May you be free. May you find peace. May you have grace and courage.

PROFESSOR SATTERFIELD: Now I'd you to change the image, and I want you to imagine you're looking in the mirror. So you're looking at yourself. And I want you to say those same mantras to yourself. May you be free. May you find peace. May you have grace and courage.

MICHAEL: May you be free. May you find peace. May you have grace and courage. May you be free. May you find peace. May you have grace and courage. May you be free. May you find peace. May you have grace and courage.

PROFESSOR SATTERFIELD: OK. Now if you could maybe just take a few more breaths, wiggle your fingers and toes a bit. You can open your eyes when you're ready. All right. How are you feeling right now?

MICHAEL: Very calm.

PROFESSOR SATTERFIELD: So physically, we get activation of the parasympathetic nervous system. So your heart rate, respiration's going down. It's sort of the anti-stress response that you're having. What was it like to look at those images and then to say those three things?

MICHAEL: It was much easier for the first image I found.

PROFESSOR SATTERFIELD: Who was the first image?

MICHAEL: And that was my wife.

PROFESSOR SATTERFIELD: Your wife.

MICHAEL: Much easier, and I felt immediately calm and positive, I guess good about saying those things to that image. It took me a moment to want to say those things to my image. But as I went along, I actually began to feel that sense of calmness and, I don't know. It's OK to say these things to myself.

PROFESSOR SATTERFIELD: Right. If you recall the work we did on the case formulation for you, when we drilled all the way down into core beliefs, and lovability and whether or not you thought you were lovable and deserving was sort of at the bottom of all of that. It's interesting that it was hard for you to say kind things to yourself.

MICHAEL: But it's the first step.

PROFESSOR SATTERFIELD: It's a first step. It's a first step. And as I mentioned, this is an exercise. It should be done most days, I would say at least five days or so a week. We ultimately shoot for at least 20 minutes, but start with five minutes. Start with seven minutes. Just do as much as you can.

PROFESSOR SATTERFIELD: I would recommend starting with an easy image like your wife or son or someone, and then include yourself. And you can even think about people that you've had conflict with. That gets a little bit tough, people that you might be angry with. And imagining them and saying kind things to them can stir things up a little bit. But you've noted just from a couple minutes that we were doing this exercise that it can really change the way that you feel physically and emotionally.

MICHAEL: Yeah, I felt that.

PROFESSOR SATTERFIELD: And you can learn something about yourself.

MICHAEL: Thanks.

PROFESSOR SATTERFIELD: OK? So why don't we put that as a homework assignment, and you'll try it out these next few weeks. Note if you have any thoughts about it or if you have any difficulties, you have any successes. That's all, like I said, grist for the mill. And bring it back next time.

MICHAEL: I'll do that. Thank you.

[VIGNETTE END]

PROFESSOR SATTERFIELD: So what do we hope this exercise will do for Michael? Most simply, it will give him some somatic quieting, and we hope a more compassionate way of thinking about others. This is especially important when given his history of anger. But remember that this practice also employs presence, focus, and in some respects, mindfulness, all that we believe is related to perspective and meaning-making.

An interesting study done by Lambert in 2013 tested the idea of whether or not a sense of belonging was linked to an individual's having meaning in life. Now, in this study, they actually did four linked studies where they looked at 644 individuals. In the very first study, it was a simple survey study, where they wanted to see if there was a correlation between feeling like you belong and having a sense of meaning—meaningfulness. They found that there was very much a strong, positive correlation. The more you felt like you belonged, the more meaning you felt you had found in life.

In study number two, they wanted to look at this relationship longitudinally. So, at time point one, they looked at an individual sense of belonging, and they wanted to see if it predicted meaning at some point down the road, about three weeks down the road, and again, they found that there was a relationship.

In studies three and four, this is where they reached in and wanted to manipulate an individual sense of belongingness. So what they did was to prime participants with feelings of belongingness. They read stories. They talked about social supports. They talked about social values. They essentially increased their sense of feeling like they were connected and they belong to other individuals. They found, as anticipated, that by increasing a sense of belonging, they were able to subsequently increase a sense of meaning. Belongingness and meaning may be different, but they do seem to be closely related to one another.

But what if someone feels like they don't belong? What if they're isolated or alone? Here's where you would break out your core CBT skills and begin working on both cognitive and behavioral levels. So consider our core CBT skills. So those cognitive skills might include journaling, so we start writing stories. We might do some self-monitoring. We might also do some cognitive restructuring. We would want to recall the habits of mind. We would want to do exercises, like the ABCD, or the DTR, the dysfunctional thought record.

We want to consider our core behavioral skills. So what activities are there that help you to feel a sense of connection? We want to do the behavioral analysis of why you are or aren't doing those particular activities. You might want to do some behavioral activation to increase the prevalence of when and how you do those activities. We want to do activity scheduling; you might want to do behavioral experiments in order to test out particularly strong, negative cognitions that cause you to feel disconnected from others. And of course, we'll want to increase social contacts, hopefully increase intimacy, and we might even want to add in somatic quieting, prayer, or mediation. So in summary, we've all been knocked to our knees, and we've all had trouble standing back up. We need to find perspective, we need to be present, and we need to connect to meaning. But remember, that meaning is constructed, it is actively built, and we can be its architect.

Let's move now to answer some frequently asked questions. The first: It seems like every time I turn on the news, there's a new disaster or a terrorist attack, or an earthquake, or a famine. How can CBT help us in the face of such pain and suffering?

My first reaction is an empathic recognition that life is full of pain and suffering, and of joys and triumphs, but there's no doubt that these horrible things happen. And CBT cannot provide us an explanation for why these things occur to innocent or to good people. But what I think CBT can provide, it can provide a toolkit to help us to understand the reactions that we're having, and if necessary, to manage or to change those reactions. I think CBT can provide tools to help us to remember to reach out to stay connected to our social supports or to our sources of meaning, so that even though we can't explain or prevent events, like disasters, we can at least manage the responses that we have to those disasters.

The second frequently asked question asks: While appealing much of the positive psychology stuff, and the CBT stuff in general, sounds kind of Pollyannaish, or maybe just derivative of the classic Norman Vincent Peale book, *The Power of Positive Thinking*. How is it different? It's a good question, and it's actually one that I get often, because when we talk about our toolkit, we talk about wrestling with cognitions, it's often when we're treating depression or anxiety, so we're lifting people up, and in essence, we are inducing or creating more positive emotion while we're decreasing negative emotion.

But remember, the goal of CBT isn't to put on rose-colored glasses and only see the glass as half full. The goal of CBT is to teach us to be fair to ourselves and to others, to teach us how to think of things in ways that are balanced and even. We want to think about thoughts as either being helpful or hurtful, and sometimes it's helpful to be sad. Sometimes it's helpful to be anxious. Sometimes it's helpful to think about the negative side of things, or if we've made a mistake, and how we might make amends. So CBT is about balance, not positive, not negative, but it gives us the tools to think about what do we need to do next and what would be most helpful.

So, for our next lecture we're going to move from the realm of positive and negative emotion. We're going to move from mental illness and mental health and psychiatry, and we're going to start talking about medical illnesses. And I hope you see that, even though we're talking about depression or talking about diabetes or cardiovascular disease, we still have an important role to play for cognitions and for behaviors. We want empower patients to connect with their providers and to be able to help in the management of their chronic diseases. Thank you.

Cognitive Behavioral Therapy and Medicine
Lecture 14

R ecently, there has been a growing acceptance of behavioral medicine—and specifically of cognitive behavioral techniques—in medical settings. This lecture will apply CBT skills to the management of chronic disease. Although initially developed for the treatment of psychopathology, CBT principles and tools have been used to understand chronic disease onset and to promote chronic disease self-management. As you will learn, for chronic illnesses, there is a strong and unavoidable role of behavior, as well as much room for improvement. CBT is a logical starting point to help improve the quality of care in medical settings.

Behavioral and Social Determinants of Health
- The biopsychosocial model includes biological, psychological, and social factors. If we want to understand the causes, as well as the contributing factors, of biological diseases, we need to look at the psychological and the social factors. CBT looks at the mind—cognition and emotion—as well as behaviors that might be directly or indirectly related to health and how much they matter.

- The skills required to practice medicine have changed dramatically over the past hundred years. The primary causes of death per individuals in 1900 were acute infectious illnesses like influenza or pneumonia. The skills of the physician were to treat those particular diseases or maybe even to try to prevent transmission of those diseases.

- In the current day, as opposed to acute infectious diseases, people are dying from chronic diseases that start slowly and build slowly—diseases like heart disease, cancer, stroke, or chronic obstructive pulmonary disease. All of these diseases have a very strong behavioral component. In order to practice medicine in the current day, it's not so much about infection prevention as it is about changing and understanding behavior.

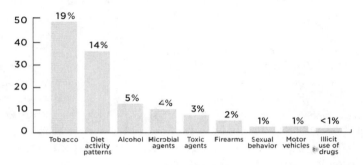

Actual (Distal) Causes of Death, Estimates for the U.S., 1990/2000

(McGinnis and Foege, JAMA 1993; Mokdad et al., JAMA 2004)

- In 2002, Michael McGinnis, Pamela Williams-Russo, and James Knickman published a paper in *Health Affairs* in which they broke down the determinants of health by percentages. They say that, on average, our genetic predisposition accounts for about 30 percent of our health. Our behavioral patterns (diet, exercise, smoking, alcohol, drug use) account for approximately 40 percent of our health. Environmental exposure to toxins accounts for about 5 percent of our health. Social circumstances (communities, education, income) account for about 15 percent of our health. Health care accounts only for about 10 percent of our health.

- In other words, the behavioral and social determinants of health account for slightly more than 50 percent of what is causing a person to get sick or stay well. Whether you're a patient or a medical provider, it would behoove you to think about the biopsychosocial model—and especially those social and behavioral determinants.

- By far, the number one cause of preventable morbidity and mortality is tobacco use (primarily smoking tobacco). About 19 percent of premature morbidity and mortality is attributable to using tobacco. A close number two comes in with obesity, the behaviors of which are diet, nutrition, and caloric intake as well as physical activity and exercise. In decreasing order, the rest of the list of top causes of preventable death is as follows: alcohol, exposure to microbial agents, toxic agents, firearms, sexual behaviors, motor vehicles, and illicit drug use.

- If 50 to 55 percent of premature morbidity and mortality is attributable to social and behavioral determinants, there is a tremendous opportunity for improvement. The challenge, though, is when life or circumstances get in the way. We all know that we're supposed to eat healthy and exercise, but do we have the resources? Do we have the opportunity? What are the competing demands? What is our level of motivation? Can we use cognitive behavioral tools to reengineer the situation?

The Chronic Care Model

- To help us understand why we do the things we do, even when we know they're unhealthy and even when we know we are at risk of having a chronic disease—we can use cognitive behavioral theory as an explanation and cognitive behavioral tools as an intervention.

- Some of the common conditions for which CBT has been applied include health anxiety, chronic pain, common symptoms like fatigue or insomnia, fibromyalgia, chronic fatigue, irritable bowel syndrome, and palliative care. With most common chronic diseases, there's always going to be an emotional and/or a behavioral and a social component.

- In 2005, about 133 million Americans suffered from at least one chronic disease, and by 2020, it is estimated that the number of people living with a chronic disease is expected to reach 157 million. About 50 percent of those people will have multiple chronic conditions, and each year, 7 out of every 10 deaths are the result of a chronic condition.

- The classic model is that prevention receives almost no attention in the medical community, so we eventually develop symptoms, see a doctor, and get a diagnosis of cardiovascular disease, or chronic obstructive pulmonary disease, or maybe even diabetes. We get a prescription, usually some form of medication, and maybe we get some education, and then we go on our way until our symptoms progress, and then we again see our doctor, who adds more pharmacotherapy.

- We know that this does work to some extent in managing symptoms, but the movement now is toward something called patient-centered care and patient empowerment. With this focus, it is not just about managing symptoms but about preventing them before they occur.

- An interesting new model proposed by Edward Wagner, called the chronic care model, is a shift in health policy and health-care system design in order to facilitate the prevention and management of chronic diseases.

- The classic model is that you have an individual primary care provider, and he or she is your primary—or maybe even your only—point of contact. If you need specialists, then you spend much of your time trying to arrange appointments and entering into all sorts of different health-care systems.

- In the chronic care model, there is a collaborative, organized health-care system of interprofessional providers, which includes physicians, nurses, psychologists, physical therapists, and occupational therapists. But there are also connections with an individual patient's community—connections with the patient and the patient's family.

- Part of the chronic care model is something called self-management and self-management support. The idea is that even if you see your primary care provider fairly often—for example, once or twice a month—that's still only 30 or 40 minutes, maybe an hour, in a particular month. You have all of those other hours in a month on your own, or with your family or community. So, we want to teach you how to self-manage your chronic disease when you're on your own.

- There have been many different innovations and trials to determine whether the chronic care model can improve the quality of care. Research has found that, over time, organizations have been able to improve their care coordination. We are broadening our team, but hopefully we're improving the collaboration within that team and improving power and empowerment for patients.

- Research on the chronic care model has shown that patients with diabetes had significant decreases to their risk of cardiovascular disease when the chronic care model was used. In addition, congestive heart failure patients were more knowledgeable, were more often to recommend therapy, and had 35 percent fewer hospital days. Furthermore, asthma and diabetes patients were more likely to receive the appropriate therapies.

Self-Management and CBT

- Self-management is defined as the individual's ability to manage the symptoms, treatment, physical and social consequences, and lifestyle change inherent in living with a chronic condition. Some of the essential skills for patients and patients' families include goal setting and action planning, self-monitoring of physical or medical symptoms, managing cognitions and emotions, managing the environment, and building and utilizing social supports.

- When it comes to self-management, there are three key areas that we want to help patients with: managing the symptoms of the illness or side effects of treatment, managing the stress and emotional impact caused by the illness, and managing and adapting to the functional impairments (social and occupational).

- In terms of managing the illness, we might be talking about managing common symptoms, such as difficulty sleeping, pain, fatigue, and nausea or changes in appetite. We might be dealing with side effects of treatment or medication that the patient needs to take. Common side effects include sedation, dry mouth, feeling that you're in a cognitive fog, or gastrointestinal distress. There are behavioral as well as cognitive strategies that might help an individual manage those symptoms.

- When it comes to managing the emotional impact, many of the same principles and practices that are used for stress management might apply. We want to see if the emotional impact includes depression, sadness, or grief. It doesn't have to be clinical depression—it could be subsyndromal, but the same behavioral and cognitive strategies might help lift an individual's mood when he or she feels the burden of illness. We also might want to look at anxiety. Is an individual worried or fearful? Is he or she avoiding things? Has the individual become hypervigilant of different symptoms that he or she might be experiencing? Are there other somatic manifestations? Here we'll want to use cognitive strategies as well as somatic quieting strategies.

- In terms of managing the functional impact, we might be talking about physical function. Has the individual's disease caused him or her to lose mobility, strength, or endurance? If so, there are behavioral strategies to begin rebuilding endurance. Has the disease affected the individual's social and occupational functioning? Has it affected his or her ability to maintain personal relationships or to perform normal job duties? Are there excessive or burdensome resource demands that are related to the individual's care, such as medical appointments, physical therapies, or medication adherence? All of these can be addressed through self-management and cognitive behavioral tools.

- In general, CBT can help with a number of mind-body factors related to disease, including anger or hostility, depression, acute or chronic stress, and loneliness or isolation. It can also help with behavioral factors, such as diet, exercise, smoking, or medication adherence.

- We potentially want to self-monitor blood pressure, blood sugar, sleep, pain, calories, fat intake, or medications. In terms of behavioral analysis, we want to use goal-setting skills. We want to build our motivation using cognitive restructuring, and maybe once we find obstacles preventing quality care, we want to use the problem-solving process of identifying the problem and testing out different solutions.

Suggested Reading

Andrasik, "What Does the Evidence Show?"

Barlow, Wright, Sheasby, Turner, and Hainsworth. "Self-Management Approaches for People with Chronic Conditions."

Feldman, Christensen, and Satterfield, *Behavioral Medicine*.

Kenny, et al, "Survey of Physician Practice Behaviors Related to Diabetes Mellitus in the U.S."

Levin, White, and Kissane, "A Review of Cognitive Therapy in Acute Medical Settings."

McGinnis and Foege, "Actual Causes of Death in the United States."

McGinnis, Williams-Russo, and Knickman, "The Case for More Active Policy Attention to Health Promotion."

Mokdad, Marks, Stroup, and Gerberding, "Actual Causes of Death in the United States, 2000."

Partnership for Solutions, "Chronic Conditions."

Perrin, Homer, Berwick, Woolf, Freeman, and Wennberg, "Variations in Rates of Hospitalization of Children in Three Urban Communities."

Satterfield, *A Cognitive-Behavioral Approach to the Beginning of the End of Life*.

———, *Minding the Body*.

Wagner, "Chronic Disease Management."

Wagner, Austin, Davis, Hindmarsh, Schaefer, and Bonomi, "Improving Chronic Illness Care."

1. What chronic illness do you have or are you most likely to contract? What self-management interventions are required (for example, stress management, medical adherence, physical activity, self-monitoring, etc.)? Is your primary care provider a believer in collaborative care? How can you get him or her to treat you as a whole person and not just as a disease?

2. If 50 percent of premature death and disease is due to behavioral and social causes, then why do we spend so few of our health-care dollars on behavior? What are the forces that keep us from doing this? What might change this situation and draw more attention to behavior?

Cognitive Behavioral Therapy and Medicine
Lecture 14—Transcript

PROFESSOR SATTERFIELD: Michael had his first big medical scare less than a year ago. He was at work, he was incredibly stressed, and he was furious at a co-worker who had yet again missed a deadline. It started with a slow burn, but quickly became a stabbing pain in his chest just behind his sternum. He started to panic when his arm began tingling. "This is it," he thought, "my first heart attack." He's rushed to the emergency room and undergoes a full work-up, and much to his relief, he's told that it's angina and not an actual heart attack. He got lucky this time.

Welcome to lecture 14 on behavioral medicine, where we'll begin to apply CBT skills to the management of chronic disease. Although initially developed for the treatment of psychopathology, CBT principles and tools have been used to understand chronic disease onset and to promote something called chronic disease self-management. This lecture translates CBT tools for use in medical settings.

Recently there's been a growing acceptance of behavioral medicine, and specifically, cognitive behavioral techniques in medical settings. And I want you to recall the biopsychosocial model. Now, in the biopsychosocial model, we had a Venn diagram of three intersecting circles. We had biological factors, psychological factors, and social factors. If we want to understand the causes, as well as the contributing factors to those biological diseases, we need to look at the psychological and the social, not a new idea, but an idea that seems to be gaining ground. Now, CBT looks at mind, cognition, and emotion, and of course, it looks at behaviors that may be directly or indirectly related to health. And exactly how much do these matter?

Now, it's important to remember that the practice of medicine, or really, the skills required to practice medicine, have changed dramatically over the past hundred years. All we need to do is look at the primary causes of death per individuals in 1900, versus, say, the year 2006. Now, about a 100 years ago, most of us were dying from acute infectious illnesses, like influenza or pneumonia. So the skills of the physician were to treat those particular diseases, or maybe even to try to prevent transmission of those diseases.

Fast forward to the current day, and folks aren't dying as much of those acute infectious diseases. It's much more about chronic diseases that start slowly and build slowly, diseases like heart disease, or cancer, stroke, chronic obstructive pulmonary disease. We know that all of these diseases have a very strong behavioral component. In order to practice medicine in the current day, it's not so much about infection prevention as it is changing and understanding behavior.

If we were to look at the determinants of health, so, what are the different contributors that cause a person to stay well or to get sick? We can look at an interesting paper published by McGinnis, Russo, and Knickman in health affairs in 2002, and here they break down the determinants of health by percentages. They say that, on average, our genetic predisposition accounts for about 30% of our health, a pretty big chunk. Our behavioral patterns, though, account for approximately 40% of our health; this would be things like diet, exercise, smoking, alcohol and drug use. Environmental exposures to toxins, to pollution, that accounts for about 5% of our health, small but still important. And our social circumstances, so our communities, our education, our income, account for about 15%. And health care accounts only for about 10%.

So, if you look at the behavioral and the social determinants of health, you're slightly over 50% of what's causing a person to get sick or causing a person to stay well. If you're a patient, or if you're a medical provider, it would behoove you, then, to think about the biopsychosocial model, and especially, those social and behavioral determinants.

So if we're to look in more depth that those behavioral determinants of health, exactly what kind of behaviors are we talking about, and how important are they? By far, the number one cause of preventable morbidity and mortality is tobacco use. This is primarily smoking tobacco, but really, it's any kind of tobacco use. And they estimate that about 19% of premature morbidity and mortality is attributable to using tobacco.

A close number two comes in with obesity, and of course, the behaviors there we're talking about are diet, are nutrition, and caloric intake, but also, physical activity and exercise. Rounding out the list are alcohol, exposure to microbial agents, toxic agents, firearms, sexual behaviors, motor vehicles, and then down at the bottom of that top-ten list are the illicit use of drugs.

So if you think about it, we have a really important opportunity. If we have 50 to 55% of premature morbidity and mortality attributable to social and behavioral factors, we have a tremendous opportunity. The challenge, though, is when life or circumstances get in the way. We all know that we're supposed to eat healthy. We all know that we're supposed to exercise. But do we have the resources? Do we have the opportunity? And what are the competing demands? And what is our level of motivation? Can we reach in with our cognitive behavioral tools and do something to reengineer that situation? So what system can help us understand why we do the things we do, even when we know they're unhealthy? Even when we know we are at risk of having a chronic disease? Well, of course we're going to take out our CBT tool kit. We can use cognitive behavioral theory as an explanation, and we can use our cognitive behavioral tools as an intervention.

So what are some of the common conditions for which a CBT has been applied? Now, of course we've talked about the psychiatric categories of depression, and anxiety, and anger, and so forth. But here we could talk about health anxiety. We could talk about chronic pain. We could talk about common symptoms, like fatigue or insomnia. We might talk about fibromyalgia, chronic fatigue, irritable bowel. We might even talk about palliative care. I think we can agree that with most common chronic diseases there's always going to be an emotional and/or a behavioral and a social component.

So what's the impact of chronic and preventable diseases? In 2005, about 133 million Americans suffered from at least one chronic disease, and by 2020, they estimated that the number of people living with a chronic disease is expected to reach 157 million; 50% of those people will have multiple chronic conditions, and each year, seven out of every ten deaths are the result of a chronic condition. Clearly, a very important area and much room for improvement.

Now, the old school model is that prevention receives almost no attention in the medical community, so we eventually develop our symptoms; we go and see our doctor; and we get a diagnosis of cardiovascular disease, or chronic obstructive pulmonary disease, or maybe even diabetes. We get our prescription, usually some form of medication, maybe we get a little bit of education, and then we go on our way until our symptoms progress a little bit more, and then we come back and they add in more pharmacotherapy. We know that this does work to some extent in managing those symptoms, but the movement now is towards something we call patient-centered care and patient empowerment. And with that particular focus, I hope we're moving more upstream, so it's not just about managing symptoms, maybe it's about preventing them before they even occur.

Now, an interesting new model proposed by Ed Wagner is called the chronic care model, and really, it is a shift in health policy and health-care-system design in order to facilitate the prevention and management of chronic diseases. So we know that most of us, in fact, probably all of us are going to have a chronic disease at some point in time. The old school model is you have an individual primary care provider, and he or she is your primary, or maybe even your only point of contact. If you need a specialist, then you spend much of your time trying to arrange those appointments and entering into all sorts of different health care systems.

In the chronic care model, we have a collaborative, organized health care system of interprofessional providers, so physicians, nurses, psychologists, physical therapists, occupational therapists. But we also have connections with an individual patient's community. We have connections with the patient and the patient's family. Now, the part of the chronic care model I want to talk about the most is something called self-management and self-management support. The idea is, even if you see your primary care provider fairly often, say, once or twice a month, that's still only 30, 40 minutes, maybe an hour over a particular month. You have all of those other hours on your own, or with your family, or with your community. So we want to teach you the skills, when you're on your own, how do you self-manage your chronic disease.

So, does the chronic care model work? And of course, there's been a lot of different innovations and trials to see if chronic care model can actually improve the quality of care. And they found that, over time, organizations have been able to improve their care coordination, and they've made an average of 48 changes in six of those core chronic care areas we've mentioned. They've found that patients with diabetes had significant decreases to their risk of cardiovascular disease when you use the chronic care model. They found that congestive heart failure patients were more knowledgeable and more often to recommend therapy, and they had 35% fewer hospital days. We know that asthma and diabetes patients were more likely to receive the appropriate therapies. So it looks like it's something that's promising. We are broadening our team, but hopefully we're improving the collaboration within that team and we're improving power, and empowerment really, for patients.

But what is thing that we're calling self-management? So, self-management is officially defined as the individual's ability to manage the symptoms, treatment, physical, and social consequences, and lifestyle change inherent in living with a chronic condition. So some of the essential skills for patients and patient families would be things such as goal setting and action planning. And I want to refer you back to our earlier lectures, where we talked about smart goals, and we talked about setting very concrete and specific action plans and looking at one-step-at-a-time progress.

We want to use the skills of self-monitoring, but here we might not be monitoring mood or social context as we have in past examples. We would be monitoring physical or medical symptoms. We want to look at managing cognitions and emotions. Remember that cognitions are related to emotions, and cognitions are very much part of motivation. If we're looking at motivation to change behavior and manage disease, we want to make sure that you have cognitions that are increasing your motivation and not decreasing.

We might want to look at ways to manage your environment. We know that the environment influences the behavioral choices that you make. So if you can make changes to your environment so that it's more supportive of healthy behaviors, then again, you're moving more towards self-management. And lastly, we want to help to build and utilize social supports. We know that individuals can manage a chronic diseases on their own, but their outcomes are better if they have at least one social support that they can turn to.

So I think of three key areas that we want to manage or to help patients to manage. And first, we want to help with the management of the symptoms, of the illness, or maybe the side effects of the treatment that an individual needs to have. Number two, we want to manage the stress and emotional impact that's caused by the illness. And number three, we want to manage and adapt to the functional impairments that might be caused by the illness. Now, I want you to know, we're not saying that cognitive behavioral therapy, or that self-management, is going to cure the disease, but it helps to manage the symptoms, the emotional and stressful consequences, as well as some of the functional impairments. So let's talk about what each of those mean.

So if we're talking about managing the illness, we might be talking about managing common symptoms, such as difficulty sleeping, having pain, having fatigue, nausea, changes in appetite. We might be looking at side effects of treatment or side effects of medication that you need to take. Common side effects include sedation, or maybe agitation, dry mouth, feeling that you're in a fog, or maybe having GI distress, again, as a consequence of your medication. There are behavioral as well as cognitive strategies that might help an individual manage those symptoms.

Part two is managing the emotional impact. So we've had a lecture already on the management of stress, and I think many of those same principles and practices might apply. We want to see if the emotional impact includes depression, sadness, or grief. It doesn't have to be clinical depression; it could be subsyndromal, but I think those same strategies, behavioral strategies and cognitive strategies, may help to lift mood when an individual feels the burden of their illness. We may want to look at anxiety. Is the individual worried, fearful? Are they avoiding things? Have they become hypervigilant of different symptoms they might be having in their body? Are there other somatic manifestations? And here we'll want to use our cognitive strategies, as well as our somatic quieting strategies.

And the last category was managing the functional impact. So we might be talking about physical function. Has your disease caused you to lose mobility, or strength, or endurance? If so, there are behavioral strategies to begin rebuilding that endurance. Has it affected your social and occupational functioning, your ability to maintain personal relationships, your ability to perform normal job duties? Or are there maybe excessive or burdensome time and resource demands that are related to your care or the need to go to medical appointments, physical therapies, or maybe adhere to referrals or even to your medications? All of these can be addressed through self-management and through cognitive behavioral tools.

So let's move to a more concrete example of a chronic disease, our number one killer, and let's look at how or where CBT might matter. So first we'll do a quick review of cardiovascular disease pathophysiology so we can see where to apply those CBT interventions. So if we're talking about the cardiovascular system, we're really just talking about plumbing and a pump. So, our heart is a pump; it beats at about 100,000 times per day, about 2.5 billion times in our life. Our pipes is our circulatory system, of course, the arteries, veins, and capillaries. And if we were to connect all of those end, to end, to end, the link would be approximately 60,000 miles. We know that our arteries are dynamic and responsive. They can basal constrict. They can basal dilate, depending on demand. The veins are really just tubes, and the capillaries are where a lot of the action happens, where gases are exchanged, where oxygen and nutrients are developed, or where waste is picked up.

The average human has about five liters of blood, about half plasma, but then a mix of different cells, red blood cells, white cells, immune cell, platelets, electrolytes, and mineral salts, all of which are important in keeping an individual's cardiovascular system, and body overall, healthy. Now, there's a lot of different diseases of the cardiovascular system that we could talk about, congestive heart failure, cardiomyopathy, aneurism, stroke, but let's focus on heart attack or myocardial infarction, since that's what was most relevant to Michael.

So, how does a heart attack occur? Well, essentially, there's a couple of different ongoing slow processes which may cause a either hardening of the arteries or narrowing of the arteries. Respectively, those are called arterial sclerosis or atherosclerosis, and often we will see that characterized by the deposition of lipids, of triglycerides, or other materials that built up in the artery and simply close the opening so that the same quantity or volume of blood is not able to get through.

So, some of the risk factors for a heart attack include, and you probably know many and of these, having hypertension or high blood pressure, what happens is that, over time, the high blood pressure causes more wear and tear to the blood vessels. In fact, it causes micro-tears, and those micro-tears serve as anchors to begin building a plaque that will eventually go on to clog those particular vessels. We know that high cholesterol, specifically, LDL, the bad cholesterol, contributes to cardiovascular disease, as well as something called a high C-reactive protein, a marker for inflammation. Behaviorally, we know that some of the risk factors include being sedentary, overweight, or smoking. Now, Michael isn't overweight, but he smokes occasionally, and he does have hypertension, and he does have high cholesterol.

Now the typical symptoms of a heart attack include sudden retrosternal chest pain, shortness of breath, nausea, vomiting, palpitations, sweating, and anxiety. It's estimated that about half of all middle-aged men and a third of women in the U.S. will develop coronary heart disease or cardiovascular disease at some point in their lives. But having a heart attack is not a death sentence, of course, survival depends on a number of factors, but on average, an MI (myocardial infarction has about a 30% mortality rate, with half of those dying before they reach the hospital. Another 10 to 15% die at some point in the subsequent year. That leaves more than half that need rehabilitation, and our hope is that rehabilitation is not just from pharmacotherapy, but includes behavior, and also includes psychological treatments and work with cognition.

Now in general, CBT could help with a number of mind-body factors related to disease, anger or hostility, depression, can help with acute or chronic stress, a sense of loneliness or isolation, or things like diet, exercise, smoking, or medication adherence. We've mentioned we want to self-monitor potentially our blood pressure, blood sugar, our sleep, pain, calories, our fat intake, or maybe how often we do or don't take our medications. We want to use our skills for goal-setting for behavioral analysis. We want to build our motivations through using cognitive restructuring, and maybe, once we find those particular obstacles preventing quality care, we want to go about our problem-solving process of identifying the problem and testing out different solutions. Let's move now to a clip of Michael, where we look at how or when he's taking his anti-hypertensives.

PROFESSOR SATTERFIELD: So next up, Michael, I thought we could talk a little bit about physical health, and the relationship between, specifically, your heart and your anger. And we had talked a bit before about how anger, and especially hostility, is related to cardiovascular disease. And we know that that's something you have. And it's something that you want to treat, as much as possible, both with behavior, with therapy, but also with medications.

And you mentioned that you're on a couple of medications. And I know for most people, my patients, but also my family, it's hard to take the medications exactly as the doctor wants you to take them. So tell me what medications you're on.

MICHAEL: Yeah. Yeah. I've got a couple. I've got a blood pressure pill, and they've also got me on the cholesterol med.

PROFESSOR SATTERFIELD: OK. So you have high blood pressure, high cholesterol. We know those are risk factors for cardiovascular disease.

MICHAEL: Right.

PROFESSOR SATTERFIELD: So we want to get those as low as we can. And you're on two pills already. So tell me how you are taking your blood pressure medicine and your cholesterol medicine.

MICHAEL: I try to take it. I would say I take it most of the time. I miss a few, I guess.

PROFESSOR SATTERFIELD: So is that once a day, twice a day?

MICHAEL: It's twice a day.

PROFESSOR SATTERFIELD: OK. So you do twice a day. And you take it most of the time. When we focus, then, on just the past week or so, how many times in the past week would you say you've missed your blood pressure pill?

MICHAEL: Maybe three or four.

PROFESSOR SATTERFIELD: OK. And for your cholesterol pill? How many times have you missed it in the past week?

MICHAEL: I would say, probably, three. Yeah, three, maybe.

PROFESSOR SATTERFIELD: OK. All right. So it sounds like in the past seven days, you've missed the blood pressure pill three or four times, and you've missed your cholesterol pill three times, or three days. So about half the time, would you say, you're missing it?

MICHAEL: I guess if I went back and thought about it each time, and really, yeah. It's probably close to half the time I'm missing it.

PROFESSOR SATTERFIELD I will tell you that you're average. So most folks that are on antihypertensive, a blood pressure pill, they have about a 50-50 chance of taking it, which is too bad, because if you don't take it, it doesn't work for you. And we know that blood pressure is one of those things that takes a while before it begins to damage your blood vessels and your heart. But eventually it does. So we want to try to get your adherence up to medications. But we don't want to jump to any conclusions about why you're missing it about half the time. So on the days you don't take it, why don't you take it?

MICHAEL: I guess, generally, I'm still forgetting a lot of the time. It's not necessarily at the top of my agenda of things to do. And maybe it's not as routine as other things that I do. So forgetting to take it. Sometimes I might be in the middle of something else. I think, it's time to take it. But then I say, not now, because I'll get to it later, another time. And then, I don't get around to it. Those are probably the most typical scenarios: either outright forgetting it, or just putting it off, and then never getting around to do it. I'll do it. I'll get it. I'll get it next time.

PROFESSOR SATTERFIELD: And then it doesn't happen.

MICHAEL: Yeah.

PROFESSOR SATTERFIELD: Yeah. OK. OK. So it sounds like it's mostly forgetting. There are other reasons. Sometimes people have side effects when they take it. Have you had any?

MICHAEL: I have not experienced any of the side effects that they talked about.

PROFESSOR SATTERFIELD: OK. So that's good.

MICHAEL: Yeah.

PROFESSOR SATTERFIELD: Another common reason: People feel uncomfortable taking pills. It makes them feel sick. Or there's a stigma associated with it.

MICHAEL: I really don't feel that, because I think that I want to get well. I want to make sure that my health is getting better. So I don't mind the idea of medication being part of that. Maybe somewhere in the background, there's a little resistance to the idea that I've got to rely on something else as opposed to on myself. But I don't feel that as a powerful factor here.

PROFESSOR SATTERFIELD: OK. All right. Other common reasons—and just to make sure we do diligence and gone down our list—sometimes it's about cost or access to the medications. Has that ever been a problem?

MICHAEL: That has not been a problem.

PROFESSOR SATTERFIELD: Not a problem. OK. And sometimes it's problems with the prescribing physician. So you disagree, or don't have a good relationship, or it's part of those dynamics. Is that part of it?

MICHAEL: Probably not as good as our relationship, but I don't feel that I would just say that because the doctor said do it, I'm not going to do it. It could be better relationship, but ….

PROFESSOR SATTERFIELD: So looks like the winner is memory. Forgetting.

MICHAEL: Seems to be it. That seems to be it. Or, if not outright forgetting, just putting it off, and thinking, somehow it'll take care of itself, or I'll catch up.

PROFESSOR SATTERFIELD: All right.

MICHAEL: Yeah.

PROFESSOR SATTERFIELD: OK. So we need to think, then, about some sort of mnemonic, a memory aid, that will help you to remember to take your meds. And what have you tried so far? Because I imagine you've tried a few things, and, maybe, they haven't worked quite so well.

MICHAEL: I really just have been relying on myself. I haven't done anything to putting something out there that's going to remind me this needs to be done. I guess I'm relying on the old brain.

PROFESSOR SATTERFIELD: OK.

MICHAEL: Which maybe isn't such a great idea.

PROFESSOR SATTERFIELD: It's working half the time. OK.

MICHAEL: OK.

PROFESSOR SATTERFIELD: All right. Well, there's different things that people can try. And some are high-tech and some are low-tech. Behaviorally, we are more likely to adhere to something if it becomes routine. And for many of us, putting on your seat belt, you sit in the car, the first thing you do is you reach over and you take the seat belt. You don't have to remember to do it, because it's become automatic. You just do it. But if you don't put on your seat belt, you get that little beepy noise that comes on. And so there's this external reminder that says, hey, you forgot to do something. So we want the equivalent of that with your medications. So what are some ideas? How could we make it automatic? And if the automaticity fails, what's that alarm?

MICHAEL: Yeah. Well, obviously, I could just program this into my devices so that I'm getting a reminder. You get a beep. You get a little message. You get whatever. So that would be, I think, the easiest thing to do. I could also, obviously, use the old-fashioned stuff of just putting notes here and there. Sticky notes, whatever. Those are things that come to mind.

PROFESSOR SATTERFIELD: OK. So we have the alarm part. I think for the automatic part, you probably want to link taking medications to something you're going to do every morning anyway. So you probably brush your teeth every morning.

MICHAEL: Brush my teeth. Have coffee.

PROFESSOR SATTERFIELD: So if you set the pill bottle right next to your toothbrush, it's a visual reminder that you need to do something. Some people pair it with breakfast. Or they sit it next to coffee grinder, or something. So just, again, visually, that it's there.

Sounds like you want to use, maybe, a smartphone or something, so that there's an alarm that just goes off. And you know what that alarm means. Of course, you have to make an agreement when the alarm goes off, you won't postpone getting the medication. So you have to take the meds.

There are some fancier ways to do it. There are apps that you can download that will even remind you exactly which medication, what dose. And you have to answer yes or no after you've taken it. And if you don't take it, it will actually notify your physician that you skipped a dose. So, maybe, a little bit more motivational.

MICHAEL: Yeah. That might be what I need, though. That might be exactly what I need.

PROFESSOR SATTERFIELD: Sticky notes are a good idea. The danger of a sticky note is you'll notice it the first few days. Then, after a while, it just blends into the background, and it becomes part of the landscape, and you don't remember it anymore. So what plan would you like to use from here on out?

MICHAEL: I like the app. I think that that's probably the thing that will keep me most responsible. It'll give me the reminder. And, as you say, it will also give me the little nudge, a motivation that if I'm not doing it, I've got to sign off. And if I don't, somebody's going to be notified. I think that that would be something that would get me into a routine.

[VIGNETTE END]

PROFESSOR SATTERFIELD: Now of course, medication adherence is just one category of interventions that we might consider, and in fact, there's an entire menu of which we might use our CBT tools. I would encourage you to, again, go to our friend, Google. Type in "Minding the Body" and "Satterfield." You will see a link for an Oxford University Press workbook called *Minding the Body*. And in this particular book, you'll see that there are four modules. One is on stress and coping specific to medical diseases. One is on mood management. The third is on social support, and social supports include family and friends, but what's interesting in this book is they also talk about how to mend or build relationships with medical providers. And the last section is on quality of life, and this includes quality of life as influenced by medical symptoms, by meaning, and also, by spirituality.

I wanted to mention just one other book that I think does a nice job of highlighting how we can import CBT skills into a primary-care visit. This is a book by Doctor Lee David from the U.K. It's called *10-Minute CBT*. Ten minutes because that's the average or so amount of time that an individual gets with their primary care provider. It gives a careful description of process and the skills required, and a little bit of the data on, even though it's not a full cognitive behavioral therapy session, why some of that structure and the approach can be helpful.

Now I think CBT is going to become even more important as we look at new models of care. We know with the Affordable Care Act that it actually mandates that behavioral health be part of anyone's insurance. Insurance companies can no longer say we're not going to treat your depression, your anxiety, or their substance use. The problem is, we don't have enough providers to meet that need, so we're going to have to teach a wider array of individuals how to do these CBT techniques. Patient-centered medical home is a popular buzzword; it's also about integration, very much like the chronic care model, and it specifically, again, includes behavioral health, but we need short-term, focused, structured, evidence-based interventions, such as cognitive behavioral therapy.

The last examples I wanted to leave you with was from the fourth edition of a textbook called *Behavioral Medicine*. In this particular textbook, they really highlight chapters on integrated medicine, stress and disease, depression, patient self-management, palliative care, and a number of other topics.

In summary, we've opened up a new and, I think, logical area of application for CBT, the realm of medical illnesses. For chronic illnesses, in particular, there's a strong and unavoidable role of behavior and much room for improvement. CBT is a logical starting point to help improve the quality of care.

For our next lecture, we'll stay on the area of behavioral medicine and tackle the always difficult topic of how to facilitate behavior change. Thank you.

Staying on the Wagon
Lecture 15

This lecture will explore the notion of long-term behavior changes, or changes that stick. First, you will learn about some of the statistics on change rates, and then you will learn about some of the leading models of change. From those models, you will discover some core concepts that are related to change—such as self-control, self-discipline, motivation, and willpower—and how they can be affected by some of the CBT skills you have been learning.

Changing Negative Behaviors

- Anyone who has tried to lose weight through diet, exercise, or other means is probably familiar with the frustrating yo-yo pattern: weight goes up, and weight goes down. In fact, evidence shows that nothing works really well for weight loss. The average weight loss is about seven to 10 pounds, and most people over a three- to five-year period gain all the weight back.

- On average, it takes about four to five attempts for an individual to quit smoking. If the individual tries to quit cold turkey, he or she only has about a seven percent chance of being successful. If the individual uses nicotine replacement therapy, such as nicotine patches or nicotine gums, he or she has about a 30 percent chance of being successful.

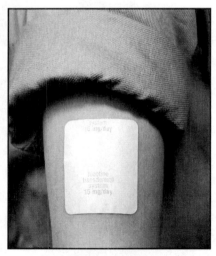

When compared with quitting smoking cold turkey, the use of nicotine replacement therapy increases smoking cessation success.

- Having a brief intervention from a medical provider can reduce your risky alcoholic drinking by about 50 to 60 percent. Treatments for alcohol dependence include detoxification or a 12-step program. Unfortunately, only 25 percent of the people who need treatment for alcoholism make it to treatment, and only about one-third of those that make it into treatment get better.

- Another example comes from medication adherence. In general, approximately 50 percent of medication doses are missed. It depends on many variables, such as the kind of medication, the cost, the availability, and whether or not your disease has obvious symptoms. Regardless of these variables, many patients forget to take, or just don't take, their medications.

- To figure out what's happening from a CBT perspective, the first thing we're going to do is gather data so that we can set a baseline of where an individual's beginning behaviors are so that we can start making a formulation, or coming up with an explanation of why the person does the things he or she does. Of course, we'll want to do a behavioral analysis. First, we want to select a behavior, and then we want to design a data-collection instrument.

- If we were going to self-monitor for someone with diabetes, for example, we might track his or her blood sugars, diet, and exercise. For someone who is overweight, we might track calories, fat, carbohydrates, weight, and physical activity. For someone who has chronic back pain, we might ask him or her to keep a pain diary, in which he or she records the intensity, frequency, or triggers of back pain and what makes it better or worse.

- When you're looking at your baseline data, you need to set your target. You need to decide where you should be and why. What is your goal? Should you set a proximal goal (what do I want to do next week or next month?) You also want to think about distal goals, which are the stars on the horizon. It's important to follow the rules of SMART goals: Goals should be specific, measurable, attainable, relevant, and timely.

- When you begin the behavioral analysis, it's important to think of recent examples of when you fell short of your goal. What happened? What were the circumstances? What were the cognitions? What were the emotions? What were the behaviors? What were the rewards? What were the punishers?

- You want to imagine back, you want to describe, you want to come up with some hypothesis, and you want to start your analysis. What happened? What were the obstacles? Were there any facilitators? What was the benefit from not acting? Was there any secondary gain? What are your most important goals and values, and can you change?

- Whether or not a person can change, and what causes a person to be a successful changer, was the subject of an interesting study done by the National Institutes of Health. They looked at the successful changers, a small subsample of individuals who were able to make dramatic changes, mostly in the realm of weight management, and keep the weight off for at least multiple years throughout the duration of the study. They wanted to determine the attributes, circumstances, or ingredients that those individuals have that others might be able to learn.

- The key ingredients were having realistic expectations, motivation and will, core skills (preferably, conditioned habits), and achievable action plans. The other ingredients these individuals had was support from significant others and from their environment.

The Transtheoretical Model

- If you're not motivated, how do you go about getting motivated? Motivation is simply defined as the activation of goal-oriented behavior. It can come from inside (intrinsic), or it can come from the outside (extrinsic).

- Some of the determinants of motivation include seeing high importance of the behavior, placing a high value on the behavior, having self-efficacy or self-confidence, and having a supportive social context or environment.

- To understand motivation, we first have to acknowledge that life is complicated, that change is difficult, and that ambivalence about change is the common condition. Ambivalence is the norm, so how do we go about resolving our ambivalence?

- The transtheoretical model, developed by James Prochaska and Carlo Diclemente, sees ambivalence not as an obstacle but as an opportunity. In the transtheoretical model, sometimes called the stages of change model, behavior change is a dynamic process that progresses through five stages.

- Stage progression is caused by utilization of 10 change processes, plus changes in self-efficacy and decisional balance—seeing the pros and cons of an activity, where hopefully the pros outweigh the cons.

- The current stage that you happen to be in should predict your future behavior, adherence, and intervention outcomes. From a clinical standpoint, your primary care provider should see how ready you are to change and then match his or her style and interventions to how ready you are.

- The five stages of change are as follows.
  - Contemplation: An individual is squarely in ambivalence—he or she can see the pros and cons of change but is not ready to change within the next six months. (An individual who is not at all ready to change and not really thinking about it is in the precontemplation stage.)

  - Preparation: An individual has decided to change but spends time building up confidence and resources to make change in the next month.

  - Action: An individual is actively in the process of change.

- Maintenance: This usually occurs after about six months of the action stage, although there is some variability.

- Lapse: This is the final stage. This occurs when an individual falls off the wagon.

- All five stages are arranged on a wheel because the model recognizes that most people can't just decide we are going to change, do it once, succeed, and be done. In fact, it usually takes multiple iterations. We move from precontemplation to contemplation, to preparation, to action, and to maintenance, and then we lapse. Hopefully, we learn something from whatever mistake we made so that the next time we go around the wheel, we have a better chance at succeeding.

Stages of Change

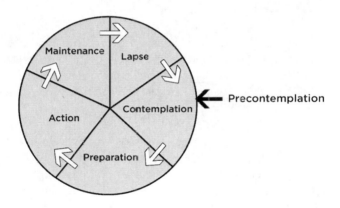

- One way to get yourself or someone to move into the preparation or action stage is a set of motivational techniques that has grown from the transtheoretical model called motivational interviewing. It was originally intended for health-care providers but has recently spread into the lay public.

- One of the motivational interviewing techniques is identifying and responding to change talk, which is any statement that suggests that the person has thought about a problem, as well as his or her need, commitment, or ability to change. When you're listening to another person talk about his or her behavior, the goal is to pick out that change statement and reflect it back to them.

- Another motivational interviewing technique is decisional balance, in which you talk about the pros of changing, the pros of not changing, the cons of changing, and the cons of not changing. Research has shown, across different behaviors, that we don't change until we see the pros of changing as outweighing the cons.

- A third strategy of motivational interviewing is called the readiness ruler, which helps us reflect and hone in on what might cause us to become more ready to change. The interviewer asks questions to provoke ideas of goals and values with regard to change but doesn't insert his or her own beliefs or value system.

- Various meta-analyses that have been done on motivational interviewing have found that across controlled clinical trials, motivational interviewing yielded moderate effects for problems involving alcohol, drugs, diet, and exercise when compared to other interviewing techniques.

- In order to facilitate change, we want to improve or increase self-efficacy, which is the belief that one is capable of performing in a certain manner to attain certain goals. People with high self-efficacy are more likely to view difficult tasks as something to be mastered rather than something to be avoided.

- We also want to think about social context. We want a supportive environment, including supportive significant others, family, and friends that help facilitate change. Health-related behaviors are highly influenced by people around us. So, if you make the decision to change, ideally other key people in your social circle can make that same decision. If not, then either change your social circle or give them clear instructions. In addition to social support, you might want to think about your social environment, removing temptations or triggers when possible.

CBT and Change

- How can CBT move us forward? The strategies we used all depend on the action plan that's developed, which in turn depends on motivation, goals, and resources. So, how do you develop an action plan?

- Action plans work if you first think about what resources you will need and put those resources in place. You need a very detailed plan with the step-by-step process that you're going to follow to facilitate change. You need a concrete and specific start date. You need to share your action plan with your social circle. There need to be regular reassessments to evaluate your progress toward your eventual goal. Importantly, you have to anticipate obstacles and expect setbacks and lapses. And you need regular consultations and adaptations to the plan if you're not able to meet those goals right away.

- Some of the CBT skills to use include having the right attitude, developing a hypothesis and testing it out, and evaluating success (or failure) and trying again.

- Inevitably, you might fall off the wagon. Often, at this point, cognitions come in the form of harsh self-criticism, which discourages us, depresses us, frustrates us, and takes away our self-confidence. We need to break out the CBT skills to challenge those harsh self-critical statements. Having a lapse is a normal and expected part of the process, and we should see it as an opportunity to learn something and do something differently next time.

Suggested Reading

Bandura, *Self-Efficacy*.

Burke, Arkowitz, and Menchola, "The Efficacy of Motivational Interviewing."

Duhigg, *The Power of Habit*.

McGonigal, *The Willpower Instinct*.

Miller and Rollnick, *Motivational Interviewing*.

Questions to Consider

1. Identify one health behavior you would like to change—for example, diet, physical activity, smoking, drinking, etc. Perform basic self-monitoring as a way to start; be sure to include frequency, quantity, triggers, outcomes, etc. After you have a week of data, consider small goals you could set.

2. Have you ever been successful in changing a behavior before (for example, stop smoking, lose weight, start exercise, etc.)? What helped you succeed? Are those lessons learned applicable to other behaviors?

Staying on the Wagon
Lecture 15—Transcript

PROFESSOR SATTERFIELD: Lose weight, stop smoking, eat your veggies, watch the carbs, don't drink too much, watch out for high-fructose corn syrup. You almost can't escape some kind of exhortation about changing your behavior these days. In fact, it's become a multi-billion dollar industry. And frankly, much of it is not evidence based. However, there is a science to behavior change. There's no magic bullet, but there is a science. What we can do?

In today's lecture, we're going to explore the notion of long-term behavior changes, or changes that stick. We'll first look at some of the statistics on change rates, then we'll take a brief detour to discuss some of the leading models of change. From those models, we'll identify some core concepts, and we'll look at what they really mean. We're going to look at concepts like self-control, self-discipline, motivation, and willpower. We'll discuss how each of these could be affected by the CBT skills we've already been learning. Now, before we go there, I want to share just a plea, or maybe a reminder, for understanding and for compassion. We all, at times, engage in behaviors that are unhealthy for us. And none of us sets out with a goal of being overweight, or having an addiction, or being totally sedentary, but life happens. Fortunately, there's something we can do about it. So, what are our chances?

First, let's look at weight loss. And for anyone who has tried to lose weight before through diet, through exercise, through any means, you're probably familiar with the frustrating yo-yo pattern; the weight goes up and weight goes down. And in fact, if you look at the preponderance of evidence, it shows us that nothing works super well. In fact, the average weight loss is about seven to ten pounds. And most people, over a three to five year period, gain all of that weight back, a little discouraging. There's only one exception to that, and that is weight-loss surgery, and there's all sorts of variations of bariatric surgeries, some which are quite extreme, some which involve bands, and there's a new one, which actually inserts a balloon and inflates the balloon in your stomach so that you have less room for food and food absorption. But regardless of the strategy you use, the aim is to lower weight and hopefully to improve fitness and nutrition.

How about for smoking or substance use disorders? Now, on average, it takes about four to five attempts for an individual to quit smoking. If they just go cold turkey, they only have about a 7% chance of being successful. If they use nicotine replacement therapy, like nicotine patches or nicotine gums, they have about a 30% chance of being successful.

How about for alcohol? We know that having a brief intervention from a medical provider can reduce your risky drinking by about 50 to 60%. We know that for treatment for alcohol dependence, there's detoxification; there's 12-step; there's all sorts of different levels, but unfortunately, only 25% of the people who need treatment for alcoholism make it to treatment, and only about a third of those that make it into treatment get better. Substance use, smoking, it waxes and wanes over time. How can we promote stronger and more lasting changes?

Another example comes from medication adherence. In our last lecture, we heard about some of the struggles that Michael was having in remembering to take his antihypertensives. In general, approximately 50% of medication doses are missed. Let me repeat that. Approximately 50 percent of medication doses are missed. It depends on all sorts of variables, the kind of medication, the cost, the availability, whether or not your disease has obvious symptoms or not, but hypertensive medications are a good example, and about 50 percent are missed. However, even if there are severe consequences, like you've had a heart transplant and you need to take immunosuppressants, many patients forget. Or if you have a glaucoma, and if you don't put one drop in your eye per day, you will go blind. Again, many patients still forget. What's happening?

So, if we think about it from a CBT perspective, we're going to roll up our sleeves, we're going to partner, and we're going to collaborate. And the first thing we're going to do is to gather data so that we can set a baseline of where an individual's beginning behaviors are and so we can start making a formulation or coming up with an explanation of why we do the things we do. Of course, you'll want to do a behavioral analysis, just like we did with Michael in the last clip when we were trying to dig a little bit deeper and understand what was underneath the reasons for him not taking his heart medication or his cholesterol medication.

So, first we want to select a behavior, then we want to design a data collection instrument. So, if we were going to self-monitor, say, for someone with diabetes, we might track their blood sugars, we might track their diet, their exercise. For someone who's overweight, it might be calories, fat, carbs; it could be physical activity, or all of the above. Or for someone who has chronic back pain, we might ask them to keep a pain diary, where they record the intensity, the frequency, or the triggers of their back pain and what makes it better or what makes it worse. Essentially, you were involved in gathering data on yourself in between visits, and in bringing that data back to your medical provider so that the two of you together can try to make sense of it and come up with some interventions.

Of course, when you're looking at your baseline data, you need to set your target. You need to decide where should you be and why. What is your goal, and specifically, your smart goal? You want to think about proximal goals, so what do I want to do next week, next month, but you also want to think about distal goals, that star on the horizon. Remember, it's important to follow the rules of smart goals where they are specific, they're measurable, they're attainable, they're relevant, and timely.

When you begin the behavioral analysis or trying to come up with that explanation of why you do the things that you do, it's important to think of recent examples of when you fell short of your goal. What happened? What were the circumstances? What were the cognitions? What were the emotions? And what were the behaviors? What were the rewards? And what were the punishers? You want to imagine back, you want to describe, and you want to come up with some hypothesis, you want to start your analysis. So what happened? What were the obstacles? Were there any facilitators? What was the benefit from not acting? Was there any secondary gain? What are your most important goals and values, and can you change?

So whether or not you can change, and what it is that causes a person to be a successful changer, was the subject of an interesting study done then by the National Institutes of Health, where they looked at the successful changers. And here they looked at that small sub-sample of individuals that were able to make dramatic changes, mostly in the realm of weight management, and keep that weight off for at least multiple years throughout the duration of the study. They wanted to see what are the attributes or the circumstances, or the ingredients that those individuals have that others might be able to learn.

So what were the key ingredients? They were having realistic expectations. So those smart goals, but also thinking about proximal or short-term goals that are realistic and achievable. They have motivation, and they have will. They have core skills, and preferably, they've conditioned habits. So for someone who's trying to manage weight, it's not a short-term project that you do for a few months, then you go back to the way you ate before. You're essentially changing for the duration of your life how you eat and how you exercise.

The other key ingredient was these individuals had achievable action plans. You always want to set the bar just a little bit above where you are now, in order to challenge yourself, but not so high that it would be discouraging when you fall short of your goal. The other ingredients these individuals had was support from significant others and support from their environment.

Now, I mentioned that they had motivation, but motivation can be sort of a slippery construct. And if you're not motivated, how do you go about getting motivated? Now, motivation is simply defined as the activation of goal-oriented behavior. It can come from inside, or be intrinsic, or it can be extrinsic, coming from outside. Some of the determiners of motivation include placing a high value on the behavior; having self-efficacy or self-confidence that you're able to do the behavior; and then, of course, having a supportive social context or environment.

So, how can we being to understand motivation? And I think, first we have to acknowledge that life is complicated, that change is difficult, and that, in fact, ambivalence about change is the common condition. Ambivalence is the norm. So how do we go about resolving our ambivalence? Well, fortunately there's a model that rests squarely in ambivalence called the transtheoretical model developed by James Prochaska and Carlo DiClemente. It sees ambivalence not as an obstacle, but as an opportunity.

In the transtheoretical model, or sometimes called the stages of change model, behavior change is a dynamic process that progresses through five stages. Stage progression is caused by utilization of 10 change processes, plus changes in self-efficacy and decisional balance, seeing the pros and cons of an activity, where hopefully the pros outweigh the cons. The current stage that you happen to be in should predict your future behavior, adherence, and your intervention outcomes. And from a clinical standpoint, your primary care provider should see how ready you are to change, and then match his or her style and interventions to how ready you are.

So what are those five stages of change? Well, for an individual who is not at all ready to change and not really thinking about it, they call that stage precontemplation. For an individual who's squarely in ambivalence, they can see the pros and the cons, but they're really not sure if they want to change; it's possible they might get ready in the next six months, but they're not ready. Stage two, then, would be contemplation.

Stage three is for the individual who's decided, OK, I need to do this. This is in my best interest, but I'm not quite sure if I have the resources. I'm not quite sure if I have enough confidence, but I would like to rally the troops, get my resources, and maybe make this change in the next month. That stage is called preparation. The stage that follows is action; so you have stopped smoking, you've started your diet, you're actively in that process. The stage after that is maintenance. Usually after about six months of the action stage, although there's some variability.

And then the last stage, which I think is an interesting feature of this model, is called lapse. All of these stages are arranged on a wheel, because it recognizes that most of us can't just decide we're going to change, we do it once, we succeed, and we're finished. In fact, it usually takes multiple iterations. We move from pre-contemplation to contemplation, preparation, action, maintenance, we lapse. We fall off the wagon, but hopefully we learn something from that mistake, so the next time we go around that wheel, we have a better chance at succeeding.

So how can you get yourself or someone to move into the preparation or action stage? Well, there is a set of motivational techniques that has grown from the transtheoretical model called Motivational Interviewing. It was originally intended for healthcare providers, but has recently spread into the lay public. So what are the specific Motivational Interviewing techniques? And I'll just mention three of them briefly.

One is being able to listen to and respond to something called change talk. The second is something called decisional balance, looking at the pros and cons. And the third is the readiness ruler. Let's talk about each of those. So first is change talk. What is change talk? Change talk is any statement that suggests the person has thought about a problem, their need, their commitment, or their ability to change. And the goal when you're listening to another person talk about their behavior is to pick out that statement and reflect it back to them. So in essence, you're steering the conversation towards that one little nugget that you heard in terms of change.

Here's an example. So I was recently talking with a patient that said, "Yeah, I know I should be better about taking my blood pressure pills, but they make me go to the bathroom all the time. It's just so inconvenient." So the change talk I heard was, "I know I should be better," so clearly they've reflected on that behavior, and part of them, at least, would like to change. So I said, "Tell me more about why you know you should be better." We steered the conversation to talking about change, and hopefully it will generate more change talk, more processing, and more thought about the behavior change.

Let's use a second example. And in the second example, we'll go back to Michael, our 50-year-old smoker who's working on his anger issues, but he's also trying to quit smoking. Now, he's down from a pack a day to three to four cigarettes every two weeks, but he's having a hard time letting go of those last few. He says, "I know I should stop, but I just can't seem to let it go. I need those cigarettes to help me cope with stress." Now, if you're listening to change talk and using Motivational Interviewing, you would hone in on, I know I should stop, and you would reflect back, Tell me more about why you know you should stop. So we've picked out that golden nugget, and we've steered our conversation right dead center to having him talk about change.

The other Motivational Interviewing technique we mentioned was decisional balance. And here you essentially take out a piece of paper, and you create a two-by-two grid. Where on one side you list the pros and cons, and across the top you might list changing and not changing. So essentially you have four cells. You want to talk about the pros of changing, the pros of not changing. You want to talk about the cons of changing and the cons of not changing. And an interesting behavior change study they've shown time and time again across different behaviors, we don't change until we see the pros of changing as outweighing the cons.

The last strategy is something called the readiness ruler. And here it just helps us to reflect and hone in on what might cause us to become more ready to change. So a question would be something like, on a scale of 0 to 10, how ready are you to stop smoking? A patient might say, "Well, maybe I'm a 3." I would say, "So it sounds like you aren't too interested right now, but I'm curious, why did you say 3 and not a 0?" I'm asking the patient to say what have they already noticed, similar to change talk, about their smoking, about their health, about their behavior that brought them up to the three. You can probably guess my next question would be, "What would it take to get you to a 4 or to get you to a 5?" I don't want to insert my own beliefs or value system, I want to know what's important to you in terms of your goals and your values that will get you to a 4 or get you to a 5.

So what support do we have from Motivational Interviewing? Well, in different meta-analysis that have been done, for example Burke's in 2003 in the journal of Consulting in Clinical Psychology, they found that across controlled clinical trials, Motivational Interviewing yielded moderate effects for problems involving alcohol, drugs, diet, and exercise, when compared to other interview techniques.

In order to facilitate change, we probably want to improve or increase self-efficacy or self-confidence. Now, it's essentially defined as the belief that one is capable of performing in a certain manner to attain particular goals. So if an individual has low self-efficacy or low self-confidence, even though their importance might be high and they're ready to change, they probably won't do it because they're afraid they might fail. So our goals, then, are to build self-confidence and self-efficacy by reminding an individual of past successes, or maybe setting very small initial proximal goals, so that they can have the experience of success, and they can feel more confident to take the next step and the next step.

We also want to think about social context. So we want a supportive environment; we want supportive significant others and family and friends that help to facilitate change. We know that our health-related behaviors are highly influenced by people around us. If all of your friends drink heavily, the chances are that you're probably going to drink heavily too. If you are a smoker, odds are many of your friends and family are probably smokers too. So if you make the decision to change, ideally other key people in your social circle can make that same decision. And if not, you might then need to think about contacts with individuals who can support the changes that you want to make.

Of course there are other changes other than social support. You might want to think about your social environment and your home environment, and removing temptations or triggers when possible. It's a classic behavioral strategy called stimulus control. So if you're wanting to decrease fat or salt intake, you make sure that most of the food in your house has low fat or low salt content so the temptation simply isn't there.

So thus far we see that you need motivation, and it can come from inside or outside. You also need confidence or self-efficacy, particularly if you'll play a big role in making or maintaining the change yourself. You'll also need to think about your social environment and how to possibly engineer things around you to promote success. But how can CBT move us forward now? Now, the strategies we used all depend on the action plan that's developed, which in turn depends on motivation goals and resources. So the important question then is, how do you develop an action plan?

Now, action plans work if you first thought about what resources you will need and you first put those resources in place. You need a very detailed plan with the step-by-step process that you're going to follow to facilitate change. You need a concrete and specific start date. You need to share your action plan with your social circle. There needs to be regular reassessments to evaluate your progress towards your eventual goal. Importantly, we have to anticipate the obstacles. We have to expect setbacks and lapses; it's all part of the process. And you'll need regular consultations and adaptations to the plan if you're not able to meet those goals right away.

So what are some of the CBT skills to use? Well, it's our regular tool box, but I think underlying all of that it's important that we have the right attitude. That attitude that it's all grist for the mill. Expect that things are going to go wrong, but then it gives you an opportunity to learn from that mistake. We want to have the attitude of seeing this as a challenge, as a puzzle. We want to develop a hypothesis about why we do the things we do, and then test out ideas to how to change it. So let's move now to our next clip, where Michael is talking about his smoking behavior.

[VIGNETTE START]

PROFESSOR SATTERFIELD: Mike, we've talked a bit about medication adherence as one behavior that's important to managing your cardiovascular disease. But there are a couple of other behaviors, too, that should probably be on our radar. We've talked about some of them before, but I wanted to check in with you. What health-related behaviors are you most concerned about when it comes to treating your cardiovascular disease?

MICHAEL: Well, outside of the meds, I guess it's the three big ones: diet, exercise, and for me, the smoking.

PROFESSOR SATTERFIELD: OK. So diet, exercise, and smoking. Which of those would you like to start talking about first?

MICHAEL: Why don't we start with smoking, 'cause we've had conversations about that in the past. I'm very aware of when I'm smoking. And I've got it down to really three or four cigarettes every couple of weeks. So I think I have made progress. But getting beyond those three or four, down below those three or four, to one, two, zero, I really haven't made a lot of progress in a while in getting there. So I'm finding that I still find that cigarette relaxing, every now and then.

PROFESSOR SATTERFIELD: Right. So let me first say, you've made a lot of progress. So you were a pack-a-day smoker for years and years and years, and now you're down, you said, to three or four cigarettes every couple of weeks.

MICHAEL: Every couple of weeks, yeah.

PROFESSOR SATTERFIELD: OK. All right. So that's going from 20 a day to three or four every couple of weeks. So that's absolutely progress. But you're right, there's no reason to stop there. Even three or four cigarettes are enough to raise your risk for having a heart attack.

MICHAEL: Yeah. And I guess I'm also concerned that the three or four, if I'm giving myself that leeway, maybe it becomes five or six, maybe it becomes a pack. So there's that concern.

PROFESSOR SATTERFIELD: OK. So why don't we focus on the three or four. And is that three or four that are spread out over two weeks, or does that usually comes in one day or after one trigger?

MICHAEL: It will vary. Sometimes it will happen as something triggers me, and I'll do two or three all at once. But I think it's more common, it's kind of spread out. And I'll say, I just need a cigarette now, and I'm going to give myself that break. So I'll take the cigarette, and that'll happen a couple, three times, so forth.

PROFESSOR SATTERFIELD: And just like with thought records, there tends to be an activated event or a trigger. And there are some thoughts about the behavior, which can make the behavior more or less likely. So let's think about the last cigarette smoked, just so that we can use a concrete example. When was the last cigarette?

MICHAEL: The last cigarette that I smoked, I was actually out of town on business. And I was at a meeting; it was a conference, OK. So I was coming out of a meeting, and this meeting, it brought up a lot of things that made me feel a little overwhelmed and a little stressed. Like, maybe these were things that these guys are talking about that I wasn't up on. And that triggered me to say, OK, just give yourself a break here with a cigarette to kind of chill out and de-stress.

PROFESSOR SATTERFIELD: OK. So the trigger was this work conference, and there were emotions of feeling stressed and overwhelmed and maybe out of your depth. And the cigarette was a way to cope with stress, but it sounds like it was also kind of a treat?

MICHAEL: It was a little bit of a treat, as well, yes. A self-soothing kind of thing. Yes, self-soothing kind of thing. Because some of the times, the thought processes is that, you've been so good that you almost owe yourself this little bit of candy, as it were.

PROFESSOR SATTERFIELD: I see. So that was the thought process. And did you do go out then? I guess you had to buy a cigarette or bum one off of somebody?

MICHAEL: No, I actually did; I went out and bought a pack. But I only smoked the one, and I've still got that pack. So this is the pack I've been working on for the last few weeks. But yeah, I did go out, and I bought a pack, and I smoked a cigarette.

PROFESSOR SATTERFIELD: OK. So let's talk about some strategies to help you get down to zero, still acknowledging you've made a lot of progress, but there's those last few steps that you want to get to. Now, given the infrequency of your smoking, you're not physiologically addicted anymore. So you're not going to have withdrawal, nicotine withdrawals, if you don't constantly keep smoking. So to me that says, you don't need the nicotine patches or the gums or the other things that I know you've tried in the past. You don't need pharmacotherapy. This is about behavior, and this is about emotion. So that's probably where we should go.

MICHAEL: Yeah.

PROFESSOR SATTERFIELD: Now, the first thing that comes to mind something we've talked a little bit about. It's called stimulus control. And it's hard to fall off the wagon if there's no supply, right? So you have a pack of cigarettes at home, which means the temptation is there. And if you get stressed or you want to treat yourself, then there's easy access to something. So what could you do about that?

MICHAEL: That would be throwing them out. Yeah, that would be one way of dealing with that stimulus.

PROFESSOR SATTERFIELD: All right. And what might prevent you from doing that?

MICHAEL: A safety net. Having that safety net there. Again, I think it's a matter of generally I feel, hey, I don't need a cigarette to deal with this. But there are times when I feel like maybe I don't need it, but I've earned the right to it.

PROFESSOR SATTERFIELD: Right. And you know, that's actually a thought that comes up often with addictions, and I'm glad you've brought it up. There is this fear of, what if something really catastrophic happens and I need that safety net? I need that one backup. Whatever the substance is, that backup drink or cigarette, or whatever it is, I need to tuck one away somewhere in the back of my dresser drawer just in case. So that's a real worry?

MICHAEL: That's a real worry. It makes it kind of sound seedy.

PROFESSOR SATTERFIELD: But it's a natural impulse. If you have relied on something for decades, in your case, just to let go of it, it generates some anxiety. Because now it feels like you're free floating, almost.

MICHAEL: Yeah, that's it.

PROFESSOR SATTERFIELD: So what do you feel comfortable doing? Throwing away the pack but keeping a backup, or would you like to not have a backup?

MICHAEL: If I'm going to get to zero, which is really my goal, here, I think I prefer to get to the point where I don't want that safety net around. It's more important to me to have zero tolerance than to have the safety. Does that make sense?

PROFESSOR SATTERFIELD: That absolutely makes sense. And I think that's sort of the most direct path to being successful, is to say, OK, just complete stimulus control, no buying cigarettes. Now, the next part is the function that that cigarette serves, and we want to find something else that can fill that same role. So it's partly stress relief, it's partly reward.

So what have you done, other times, because you're only smoking three or four cigarettes in a week? I would guess stress comes up more often than that. So what do you do in lieu of smoking cigarettes?

MICHAEL: In lieu of the cigarettes.

PROFESSOR SATTERFIELD: Yeah.

MICHAEL: I have actually done some light exercise, when it's possible to do so. Just getting out, even at work sometimes, if I've got an opportunity for a break. Maybe you are feeling a little stressful, maybe even feeling that need to go out and have a cigarette, instead 10 minutes, go outside, brief walk.

PROFESSOR SATTERFIELD: All right.

MICHAEL: Something like that. I've done that. Other things that I've done that have worked are really thinking about some of the things that we've talked about, in here, and just taking an opportunity to write down what's going on here, what my desire or need is, and breaking it down and actually separating it from myself.

So that's something that doesn't really have so much of an obvious reward element to it, except I guess I begin to think of it as, well, the reward is you're getting to where you want to be. So if it helps you not to smoke, then go through that process. So there's a couple of things that I've done in lieu of actually having a cigarette.

PROFESSOR SATTERFIELD: Sure. And it's interesting to think about rewards and punishments, for lack of better terms, for the pros and cons. And the pro of smoking the cigarette is, you get the reward right away. You get the taste, you get this sensation, you get the physiologic experience of the nicotine. The punishment, I guess, the downside, later; well, let me ask you. Is there a downside later, after you've smoked that cigarette?

MICHAEL: Yeah, you don't feel so great, really don't. You don't. It's all about the in-the-moment relief. Sometimes that's the most important thing, and you have a cigarette, but then you do feel not so great afterwards.

PROFESSOR SATTERFIELD: So in that moment, when you're tempted, to having the thought of, it's not worth it.

MICHAEL: It's not worth it. What's beyond it, what's on the other side of it. I guess I also should say that probably not so much, obviously, when I'm at work I'm feeling that. But if I'm at home and I'm thinking, I've got that urge, sometimes I do replacements that really aren't that great of things. Treat yourself to whatever, a scoop of ice cream or whatever it is. Yeah, sometimes I do that, I should admit.

PROFESSOR SATTERFIELD: OK. And I think that's common and all things in moderation. We know ice cream, even though not the healthiest in the world, in moderation, probably not a big deal.

MICHAEL: Yeah.

PROFESSOR SATTERFIELD: All right. So we have some ideas, then, about how you'll work on getting those cigarettes down. And I think what we should do so there's some accountability in reporting back is, maybe not next session, but in two sessions we'll check in again about your smoking and see if you've been able to get that amount down from three or four, maybe to zero.

MICHAEL: OK, let's do that.

PROFESSOR SATTERFIELD: All right.

[VIGNETTE END]

PROFESSOR SATTERFIELD: The last piece I would like to talk about is the inevitability that maybe things won't work out quite the way you wanted. You're traversing your travel across that wheel of change and maybe you get to the lapse stage; you fall off the wagon. And often what happens is we have cognitions, and those cognitions come in the form of harsh self-criticism. That harsh self-criticism discourages us, depresses us, frustrates us, and takes away our self-confidence. We can break out those cognitive behavioral therapy skills, and we can challenge those harsh self-critical statements. Having a lapse is a normal and expected part of the process, and we should see it as an opportunity to learn something and do something a little bit different next time.

So what do you need to change? What are the key ingredients? Well, we want to have realistic expectations. We want to make sure that we maximize your motivation or will to change. We want to make sure that you have those core CBT behavior-change skills in place, and preferably you're working towards having conditioned habits that are sustainable over the rest of your life. And we want to make sure that you have achievable, yet flexible, action plans, along with support and environmental help.

Let's end by looking at one of our frequently asked questions. This patient asks, "I've tried everything in the world to stop smoking, and I just can't seem to do it. My doctor tells me I must have some self-destructive streak, or an unconscious death wish. Is there anything to that? Could it be some sort of core belief?" Well unfortunately, I've heard this before. I've heard it in other contexts when children aren't doing well in school, and they blame the child, when people become sick, and they blame the patient. To me, this sounds a little bit like blaming the patient. No. I don't think it's because you have a death wish, I think it's because nicotine is highly addictive, and it's very difficult to stop smoking. You need support; you need resources, maybe nicotine replacement therapy. But together, with enough iterations around that wheel, enough support, and maybe some pharmacotherapy, you can successfully quit smoking.

So I hope you'll join us, then, for our next lecture, where we continue along the lines of talking about behavior change, but in the context of managing weight. Thank you.

Thinking Healthy: Weight and Nutrition
Lecture 16

In this lecture, you will learn about a range of weight issues, including weight gain, weight loss, and, more importantly, fitness and wellness. CBT—with its focus on motivation, cognition, and behavior—has quite a few tools to offer, and you will learn what they are and if they really work. In essence, it is really difficult to change when it comes to weight management, but the best chance we have is probably slow and steady interventions through CBT.

The Epidemiology of Weight

- About 69 percent of men and women over the age of 20 are considered overweight or obese, and about 36 percent are considered obese. The rates of people who are overweight and obese have been rising dramatically over the past few decades for adolescents and adults. By the year 2030, 58 percent of the world is predicted to be overweight.

- Using the biopsychosocial model as a guide, we want to look at biological explanations, stress and other psychological variables, and the social environment for ways to change health behaviors. Like stress, obesity is an epidemic. There are many environmental pressures to make bad food choices. But are we really behaving differently when it comes to food? And how are we supposed to be eating?

- Many people are familiar with the old food pyramid with the carbohydrates on the bottom, then the fruits and vegetables, and finally the dairy, meat, oils, and sweets closer to the top of the pyramid. The pyramid was revised about every decade until recently, when it was scrapped completely.

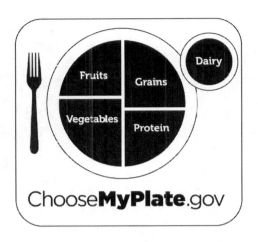

ChooseMyPlate.gov

- Today, we have MyPlate, and it's a relatively simple graphic—a bird's eye view of a plate with a little cup of dairy next to it. The plate looks like it's been approximately cut into four quadrants: one each for fruits, vegetables, grains, and protein. There are slightly larger portions of vegetables and grains and slightly smaller portions of fruits and protein.

- Unfortunately, people follow these simplified dietary recommendations only 2 percent of the time. And to count as following those recommendations, you only have to be compliant at 70 percent of your meals.

- The most commonly eaten vegetable is the potato, in the form of French fries or potato chips. The second most commonly eaten vegetable is the tomato, in the form of ketchup or pizza or pasta sauce. The third most commonly eaten vegetable is onions, and the fourth is iceberg lettuce, which is mostly water with little nutritional value.

- Why are we not making very good food choices in terms of what we eat? It might be partly ignorance—but that can't be all.

- About 60 percent of U.S. adults don't exercise regularly. But about 73 percent believe that they're in fair to excellent physical condition. About 25 percent of the population is sedentary, and it's estimated that this costs the U.S. health-care system 76 billion dollars per year.

- It's tempting to attribute our rising overweight and obesity rates to a failure in willpower—some sort of decline in character—but think of it in another way: If you gave a test to 100 people and 70 of them failed, would you assume that they were all lazy or lacked willpower, or would you begin to wonder about that test and what made it so difficult?

Energy Balance and Weight Loss
- Energy balance is the key to the regulation of body weight—calories taken in versus calories burned off. But it really isn't that simple, because our rate of energy expenditure or metabolism might vary.

- Energy expenditure occurs in three different ways: basal metabolic rate (about 60 percent of the total calories burned); thermic effect of food, which is the energy it takes to eat and digest your food (about 10 percent of the total); and activity thermogenesis, which is the calories burned from physical activity and exercise (about 30 percent of the total).

- The high percentage of our basal metabolic rate is partly why losing weight is so difficult. The body slows our metabolic rate when we're dieting. Our metabolic rate also slows as we age—in part due to the loss of lean muscle mass that burns calories much more quickly. So, as we age, it gets harder and harder to keep the weight off, and the more we diet, the more we run the risk of slowing down our metabolism.

- In addition, our food environment and even our culture make it extremely difficult to make good food choices. Think about your own family or cultural experience. Food is often tied with celebrations (birthdays) or holidays (Thanksgiving). It's also tied symbolically to feeling cared for or loved.

- Of course, those familial and cultural influences occur in a broader environment that influence our choices. This is partly about socioeconomic status, but there also are broader social influences. For example, about 50 million people eat at McDonald's per day, and one-quarter of the nation's vegetable consumption is French fries.

- In 1970, about 26 percent of our food dollars were spent eating out. That has increased to about 41 percent in 2005. Our portion sizes also have changed dramatically in the past 20 years. The National Heart, Lung, and Blood Institute reports that two pieces of pizza used to be around 500 calories, and now it's about 850 calories, for example.

- About 50,000 schools serve fast food for lunch. Physical education has been cut; it's no longer mandatory in many schools. The average child has spent more hours watching television than going to school by the time he or she graduates from high school. And children are on the Internet much more than they watch television.

- When we're stressed, it affects our food choices and our motivation to exercise. When we're stressed, 65 percent of us eat more candy or chocolate, 56 percent eat more ice cream, 53 percent eat more potatoes or corn chips, 49 percent eat more cookies, and only 8 percent eat more vegetables.

- What are some of the implications? We might need to think about reengineering food availability and changing our habits of how we respond to stress. We might want to limit our exposures to bad food. We might want to think about other stress-reduction strategies to manage our moods that don't involve reaching for candy or cookies. When we're stressed, we need to schedule an increased amount of time to sleep, and we need to exercise more, not less.

Overweight and Obesity among Adults Age 20 and Older

United States, 2009–2010

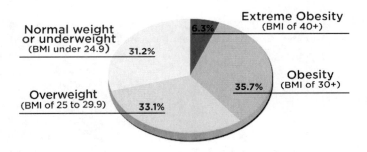

Normal weight or underweight (BMI under 24.9) — 31.2%

Overweight (BMI of 25 to 29.9) — 33.1%

Extreme Obesity (BMI of 40+) — 6.3%

Obesity (BMI of 30+) — 35.7%

CBT for Exercising and Dieting

- The National Institutes of Health did a meta-analysis of 48 randomized controlled trials, in which they found that there was an average weight loss of eight percent over a period of one year. At a three- to five-year follow-up, there was zero weight loss.

- More realistic initial goals for weight loss are to be as fit as possible at your current weight and not to worry so much about the number and to prevent further weight gain as you get older. If you can be successful at the first two, then the third goal should be to begin weight loss.

- Both dieting and exercise are important, but if your goal is to lose pounds, dieting will probably get you there quicker than exercise will. Ideally, you would do a little bit of both.

- Some of the skills that are helpful when dieting include self-monitoring (knowing your baseline, or where you're starting), stimulus control (removing temptation from your environment), cognitive restructuring (what thoughts do you have when you're deciding what to eat or what not to eat?), and motivational enhancement (such as motivational interviewing in the transtheoretical model).

- There are a number of well-designed CBT programs for weight management and physical activity, but most of them have been shown to have fairly modest effect sizes. One of the best models comes from Judy Beck, daughter of Aaron T. Beck, the father of CBT. In her book *The Beck Diet Solution*, she plans out a 42-day action plan to help individuals realize their exercise and weight-loss goals.

- The plan starts with self-monitoring and a behavioral analysis. What really makes you eat? Why do you really want to lose weight? How do you think like a thin person? This moves you into the realm of cognitive restructuring.

- Some of the habits that she talks about include paying attention to what foods you select at the grocery store, taking time to plan and prepare meals, thinking about the choices you're making, serving food on smaller plates, eating slower and without distraction, and pausing for 20 minutes after a serving before you decide you need more.

Taking the time to plan meals is a good habit to have when you are trying to manage your weight.

- More than 100 studies on weight loss and CBT have been conducted, all testing slight variations on the model or populations and all having behavioral interventions as number one and cognitive interventions as number two.

- For example, in 2012, Eduardo Pimento conducted an international study looking at a small sample of middle-aged women. They used an eight-week randomized controlled trial of CBT and were able to show decreased weight, decreased body mass index, decreased waist circumference, and improved eating habits. But the effects were modest.

- In 2011, Denise Wilfley and colleagues conducted a comprehensive literature review focusing on children and adolescents. They used behavior therapy supplemented with cognitive restructuring, and they found that this combination was the strongest nonmedical treatment for children and adolescents. They used self-monitoring and stimulus control, both of which are invaluable behavioral components.

- The U.S. Preventive Services Task Force recommends multimodal approaches to weight management and specifically lists CBT as a core ingredient.

- A number of large longitudinal studies have shown that it's not just about fat—it's also about fit. An overweight but fit person is much better off than a thin person who is unfit. In fact, even small improvements in fitness can have substantial benefits.

- There are many benefits of physical activity. It increases in cardiorespiratory fitness, reduces morality, decreases risk of chronic diseases (such as cardiovascular disease, hypertension, diabetes), and increases psychological well-being.

- Greater health benefits are associated with greater levels of activity, but exercise does not need be intense or prolonged to be beneficial. If possible, you should aim for 60 to 90 percent of your maximum heart rate; you can derive your maximum heart rate by subtracting your age from the number 220. The greatest relative benefit may be gained by previously sedentary people becoming even slightly active.

- In 2011, Chi Pang Wen and colleagues published by a study of 416,000 subjects that were followed over a period of eight years. In this study, they found that inactive people who increased their physical activity by just 15 minutes per day reduced their risk of death by 14 percent and increased their life expectancy by three years. Each additional 15 minutes of exercised lowered their risk by an additional four percent.

Suggested Reading

American Dietetic Association, *Complete Food and Nutrition Guide.*

Beck, *The Beck Diet Solution.*

Flegal, Carroll, Ogden, and Curtin, "Prevalence and Trends in Obesity among U.S. Adults."

Franz, VanWormer, Crain, Boucher, Histon, Caplan, Bowman, and Pronk, "Weight-Loss Outcomes."

Gardner, Kiazand, Alhassan, Kim, Stafford, Balise, Kraemer, and King, "Comparison of the Atkins, Zone, Ornish, and LEARN Diets for Change in Weight and Related Risk Factors among Overweight Premenopausal Women."

Jacobs, Newton, Wang, Patel, McCullough, Campbell, Thun, and Gapstur, "Waist Circumference and All-Cause Mortality in a Large U.S. Cohort."

Pimenta, Leal, Maroco, and Ramos, "Brief Cognitive-Behavioral Therapy for Weight Loss in Midlife Women."

Wen, Wai, Tsai, Yang, Cheng, Lee, Chan, Tsao, Tsai, and Wu, "Minimum Amount of Physical Activity for Reduced Mortality and Extended Life Expectancy."

Wildman, Muntner, Reynolds, McGinn, Rajpathak, Wylie-Rosett, and Sowers, "The Obese without Cardiometabolic Risk Factor Clustering and the Normal Weight with Cardiometabolic Risk Factor Clustering."

Wilfley, Kolko, and Kass, "Cognitive Behavioral Therapy for Weight Management and Eating Disorders in Children and Adolescents."

1. More than two-thirds of the U.S. population is now overweight or obese, despite the billions we spend on healthy foods, diets, gyms, personal trainers, technological gadgets, etc. What would be the most effective and efficient intervention to address this problem? Justify your choice, and consider the pros and cons of what you recommend.

2. The rate of increase for childhood obesity has leveled off in recent years. What do you think caused this success? Why hasn't it worked for adults?

Thinking Healthy: Weight and Nutrition
Lecture 16—Transcript

PROFESSOR SATTERFIELD: Nearly 70% of Americans have it. About 40% of us are trying to change it. We spend a collective total of nearly $500 billion per year on it. It's been closely linked to heart disease, stroke, cancer, and early death. What are we talking about? We're talking about being overweight or obese. We're obsessed with fatness, and to a lesser extent, fitness. But this obsession has done little to stop what is being called an epidemic obesity. What is going on? In this installment, we'll tackle this and other vexing questions regarding weight, weight gain, weight loss, and I think more importantly, fitness and wellness. CBT, with its focus on motivation, cognition, and behavior, has quite a few tools to offer. Let's see what they are and if they really work.

So first we'll want to calibrate our language, our terminology, and I want to talk just a little bit about the epidemiology of weight. Now, the number we most commonly see is our weight in pounds. In a medical setting, we'll often use something called the BMI, or the body mass index. Your body mass index is simply proportion of your weight to your height, and specifically, it's your weight in kilograms divided by your height in meters squared. Since that's an awful lot of math to do in your head, the easiest way to figure your BMI is to go online, type in BMI calculator. You can enter in your weight in pounds and your height in feet and inches, and there you'll get a number.

An alternative to BMI is something called waist-to-hip ratio, or the gut-to-butt ratio. The goal is that, for men, your waist-to-hip ratio would be less than .95, and for women, it would be less than .80. For individuals who have a BMI between 18.5 and 24.9, that's considered what's called a normal body mass index, or a normal weight. For folks from 25 up to 29.9, that's considered overweight. And anyone 30 and above, is considered obese.

In terms of the epidemiology, we know that about 69% of men and women over the age of 20 are considered overweight or obese, that's 25 and above; and 36% are considered obese, or a BMI of 30 or higher. We know that the rates of overweight and obesity have been rising dramatically over the past couple of decades for adolescents and for adults. And we believe by the year 2030 that a full 58% of the world is predicted to be overweight.

So when we hear statistics like this, I hope that you've developed the habit to step back and start thinking about a formulation, to start thinking about behavioral and analysis. And I would recommend that we could go back and use our model—the biopsychosocial model. So we would want to look for biological hypotheses. We would want to look at psychological hypotheses, such as stress or other psych variables. And we would also want to look at social relationships and the social environment.

So we've already talked a good bit about stress. We know that it, too, is an epidemic, and we also know that there are many environmental pressures to make bad food choices, but are we really behaving differently when it comes to food, and how are we supposed to be eating? So let's take a look at nutrition statistics. Now, most of us are familiar with the old food pyramid, with the carbs on the bottom; then the fruits and vegetables; then the dairy, meat, oils, and sweets up closer to the top of the pyramid. Now, this pyramid was revised about every decade or so until just recently, when they scrapped the pyramid completely. Today, we have something called My Plate, and it's a relatively simple graphic, a bird's eye view of a plate with a little cup of dairy next to it. The plate looks like it's been approximately cut into four quadrants. We have a quadrant for fruit, for vegetables, for grains, and for protein. A slightly larger portion of vegetables, slightly smaller portions for the fruits, and for the protein.

So how do we do in terms of following these simplified dietary recommendations? Well, not so good. We follow these recommendations only 2% of the time. And to count is a yes, to count as following those recommendations, you only have to be compliant 70% of your meals. If we look at the most commonly eaten vegetable, it's the potato, but usually in the form of French fries or potato chips. Second most commonly eaten vegetable is the tomato, in the form of ketchup or pizza or pasta sauce. Third is onions. And fourth is iceberg lettuce, which is mostly water with little nutritional value.

So, we're not making very good food choices in terms of what we eat. But that only begs the question of why. It may partly be ignorance, but it can't be that simple. Well, we're not eating so well, but what about physical activity? What about exercise? How are we doing there? Well, we know that about 60% of U.S. adults don't exercise regularly, but 73% of us believe that we're in fair to excellent physical condition, and a full 25% of the population are fully sedentary, and it's estimated that this costs the U.S. health care system a full $76 billion per year.

Now, it's tempting to attribute our rising overweight and obesity rates to a failure in willpower, some sort of decline in character, but think of it in another way. If you gave a test to 100 people, and 70 of them failed, would you assume they were all lazy or unintelligent or lacked willpower, or would you begin to wonder about that test and what made it so difficult? So let's go back and look at some biological explanations, some social and environmental explanations, and take a look again at the role that stress might play. And let's remember that CBT is particularly well suited to address stress and behavior.

So we know that energy balance is the key to the regulation of body weight; this is the classic calories taken in versus calories burned off. But we also know that it really isn't that simple, since our rate of energy expenditure or metabolism may vary. Now, energy expenditure occurs in three different ways. The first is our basal metabolic rate, and that's about 60% of the total. Second is the thermic effect of food, about 10% of the total, and that's the energy it takes to eat and digest your food. And the third is activity thermogenesis, and that burns off about 30% of your calories, and that's the physical activity and the exercise.

The high percentage of your basal metabolic rate is partly why losing weight is so hard. The body slows our metabolic rate when we're dieting. Our metabolic rate also slows as we age, in part due to the loss of lean muscle mass that burns calories much more quickly. So, as we age, it gets harder and harder to keep the weight off, and the more we diet, the more we run the risk of slowing down our metabolism, but that's not all. Our food environment and even our culture, make it extremely difficult to make good food choices.

So think from your own family experience or your own cultural experience. When does food make an appearance? Food is often tied with celebrations, the wedding cake and the birthday cake, or it's tied with holidays, the Thanksgiving feast or the Christmas or other holiday feast. It's also tied symbolically to feeling cared for or to feeling loved. For me, it was my grandmother's blackberry cobbler. She would cook an entire cobbler for the family. She would cook a second cobbler just for me, given me a serving spoon, and I would eat myself into a happy food coma. Nothing better.

So when we're talking about changing food choices, we have to remember that it brings with it all of that history, all of that meaning, and all of that symbolism. Now of course, it is about family and it's about culture, but it's also about other social determinants, such as socioeconomic status and education. We also have to remember that there are broader social influences. For instance, McDonald's advertising budget is ten times the NIH budget for healthy eating. About 50 million a day eat at McDonald's, and a quarter of the nation's vegetable consumptions are French fries.

In 1970, about 26% of our food dollars were spent eating out. That has increased to about 41% in 2005. Our portion sizes have also changed dramatically in the past 20 years. NHLBI, the National Heart, Lung, and Blood Institute, has a terrific online portion distortion quiz. They show us that two pieces of pizza used to be around 500 calories, and now it's about 850 calories. A bagel used to be around 140 calories, but now it's all the way up to 350 calories. And an average cup of coffee used to be 45 calories, but now it's 330 calories, compliments of the Grande Starbucks.

If we look at broader media influences, the average child watches around 10,000 TV ads; 95% of those ads are for sugary cereals, sodas, candies, and fast food; 50,000 schools serve fast food as their "nutritious" school lunch; and physical education, or PE, has been cut. It's no longer mandatory in many different schools. The average kid has spent more hours watching TV than going to school by the time they graduate from high school. And what about the Internet? They watch that way more than TV.

So it's important that we remember, when we're talking about psychological variables, such as stress and obesity, we're talking about stress on a physiologic level, but we're also talking about stress on a behavioral level. When we're stressed, it affects our food choices. When we're stressed, it affects our motivation to exercise. So, what do we eat when we're stressed? Well, 65% of us eat more candy or chocolate; 56% eat more ice cream; 53% eat more potatoes or corn chips; 49% eat more cookies; and only 8% of us eat more vegetables.

So, what are some of the implications? We might need to think about reengineering food availability and changing our habits of how we respond to stress. We might want to limit our exposures to bad food. We might want to think about other stress-reduction strategies to manage our moods, other than reaching for the candy or for the cookies. We probably want to schedule an increased amount of time to sleep when we're stressed, even though we're busy and feel that we don't have the time. And we actually need to exercise more, not less, when we're stressed.

So I often get the question of whether or not an individual should exercise or diet. If their BMI is 26, 27, 28, they're technically in that overweight category, but maybe they don't have many health consequences as of yet. I tend to go by the NIH guidelines, which say, if you are overweight, in other words, your BMI is between 25 and 30, if you are overweight and you have two or more cardiovascular risk factors, such as hypertension or high cholesterol, then you should try behavioral modification, diet, exercise, better food choices.

If you are obese, you're BMI is over 30, and you're unable to lose 10% of your weight, then you could consider adding pharmacotherapy into your behavioral modification program. If your BMI is over 40, you're already doing behavioral modification, you've already tried pharmacotherapy, then you could also consider weight loss surgery. And of course, that's an evaluation you would want to do with your primary care physician.

So what does the data tell us in terms of the outcomes for behavior modification for all of these different kinds of diets and exercise? And here I don't want parse it into specific kinds of diets, but I want to look at a large meta-analysis that NIH did of 48 different randomized control trials. In these 48 trials they showed that there was an average weight loss of 8% over one year, and at the three to five year follow up, there was zero weight loss.

So, essentially, everyone increased their weight back up to where they had started. Sort of discouraging in a way, but remember: Those individuals were able to lose initially, and at least they prevented weight gain, even though they gained that weight back.

So I think maybe some more realistic initial goals would be to first be as fit as possible at your current weight and don't worry so much about the number. The second goal would be to prevent further weight gain. We know that as we get older, we tend to gain more weight. So if you can put the brakes on that, that should certainly be considered a success. If you're good at number 1 and number 2, then number 3 would be, "OK, now we can think about decreasing BMI or decreasing your actual weight."

So, what are some of the skills that we should think about in terms of dieting and exercise? Well, both of them are important, but if your goal is to decrease that number, to lose pounds, dieting will probably get you there quicker than exercise will. Ideally, you would do a little bit of both. But what skills would be helpful, especially for dieting? Well, it takes us back to our usual list of self-monitoring, so you need to know your baseline at where you're starting; we might use stimulus control, so removing temptation from your environment; cognitive restructuring, so what thoughts do you have when you're deciding what to eat or what not to eat; and we might use some of those motivational enhancement strategies that we talked about with the transtheoretical model and motivational interviewing.

There's a number of well-designed CBT programs for weight management and physical activity, but most of them have been shown to have a fairly modest effect size. One of the best articulated and demonstrated models comes from Judy Beck. And of course, her name sounds familiar, because her father was Aaron or Tim Beck, the father of cognitive behavioral therapy. Judy Beck wrote a book called, *The Beck Diet Solution*, in 2008, a best seller that very carefully plans out a 42-day action plan to help individuals realize their exercise and weight-loss goals. In that book they start with self-monitoring and a behavioral analysis. What really makes you eat? Why do you really want to lose the weight? How do you think like a thin person? And here that really moves you into the realm of cognitive restructuring.

So what's an example of some of the habits that she talks about? So what foods do you select when you go to the grocery store? Many of us go on autopilot as we're zooming through our familiar grocery store, and we pick the same sorts of foods. You want to shift those habits, taking time to plan and prepare meals and thinking about what choices you're making, serving your food on smaller plates, eating more slowly and without distraction, or pausing for 20 minutes after a serving before you decide you need more, and this is from a basic physiologic explanation of how and when we feel satiety, and it takes us about 20 minutes before we feel satiated after we've eaten.

So, what's the evidence for CBT and weight loss? Remember that CBT started in psychiatry as a treatment for mental illness, and the strongest evidence for CBT and management of eating comes from studies of binge eating and bulimia. It's also a key ingredient for the treatment of anorexia, a disorder which is at the other extreme end of the spectrum. But what about for run-of-the-mill weight loss? Well, we've had over about 100 studies, all testing slight variance to the model or to different populations, and all have behavioral interventions as number one and cognitive interventions as number two.

So an example would be from Pimenta in 2012. This was an international study looking at a small sample of mid-life women. They used an eight week randomized control trial of cognitive behavioral therapy. They were able to show decreased weight, decreased body mass index, decreased waist circumference, and improved eating habits, but the effects were modest. In fact, in most of these studies, we're back to that number that NIH has given us from their meta-analysis, the weight loss of about 8 to 10%.

What about evidence for youth? And I wanted to mention just one study thought by Denise Wilfley in 2011. This was a comprehensive literature review focusing on children and adolescents, where they used behavior therapy supplemented with cognitive restructuring, and they found that that combination was the strongest non-medical treatment for youth and for adolescents. They used self-monitoring, they used stimulus control—both invaluable behavioral components. The U.S. Preventive Services Task Force, in fact, recommends multimodal approaches to weight management and specifically lists CBT as a core ingredient.

355

A number of large longitudinal studies have shown us that it's not just about fat. It's also about fit. An overweight but fit person is much better off than a thin person who is unfit. In fact, even small improvements in fitness can have substantial benefits. So some of the benefits of physical activity, increases in cardiorespiratory fitness, we know there's an overall reduction in morality, better management, or even prevention of cardiovascular disease, hypertension, diabetes, and the list goes on and on, and I think we should make sure we add to that list a decrease in stress, and an increase in psychological well-being.

Well, how much physical activity do we need to have? And honestly, it's a little frustrating if you follow the literature, because it seems like the amount continues to change. But the point that I hope you'll take away from this is that greater health benefits are associated with greater levels of activity. But exercise does not need be intense, nor does it need to be prolonged to be beneficial. If possible, you should aim for 60 to 90% of your maximum heart rate. You can derive your maximum heart rate by taking the number 220, [subtracting] your age, and then you would want to be approximately 60 to 90% of that number.

We know that the greatest relative benefit may be gained by previously sedentary people becoming even slightly active. In fact, I wanted to share one interesting and very promising study done by Ching-Pang Wen in Taiwan. This was published by "The Lancet" in 2011 and included a whopping 416,000 subjects that they followed over a period of eight years.

In this study, they found that inactive people who increase their physical activity by just 15 minutes per day reduced their risk of death by 14% and increased their life expectancy by three years. And I want to repeat that, because I think it's rather extraordinary. Inactive people who increased their physical activity by just 15 minutes per day reduced their risk of death by 14% and increased their life expectancy by three years. Each additional 15 minutes of exercised lowered their risk by an additional 4%. Just 15 minutes a day. I hope that seems doable.

Next, let's move to a clip of Michael. Michael is trying to increase his physical activity levels, and he's encountering some challenges.

[VIGNETTE START]

PROFESSOR SATTERFIELD: So Michael, let's continue talking about health-related behaviors that are important in managing your cardiovascular disease. And on our list, I have medication adherence, smoking, diet, and physical activity. So which of those should we pick up?

MICHAEL: Let's talk about physical activity, I think.

PROFESSOR SATTERFIELD: Physical activity.

MICHAEL: Yeah.

PROFESSOR SATTERFIELD: OK. All right. So we know that physical activity and cardiovascular health are very much related to one another. And we know that oftentimes, we're told our level of exercise should be here, but in reality, we're down here somewhere. But I don't want to assume. So let me just ask first, what is your current level of physical activity?

MICHAEL: Well, it's pretty low, I think. A lot of things get in the way. But I would say I might be getting an hour a week.

PROFESSOR SATTERFIELD: An hour a week.

MICHAEL: Yeah.

PROFESSOR SATTERFIELD: OK. Well, let's maybe take a step back and make sure we're defining physical activity the same way. And you might have noticed that folks now talk more about physical activity versus exercise. And that's because exercise sounds like it's something that you do in a gym. It's something you have to have a special outfit for, and special shoes, or whatever. And really, physical activity is physical activity. It all counts, and it all contributes to cardiovascular health.

Walking to work, or walking across the parking lot, or taking the stairs instead of the elevator—that's all physical activity. And we think of that as summing across the course of the day, or over the course of a week. So that all counts.

MICHAEL: OK.

PROFESSOR SATTERFIELD: So for you, when you said an hour a week, what kind of physical activity is that?

MICHAEL: Well, I was thinking more about I walk. And it's that setting; I wasn't really thinking about it as, OK, do I walk? How many steps do I take during the day? But do I go out and take x minutes to walk? That's the sort of thing I was talking about.

I used to be a tennis player. I was never great, but I played tennis somewhat regularly once upon a time. I haven't done that in a long time. So, nothing structured like that, though it would be nice to do that. So I guess what I'm saying, roughly an hour a week. I'm thinking more walks around the neighborhood.

PROFESSOR SATTERFIELD: OK. And maybe it's good, then, to think of physical activity in these two buckets. One is incidental physical activity, walking to work, or from the car, or up the stairs. And then there's the time that's specifically set aside or dedicated to physical activity. That can still be things you enjoy, like tennis or going for walks or whatever. But it's really time that you've used specifically earmarked for physical fitness, if you will.

MICHAEL: Yeah. OK.

PROFESSOR SATTERFIELD: And that's about an hour a week.

MICHAEL: Yeah. That's about an hour a week.

PROFESSOR SATTERFIELD: And ideally, what we want to do is we want to increase both of those. So how much physical activity should you be getting, do you think?

MICHAEL: I would say probably 45 minutes? Maybe even an hour a day?

PROFESSOR SATTERFIELD: OK. All right. You know, it's been hard to pin down because the recommendations from the experts often change. But now the recommendation is to exercise on more days than not, and to try to get—it depends on the intensity of the exercise—but to try to get 45 minutes to an hour a day if possible. Now that's a pretty high goal I think for a lot of us. But remember, all physical activity counts. So maybe the sum total will get you closer there. So what's your first goal? You're doing about an hour a week now. We want to increase that as much as we can. What would be a goal you'd like to set for yourself?

MICHAEL: For the whole week in terms of time?

PROFESSOR SATTERFIELD: Yeah. Sure.

MICHAEL: I guess it would be good to be doing—I don't know. Maybe reasonably 20 to 30 minutes, five days a week?

PROFESSOR SATTERFIELD: Twenty to 30 minutes, five days per week. And what activity would you be doing? Is that walking?

MICHAEL: I'm thinking walking. And definitely since we're broadening, and we're talking about physical activity, whereas I've been thinking really more of the structured exercise time, if I broaden it out, I can definitely take stairs at work. There are places that I might take the car to that I could walk to. So I could include those things. So the question then becomes, how do I monitor that? I mean, I've got to keep it all in my head. I don't know.

PROFESSOR SATTERFIELD: And I think you're doing a good job in thinking about specific goals. And remember our acronym for goals is SMART, S-M-A-R-T. So S is you want it to be specific, and you've specified 20 to 30 minutes of walking five days per week each week. And that includes the incidental walking, but it can also include earmarked time where you go for an extra walk.

So S for specific, M measurable. So that's sort of that point I think you're getting at. So we want to be able to measure the amount that you're walking. So you use 20 to 30 minutes. So you could time it. That might get a little bit tricky if it's walking up the stairs or across the parking lot. So what other way could you measure it?

MICHAEL: Well, I guess you could measure—I know there's a lot of talk out there, and even some apps I've heard about, where you measure the number of steps you take.

PROFESSOR SATTERFIELD: Sure. Sure.

MICHAEL: Rather than time, I might be talking about x number of steps.

PROFESSOR SATTERFIELD: Steps. Right. Right. And you're right. In most smartphones, there's an accelerometer that counts your steps. And there's also some inexpensive devices that you can buy and wear on your belt clip, or some of them are bracelets that you can wear that count the steps. So we just want to get a sense of, you may even try walking 20 or 30 minutes and see how many steps that is, so you can set your goal, and figure out how many steps per day you need to do for that.

So SMART goals, specific, measurable, attainable. So do you think it's realistic to do that given your schedule and where you are now?

MICHAEL: It may be a little much for right now. There're some reasons I don't go and get the exercise now. We can assume there are going to continue to be issues, not having time, other commitments that I have. These are things that typically will get in the way. So maybe I should think more about getting this kind of exercise two or three times a week?

Or maybe I should just adjust it once I've got an idea of how many steps are in 30 minutes. I should say, well, it's more like two hours a week. And how many steps would that be? But I'm thinking out loud here.

PROFESSOR SATTERFIELD: OK. OK. And I want you to set the goal. There's no right amount. It's thinking realistically what is going to be attainable for you. You want it specific, measurable, attainable. And the last two, you want it relevant and timely. We know that physical activity is very much relevant to your cardiovascular health. So we're not off on a tangent. We know it's relevant.

And timely is, is this a good time for me to do it? Sounds like you're busy now, but I know you have a high-pressure job, and you're pretty much always busy it seems like. There might be other things going on. Do you think this is a good time to start something?

MICHAEL: I think it is. I think it is. Because if you're going to value something, if you're going to say your health is important, your point is well taken. You're always busy, so it may as well be now.

PROFESSOR SATTERFIELD: And we also want it timely in a sense of there's going to be follow-up, there's going to be accountability. We have a defined time frame. So when would you like to start this?

MICHAEL: Well, maybe insofar as we can always check in with each other, starting after this session. Maybe we set a goal, and then the next session or two sessions from now, we come back and we monitor. We check up on what's going on. I think that that will be really helpful for me on that accountability front.

PROFESSOR SATTERFIELD: OK, good. Good. So I want to make sure that I've done a good job facilitating this discussion and sort of helping you develop this treatment plan. So can you repeat back what it is that you're going to do in terms of physical activity?

MICHAEL: I am going to shoot for realistically three times a week, 30 minutes. So a total of 90 minutes a week. And the kind of activity we're talking about is mostly walking. But we're thinking not necessarily about just the walking, as I said. The next 30 minutes, I'm going to walk around the neighborhood. We're talking about walking that might be walking up steps at work. Might be walking across the parking lot, or to the cafe instead of driving to it. In order to monitor that, I'm going to look at what's available to me in terms of counting the steps. And one good thing that I can do is to set this up is just check what is for me 30 minutes. How many steps is that? And then, can plug that back into the 90 minutes. How many steps am I trying to get this week? And then we'll come back, and we'll see how I've done.

PROFESSOR SATTERFIELD: OK. That sounds perfect.

MICHAEL: OK.

[VIGNETTE END]

PROFESSOR SATTERFIELD: So as we think about the complex field of weight management and fitness, I hope that we can remember to pull forward our biopsychosocial model; I hope we can pull forward the transtheoretical model and stages of change; and I hope we can use some of those core behavior change principles that we've talked about in the past few lectures.

We've covered the scope of weight issues, the epidemiology of weight, and how tough it is to change. In essence, the cards are really stacked against us. But the best chance is probably slow and steady interventions through cognitive behavioral therapy is recommended by the U.S. Preventive Services Task Force.

I'd like end by moving to our next FAQ, or frequently asked question, and the question is weight management is obviously important for medical reasons, but the issue of weight seems to cut more deeply than that. Why do we care so much about our shapes, if we are healthy? Again, a very good question, and I think you've touched on a really important issue here, and it gets to the issue of self-worth and what messages our society has given us. It's not just about your cholesterol, your hypertension, or your cardiorespiratory fitness. It's about what you look at as an individual and what the marketers have told us valuable or not valuable.

It's very easy for a child to mistakenly equate the way they appear with whether or not they're lovable, with whether or not they'll be rich, successful, or desirable. And it's exactly those sorts of associations that we need to break, and I've been encouraged by seeing more and more of a movement to move away from airbrushing, to move away from the super skinny supermodels, and to look at a realistic body image and body weight.

Please join us next time, where we continue talking behavioral medicine in the context of substance use disorders. Thank you.

Behavioral Therapy for Chemical Addictions
Lecture 17

The misuse and abuse of alcohol and drugs continue to be a central challenge both to our society and health-care system. Like other mental illnesses or diseases of the brain, substance use disorders carry a great amount of stigma, blame, and misinformation. In this lecture, you will be exposed to the basics of substance use disorders, and you will learn what second- or third-wave CBT therapies might be able to offer in terms of treatment.

Substance Use Disorders

- About 52 percent of people are regular drinkers, which is defined as someone who has at least 12 drinks over a one-year period. About 23 percent of people are defined as risky drinkers. About 7.2 percent of people have a diagnosable alcohol use disorder, which equates to about 17 million adults.

- Drinking often starts early. In fact, about 24 percent of eighth graders consume alcohol, and about 64 percent of twelfth graders consume alcohol. About 50 percent of college students binge drink, causing about 1,800 deaths per year.

- Alcohol use continues into older age. Research showed that about 3 percent of older adults met the full criteria for an alcohol use disorder or alcoholism. At-risk drinking was reported in 19 percent of individuals aged 50 to 64 and in 13 percent of respondents aged 65 and higher. Binge drinking was reported in 23 percent of individuals aged 50 to 64 and still in 15 percent of individuals over the age of 65.

- The medical complications of alcohol use include hypertension, stroke, cardiomyopathy, cirrhosis of the liver, pancreatitis, and mouth, throat, and liver cancer. In fact, 25 to 40 percent of patients who occupy general hospital beds are thought to have alcohol problems.

- Research showed that about 9.2 percent of Americans, or about 24 million people, 12 years old or older used an illicit drug in the past year. The most commonly used illicit drug was marijuana, at 14 percent use at any time in the past year or 7.3 percent use in the past month. Marijuana can be addictive, and about 9 percent of individuals who regularly use marijuana develop a substance use disorder.

- A rising and more recent category of abuse is with prescription medication, including painkillers (such as Oxycodone, Vicodin, and Percocet), tranquilizers (such as Valium, Xanax, and Ativan), and stimulants (such as Adderall and Ritalin).

- In 2009, 7 million Americans reported current (within the past month) nonmedical use of prescription drugs—more than the number of individuals using cocaine, heroin, hallucinogens, and inhalants combined. And that number continues to rise, especially with painkillers.

- In fact, prescription drug overdose was the leading cause of injury death in 2012. And among people aged 25 to 64 years old, drug overdose caused more deaths than motor vehicle traffic accidents.

- There are many psychosocial aspects or social consequences related to substance use disorders or the use of substances. Alcohol is involved in one-half to two-thirds of all homicides and at least one-half of serious assaults. About 70 percent of incarcerated individuals have a substance use disorder. It accounts for one-third of all criminal justice costs and about 50 percent of all cases of child abuse and neglect.

- There is a continuum of substance use, from abstinence, to low risk, to at risk, to substance use disorders, which can be mild, moderate, or severe. In order to be diagnosed with a substance use disorder, you have to meet a minimum or two diagnostic criteria out of a total list of 11. If you have two to three of these criteria, you're considered mild. If you have four to five, you're considered moderate. If you have six or more, you're considered severe. The 11 criteria are as follows.

o   Failing to fulfill obligations

o   Hazardous use

o   Social/interpersonal problems

o   Tolerance

o   Withdrawal

o   Being unable to cut down

o   Using more than intended

o   Neglecting important activities

o   Spending a lot of time getting the substance

o   Psychological or physical problems

o   Craving

Screening for Substance Use Disorders

* Commonly used screening tests for alcohol and drug use include a single-question screener for alcohol put out by the National Institute on Alcohol Abuse and Alcoholism (How many times in the past year have you had x or more drinks in a day?; $x = 5$ for men and 4 for women or anyone over the age of 65) and the 10-question Alcohol Use Disorders Identification Test that focuses on recent alcohol use, dependence symptoms, and alcohol-related problems.

* The National Institute on Alcohol Abuse and Alcoholism also puts out a single-question screener for illicit drugs: How many times in the past year have you used an illicit substance or a prescription

medication for nonmedical reasons or because of the way it made you feel? In addition, a questionnaire that is often used is the Drug Abuse Screening Test.

- SBIRT (screening, brief intervention, referral to treatment) is an increasingly popular public health approach to doing screening and brief intervention for substance use disorders in primary care settings. Following this approach, you quickly assess the use and severity of alcohol, illicit drugs, and prescription drug abuse. Then, the brief intervention is a three- to five-minute motivational and awareness-raising intervention given to risky or problematic substance users. The final step involves referrals to specialty care for patients with substance use disorders.

- A recent meta-analysis of SBIRT suggests an overall reduction of 56 percent in the number of drinks. Research has shown that brief interventions can reduce alcohol use for at least 12 months in patients who are not alcohol dependent.

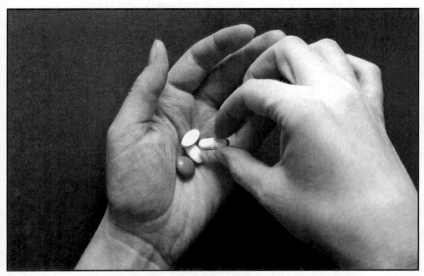

In 2009, 7 million Americans reported current (within the past month) nonmedical use of prescription drugs.

- Brief interventions are really for people who are at-risk users. But what about people with full-blown substance use disorders? In 2012, an estimated 23.1 million Americans needed treatment for a problem related to alcohol or drugs, but only about 2.5 million people—or a little more than 10 percent—received treatment at a specialty facility. That means that there are millions of people who simply aren't getting into treatment.

Treatments for Substance Use Disorders

- The most commonly used form of treatment for substance use disorders is a 12-step program, such as Alcoholics Anonymous or Narcotics Anonymous, that uses a peer-to-peer individual and group counseling model.

- In 2013, there were about a million people that were involved in some sort of 12-step program, and there were about 60,000 meetings occurring somewhere in the United States. Studies have shown that the effectiveness rate is only about five to 10 percent—but that's for people who stick with it. Unfortunately, 90 percent of the people who go to a meeting drop out in the first 90 days.

- The community reinforcement approach (CRA) is a different type of treatment. There are four main components of the CRA.
  - The first component is a functional analysis of substance use, in which the triggers, or the antecedents, of use as well as the positive and negative consequences are explored.

  - The second element is called sobriety sampling. The idea is that movement toward abstinence begins with the client's agreement to sample a brief period of abstinence.

  - The next part of CRA is the actual treatment plan, in which you want to establish meaningful, objective goals that are selected by the client and negotiated with the clinician. You want to establish specified methods for obtaining those goals. Some of the tools used are the Happiness Scale and a Goals of Counseling form.

○ They might add behavior skills training, in which they teach three basic skills through instruction and role playing: problem-solving skills, communication skills (specifically, helping people have a positive interaction style even in the face of conflict), and drink/drug refusal training. The next skills training is job skills training, in which they teach the basic steps and skills necessary for getting and keeping a job. Other components might include social and recreational counseling, relapse prevention, and relationship counseling.

- Mindfulness-based relapse prevention (MBRP) is another type of therapy. It was initially developed by Alan Marlatt and is currently being studied by Sarah Bowen. This kind of therapy is in the realm of third-wave therapies, with their focus on mindfulness and acceptance. MBRP uses the acronym SOBER: stop, observe, breathe, expand awareness, and the respond mindfully.

- In a study that was published in 2014, Sarah Bowen looked at 268 individuals with substance use disorders. She analyzed three different kinds of treatment: CBT relapse prevention, MBRP, and treatment as usual. For individuals in aftercare following initial treatment for substance use disorders, CBT relapse prevention and MBRP were superior to treatment as usual.

- At the 12-month follow-up, MBRP offered an added benefit over CBT and treatment as usual in reducing drug use and heavy drinking. Targeted mindfulness practices may support long-term outcomes by strengthening an individual's ability to monitor and skillfully cope with discomfort associated with craving or negative affect.

- Therapeutic education system (TES), developed by Lisa Marsch and colleagues at Dartmouth University, is delivered in a different modality. With TES, there are 62 Internet modules. In 2014, a team led by Aimee Campbell and Edward Nunes looked at 507 individuals using alcohol and drugs and working their way through the 62 Internet modules. They found that TES was superior to treatment as usual on both adherence and abstinence.

- TES uses a contingency management system to get people to do the modules. There are a number of different variants on contingency management where you use lotteries or payments as a reward for someone who, for example, comes in and gives a urine sample to prove that he or she hasn't been using drugs.

- But does contingency management work, and should we pay people to not engage in unhealthy behaviors? In 2013, Nadine Farronato and colleagues did a systematic review of CBT versus contingency management for cocaine addiction. They found that contingency management produced very rapid results in the beginning of treatment and CBT produced results toward the end and after treatment had ended. About half of the studies that did a combination of the two showed better results, but half showed no advantage.

- In 2011, Kate Cahill and Rafael Perera reviewed 19 different smoking-related studies, with a total of about 4,500 different subjects. Only one large study out of 19 showed that payments for abstinence were beneficial. The incentives did increase participation, but the initial success faded after the rewards went away. It seems like incentives are just one extrinsic motivator, and the results are mixed for now.

- Community reinforcement approach and family training (CRAFT) is a recent outgrowth of CRA that focuses on how to help the families and loved ones of those abusing alcohol or drugs. The goal of CRAFT is to use positive communication to reinforce positive behaviors while taking care of yourself and using others' social supports. You want to highlight positive interactions, positive conversations, times when your loved one is sober or not using, and times when he or she has been reliable. Thus far, the research results are positive.

Suggested Reading

Babor, McRee, Kassebaum, Grimaldi, Ahmed, and Bray, "Screening, Brief Intervention, and Referral to Treatment (SBIRT)."

Babor, Higgins-Biddle, Saunders, and Monteiro, *AUDIT: The Alcohol Use Disorders Identification Test.*

Blazer and Wu, "The Epidemiology of At-Risk and Binge Drinking among Middle-Aged and Elderly Community Adults."

Bowen, Chawla, and Alan Marlatt, *Mindfulness-Based Relapse Prevention for Addictive Behaviors.*

Cahill and Perera, "Competitions and Incentives for Smoking Cessation."

Campbell, Nunes, Matthews, Stitzer, Miele, Polsky, Turrigiano, Walters, McClure, Kyle, Wahle, Van Veldhuisen, Goldman, Babcock, Stabile, Winhusen, and Ghitza, "Internet-Delivered Treatment for Substance Abuse."

Carroll, Kiluk, Nich, Gordon, Portnoy, Martino, and Ball, "Computer-Assisted Delivery of Cognitive-Behavioral Therapy."

Carroll, Ball, Martino, Nich, Gordon, Portnoy, and Rounsaville, "Computer-Assisted Delivery of Cognitive Behavioral Therapy for Addiction."

Carroll, Ball, Martino, Nich, Babuscio, and Rounsaville, "Enduring Effects of a Computer-Assisted Training Program for Cognitive Behavioral Therapy."

Fanning and O'Neill, *The Addiction Workbook.*

Farronato, Dürsteler-Macfarland, Wiesbeck, and Petitjean, "A Systematic Review Comparing Cognitive-Behavioral Therapy and Contingency Management for Cocaine Dependence."

Gruber, Pope, Hudson, and Yurgelun-Todd, "Attributes of Long-Term Heavy Cannabis Users."

Martin, "The Epidemiology of Alcohol-Related Interpersonal Violence."

Smith, Schmidt, Allensworth-Davies, and Saitz, "Primary Care Validation of a Single-Question Alcohol Screening Test."

1. Recreational marijuana is now legal in several states (including Washington, Oregon, Colorado, and Alaska). What are the primary arguments for and against the legalization of marijuana? Will it create a spike in substance use disorders?

2. Are sexual or Internet addictions really the same as chemical addictions like addictions to alcohol or drugs? How might they be similar or different? Are these behavioral addictions modern, or are there historical examples?

Behavioral Therapy for Chemical Addictions
Lecture 17—Transcript

PROFESSOR SATTERFIELD: Donovan was the apple of his mother's eye, always so sweet, so smart, and just a little bit shy. He did well in school and got into a good college. He studied hard. He got a good job on the other side of the country. She worried about him but knew that he needed to live his own life. Six months, 12 months go by, she hears from his less and less. And when he does call, he seems distracted, or sleepy, or irritable. He loses his job, and he starts waiting tables, but insists it isn't his fault. It's only temporary.

Two years after he graduated college, she got the call that every mother dreads. It was the ER at San Francisco General Hospital. Donovan had been found unconscious and barely breathing, an apparent accidental overdose from IV heroin use. How could this possibly happen? Her father, his grandfather, was maybe an alcoholic but heroin? How was that even possible? She bought the next ticket to San Francisco, her life now turned upside-down.

The misuse and abuse of alcohol and drugs continue to be a central challenge to our society and health-care system. Like other mental illnesses or diseases of the brain, substance-use disorders carry a great deal of stigma, blame, and misinformation. Let's review the basics of substance-use disorders and what second- or third-wave CBT therapies might be able to offer.

Let's first look at the prevalence of alcohol use and alcohol-use disorders. We know that approximately 52% of the population are regular drinkers, and a regular drinker is defined as someone that has at least 12 drinks over a one-year period. We know that 23% of the population would be defined as what's called risky drinkers. And 7.2% of the population would have a diagnosable alcohol-use disorder, that's about 17 million adults. But drinking often starts early, in fact, 24% of eight graders consume alcohol, and 64% of twelfth graders consume alcohol. We know that 50% of college students binge drink, causing about 1800 deaths per year and around 700,000 physical or sexual assaults.

Alcohol use continues into older age. We know that 3% of older adults meet full criteria for an alcohol-use disorder, or alcoholism. At-risk drinking was reported in 19% of individuals aged 50 to 64 and in 13% of respondents aged 65 and higher. Binge drinking was at 23% for individuals aged 50 to 64 and still at 15% for individuals over the age of 65. We know the medical complications of alcohol use include possible hypertension; stroke; cardiomyopathy; cirrhosis of the liver; pancreatitis; increase in mouth, throat, and liver cancer, just to name a few. In fact, 25 to 40% of patients who occupy general hospital beds are thought to have alcohol problems.

But what about the epidemiology of drug use? We know that about 9.2%, or around 24 million, Americans age 12 or higher used an illicit drug in the past year. The most commonly used was marijuana at 14% use at any time in the past year, or 7.3% of use in the past month. We do know that marijuana can be addictive, contrary to popular belief, and about 9% of individuals who regularly use marijuana go on to develop a substance-use disorder.

A rising and more recent category of abuse is in the category of prescription medication. And here we're talking about things like pain killers, Oxycodone, Vicodin, Percocet; tranquilizers, such as Valium, Xanax, and Ativan; or stimulants, such as Adderall or Ritalin. In fact, in 2009, 7 million Americans reported current, within the past month, non-medical use of prescription drugs, and that's more than the number of individuals using cocaine, heroin, hallucinogens, and inhalants combined, and that number continues to rise, especially with pain killers. In fact, prescription drug overdose was the leading cause of injury death in 2012, and among people aged 25 to 64 years old, drug overdose caused more deaths than motor vehicle traffic accidents.

Of course, there are many psychosocial aspects or social consequences related to substance-use disorders, or just the use of substances. Alcohol is involved in a half to two-thirds of all homicides and at least one-half of serious assaults. We know that 70% of incarcerated individuals have a substance-use disorder; it accounts for a third of all criminal justice costs and about 50% of all cases of child abuse and neglect.

But when we talk about substance use, we want to remember that we're thinking about use along a continuum, and at one end of the continuum, we have complete abstinence, not using at all. The next level over would be low-risk, so occasional use. Moving in to at-risk, so the individual, the in terms of quantity or the occasions in which they use, might place themselves or others at risk for negative consequences. Then at the far end of the spectrum, we have the substance-use disorders, and those might be mild, moderate, or severe.

Let's a quick quiz. I'm going to read four different case descriptions, and I want you to decide which of these patients is an at-risk drinker. So case one is a 45-year-old woman who drinks one to two glasses of wine each night. Is she an at-risk drinker? Case two, a 70-year-old man who drinks one to two beers each night. Is he an at-risk drinker? Case three, a 25-year-old woman who drinks four to five drinks once per week when she goes out with her friends. And the last one, a 40-year-old man who drinks one to two glasses of wine each night. Which of those four is an at-risk drinker?

It's a little bit of a trick question, because in fact, three of those individuals would technically be considered at-risk drinkers. The 45-year-old woman drinking one to two glasses per night is at-risk. The 70-year-old man who drinks one to two beers each night is at-risk. The 25-year-old woman who drinks four to five drinks once per week is also at-risk. So let's go ahead and define what we mean by at-risk substance use. And remember, by *at-risk*, we're looking at drinking patterns or quantities that might place an individual at risk for medical complications or maybe social problems.

For a male who's under the age of 65, you can drink, on average, two drinks per day, but no more than 14 drinks per week. That number drops for women, on average one drink per day and no more than seven drinks per week. For anyone over 65, it's an average of one drink per day, no more than seven drinks per week. In terms of binge drinking for men under 65, if they drink more than four, it's considered a binge drink. For women, if they drink more than three drinks, it's considered a binge. For individuals over 65 years old, if they drink more than three drinks, it's actually considered a binge.

Now, you may wonder where these particular numbers come from, and they really come from the medical literature, where we look at individuals who've had complications, medical or social, from their use of alcohol or drugs, then we look at how much those individuals used and at what point they crossed the threshold that might place them at risk. Now this isn't saying that they have an alcohol-use disorder or any sort of drug-use disorder, but they're in that at-risk category, where we probably want to take a little bit of a closer look.

Now, what about for illicit drugs? So for illicit drugs, any use is considered at risk. And for prescription drugs, any unadvised or any non-medical use of a prescription medication also places an individual at risk. Now remember, at-risk just means exactly what it says, you're at risk. And it should be a focus of further inquiry and investigation to see if it might be a problem. It might not, but it might be a problem.

Now, as I mentioned, out on the far end of that spectrum, we have substance-use disorders. And in order to be diagnosed with a substance-use disorder, you have to meet a diagnostic criteria. There's a total list of 11, and you need a minimum of 2 of these diagnostic criteria. If you have 2 to 3 of these criteria, you're considered mild; 4 to 5, you're considered moderate; if you have 6 or more, you're considered severe. So what are those 11 criteria?

So the first is a failure to fulfill work or social obligations as a consequence of substance use. The second is that you use at times even when it might be hazardous, so this is the classic do not operate dangerous machinery or drive a car while you're drinking or using drugs; individuals who do that would then get a point on this diagnostic criteria. Number three would be, has your substance use cause social or interpersonal problems? Next would be tolerance, so do you have to use more and more of the substance in order to have the same effect? Next would be withdrawal, so if you abruptly stopped using the substance, do you have a physiologic reaction because your body needs to have that substance? You've developed an addiction. Are you unable to cut down despite repeated attempts and maybe even a desire to cut down? Are you using more than you initially intended to use? Do you neglect important activities or spend a lot of time getting the substance? Had there been psychological or physical problems, like medical problems, that have come up as consequence of your substance use? And last, do you have a psychologic or physiologic craving to have more of the substance?

Now, when you go to a primary-care setting, they often use very brief screening tests around alcohol and drug use. We know that alcohol and drug use are relevant to a lot of different medical disorders, and it probably should be on the map for any primary care clinician. So if we're looking in the category of alcohol, there is one commonly used, single-question screener put out by NIAAA, the National Institute on Alcohol Abuse and Alcoholism. The second most commonly used screener is something called the AUDIT, and let me describe each of those.

So the NIAAA single-question screener is as follows. Let's assume you're a man and you are under the age of 65, how many times in the past year have you had five or more drinks in a day? So how many times in the past year have you had five or more drinks in a day? If the answer is anything other than 0, that individual is considered "at risk," and you might go on to do a more in-depth screener. Incidentally, that number changes to, have you had four or more drinks in a day for women or for anyone over the age of 65.

Now, I mentioned the AUDIT, and AUDIT stands for Alcohol Use Disorders Identification Test. It is a 10-question survey, which focuses on use, but also focuses on potential dependent symptoms, or consequences of using alcohol. The cut-off score on the AUDIT, which is freely available online, is 8 or above. If you're 8 or above, you are in that at-risk category. You may just need some simple advice, or you may just need to cut down and take it easy a bit. If your scores are in 16 to the 19 range, you might need some brief counseling. If your scores are 20 or higher, you might need a referral to a specialist.

If we're looking in the category illicit drugs, there's also a single-question screener from National Institute on Drug Abuse, which simply asks, "How many times in the past year have you used an illicit substance or used a prescription medication for non-medical reasons or because of the way it made you feel?" Single question, and if you're answer is anything other than 0, again, you're at risk. The questionnaire that is often used is the DAST, and that's the Drug Abuse Screening Test.

Let's move on to do a brief demonstration of alcohol screening, and we'll look at a clip from Carol.

[VIGNETTE START]

PROFESSOR SATTERFIELD: Can you tell me a little bit about the alcohol use? You said that you have a glass of wine before bed to help you sleep?

CAROL: Mm-hm.

PROFESSOR SATTERFIELD: So how many days per week do you usually drink alcohol?

CAROL: I mean, I don't really drink it a whole lot on the weekends, but on weeknights, I'll have probably a glass or two. So we'll say five days a week.

PROFESSOR SATTERFIELD: OK. So five days a week, and you said a glass or two. So how often is it one, and how often is it two?

CAROL: That's a good question. I guess it's probably closer to two than one most nights. But I don't fill it to the brim or anything.

PROFESSOR SATTERFIELD: And that was my next question. So glasses are small or glasses are big? So do you have a sense of how many ounces?

CAROL: I measure, actually. So it's five-ounce glasses.

PROFESSOR SATTERFIELD: It's five-ounce glasses. OK. And so more commonly, two than one. And sounds like you're drinking somewhere, then, between maybe seven to 10 glasses per week?

CAROL: That's probably accurate.

PROFESSOR SATTERFIELD: And are you comfortable with that amount, or is that something that worries you a little bit?

CAROL: I'm not worried about it. I don't feel like I need it necessarily, and I don't get drunk, or anything like that. But it'd be nice to not, I guess, feel like, it'd be nice to feel like it doesn't help me fall asleep. Like it doesn't have to be there.

PROFESSOR SATTERFIELD: Right. Right. It's sort of a crutch that you use to help you fall asleep. It would be nice to drink for the enjoyment, or with your meal, or whatever reason, and not have to use it as a medication almost. I'm just going to maybe bookmark this as something that we can talk about later too, because for a woman your age, what's considered moderate drinking is no more than seven drinks per week. So if you're sometimes up above seven, it doesn't mean that you have a problem with alcohol, but it means you're drinking a little bit over what would be considered moderate drinking for a woman your age. And we'll want to keep an eye on it and make sure that it doesn't become, again, a crutch, like we said, that then becomes its own sort of problem.

BOTH: OK.

[VIGNETTE END]

PROFESSOR SATTERFIELD: So what would we do with Carol? Honestly, alcohol is now on my list for her. I've flagged it, not necessarily as her most important problem, but something that I want to pay attention to. I haven't yet seen other indicators that alcohol is truly a problem, but she is drinking in the risky category; she is drinking more than seven drinks per week on average. I will encourage her to cut back to safe levels, and I will regularly reassess her.

Next I'd like to talk about an increasingly popular public-health approach to doing screening and brief intervention for substance-use disorders in primary-care settings, and it's something that's called SBIRT, or S-B-I-R-T, where the S stands for screening. You quickly assess use and severity of alcohol, illicit drugs, and prescription-drug abuse. This is often done with a quick questionnaire that's in the waiting room before your primary-care appointment, sometimes done on a computer tablet or at home on a patient health portal. The BI stands for brief intervention, and the brief intervention is three- to five-minute motivational and awareness-raising intervention given to a risky or problematic substance user.

So if you do your screening and you score in the at-risk category, then a nurse, or your primary care physician, or a behavioral health specialist would then spend about three to five minutes with you talking about ways to reduce risk and providing some basic education about your level of use. The RT stands for Referrals to Treatment. And these are for individuals who aren't just risky users, but you suspect that they might have a full-blown alcohol-use disorder or substance-use disorder in general. The RT, referrals to treatment, means then you would work with that individual to prepare them to accept a referral to specialty care. Then you would actually facilitate that referral and help them to make that connection.

But does SBIRT work? The recent meta-analysis suggests an overall reduction of 56% in the number of drinks. Research has shown that brief interventions can reduce alcohol use for at least 12 months in patients who are not alcohol dependent, and if you think about it, that three to five-minute intervention, just reaching out to someone before they have a full-blown use disorder and saying, "Hey, you know what, the amount you're drinking is actually not safe, and here's why I'm worried, and here's some things that you can do about it," might reduce drinking as much as 56% over a period of 12 months.

Now, as I mentioned, brief interventions are really for people who are at-risk users. But what about people with full-blown substance-use disorders? In 2012 an estimated 23.1 million Americans needed treatment for a problem related to alcohol or drugs, but only about 2.5 million people, or a little more than 10%, received treatment at a specialty facility. That means that there are millions of people who simply aren't getting into treatment.

So, what are the most commonly used forms of treatment for substance-use disorders? Well, the most commonly used is a 12-step program, things like Alcoholics Anonymous, or Narcotics Anonymous that uses a peer-peer individual and group counseling model. Now, the data shows us that in 2013 there were about a million people that were involved in some sort of 12-step program, and there were about 60,000 meetings occurring at some place around United States

In terms of the efficacy of this particular approach, studies have been quite difficult, because with Alcoholics Anonymous, as the name implies, they like to keep things anonymous. So it's been difficult for researchers to go in and to study. But in the studies that have been done, it looks like the effectiveness rate is actually a little bit disappointing. It's about 5 to 10% effective, but that's for people who stick with it. I think the primary problem with 12-step is that 90% of the people that go to an AA meeting drop out in the first 90 days. For the folks that stay, it works, but you have to get people to stay.

I wanted to share a different type of treatment, one that we haven't talked about in our toolbox as of yet. It's called CRA, or the community reinforcement approach. Now, me, being a dyed-in-the-wool cognitive behavioral therapist, I read their treatment manuals and I think, ah, this is CBT, but there are some important differences, and they've added in, I think, some really interesting elements in terms of thinking about community support and social relationships. CBT often very much on the individual or maybe the couple, maybe the family, a lot less in thinking about a supportive community.

So, there are a number of different components, four main components, for the community reinforcement approach. The first, they want to do a functional analysis of substance use. So they want to come up with those explanations of what are the triggers or the antecedents of use, and they want to explore the positive and the negative consequences. So here we're talking about rewards and punishments, and there are rewards to using alcohol and drugs; it's part of the reason why people use them. But we want to look at both sides of the coin.

The second element is something they call sobriety sampling. Now here, they think that movement towards abstinence begins with the client's agreement to sample a brief period of abstinence. Now remember, there's no failure here; it's all grist for the mill. So you'll talk to an individual, you will get their agreement that they won't drink for 7 days, or 10 days, or 30 days, whatever number you agree to. They go out and they try that experiment, if you will, that sobriety sampling, and see what happens. Sometimes people can't do it, sometimes they can do it, but either way, they learn important information that helps to feed their functional analysis and helps to shape their subsequent treatment approach.

Now, the next part of CRA is the actual treatment plan itself, where you want to establish meaningful, objective, smart goals that are client selected and negotiated with the clinician. You want to establish specified methods for obtaining those goals, and here we might be pulling out some of those tools from our CBT toolbox. But they add additional tools, such as the Happiness Scale, so they're not just looking at negative emotions but also positives. And they use things such as a Goals of Counseling form to help the individual track their progress towards their goals.

They may add in a component of behavior skills training, where they teach three basic skills through instruction, and they also use a lot of role-playing with the facilitator or with the therapist. So they will look at problem-solving skills. Obstacles always arise; you may need to be nimble on your feet in terms of responding to problems. They teach communication skills and particularly help people to have a more positive interaction style, even in the face of conflict.

They also teach something that's quite important called drink and drug refusal training. Remember that our social networks are very powerful in terms of influencing our behavior. So one of the things that causes an individual to fall off the wagon, they've decided not to drink or not to use drugs, but guess what, their best friend, their neighbor, their significant other comes and offers it to them, so they need to develop their communication skills in terms of refusing drinks or drugs but still salvaging that relationship. The next skills training comes in the job skills department. Often, individuals who may have been using substances for a long period of time, they've either forgotten or they lack the basic steps and skills necessary for getting and for keeping a job.

Some of the other components would include social and recreational counseling. Often folks will need to establish new social contacts and new relationships or maybe new positive social or recreational activities that don't involve alcohol or drugs. You want to think about relapse prevention. There's a number of different strategies that are effective in helping a person stop using, but the real test comes in, can they stay clean for 30 days, 60 days, 90 days, 6 months, 5 years and so on? They teach clients to identify high-risk situations, and they teach them to anticipate or to cope with potential relapses. Another important part that CRA adds is relationship counseling. They know that substance-use disorders plays a great, tremendous stress on the individual and their significant others. It teaches them how to improve the interaction between client and his or her partner.

The next type of therapy that I wanted to talk about is similar to some of the things that we've talked about in the past when we've talked about cognitive therapy in contrast to mindfulness-based cognitive therapy for the treatment of depression. But here were talk about substance abuse. Cognitive behavioral therapy is still a leading player, but we've added something now called Mindfulness-based Relapse Prevention or MBRP. This was initially developed by Alan Marlatt in Washington State and is currently being studied by Sarah Bowen. And here, I really want you to think back to those third-wave therapies with their focus on mindfulness and sometimes accepting the storms that come in, the cravings that might come in in terms of substance abuse, and not necessarily wrestling with them, but just letting them diminish and to leave on their own.

So in MBRP, they user the acronym SOBER, where the S stands for Stop; the O stands for Observe; the B stands for Breathe; the E stands for Expand Awareness; and the R stands for Respond Mindful. So, if we think about substance-use disorders, an individual will often see a trigger; that trigger may activate a physiologic or psychologic craving to reach out and smoke that cigarette, to have that drink, to use drugs. What SOBER does is it teaches an individual to slow down. It gives them that couple-second pause so that their frontal lobe, that executive functioning, can kick in and say, "Wait a minute. Is this really what you want to do? Is this in service of your values and your goals, or can we have you step outside of the situation, or maybe call somebody for help?"

Now, an example of a strategy often used as part of mindfulness-based relapse prevention is something called surfing the urge, and it's something that we use with Michael. And just to remind you, Michael used to be a pack-a-day smoker, so he was physiologically addicted to nicotine. When he stopped smoking, he would have cravings for nicotine. Now, often, when an individual has a physiologic craving, they imagine that the intensity of that craving will just continue to go up, and up, and up, and up until they just can't stand it anymore.

But we know that the way cravings work, yes, there is a physiologic increase to that craving, but it hits a plateau; it stays at that plateau for a relatively short period of time; then that craving begins to decrease. So really, all you need to do is to buckle your seat belt while you're having that craving, and this too shall pass. So surfing the urge first teaches the skills of mindfulness and of awareness, but it tells the individual, you have this wave coming in, rather than allow yourself to get hammered by that wave, take out your surfboard and surf that urge into the shore, step off, and go about your way.

So how about evidence for mindfulness-based relapse prevention? And this is a study by Sarah Bowen that was published in 2014. She looked at 268 individuals with substance-use disorders, and she looked at three different kinds of treatment. She looked at cognitive-based or cognitive behavioral therapy that focused on relapse prevention; she looked on mindfulness-based relapse prevention; and she looked at treatment as usual. For individuals in aftercare following initial treatment for substance-use disorders, CBT relapse prevention and mindfulness-based relapse prevention were superior to treatment as usual. At 12-month follow-up, mindfulness-based relapse prevention offered an added benefit over CBT and treatment as usual in reducing drug use and heavy drinking. So it looks like maybe targeted mindfulness practices can support long-term outcomes by strengthening an individual's ability to monitor and skillfully cope with discomfort that comes from those cravings.

The next system that I wanted to introduce is something called TES, which stands for the Therapeutic Education System. And I wanted to illustrate this because it's delivered in a different modality. In TES, we have 62 Internet modules, so it's quite extensive. Again, as a CBT person, I see them and I think, "This has lots of CBT," but it's based primarily on CRA, the Community Reinforcement Approach developed by Lisa Marsch and her colleagues at Dartmouth University, and recently evaluated in a paper by Campbell in 2014, where they looked at 507 individuals using alcohol and drugs and working their way through these 62 Internet modules. What they found was that TES was superior to treatment as usual on both adherents and abstinence. So it looks like their treatment approach, CRA, delivered through an Internet modality, was helpful and successful.

Now, one of the interesting features of TES is that it uses a contingency management system to get people to do the modules. So essentially what happens is every time you use the module, you get a sort of lottery ticket that makes you eligible to win, say, $100 in prize money. Each time you take another module, you get another ticket, and your odds continue to go up There's a number of different variants on contingency management where you use lotteries or rewards or payments as a reward for someone, who, say, comes in and gives a urine sample and you can prove that they haven't been using.

But does contingency management work, and should we pay people to not engage in unhealthy behaviors? I want to share just a couple of studies on this topic. The first is by Farronato in 2013, and they did a systematic review of CBT versus contingency management for cocaine addiction. They found that contingency management produces very rapid results in the beginning of treatment and CBT produced results towards the end and after treatment had ended. About half of the studies that did a combination of the two showed better results, but half the studies showed that a combination didn't really matter, and they weren't very supportive of contingency management. In another study done looking at smoking, it was a Cochrane review by Cahill and Perera in 2011; they looked at 19 different studies, total of about 4,500 different subjects. There was only one large study out of their 19 studies, showed that payments for abstinence were beneficial. The incentives did increase participation, but the initial success faded after the rewards, and they went away.

So, it looks like incentives are just one extrinsic motivator, and it looks like the results are mixed for now. However, a more common scenario is when a family or a friend is trying to get their loved one to cut down or to quit using entirely. It's estimated that for every one substance abuser, there are five family members affected. So what should families do? Now, the last modality I wanted to talk is something called CRAFT. Now, this is CRA, as we've talked about before, but they've added an FT, which stands for family training. Now, CRAFT is a more recent outgrowth of CRA that focuses on how to help the loved ones of those abusing alcohol or drugs.

Now, I found a couple of books and websites about CRAFT that I thought were good and quite helpful. One was by Jeff Foote called *Beyond Addiction* and another by Robert Meyers called *Get Your Loved One Sober*. There's a website called the20minuteguide.com, with 20 using the numbers 2, 0. This website includes instructions, motivational messages about how to take care of yourself, how to communicate with your loved one, and how to get help if you need it.

The goal of CRAFT is to use positive communication to reinforce positive behaviors while taking care of yourself and using others' social supports. You want to highlight positive interactions, positive conversations, times when your loved one is sober or not using, times when they've been reliable. Some might say, "Is this enabling?" But remember that there is an important distinction. When you are enabling, you're increasing an individual's drug use behavior by removing negative consequences. You cover for them at work. You pay for them to have their car fixed, which they crashed when they were using. That might be enabling. A positive reinforcement increases non-drinking behavior. And thus far, the research results are positive.

Let's move on to ask one of our frequently asked questions, and this patient asked, "Other than surfing the urge to deal with cravings, what are some other strategies to cut down?" It really depends on the substance, and it depends on the severity of use, but the first thing that I would do is self-monitoring or some sort of substance use diary, where you not only want to record use, but you want to record the antecedents or the triggers, as well as the consequences. You might them think about removing triggers. If an individual is triggered because they drive by a bar on their way home from work, change the route that you drive so that you are able to avoid that trigger. You might also make some temporary or even permanent changes in your social circle. Remember our friends and family have a big influence on the behavioral choices we make. If they are pushing you in unhealthy directions, maybe it's time to have different social supports. Another helpful website to go to—and this is particularly for folks who might be in that at-risk drinking category—is called the Drinker's Checkup, which you can find on Google.

So, where does that leave us? Well, for Donovan, we really don't have very much information about his IV heroin use. We can hope that this was a one-time accident and that he might learn from that accident. Of course, if his use is much more developed than that, there's both pharmacotherapies as well as psychotherapies that might help. For Carol, we'll probably want to watch and wait. For Michael, he's made a lot of progress already with his smoking, and we'll want to help him build on those successes.

In our next lecture, we'll tackle the topic of insomnia. Thank you.

Getting a Good Night's Sleep
Lecture 18

Insomnia is defined as difficulty with the initiation, maintenance, duration, or quality of sleep that results in the impairment of daytime functioning, despite adequate opportunity and circumstances for sleep. In this lecture, you will learn that the same toolbox of CBT skills and strategies—assessment, self-monitoring, behavioral analysis—can be helpful for insomnia, as well as for energy and fatigue. In addition to insomnia, you will learn about normal sleep, including quantity, frequency, and stages of sleep.

Insomnia

- Most research studies adopt an arbitrary definition of insomnia as a delay of more than 30 minutes in sleep onset or a sleep efficiency of less than 85 percent. Your sleep efficiency is simply the ratio of time asleep to time spent in bed times 100.

- Fewer than half of Americans say that they get a good night's sleep on most nights. About 10 percent of the U.S. population has chronic insomnia, with chronic being defined as lasting more than one month. Higher rates of insomnia are found in people with chronic pain, psychiatric disorders, and alcohol or drug addictions, and the prevalence of insomnia rises with age.

- There is a large societal and economic impact of insomnia. In fact, *Business 2.0* estimates the American "sleeponomics" to be worth about 20 billion dollars per year, including everything from the more than 1,000 sleep clinics conducting overnight tests for disorders like apnea, to countless over-the-counter and herbal sleep aids, to how-to books and sleep-encouraging gadgets and talismans.

- Why do we sleep? What is the function? We don't actually know for sure, but we do know some of the medical consequences if an individual is sleep deprived. Anyone who has missed a night of sleep is very familiar with the compulsion for sleep the next day and the impairment in functioning and mood.

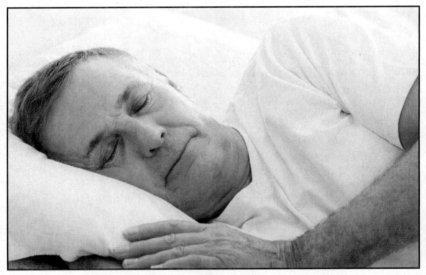

We don't know exactly why we sleep, but we do know the consequences of a lack of sleep.

Sleep

- On average, we need to have about seven to eight hours of sleep per night. Sleep is organized into five sleep stages that are systematically spread across time: stages one, two, three, and four (non-REM sleep stages) and rapid eye movement (REM) sleep, in which we do our dreaming.

- Each stage has a characteristic pattern on an electroencephalogram (EEG) that measures brain activity. A sleep hypnogram is a special kind of graph that plots stages of sleep over time—usually only the EEG activity. This type of graph shows the different stages of sleep and the multiple sleep cycles that occur over the night.

Hypnogram

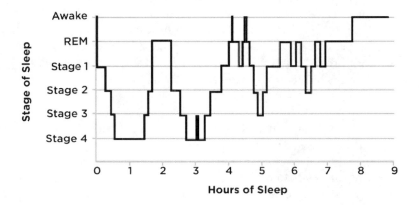

- A full cycle of sleep includes all five stages and is typically 90 to 100 minutes long, with a total of four to six cycles over the course of any given night of sleep. In general, the healthy young adult non-REM sleep accounts for about 75 to 90 percent of sleep time, and REM sleep accounts for about 10 to 25 percent.

- The proportion of time we spend in slow-wave sleep changes as we age. Men 20 to 29 years of age spend about 21 percent of their total sleep in slow-wave sleep. Once they reach ages 40 to 49, slow-wave sleep drops to about 8 percent, and those aged 60 to 69 only spend about 2 percent of their sleep time in slow-wave sleep. We really don't know why this is the case, but it's fairly well accepted that our sleep architecture changes as we grow older.

- There are two biological systems that make us sleep: circadian rhythms and the sleep homeostatic drive. There are psychological factors, such as expectations, scripts, behaviors (especially things you do right around bedtime), stress, mental fatigue, and depression. There are also social, cultural, or environmental factors (such as the sleep environment, which might make it easier or more difficult for you to fall asleep).

- Circadian rhythms essentially refer to our body's biological clocks. We have a number of automatic processes, such as body temperature or even normal cortisol secretion, that have daily diurnal rhythms, so something has to keep track of what time it is. We've all had the experience of waking up before our alarm clock or of knowing that it's around 3 pm in the afternoon because you are starting to get sleepy. It's all about circadian rhythms.

- We think of the sleep homeostatic drive as the yin to the yang of the circadian rhythm system. Our circadian rhythms help promote wakefulness during the day while our sleep homeostatic drive creates a drive for sleep that accumulates throughout the day and maximizes before bedtime. If you are sleep deprived, you might feel this profound and powerful drive to fall asleep at any time during the day.

- If we want to think about the psychological, behavioral, social, and environmental factors of sleep, we can combine them into something called sleep hygiene. Sleep hygiene is essentially a list of conditions that we believe are helpful or hurtful in terms of helping an individual get a good night's sleep.

Sleep Hygiene
- Keep regular bedtime and wake-up times.
- Keep the bedroom quiet, comfortable, and dark.
- Do a relaxation technique for 10 to 30 minutes before bed.
- Get regular exercise.
- Don't nap.
- Don't lie in bed feeling worried, anxious, or frustrated.
- Don't lie awake in bed for long periods of time.
- Don't use alcohol, caffeine, or nicotine.
- Turn off your television, cell phone, and computer.

Energy and Fatigue

- Fatigue can be caused by a number of factors and is usually the body's way of slowing us down so that it can recover, often by helping us go to sleep. We often complain that we don't have enough energy—hence the market for energy drinks and the vast success of Starbucks coffee.

- But how can we assess what level of energy is normal? Why is it that some people are still fatigued even after a good night's sleep? How can some people be exhausted even if they haven't exerted themselves?

- Sleep and fatigue are closely related to one another, but they're not entirely the same. Fatigue is one of the most commonly presented symptoms in a primary care practice. In typical clinical practice, fatigue is evaluated with one item only: On a scale of 1 to 10, with 10 being the most severe, what is your average level of fatigue? Any patient who reports a rating of 4 or higher warrants a further workup.

- Things that might be assessed at this point include stress, depression or other mental health issues, nutrition, medications (over the counter or prescription), quality of sleep, chronic pain, anemia, thyroid function, or a number of other medical conditions that might help to explain your fatigue.

- There are targeted interventions that we might try for any of these factors, but first we need to start with assessment. One way to measure sleep is with a sleep diary, which is essentially self-monitoring for sleep.

- In a sleep diary, we want an individual to write down the time entering and leaving bed, sleep onset latency (how long it takes to fall asleep), number and duration of awakenings during the night, time of final awakening, napping, subjective sleep ratings of the quality of sleep, daytime sleepiness, medications/alcohol, and sleep efficiency.

- There are a number of new technological tools for assessing sleep, such as Fitbit or other technologies that you can strap to your wrist. You wear it while you sleep, and these devices are able to deduce how well you slept that night. This is much easier than a sleep diary, but it doesn't give you as much information.

- If you were interested in measuring fatigue, there are a number of questionnaires—many from the cancer literature and some from the chronic fatigue literature—that measure fatigue intensity, consequences or impact of fatigue, timing of fatigue, related symptoms, and self-care actions.

CBT for Insomnia

- There are CBT interventions that have been especially designed for insomnia. In fact, there's a subtype of CBT called CBT-I, where the "I" stands for insomnia. This particular subset of CBT focuses on changing sleep habits, altering schedules and sleep environments, and challenging misconceptions about sleep. CBT-I starts with an assessment (usually a detailed sleep diary), moves to a formulation for likely causes, and includes psychoeducation on sleep and sleep hygiene.

- Another intervention for people with insomnia is stimulus control therapy. For example, the patient is told only to go to bed when he or she feels sleepy, only to use the bed for sleep and sex (not for work), and to get out of bed if he or she is not able to fall asleep within 30 minutes.

- This is similar to a type of therapy called sleep restriction therapy, which is used for people who are spending a lot of time tossing and turning in bed. For this type of therapy, patients reduce the number of hours they spend in bed to their estimated sleep time. Then, they increase the amount of time they spend in bed in 15-minute increments until their sleep efficiency is up to about 90 percent.

- Patients also might try progressive muscle relaxation, imagery, or other somatic quieting as relaxation strategies to help ease them into sleep. In addition, they might try some cognitive restructuring if right before bedtime they are having cognitions that make them anxious or activated or make it more difficult to sleep.

- Two large meta-analyses have shown that CBT, in comparison to a placebo control, yielded improvement in sleep latency and total sleep time in about 50 to 60 percent of people. However, that leaves a pretty good chunk of the population that it didn't work for.

- Sleep hygiene and other interventions can be tried, but there are also sleep medications or sleeping pills that fall into a few different categories: sedatives/hypnotics, benzodiazepines, benzodiazepine agonists (such as Ambien, Sonata, and Lunesta), and antidepressants. Over-the-counter drugs include diphenhydramine (Benadryl and Tylenol PM) and melatonin.

- It's estimated that about 50 million prescriptions for sleep aids are written every year, and they cost about 4 billion dollars. These drugs can certainly put a person to sleep, but sleep is very complex, and we just can't have the same quality of sleep with pharmacotherapy.

- In fact, a randomized controlled trial that was published by Gregg Jacobs and colleagues in 2004 looked at CBT versus medications versus a combination versus a placebo. They had four different conditions. They found that CBT outperformed medications and that there was no advantage to using the combination of CBT plus medications.

- In a systematic review by Matthew Mitchell and colleagues in 2012, they found that CBT-I for insomnia was superior to medications overall.

Suggested Reading

Jacobs, *Say Goodnight to Insomnia*.

Jacobs, Pace-Schott, Stickgold, and Otto, "Cognitive Behavior Therapy and Pharmacotherapy for Insomnia."

Mendoza, Wang, Cleeland, et al, "The Rapid Assessment of Fatigue Severity in Cancer Patients."

Mitchell, Gehrman, Perlis, and Umscheid, "Comparative Effectiveness of Cognitive Behavioral Therapy for Insomnia."

Morin, Colecchi, Stone, Sood, and Brink, "Behavioral and Pharmacological Therapies for Late-Life Insomnia."

Piper, Dibble, Dodd, et al, "The Revised Piper Fatigue Scale."

Sivertsen, Omvik, Pallesen, Bjorvatn, Havik, Kvale, Nielsen, and Nordhus, "Cognitive Behavioral Therapy vs. Zopiclone for Treatment of Chronic Primary Insomnia in Older Adults."

Smith, Perlis, Park, Smith, Pennington, Giles, and Buysse, "Comparative Meta-Analysis of Pharmacotherapy and Behavior Therapy for Persistent Insomnia."

Questions to Consider

1. Is a decline in the quality of sleep an unavoidable consequence of age? What can you do that might mitigate the negative effects of lower-quality sleep?

2. Despite decades of research, we still don't have a clear idea of why we dream. What are the beliefs you hold about dreams and dreaming? Are they random noise? Are they worthy topics for exploration in psychotherapy (for example, dream analysis)?

Getting a Good Night's Sleep
Lecture 18—Transcript

PROFESSOR SATTERFIELD: Catch some shut-eye. Get your Zs. Counting sheep and sawing logs. Those little slices of death being reborn, dipped again in God. Sleep that knits up the raveled sleeve of care. Writers and thinkers since the time of Gilgamesh have been waxing poetic about the power and beauty of sleep and that special pain of insomnia. It touches us in a very primal and powerful place.

Insomnia is defined as difficulty with the initiation, maintenance, duration, or quality of sleep that results in the impairment of daytime functioning despite adequate opportunity and circumstances for sleep. Most research studies adopt an arbitrary definition of a delay of more than 30 minutes in sleep onset or a sleep efficiency of less than 85%. And your sleep efficiency is simply the ratio of time asleep to time spent in bed, times 100.

Fewer than half of Americans say they get a good night's sleep on most nights. About 10% of the U.S. population have what is called chronic insomnia, with chronic being defined as lasting more than one month. You see higher rates of insomnia in people with chronic pain, psychiatric disorders, alcohol or drug addictions, and the prevalence of insomnia rises with age.

We know that there is a large societal and economic impact. In fact, Business 2.0 estimates the American sleeponomics to be worth about $20 billion a year. And that includes everything from the 1,000-plus sleep labs to ongoing overnight tests for things like sleep apnea to over-the-counter medications, herbal supplements, how-to books, and all sorts of gadgets and gizmos meant to help us get a good night's rest.

But why do we sleep and exactly what is the function? Well, we don't actually know for sure, but we do know some of the medical consequences if an individual is sleep deprived. For anyone who's missed a night of sleep, you are very much familiar with the compulsion for sleep the next day, and the impairment in functioning, the impairment in mood. But let's look first at what normal sleep is. We will look at quantity, frequency, and we'll look at different stages of sleep or what's called Sleep Architecture.

Now, on average, we need to have about seven to eight hours of sleep per night. Sleep is organized into five sleep stages that are systematically spread across time. They're named stages one, two, three, and four; these are the non-REM sleep stages. And the fifth stage is REM sleep or Rapid Eye Movement sleep, where we do our dreaming. Each stage has a characteristic pattern on an EEG, or an Electroencephalogram, that measures brain activity. If you want to measure your stages of sleep across a particular night of sleep, you would use a sleep hypnogram that uses EEG measurements overtime.

Now, a full cycle of sleep includes all five stages, and it's typically 90 to 100 minutes total. And you have a total of four to six cycles over the course of any given night of sleep. In general, the healthy young adult non-REM sleep accounts for about 75 to 90% of sleep, and REM sleep account for about 10 to 25%. And again, total sleep time in a healthy adult is about seven to eight hours.

Now, we know that the proportion of time we spend in slow-wave sleep changes as we age. Men 20 to 29 years spend about 21% of their total sleep in slow-wave sleep. Those aged 40 to 49, it drops down to about 8%, and those aged 60 to 69 only spend about 2% of their sleep time in slow-wave sleep. Why? Well, again, we're not really sure, but it's fairly well accepted that we see these changes in sleep architecture as we grow older.

So what is it that makes us sleep? And I'll just touch on a couple of different explanations, and here we're going back to use our biopsychosocial model, where there's two biological systems—circadian rhythms and something called the sleep homeostatic drive. There are psychological factors, such as expectations, scripts, behaviors, especially things that you do right around bedtime. Stress or mental fatigue or depression might also be factors. And then of course there's social, cultural, or environmental factors, such as the sleep environment that might make it easier or more difficult for you to fall asleep.

So let's just talk briefly about circadian rhythms. And circadian rhythms, essentially, refer to our body's biological clocks. So we have a number of automatic processes, like body temperature, or even normal cortisol secretion, that have daily diurnal rhythms. So something goes up, something goes down; it's essentially meant to give you the right level of energy or alertness at the right period of time. We've all had the experience of waking up before our alarm clock or knowing that it's around 3:00 pm or so in the afternoon, because you feel that dip in energy, and you start to get a little bit sleepy. It's all about circadian rhythms.

There's also the sleep homeostatic drive. And we think of the sleep homeostatic drive as the yin to the yang of the circadian rhythm system. So, our circadian rhythms help promote wakefulness during the day, while our sleep homeostatic drive creates a drive for sleep that accumulates throughout the day and maximizes before bedtime. If you are sleep deprived however, you might feel this profound and powerful drive to fall asleep at any time during the day.

Now, if we want to think about both the psychological as well as social or environmental factors, we can pull them all together and talk about something called sleep hygiene, and sleep hygiene is essentially a system, or really, a list of conditions that we believe are helpful or hurtful in terms of helping an individual get a good night's sleep. So a list of sleep hygiene, and again, it includes both behavioral as well as psychological, environmental, it's things such as keeping a regular bedtime and a regular wake-up time even on the weekends; keeping your bedroom quiet, comfortable, and dark; having a period of relaxation time before bed of 10 to 30 minutes, and for many individuals, this might be reading a book; getting regular exercise, but not exercising within an hour or two before bed time; not taking naps during the day, or if you do find that you need to nap, not napping after 2:00 pm, and trying to do what they call power naps, or just 20 to 30 minutes, so it doesn't disrupt your ability to go to sleep at night.

Other recommendations include if you do wake up in the middle of the night, which is quite common and nothing necessarily to worry about, don't lie in bed feeling worried or frustrated for more than 20 or 30 minutes. Get up and do something that is relaxing. Don't use alcohol, caffeine, or nicotine, again, particularly with any sort of proximity to your bedtime, and to make sure to turn off TVs, cellphones, and computers. And many of us love to look at our iPads or our iPhones, those glowing screens right before bed, and there's recent research to show us that that actually wakes us up and activates us.

But what about energy or fatigue? We're all familiar with the experience of being tired or fatigued, and fatigue can be caused by a number of factors, and it's usually the body's way of slowing us down so that the body can recover, often by helping us go to sleep. But we often complain that we don't have enough energy, hence the market for energy drinks and the vast success of Starbucks. But how can we assess what level of energy is normal? Why is it that some people are still fatigued, even after a good night's sleep? Or how can some people be exhausted, even if they haven't exerted themselves?

We know that sleep and fatigue are closely related to one another, but they're not entirely the same. Fatigue is one of the most commonly presented symptoms in a primary care practice, and there's really a very simple and unsophisticated way to assess it. It's usually with one item, where the clinician will ask, on a scale of 1 to 10, with 10 being most severe, what is your average level of fatigue? Any patient that says they have a 4 or higher warrants a further workup.

So what are the things they might work up or look for? They will look for stress. They will look for depression or other mental health issues. They might look for nutrition or whether it's a side-effect of medications, over-the-counter or prescription, that you might be on. They might look at your quality of sleep; they might want to do a hypnogram or a sleep study; maybe it's chronic pain, anemia, thyroid function, or a number of other medical conditions that might help to explain your fatigue.

Now, for Maria, she has both insomnia and fatigue. Both are key symptoms of depression, and insomnia most likely worsens her fatigue. Now, treating her depression without any special attention to sleep or fatigue may be sufficient, but there are targeted interventions that we might try. First, though, we need to start with assessment.

So what we would do with Maria, or really, any patient, is do something called a sleep diary, which is essentially self-monitoring for sleep. We want an individual to write down the time entering and leaving bed. We might want to look at sleep onset latencies, so how long does it take to fall asleep, number and duration of wakenings during the night, final awakening, napping, subjective sleep ratings of the quality of sleep, whether or not you're sleepy and able to function the next day. Of course, we want to look at those hygiene factors as well. There are a number of new technological tools, such as a Fitbit or other technologies, which you can strap to your wrist. You wear it while you sleep, and they're able, through an algorithm, to deduce how well you slept that night. Certainly much easier than a sleep diary, but doesn't quite give you as much information. If you were interested in measuring fatigue, there's a number of questionnaires, mostly from the cancer literature or from the chronic fatigue literature, all measuring intensity, consequences, or impact of the fatigue, timing-related symptoms, and self-care. Let's move then to our first clip of Maria, where we are assessing her quality of sleep.

[VIGNETTE START]

PROFESSOR SATTERFIELD: Maria, why don't we switch gears now and talk a little bit about sleep, and specifically, about insomnia.

MARIA: OK.

PROFESSOR SATTERFIELD: And as we mentioned before, that's one of our goals. And it's very important for energy, and mood, and for well-being. And I think before we begin exploring different interventions, we just need more data. So we need more information on how you sleep. So would it be OK if I ask you some questions about how you're sleeping or not sleeping?

MARIA: Of course.

PROFESSOR SATTERFIELD: OK. So if we just think about, say, the past week, so keep it fairly recent, on average, about how many hours of sleep per night do you get? And that's sort of summed up over the course of a night.

MARIA: Well, I don't know. Maybe four or five?

PROFESSOR SATTERFIELD: So four to five hours per night. That's average. And what time do you usually go to bed for the first time?

MARIA: Well, I try to go to bed when my husband goes to bed, and that's around 10 o'clock. But I don't usually fall asleep then.

PROFESSOR SATTERFIELD: OK. So 10:00 pm. And sounds like some trouble falling asleep.

MARIA: Yeah. But I'm usually, you know, my brain is just going and going at the end of the day like that.

PROFESSOR SATTERFIELD: All right. So a lot of thoughts.

MARIA: Yeah. Yeah, a lot of thoughts.

PROFESSOR SATTERFIELD: And about how long does it usually take you to fall asleep?

MARIA: I don't know. I try not to look at the clock, but sometimes I do, and it's after midnight.

PROFESSOR SATTERFIELD: OK. So it can take two hours or so?

MARIA: Can take that long, yeah. Sometimes it's faster than that.

PROFESSOR SATTERFIELD: OK. So it can be up to two hours. And once you fall asleep, do you stay asleep or do you wake up in the middle of the night?

MARIA: Sometimes I wake up in the middle of the night and just sort of lie awake and think about things again, you know?

PROFESSOR SATTERFIELD: What wakes you up?

MARIA: I don't know. Just anything. I just wake up, I guess. I just wake myself up.

PROFESSOR SATTERFIELD: OK. So it's not noise in the house, or going to the bathroom, or hunger?

MARIA: Oh, sometimes my husband gets up. Sometimes he's getting dressed in the middle of the night, and I have to get him back to bed. But he thinks he's going to work. But it isn't always that. Sometimes I just wake up and lie there, just worrying.

PROFESSOR SATTERFIELD: OK.

MARIA: Thinking about things.

PROFESSOR SATTERFIELD: All right. And what time do you get up in the morning, or get out of bed in the morning?

MARIA: Oh, I usually get up by 6:30 or so.

PROFESSOR SATTERFIELD: All right. So ideally, if you're in bed from 10:00 to 6:30 that would be eight and a half hours.

MARIA: Yeah, that would be eight. That'd be wonderful.

PROFESSOR SATTERFIELD: You're getting four to five now, so there's a lot of time trying to fall asleep, getting up and of the night.

MARIA: Yeah.

PROFESSOR SATTERFIELD: Do you ever wake up, say, before 6:30, like, 4:00 or 5:00 in the morning and you just can't …?

MARIA: Yeah, and then I figure, well, you know, I'm going to get up in an hour anyway, so I just stay awake.

PROFESSOR SATTERFIELD: Right. OK. All right. So the reason I ask some of these questions, we want to get a sense, again, a baseline where you're starting. But we also wanted to see if there's a consistent pattern to your insomnia. Some people just have trouble falling asleep. Some people just have the issue of waking up too early in the morning. I think it's a mixed bag for you.

MARIA: Yeah.

PROFESSOR SATTERFIELD: OK. All right. My next set of questions are about common things that affect the quality of our sleep, and you probably know many of these already. First question is about stimulants like caffeine. Are you a coffee or tea drinker?

MARIA: I try not to drink coffee or tea after noon, more or less. Yeah.

PROFESSOR SATTERFIELD: All right.

MARIA: Sometimes I have a little chocolate at night. A little piece of chocolate. I don't know if that affects it or not. But I know that has a little caffeine.

PROFESSOR SATTERFIELD: Yeah, yeah. OK. So sounds like you're fairly careful with the caffeine.

MARIA: Try to be.

PROFESSOR SATTERFIELD: How about alcohol? Sometimes people will have a nightcap or a glass of wine at the end of the day to relax.

MARIA: Yeah, sometimes I have a glass of wine. Yeah.

PROFESSOR SATTERFIELD: OK. About how often, would you say?

MARIA: A couple times a week. Something like that, yeah.

PROFESSOR SATTERFIELD: And I ask, you know, alcohol is a depressant. It relaxes us. And it often helps people fall asleep. The problem is it affects sleep quality, and then you'll often wake up in the middle in the night, or wake up too early. But it sounds like it's not sort of a regular thing that you do.

MARIA: I think it's other things. I've always had a glass of wine occasionally. It hasn't bothered me before.

PROFESSOR SATTERFIELD: Sure. OK. Now, tell me about your sleep environment. And I'm interested in things like temperature, sound, comfort.

MARIA: Comfort?

PROFESSOR SATTERFIELD: Yeah.

MARIA: Well, I sleep with Jack, still. He's like a space heater. I'm kind of cold myself, but he's so warm. I don't even have to be touching him, you know? I could be just, like, six inches away and warm as toast because he's so warm. He does snore some, but you now, I just think, when he's snoring, he's still alive, at least. I know that he's alive if he's snoring. So it doesn't really bother me that much. He's always snored.

PROFESSOR SATTERFIELD: OK. So sleep environment, sounds like that's, again, not the cause. That's OK.

MARIA: It just seems like it's just the worries, you know? Just thinking about things so much.

PROFESSOR SATTERFIELD: And how often does he interrupt your sleep by getting up, or thrashing about or?

MARIA: No more than one time in a night, usually. Sometimes he'll get up and go to the bathroom on his own. Sometimes he can still do that. And that doesn't bother me.

PROFESSOR SATTERFIELD: All right. Now, what about daytime napping? That's often when people try to catch up on their sleep. But they sleep during the day, and then it's harder to sleep at night.

MARIA: Yeah. If he falls sleep in the afternoon, I'll try to get in a little sleep. I don't always feel like sleeping at that time of day, but I do try sometimes to get a nap.

PROFESSOR SATTERFIELD: And is that usually 20 minutes, 30 minutes, two hours?

MARIA: It's not two hours, but it might be 30 minutes, yeah.

PROFESSOR SATTERFIELD: OK. And how about physical activity? We know in general, exercise, physical activity improves sleep, unless it's done right before bedtime, then you're sort of activated and it's harder to go to sleep.

MARIA: Yeah. I probably don't exercise enough. I don't do anything, really, in the evenings. I'm tired at that point, so I don't exercise then. I wish I exercised more. I used to exercise more. Maybe I'd sleep better I did.

PROFESSOR SATTERFIELD: OK. All right. Well, what I'll do is, before you leave today, I'll give you a handout on recommendations for something they call sleep hygiene. And sounds like you're doing most of them already. And that's attention to stimulants, and alcohol, and sleep environment, and physical activity, and daytime naps, and so on.

MARIA: Will I have to give up chocolate?

PROFESSOR SATTERFIELD: You won't have to give up chocolate. So we'll give you that. It sounds like you pretty much maximized many of those already. But I think it's good, still, to have the information. The other thing we'll need is to have you collect data, do self-monitoring on your sleep. And I wanted to propose that we do this in sort of a new, higher-tech kind of way, by using a device that tracks your sleep. Have you seen these before?

MARIA: Yeah. I think my son has one of those. He's a big fitness buff. He runs marathons and things.

PROFESSOR SATTERFIELD: OK. All right. Well, essentially, what it does is it electronically records physical activity, things like steps, throughout the day. But we're going to use it for sleep. And based on your body movements, it's able to deduce the quality of sleep that you have.

And we, in the past, have used paper sleep diaries. And I'll still give you a form where you can record extra things. But it was difficult for people, because you don't want to interfere with their sleep by having them fill out a sleep diary, or maybe the next morning, they may not know exactly how much they slept or the quality. But this gives you a little more of an objective measure of, how many hours are you sleeping? What was the quality of sleep?

What we won't have, and what you can fill out on a sleep diary that I'll give to you is, if there weren't any external factors that influenced your sleep. Your husband got up at 2:00 am and started getting dressed for work. So we'll want to know, sort of, when those things occur, and what they are, and if there's anything we can do about it. So what you would do is just put this on before bedtime. It will collect data for you. And I'll show you how you can either, on your own, you can sync it to your computer, iPad, some of these even connect to your phone. Either your son can show you, or I could show you right afterwards.

MARIA: OK. Thank you.

PROFESSOR SATTERFIELD: All right? So I want to make sure I did a good job explaining how you're going to track your sleep. And there's sort of two parts. One's the bracelet, and one's the sleep record. So how will you use this?

MARIA: So I'll figure out how to use the Fitbit, and my son can probably tell me how to use that. I'll talk to him. And then I'm going to fill out anything that happens in the night that affects how I sleep on that form that you'll get me.

PROFESSOR SATTERFIELD: Anything else you think we should be recording on that form, because remember, we want to keep it collaborative.

MARIA: Um, well, maybe when I have a good night's sleep. If I get one, I'll write that down.

PROFESSOR SATTERFIELD: Yeah. Perfect. And I think we want to identify obstacles to sleep, but we also want to identify facilitators. So the positives. So let me give you both of these. And we'll see how you did next week.

MARIA: Thank you. Thank you.

[VIGNETTE END]

PROFESSOR SATTERFIELD: As I mentioned, there are CBT interventions that have been especially designed for insomnia. In fact, there's a subtype of CBT called CBTI, where the I stands for insomnia. And in this particular subset of CBT, you focus on changing sleep habits; altering schedules and sleep environment; challenging misconceptions about sleep, cognitions such as "If I don't get a good night's sleep, tomorrow will be terrible," or cognitions such as, "If I wake up in the middle of the night, that means something must be wrong." Of course, it starts with an assessment; it starts with a formulation, and includes psychoeducation on sleep and sleep hygiene.

Other interventions we might use for Maria are things such as stimulus control therapy. An example there is that she would be told only to go to bed when she feels sleepy. She would have the same time to get up every morning, but only going to bed when she's sleepy, and only using the bed for sleep and sex, not for work; you don't want your bed to be associated with the stress of work, and to get up out of bed if she's not able to fall asleep within 30 minutes. This is similar to a type of therapy called sleep restriction therapy, where essentially folks are spending a lot of time tossing and turning in bed. You shrink the amount of hours that they spend in bed until you can increase their level of sleep efficiency up to about 90%.

Now of course we might use some progressive muscle relaxation, some imagery, or other somatic quieting as a relaxation strategy to help ease her into sleep. The other thing we try is to do some cognitive restructuring if we find that right before bedtime she's having cognitions that make her anxious or activated, or make it more difficult to sleep. Let's move to look at our second clip of Maria.

[VIGNETTE START]

MARIA: Well, I filled out this form that you gave me about sleep and thoughts that I had about it. And I don't know if I did it all right, but I took a crack at it.

PROFESSOR SATTERFIELD: OK, good.

MARIA: So when I'm getting ready for bed, the feelings that I'm having, I'm sort of anxious and worried. I don't know why. It may be just at night, you feel more afraid, you know? And it gets dark and everything seems a little worse than it does during the day. And so, when I lie down to go to sleep, even though two hours before, I was so exhausted, I could hardly keep my eyes open, when I lie down, then there I am, wide awake again. And thinking about things, and thinking about things.

PROFESSOR SATTERFIELD: OK. So it looks like you did a thought record about thoughts you have before bed. Is that right?

MARIA: Yeah.

PROFESSOR SATTERFIELD: OK. You chose the seven-column version instead of the ABCD, which is terrific. So that's good. Do you want to just walk me through these different columns, starting with the trigger?

MARIA: OK. Yeah. Well, the trigger was the getting ready for bed. I wanted to see how I felt about it, and why I was having so much trouble. But just getting ready for bed. And then the feelings that I was having was that I was anxious, and stressed, and kind of wired I guess. Just kind of like I wanted to go to bed and go to sleep, but I didn't want to go to sleep. I was afraid to let go or something.

PROFESSOR SATTERFIELD: Right. And wired is not a feeling you want before bed.

MARIA: That's right. That's right. And that's exactly when it happens. Because if I were wired in the morning, I'd be fine. But I'm wired at night instead.

PROFESSOR SATTERFIELD: OK. And I saw where you wrote "anxious." You have wired, and you have sadness, and tell me about these intensities that you rated those emotions.

MARIA: Well, the anxiety and being worried, that was pretty intense, you know? Maybe 6 out of 10. Something like that. And the sad, well, I was just looking at Jack in bed, and you know, that's so constant. I don't know. Maybe a 40 out of 100. Four out of 10.

PROFESSOR SATTERFIELD: OK. All right. So we have anxiety at about a 6 out of 10, sadness about a 4 out of 10 or so.

MARIA: Yeah, something like that.

PROFESSOR SATTERFIELD: OK. All right. And here, you've captured some of the thoughts that you were having. So what were they?

MARIA: Right. Oh, the thing I'm thinking is, I can't get to sleep. And if I can't get to sleep, I'll feel horrible in the morning. And if I feel horrible in the morning, I won't be able to do what I need to do. And then, of course, that makes me more worried and anxious. And so it's just kind of a spiral down.

PROFESSOR SATTERFIELD: Right. Right. You see this, almost, chain reaction. I don't sleep, and then I feel bad, and then I can't do the things I need to do and then.

MARIA: Exactly, exactly. Yeah. How am I going to get enough sleep? How could I possibly?

PROFESSOR SATTERFIELD: What was at the end of that chain? So you don't sleep, you'll feel miserable in the morning, you'll be really tired, you won't be able to take care of Jack, and then what's the catastrophe, I guess, at the end, or the disaster that would happen?

MARIA: Well, I thought that was it. Not being able to take care of Jack. Something will happen to him and I won't be able to cope. Or he'll be unhappy and I'll be useless.

PROFESSOR SATTERFIELD: OK. OK. So he'll suffer in some way?

MARIA: Uh-huh. Yeah. Yeah.

PROFESSOR SATTERFIELD: If you don't sleep? That's a lot of pressure. That's lot of pressure, right, to put on yourself, though.

MARIA: Yeah.

PROFESSOR SATTERFIELD: OK. All right. And these next two columns were designed to help you weigh the evidence for and against. So let's talk about the evidence that supports this idea that, if you don't sleep, then he's going to suffer the next because you'll be able to take care of him.

MARIA: OK. Well, if I don't sleep, sometimes I don't sleep. And then, the next day, I do feel terrible. And then I'm just not very good at all, the things that happen, and I'm more irritable. And I wish it weren't happening. And you know, I'm just not that good with him. Nothing terrible happens. He hasn't died. But you know, it's not a good feeling.

PROFESSOR SATTERFIELD: OK. So you're not on your A game, for sure. But it's not the worst-case scenario it sounds like.

MARIA: No. Nobody died.

PROFESSOR SATTERFIELD: OK. And one of those habits of mind that we've talked about is the all or none thinking, the black or white thinking. And I think, especially when you're feeling anxious and vulnerable, and maybe going to bed, everything seems black or white, that it's going to be worst-case scenario.

MARIA: It always seems worse at night.

PROFESSOR SATTERFIELD: Well, tell me any other evidence you have for or against that thought of, if you don't sleep, he's going to suffer tomorrow.

MARIA: Well, sometimes when I don't sleep, he's more irritable the next day, or things happen to him like might happen to him in the night, and I wouldn't notice it because when I did get to sleep, I would be so dead to the world myself. But that doesn't happen that often. Usually, I do wake up when he wakes up.

PROFESSOR SATTERFIELD: Sure. And I know you have a home health worker, and you've been thinking of increasing hours. She comes in the morning at least a couple times a week.

MARIA: Yes, and we have a different one now, too.

PROFESSOR SATTERFIELD: Oh, good. Good. How's she?

MARIA: Yeah. It's actually working out pretty well. She's young, but she's nice. And Jack seems to like her. He was even flirting with her.

PROFESSOR SATTERFIELD: OK. [LAUGHS]

MARIA: It explains to me, here's a man who can't control his bowel or his bladder, and he doesn't know what he's had for breakfast, and he still remembers how to flirt. How do you scientists explain that?

PROFESSOR SATTERFIELD: Right, right. I don't have an explanation. Human nature, right? So how about on the nights before she's going to come? Are you able to just hand things off to her so you can sleep in late?

MARIA: Yes. There are some things that I can hand off to her when she comes. Yes. She can get him breakfast and get him dressed. If I can sleep. Usually I'm awake anyway by that time. But at least I don't feel as pressured.

PROFESSOR SATTERFIELD: OK. All right. Now, there's a couple of strategies, before we get to the alternative thought or the dispute box, really. We can talk about evidence for and against, but we can also talk about statements or thoughts that are more helpful, that might be about a behavior, a way to cope that might help you. So you're in bed, and you're feeling anxious, and you're feeling a bit keyed up. And you can continue to ruminate and think about those sorts of things and wrestle with your thoughts. Or is there an alternative of something else you could do while you're there in bed?

MARIA: Well, sometimes I try to think about something that's pleasing to me. Like, when I was a teenager, we lived in a little house, it was a white brick house with green roof. And it had beautiful flowers all over the front of it, roses in all different colors. And I just remember those roses and the way they smelled, and sometimes, if I can think about that, I can stop the cycle of going on and on.

PROFESSOR SATTERFIELD: So it sounds like you're using some guided imagery.

MARIA: Yes! Thanks to you.

PROFESSOR SATTERFIELD: And the helps to take your mind away, and to a more pleasant place.

MARIA: And sometimes I just try to tell myself, you know, it doesn't help to worry about it. The next morning, it's usually not as bad as I imagined it was at night. And I'm just spinning my wheels for nothing.

PROFESSOR SATTERFIELD: So that's an important thought to remember and to write down. Oftentimes, things seem worse at night. And in the morning, they seem much better. Things often don't turn out as bad as I think they might. So those are important thoughts to capture. And I think, on the behavioral side, the guided imagery is a great idea. I know you've also practice the progressive muscle relaxation and you've done some deep breathing as well. You've tried a little bit of meditation. So there's a whole menu of things that you can try.

MARIA: I've tried playing the tape with your voice, and that helps me sleep, sometimes. I'm able to fall asleep with that.

PROFESSOR SATTERFIELD: Oh, good. And if you fall asleep in the middle of the exercise, you know, excellent.

MARIA: You won't be hurt.

PROFESSOR SATTERFIELD: Not at all. Not at all. So I think for tonight, or tomorrow night, or whenever these anxious thoughts come up again if you have a couple of those pre-written, pre-analyzed alternate cognitions, things always seem much worse at night, things will be better in the morning, worst case scenario is very unlikely, I get help from the new home health worker. If I really need to, I can ask for more help. And you can then kick into guided imagery or some sort of relaxation to help, again, turn down that anxiety. All right? Is that something you can try?

MARIA: Yes. Yes, it is. Thank you.

PROFESSOR SATTERFIELD: So do that, and come back next time and let me know how it went.

MARIA: OK. I'll do that.

[VIGNETTE END]

PROFESSOR SATTERFIELD: But do these treatments work? I wanted to share two large meta-analyses that show that CBT, in comparison to a placebo control, yielded improvement in sleep latency and total sleep time in about 50 to 60% of people. That does leave a pretty good chunk of the population that it didn't work for. We might try sleep hygiene; we might try other interventions, but there are also sleep medications or sleeping pills, and they fall into a couple of different categories, sedatives or hypnotics, benzodiazepines, or their cousins of benzodiazepines, agonists, things like Ambien, Sonata, and Lunesta, or sometimes small doses of antidepressants that are sedating are also used. There might be over-the-counter drugs, such as diphenhydramine, brand name is Benadryl, things that they put in Tylenol PM, melatonin, and so on.

It's estimated that about 50 million prescriptions are written every year, and it costs about $4 billion dollars, all these different sleep aids. But do they work? Well, the answer is, they sort of work. We can certainly put a person to sleep, but I would encourage you to remember how complex sleep is. We proceed through those five different stages for about 100 minutes, then we cycle back around and we do it all over again. Imagine the complexity that a pill or a drug would have to have in order to change the way it works, five different times and then cycle back around and do it all over again. We just can't have the same quality of sleep with pharmacotherapy.

In fact, if you look at randomized control trial that was published by Jacobs in the Journal of the American Medical Association Internal Medicine in 2004, they did a randomized control trial of CBT versus meds, versus a combination, versus a placebo. So they had four different conditions. They found that cognitive behavioral therapy actually outperformed medications, and there was no advantage to using the combination of CBT plus medications. In a systematic review by Mitchell in 2012, they found that CBTI for insomnia was superior to medications overall.

So in summary, we see that that same toolbox; those same CBT skills; those same protocols, doing an assessment, doing self-monitoring, doing a behavioral analysis, those strategies can be helpful for insomnia. Those strategies could even be helpful for energy and fatigue.

We continue in our theme of behavioral medicine in our next lecture when we talk about chronic pain. Thank you.

Mastering Chronic Pain
Lecture 19

Whether minor or severe, chronic pain is regularly experienced by 15 to 20 percent of Americans each year. Both cognitive and behavioral factors influence the experience of pain and the intensity of suffering. In this lecture, you will learn about pain, how it is measured, and how psychological factors can alter the experience of pain. You also will learn about mind-body factors and chronic pain, including gate theory, depression, anxiety, positive emotions, and stress. Furthermore, you will learn how well the CBT toolbox works for pain.

Pain

- The International Association for the Study of Pain defines pain as an unpleasant sensory and emotional experience associated with actual or potential tissue damage. The largest cause of acute pain is surgery. Approximately 46 million procedures are performed each year, and most patients report moderate to severe pain post-surgically, even in the face of current treatments and techniques.

- In general, acute pain is thought to be an important and adaptive signal. It tells us of imminent tissue damage. It only takes one touch of a hot stove to learn not to touch that hot stove. There are diseases such as Hansen's disease, commonly called leprosy, where an individual is unable to feel pain, and as a consequence, he or she suffers ongoing tissue damage.

- But there are also times when pain misinforms us—like in the case of fibromyalgia, a chronic pain disorder—or is so intense that it overwhelms us. Fortunately for some, pain can be entirely suppressed so that we can think clearly and escape danger.

- The process of being able to feel pain is called nociception. There are four basic steps.

- Transduction: where nociceptors, or pain receptors, transduce noxious stimuli into nociceptive impulses.

- Transmission: where electrical impulses are sent via afferent nerves to the spinal cord and then along sensory tracts to the brain.

- Modulation: the process of dampening or amplifying pain related to the neural signal (hugely important for mind-body medicine).

- Perception: the subjective experience of pain that results from transduction, transmission, and modulation plus psychological and social factors at play within the individual.

- Chronic pain has usually been defined arbitrarily as pain that persists for three to six months or longer, or beyond the period of expected healing. Ongoing or progressive tissue damage may be present in some types of chronic pain, including progressive neuropathic pain and some rheumatologic conditions. In other cases, chronic pain may be present when tissue damage is stable or even undetectable.

- Unlike acute pain, chronic pain is now thought to be a disease of the central nervous system that involves some sort of maladaptive reprogramming of the brain and/or spinal cord. The brain can generate terrible pain in a wound that has long healed or even chronic pain in a limb that has been amputated and no longer exists.

Chronic pain, such as the pain experienced by arthritis sufferers, is thought to be a disease of the central nervous system.

- On average, 15 to 20 percent of Americans experience chronic pain each year—approximately 46 million people. Headache is the most common, followed by back pain, arthritis pain, and other musculoskeletal pain.

- We need to distinguish acute pain from chronic pain. We think of chronic pain as a syndrome—really as an entirely different disorder. In a way, it takes on a life of its own. In addition to the reprogramming of the brain, chronic pain also has potentially devastating consequences on mood, depression, anger, anxiety, social relationships, finances, and image. You can think of chronic pain as a chronically stressful condition that essentially keeps the stress response turned on all the time.

Measuring Pain
- In a medical setting, pain is now called the fifth vital sign, and it's regularly assessed. Clinicians assess the sensation, or nociception, of pain. They simply ask, on a scale of 1 to 10, with 10 being the most intense, what's your average pain? They also might ask you, what's the highest pain you've experienced in the past week? What's the lowest? What makes it better? What makes it worse? Clinicians might show younger individuals a series of happy to sad faces and have them point to which of those best matches the intensity of the pain they feel.

- Clinicians also might do some functional impairment measures. They are looking for impairment in activities of daily living as well as social or occupational impairment as a consequence of your pain.

- You also might be asked to rate, on a scale of 1 to 10, your level of emotional suffering. It's important to distinguish between the physical sensation of pain and the emotional suffering that might be tied to pain; they're often correlated with one another, but they might be quite different.

- Keep in mind that there is no objective measure of pain; there is no lab test. It's all based on self-report.

The Role of the Central Nervous System

- The central nervous system is involved in pain. The central nervous system is the seat of cognition, emotion, and expectation. The central nervous system also is important in directing the transduction from the psychological experience of pain into the biological, and vice versa.

- The nociceptors transmit signals to the spinal cord, which then transmit to the central nervous system or to the brain, where perception and modulation might occur. Modulation of pain happens all the time. For example, soldiers on the battlefield might not realize they've been injured and feel no pain until they're in a safer context, and then they begin to feel pain.

- In response to the growing awareness of mind-body phenomena in the realm of pain, the gate control theory of pain was first described in the early 1960s by Ronald Melzack and Patrick Wall. In this theory, pain signals encounter what are called nerve gates in the spinal cord that open or close depending on a number of factors, possibly including instructions coming down from the central nervous system.

- When the gates are open, pain messages can get through, and pain can be intense. When the gates close, pain messages are prevented from reaching the brain and may not even be experienced at all. It essentially gives us one mechanism for modulation that takes place in the spinal cord.

- A number of observational studies on the variability of pain experience have suggested that gate control might actually be true. Something must be happening to modulate the experience of pain, which has been well documented. For example, we know that pain transmission seems to have a limited bandwidth. You have, for example, A fibers that send fast and sharp pain, and you have C fibers that send slow and dull pain. If you stub your toe or hit your hand, the A fibers are activated. You might rub your toe or hand to stimulate the C fibers, which then displace the A fibers signal.

- Positive or negative emotions can influence the experience of pain. For example, if a clinician puts an individual in a burn test condition, the patient usually holds something that looks like a soldering iron. Once it starts to get hot, the clinician waits to see how long the individual can hold on to the hot rod before feeling like it's burning him or her. When a person is in a positive mood state, he or she will hold on to the rod longer and the pain sensation is diminished.

- The opposite is true if a person is depressed, which tends to intensify the sensation of pain. Stress, depending on the circumstance, can either intensify or diminish pain.

- A study by Irene Tracey at Oxford showed that thinking about pain increases the sensation of pain. Subjects were asked to think about their chronic pain, and they showed an increased activation in their pain-perception circuits.

- Distraction, on the other hand, can be a good pain reliever. In another study, Dr. Tracey's subjects were asked to do a complex counting task while they were being burned with a heat wand. Their perception of pain was much less while distracted, and corresponding brain imaging showed lower activation in pain centers.

- Distraction could be interfering with cognitions that would otherwise amplify the experience of pain. Distraction might be causing some sort of reduction in tension, or maybe it's some form of somatic quieting.

Stress and Pain
- In conditions of extreme stress—like trauma—our experience of pain may be entirely shut down. But even more, minor acute stressors are known to produce something called stress-induced analgesia. Our fight-or-flight system and our HPA axis stress response not only lead to the release of epinephrine and cortisol, the stress hormones, but they also promote the release of beta-endorphins, part of the family of endogenous opiates, our internal pain killers.

- Our stress response systems and the chemical messengers they release were really intended for short-term situations and not the more common stressors we encounter today, which are often of a chronic nature.

- Chronic stress does not produce analgesia. In fact, it sometimes produces hyperalgesia, or increased sensitivity to pain. We don't fully understand how this happens, and there are most likely a number of different mechanisms, most of which include some sort of structural rewiring of the central nervous system triggered by high levels of gluccocorticoids.

- If stress seems to be playing a major role, then it is time to move to our strategies for stress management. This might include various somatic quieting, working with primary or secondary appraisals, better use of coping resources, or adding in new activities that help mitigate the effects of stress.

Treating Pain

- When it comes to treating pain, most people immediately think of pharmacotherapy—these are the drugs in the opioid family like morphine, hydrocodone, or oxycodone. These drugs work because of their similarity to our bodies' own pain relievers, the endogenous opiates.

- There are several non-pharmacological treatments. The chronic care model encourages more patient empowerment and self-management. If we think of chronic pain as a chronic disease, it might benefit from this model.

- A core skill is self-monitoring, but in the case of pain, this would involve creating a self-monitoring form, such as a pain diary, to collect data and then creating a treatment package.

- In a treatment package, we might have pharmacotherapy as one tool to combat chronic pain, but we might also want to think about practical, structural, or even mechanical interventions. This would include things like physical therapy, occupational therapy, environmental changes, having pull bars in your home, and using walkers, braces, wraps, ice, heat, or massage.

- Part of the treatment package should also include the psychological. We would want to include some cognitive strategies, including assessing an individual's expectations for and attitude about his or her pain. We want to challenge maladaptive cognitions, including catastrophizing, all-or-none thinking, and maximizing/minimizing. We also want to use cognitive strategies for stress management.

- We want to add some behavioral strategies to the pain management package. Behavioral strategies include physical therapy and massage, graded or graduated physical activity (exercise starting at a modest level and slowly building until a person has more flexibility, strength, and endurance), and somatic quieting.

- A critical behavioral element is activity scheduling. Lower activity levels mean less reward and reinforcement—and often lower mood. We want an individual to start scheduling positive activities. We can have him or her engage in pleasure predicting, in which the patient rates his or her predicted enjoyment of a prospective activity on a scale of 1 to 10. Then, after the patient does the activity, he or she rerates the level of pleasure actually experienced. Almost always, the patient finds that he or she enjoyed it more than predicted.

- Once you have more data from the patient, you can start identifying potentially helpful interventions. If cognitions are amplifying suffering, then you should do some thought records. If there are very few physical or social activities, then you might want to do graduated exercise or physical therapy and some activity scheduling. If it's depression, then you might want to add social contacts and positive activities.

- In 2012, Amanda Williams, Christopher Eccleston, and Stephen Morley looked at CBT versus treatment as usual or wait-list controls and found that CBT has statistically significant but small effects on pain and disability and moderate effects on mood and catastrophizing. By six to 12 months, the main effect was on mood.

- A review of behavioral treatments, including CBT, for chronic low back pain concluded that behavioral treatments were more effective than usual care for pain post-treatment but not different in intermediate- to long-term effects on pain or functional status.

- A review of behavioral treatment for headaches by Frank Andrasik in 2007 describes CBT-based interventions (relaxation, biofeedback, and cognitive therapy) as reducing headache activity by as much as 30 to 60 percent on average across studies.

- Other meta-analyses have supported the efficacy of psychological treatments, including CBT, in reducing arthritis and fibromyalgia pain.

Suggested Reading

Andrasik, "What Does the Evidence Show?"

Astin, Beckner, Soeken, Hochberg, and Berman, "Psychological Interventions for Rheumatoid Arthritis."

Caudill, *Managing Pain before It Manages You.*

Glombiewski, Sawyer, Gutermann, Koenig, Rief, and Hofmann, "Psychological Treatments for Fibromyalgia."

Henschke, Ostelo, van Tulder, Vlaeyen, Morley, Assendelft, and Main, "Behavioural Treatment for Chronic Low-Back Pain."

Knittle, Maes, and Gucht, "Psychological Interventions for Rheumatoid Arthritis."

Williams, Eccleston, and Morley, "Psychological Therapies for the Management of Chronic Pain (Excluding Headache) in Adults."

1. Research has shown that distraction can be an effective way to reduce the sensation of pain. However, research also has shown that mindfulness (focusing on the pain, for example) also can be helpful in reducing pain. How is this possible? What might explain the effectiveness of each?

2. Recent neuroscience research has shown that social rejection or a romantic breakup "light up" similar brain areas as physical pain. Try applying the concepts of transduction, transmission, modulation, and perception to this sort of psychic pain. What implications would this have for psychotherapy or psychological coping in general?

Mastering Chronic Pain
Lecture 19—Transcript

PROFESSOR SATTERFIELD: During Maria's intake, she said she hurt all over, a sort of full-body ache that couldn't be touched with pills. She also mentioned her sometimes debilitating osteoarthritis, especially in her hip and her knees, and her regular back problems made worse by having to care for her husband. She's afraid of pain pills, mostly because she wants to be alert and clear, and she fears addiction. She wanted to know if CBT could help.

Whether minor or severe, chronic pain is regularly experienced by 15 to 20% of Americans each year. Both cognitive and behavioral factors influence the experience of pain and the intensity of suffering. We'll talk about the pain process, transduction, transmission, modulation, and perception. We'll learn how psychological factors can alter the experience of pain, but first we'll define pain and all of its facets and how we measure it. Then we're going to look at those mind-body factors with chronic pain, including something called Gate Theory, and of course, looking at depression, anxiety, positive emotions, and stress, and we'll take out that CBT toolbox and see how well it works for pain.

The International Association for the Study of Pain defines pain as an unpleasant sensory and emotional experience associated with actual or potential tissue damage. So what's the largest cause of acute pain? It's surgery. Approximately 46 million procedures are performed each year, and most patients report moderate to severe pain post surgically, even in the face of current treatments and techniques. But why do we have pain? In general, acute pain is thought to be an important and adaptive signal. It tells us of imminent tissue damage. It only takes one touch of that hot stove to learn not to touch that hot stove. And we know that there are diseases such as Hansen's disease, or what's commonly called leprosy, where an individual is unable to feel pain, and as a consequence, they suffer quite a bit of ongoing tissue damage. But there are also times when pain misinforms us, like in the case of fibromyalgia, a chronic pain disorder, or is so intense that it overwhelms us. Fortunately, for some, pain can be entirely suppressed so we could think clearly and escape danger.

But how does pain work? The process of being able to feel pain is something called nociception, and there are four basic steps. The first step is called the transduction, and this is where nociceptors or pain receptors, transduce noxious stimuli into nociceptive impulses. We have all sorts of nociceptors throughout our body; some are sensitive to crush or pressure; some are sensitive to temperature; and some are sensitive to chemicals.

We then have transmission, where the electrical impulses from the nociceptors are sent via afferent nerves to the spinal cord, and then along sensory tracks to the appropriate part of the brain. Transduction leads to transmission. The third step is called modulation, and this is the process of dampening down or of amplifying the pain signal related to the neural transmission. Now, this is hugely important for mind-body medicine, because there seem to be factors which can either increase the intensity, amplification, or dampen it down. And the fourth and final step is called perception, where the subjective experience of pain that results from transduction, transmission, and modulation, plus psychological and social factors are at play within the individual.

But what about chronic pain? Now, chronic pain has usually been defined arbitrarily as pain that persist for three to six months or longer, or beyond the period of expected healing. Ongoing or progressive tissue damage may be present in some types of chronic pain, including progressive neuropathic pain in some rheumatologic conditions. In other cases, chronic pain may be present when tissue damage is stable or even undetectable.

Unlike acute pain, chronic pain is now thought to be a disease of the central nervous system that involves some sort of maladaptive reprogramming of the brain and/or the spinal cord. The brain can generate terrible pain in a wound that has long healed or even chronic pain in a limb that has been amputated and no longer exists. On average, 15 to 20% of Americans experience chronic pain each year, approximately 46 million people. Headache is the most common, followed by back pain, arthritis pain, and other musculoskeletal pain.

Let's talk a little bit about the psychology of chronic pain, and it's important to remember that we need to distinguish acute pain from chronic pain. We think of chronic pain as a syndrome, really, as an entirely different disorder. In a way, it takes on a life of its own. We mentioned the reprogramming of the brain, but that's not all that's happening. It also has potentially devastating consequences on mood, depression, anger, anxiety, effects on social relationships, finances, and self-image. You can think of chronic pain as a chronically stressful condition that essentially keeps the stress response turned on all the time, and by now, you're familiar with some of the medical consequences of chronic stress.

So how do we measure pain? In the medical setting, pain has now been called the fifth vital sign, and it's regularly assessed or should be, at every medical visit. So first they want to assess the sensation or the nociception of pain, and they simply ask, on a scale of one to ten, with ten being the most intense, what's your average pain? They may ask you what's the highest pain you've experienced in the past week? What's the lowest? What makes it better? What makes it worse? For younger individuals, they may show them a series of happy to sad faces and have the child point to which of those best matches the intensity of the pain that they've felt.

They might also do some functional impairment measures, and here we're looking for impairment in activities of daily living and things you used to be able to do at home, social activities you used to be able to engage in, or activities at work. We want to know if there's a social or occupational impairment as a consequence of your pain. Now, this one is especially important, because if pain medications are prescribed, we don't want them to just make an individual numb or turn down that sensation of no susception. We want pain medications, or really, any treatment for pain, to decrease functional impairment and improve functioning in general.

You might also be asked to rate, on a scale of one to ten, what is your level of emotional suffering, and it's important to distinguish between the physical sensation of pain and the emotional suffering that might be tied to pain. They're often correlated with one another, but they might be quite different. In the end, it's important to remember, there is no objective measure of pain; there's no lab test. It's all based on self-report.

So I mentioned that the central nervous system was involved in pain, but what exactly happens there and what does it do? In our CNS, or central nervous system, we know that that's the seat of cognition, emotion, and expectation, so you can already start drawing some connections between the experience of pain in the central nervous system through those pathways. We also know that the central nervous system is important in directing the transduction from psychological experience of pain into the biological, and vice versa. We know that the nociceptors transmit their signals to the spinal cord, which then transmit to the central nervous system or to the brain, and there we see things such as perception and modulation that might occur. We know that modulation of pain happens all the time, and we've all heard stories about, say, soldiers on the battlefield that don't realize they've been injured and feel no pain until they're in a safer context, and then they begin to feel that pain.

In response to the growing awareness of mind-body phenomenon in the realm of pain, the gate control theory of pain was first described in the early 1960s by Ronald Melzack and Patrick Wall. In this theory, pain signals encounter what they call nerve gates in the spinal cord that open or close, depending upon a number of factors, possibly including instructions coming down from the central nervous system. When the gates are open, so to speak, pain messages can get through, and pain can be quite intense. When the gates close, pain messages are prevented from reaching the brain and may not be even be experienced at all. It essentially gives us a mechanism for modulation that takes place on a level of the spinal cord.

So what's the evidence for gate control? A number of observational studies on the variability of pain experience have suggested that gate control might actually be true. Something must be happening to modulate the experience of pain, which has been well-documented. For example, we know that pain transmission seems to have a limited bandwidth. You have, for example, A fibers that send fast and sharp pains, and you have C fibers that send slow and dull pain. If you stub your toe or hit your hand, the A fibers, the fast, sharp sensation fibers are activated. What you will immediately do is you will grab your hand or your toe, and you'll rub it; you'll squeeze it to stimulate the other fibers, the C fibers, that will then displace the A fiber signal. So it's a very mechanical, simple example of how you can switch or displace a pain signal, thus change your experience of the pain.

But what would open or close the gate in the spinal cord? Well, we know that positive or negative emotions can influence the experience of pain. For example, if you put individuals in a burn test condition, you essentially will induce either positive or negative emotions in an individual, and you usually have them hold something that looks kind of like a soldering iron. They will turn it on. It starts to get hot, and they wait to see how long the individual can hold on to that hot rod before they feel that it's starting to burn them. Now, whether this is good or bad is up to you, but when you're in a positive mood state, you will hold on to that rod a little bit longer and your pain sensation has actually been diminished. The opposite is true if you're depressed, which we know tends to intensify the sensation of pain. And stress, depending on the circumstance, can either intensify or diminish; it's either opening or closing those gates.

A study by Irene Tracey at Oxford showed that thinking about pain has the power to sometimes increase the sensation of pain. Subjects were asked to think about their chronic pain, and they showed an increased activation in their pain perception circuits. Distraction, on the other hand, can be a good pain reliever. In another study, Dr. Tracey's subjects were asked to do a complex counting task while they were being, again, burned with that heat wand. Their perception of pain was much less while distracted, and corresponding brain imaging showed a lower activation in their pain centers. Other studies have found that listening to tones or even to music as a form of distraction can decrease pain sensations.

But why might distraction work? It could be interfering with cognitions that would otherwise amplify the experience of pain. Distraction might be causing some sort of reduction intention, or maybe it's some form of somatic quieting. Let's look, though, at a quick example of a new patient, Sarah, who's learning how to do guided imagery as a way to relax and escape her pain. Note that when you see this clip, she's already gone through a series of breathing exercises, through progressive muscle relaxation, and now we're right at the point where she's going to start some guided imagery.

[VIGNETTE START]

PROFESSOR SATTERFIELD: You can keep your eyes closed. And now I want you to imagine you are in your paradise. For some people, it's a beach. For some people, it's the woods. It might be the city. Who knows? It's up to you. But I want you to imagine you're there. I want you to imagine the temperature. Is it bright? Is it dim? Is it warm? Is it cool? This is your world, and you control it. You are absolutely safe. You are absolutely in charge. I want you to imagine any sounds that you hear. Is there music? Are there birds? Are there any smells that are there? Do you smell flowers, or maybe chocolate chip cookies? Whatever is paradise for you.

Give yourself this treat. This is your space. You created it, and you can go back there any time you want. It only takes a moment. You can paint the picture any time you want. So I want you to take one last look around, but know that you'll be back. And maybe next time, you're going to stay a little longer. This is yours. You can go back because you deserve it. OK, so say goodbye. Wiggle your fingers a little bit. And when you're ready, go ahead and open your eyes.

SARAH: Wow.

PROFESSOR SATTERFIELD: Tell me what you are feeling right now.

SARAH: Relaxed. Very, very relaxed. It feels good.

PROFESSOR SATTERFIELD: I bet it's a while since you felt relaxed.

SARAH: No tension.

PROFESSOR SATTERFIELD: Do you want to share what your paradise was, or you want to keep that secret?

SARAH: Oh, I'll share it. It's a log cabin up on a mountain. I can see 100 miles, with a porch across the front. Sunny October, my favorite time of the year with all the foliage, and fire in the fireplace, and I can smell ginger snaps.

PROFESSOR SATTERFIELD: Perfect. I love your imagination. Perfect.

SARAH: Sounds like paradise to me.

PROFESSOR SATTERFIELD: Yeah, me too. And remember, you can go back there anytime you want. So what I think we'll do from here is, how about we give you a homework assignment to go back there at least once every week? I mean, the more often, the better, but I know there's a lot that's on your plate. So whenever you're feeling tense, that should be your clue of maybe you can go to the bedroom or somewhere quiet and close a door and take a few minutes to do some breathing, maybe do some progressive muscle relaxation, do some imagery, if that's what you want, and then hopefully get back to this place where you are right now.

SARAH: OK. All right, good. Thank you.

PROFESSOR SATTERFIELD: Sure. You're welcome.

[VIGNETTE END]

PROFESSOR SATTERFIELD: Relaxation and guided imagery are just one set of tools to address chronic pain. They may work through somatic quieting, but they may also work through their effect and decreasing stress.

So let's talk a bit about stress and pain. Now, in conditions of extreme stress, like trauma, our experience of pain may be entirely shut down, but even more minor, acute stressors are known to produce something called stress-induced analgesia. Our-fight-or-flight system and our HPA access stress response not only lead to the release of epinephrine and cortisol, the stress hormones we've talked about before, they also promote the release of beta-endorphins, our endogenous opiates, or our internal pain killers.

How do we know this? Well, from early animal research, where animals were subjected to various stressors, then blood endorphin levels were measured. In human studies, researchers use things like foot shocks, exercise stress, social stress tests, and other methods to elicit a less stress response, measure endorphins, and in some cases, block endorphins using a drug called naloxone. It's generally thought to be evolutionary, and it's thought to be adaptive.

As we've learned though, our stress-response systems and the chemical messengers they release, were really intended for short-term situations and not the more common stressors we encounter today, which are often of a chronic nature. Chronic stress does not produce analgesia. In fact, it sometimes produces hyperalgesia, or increased sensitivity to pain. We don't fully understand how this happens, and there are most likely a number of different mechanisms, most of which include some sort of structural rewiring of the central nervous system triggered by the higher levels of glucocorticoids or those stress hormones which we've mentioned before.

Now, if stress seems to be playing a major role, then it's time to move to our strategies for stress management. This might include various somatic quieting, working with primary or secondary appraisals, the cognitions about the stressor, or your coping resources. We might encourage a person to have better use of those coping resources or social supports or adding in new activities that help to mitigate the effects of stress.

So, how do we treat pain? Most people immediately think of pharmacotherapy, and these are the drugs in the opioid family, usually like morphine, hydrocodone, or oxycodone. And these drugs work because of their similarity to our body's own pain relievers, the endogenous opioids that we've talked about before. But let's expand our idea of treatment, and let's look at several non-pharmacologic treatments.

Now, recall the need for new attitudes towards the management of chronic disease when we talked about the Chronic Care Model. We wanted to encourage more patient empowerment and patient self-management. And if we think of chronic pain as a chronic disease, it would certainly fit into that category that might benefit from the Chronic Cure Model. Remember one of the core skills was in self-monitoring, but in this case, we would be creating a self-monitoring form like a pain diary. We would need to create that diary to collect data and then to create a treatment package.

So, what would be in a treatment package? What sorts of things would we want to piece together? We might have pharmacotherapy as one tool in our tool kit to combat chronic pain, but we might also want to think about practical, structural, or even mechanical interventions, so that would be things like physical therapy, occupational therapy, changes in your environment, having pull bars in your home, using walkers, using braces or wraps, using ice, using heat, using massage. All of those things packaged together can have a fairly substantial impact depending on the individual's pain and the source of pain.

But part of that treatment package should also include the psychological, and in that package we would want to include some of the cognitive strategies that we know about. First, we want to look at an individual's expectation, expectations for their level of functioning, expectations for their pain, but also expectations for their pain-control strategies. When a patient tells me that their goal is to feel numb all of the time, I get very worried, because first of all, it's an unrealistic goal, and secondly, I wonder if maybe they're looking for that numbness as a way to avoid something that might be more psychologically painful.

We would also want to look at an individual's attitude. Had they become helpless, or hopeless, or even depressed as a consequence of the pain that they've been experiencing, maybe over a long period of time? We might want to look at and challenge some maladaptive cognitions. Recall those habits of mind that we've talked about before. Is an individual catastrophizing? Are they using all their non-thinking? Are they using maximizing or minimizing? Or, another habit of mind that we haven't talked about much is called emotional reasoning, where an individual deduces, again, on an implicit level, that if I feel something with a really strong emotional charge, that must mean it's true. Actually, it just means you have a strong emotional charge, and it's going to be a little bit harder to step outside of that emotion and to rationally look at a particular situation. Then, of course, we want to use some of those cognitive strategies for stress management, where we might look at accuracy of appraisals.

So let's take a moment, then, to look at what a cognitive exercise might look like if we are looking at the habits of mind of an individual who has chronic pain. Let's say that we're doing an ABCD, where we look at the activating event, the beliefs, the consequences again, which are both emotions and behavior, as well as the disputation, or this is where you restructure or rework those thoughts.

Let's say that the activating event is having a stabbing back pain. It doesn't have to be an external event, it's just whatever triggers this cascade of cognitions and emotions and reactions. So let's say the individual has an activating event of stabbing back pain. It triggers the cognitions, or beliefs, of, "I can't take this. This is horrible. My life has been ruined by this pain." The consequences they have driven by those beliefs in cognitions, they feel depressed, they feel hopeless, they stay at home, and they decide to take more of their pain pills.

If they decide that those consequences are not what they were after, they're not helpful, instead, they're hurtful, then you want to go to the D box, the dispute box. And to create that dispute box, remember to think about those habits of mind. Is this individual relying on some of those habits of mind? Are these thoughts balanced? Can you look at the other side of the coin? If you had a friend or a loved one that was saying these things, what might you say in return to help them think about a more balanced approach? What would be some more helpful, but still accurate and believable, cognitions?

So the disputations might include things like, "Yes, this physical pain is intense, but it's familiar, and I have a plan to manage it. I can take my meds. I can stretch. I can use ice. I can use distraction. I can pray. Or I can meditate." Another dispute might be, "I had pain yesterday, and I had pain the day before that, and the day before that, and you know what, I survived. It stinks, but it's beyond my control. I can manage this." Or another example is, "Even though I hurt, I always feel better if I make it out somewhere, if I accomplish something, or if I see someone. Isolation hurts too. I can choose not to be isolated."

If we're still thinking about that pain package, that pain-management package, we have our structural, functional, mechanical tools; we have our pharmacotherapy; we have our cognitive therapy. Now we want to add in some additional behavioral strategies. We've mentioned things like physical therapy and massage, which of course can be helpful. We might want to think about something called graded or sometimes called graduated physical activity, and essentially, this is exercise starting at a very mild, modest level and slowly working the way up until a person has built more flexibility, strength, and endurance. This is something you might start with a physical therapist, but then you would continue it on your own. Another common behavioral activity would be somatic quieting. Remember, we think of chronic pain as a chronic stress response. That means that the individual's HPA access, their sympathetic nervous system, are working on overdrive, so it's going to take an equal amount of counter-action in order to turn down the volume on those overactive stress response systems.

Now, a critical behavioral element is activity scheduling, and if you recall activity scheduling from our depression lectures, we talked about the activity record, where an individual writes down their activities. But then they can prospectively plan activities that they know are going to have a lifting effect on their mood. And for individuals who are in pain, they may not be depressed, but often, what happens is they find themselves pulling away from sources of enjoyment, or support, or social relationships. Remember that lower activity levels mean less reward, less reinforcement, and eventually those might even lead to depression. So we want an individual to start scheduling those positive activities.

But what happens and what often comes up when an individual is in pain? And I've seen this many, many times with patients. We'll talk about the relationship between activities and mood. We'll talk about the importance of scheduling activities, but the response I often get is, "Yes, but I hurt. Yes, I would love to do that, but I have pain. Yes, I could schedule that, but I won't enjoy it, because the whole time I'm going to be thinking about my pain."

If you remember with depression, we had a similar objection saying, "Yeah, I could do that but I won't enjoy it," so we did something called pleasure predicting. If we can get the patient to suspend their disbelief temporarily, to go ahead and prospectively schedule one thing, I will ask them on a scale of 1 to ten, 10, much do you predict you're going to enjoy yourself? They make their prediction. They write it down. Then, the next week, they go and actually do that activity. Once they finish, they re-rate the level of pleasure that they actually experienced, and almost always, not every time, but almost always, they find that they enjoyed it more than they had predicted. Chronic pain, like depression, often causes people to make very pessimistic predictions, and it's a matter of giving them that extra boost they need to go out and test out those assumptions.

So, if you're interested in the sketch of a more comprehensive and long-lasting CBT plan to manage pain, I would encourage you to look at the bestselling book written by Margaret Caudill called *Managing Your Pain before It Manages You*, now, on its third edition. You can imagine some of the elements that are included. They start with assessment and formulation. They move into behavioral analysis and problem solving. They create a pain package plan and something called a panic plan, meaning, when everything you've tried just doesn't work, and that pain shoots up, what do you do? When do you call your doctor? When do you call your social supports? When is it OK to ramp up the pain meds? And it's always helpful to think about those things in advance so you know that you have a plan in place.

The program also goes on to look at the roles of mood, stress, and social supports. If we were to think about assessment and formulation from a CBT perspective, we, of course, would want to do a semi-structured interview first that's always our gold standard. We would want to do self-monitoring. And here, we would use a pain diary. There's a number of examples available online including, if you type in, "Minding the Body, Satterfield," you'll go to an Oxford University Press website that talks about a workbook. You can click on the link for a companion site and then download the forms for free. In a typical pain diary, it has days of the week across that you fill in data at least three times per day, rating your physical sensation. You also rate your suffering. You want to record circumstances, triggers, and context. And you want to record what you tried and whether or not it was helpful or hurtful.

Now, this pain diary gives you a baseline, but it also gives you an idea of whether there are current strengths or strategies to keep, or maybe even to ramp up. It also helps us to see particularly vulnerable times so activities can be arranged around those times, and it gives you a more objective assessment of how interventions work or didn't work. Once you have your data, you want to move to formulation. You can start identifying potentially helpful interventions. If cognitions are amplifying suffering, then you'll want to do some thought records. If there's very little physical activity or social activities, then you might want to do graduated exercise or physical therapy and some activity scheduling. If it's depression, then you might want to add in social contacts and positive activities.

What does the data show us? If we look at a Cochrane review by William Eccleston and Morley in 2012, they looked at CBT versus treatment as usual or weightless controls, and they found that CBT has statistically significant, but small effects on pain disability, moderate effects on mood and catastrophizing. And by 6 to 12 months, the main effect was on mood. So, again, it's not reaching in and fixing the pain, but it's already altering and changing an individual's mood and potentially changing some of those habits of mind.

A Cochrane review of behavioral treatments, including CBT, for chronic low back pain included 30 randomized controlled trials and concluded that behavioral treatments were more effective than usual care for pain post-treatment, but no different and immediate to long-term effects on pain or functional status. A review of behavioral treatment for headaches by Andrasik in 2007 describes CBT-based interventions, relaxations, biofeedback, cognitive therapy, and he was able to reduce headache activity by as much as 30% to 60% on average across those different studies.

These effects surpass those various controlled conditions and were typically sustained over time including years after treatment. Now other meta-analyses have supported the efficacy of psychological treatments, including CBT and reducing arthritis pain, fibromyalgia. And most of the studies in these reviews compared interventions with various CBT techniques to usual care or weightless controls.

So I'd like to move to our next frequently asked question, and this is, again, one that often comes up in a primary care setting, and since I often work with medical patients, I hear this one a lot from both patients and providers. They say, if you recommend cognitive interventions for pain, aren't you in a sense saying that the pain is all in your head? That seems rather unhelpful and unsupportive. My response usually has a couple of elements. First of all, go for empathy first; that's usually the safe route, and you want to acknowledge that that individual's suffering, and they may have had negative encounters with the medical establishment that doubted that they were experiencing pain.

I find those doubts about pain to be unhelpful. If a person says they're suffering, they're suffering. If they say they have pain, they have pain. But at the same time, it's important to remember that mind and body are very much related, and just because we're going to look at the stress, the cognitions, and the behaviors associated with pain, doesn't mean that we're saying that your pain is not real. We're saying that it's all connected. And if we're going to come at this from a medical perspective, as we should, we should also try all avenues and come at this from a cognitive and behavioral perspective as well.

So I hope that you'll stick around for the next lecture. We're going to broaden our purview and we're going to look at not just the individual and their health, but we're going to look at the health of relationships. Thank you.

Building and Deepening Relationships
Lecture 20

Many people have argued that we've evolved multilayered, complex social relationships in order to help us survive and thrive and we've developed some rather complex and nuanced rules about how those relationships should work—rules that are always evolving and only partly derived from biology. It's cliché to say that people need people and that this idea of love and attachment is, of course, the thing that music, art, literature, and movies are made of. But is it true? Can't being alone or even totally isolated be just fine? In this lecture, you will learn about the health of relationships.

Social Relationships

- In his classic studies, Harry Harlow studied maternal separation and social isolation in infant monkeys taken from their mothers. He began to systematically tease apart what it was that made infants bond to their mother. He assumed that it was food and survival.

- Harlow took infants away from their mothers and placed them in a variety of different conditions with fake mothers made of either wire or terry cloth, complete with a fake face that the infants came to recognize. The infants bonded to their "mom."

- He then wanted to see if food was the key factor or if it was touch and sensation. He put two mothers in the cage: a wire one and a cloth one. Sometimes the wire mother had a bottle connected to the food, and sometimes it was the cloth mother. In both instances, regardless of where the food was located, the infants clung to the cloth mother. They received all of their nurturance and love from touch—it wasn't just about food.

- But what about the widower who dies shortly after his wife, even though he seemed to be in fine health? What about the socially isolated elderly man who can't seem to bounce back after a relatively mild heart attack? What about the 35,000 suicides per year involving many people who are socially isolated and depressed?

- While true that some people are more social than others—extroversion and introversion are real—we all need relationships. We don't have to be popular, but we need at least one key relationship to help us get by in life. Not having any relationships is bad both for your mental health and your physical health.

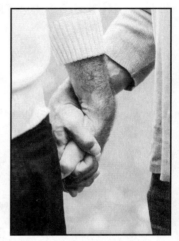

We all need at least one key relationship to help us get by in our lives.

- If relationships are so critical, then why are there so many people who are lonely? How do you assess both the quality and quantity of relationships? How can you explain a deficiency in either?

- Impairments in social functioning can come from a variety of places, but there are mainly two places that therapists should look.
  - Does the client have a skills deficit in terms of human interaction? This is derived partly from self-report but also from observation and maybe from some in-session exercises.

  - Does the patient have sufficient skills but something is blocking the use of those skills? For example, maybe social anxiety plays a part. Maybe the client knows what to do but is so anxious that he or she is not able to perform those particular skills.

- Of course, the therapist should look for other diagnoses, such as depression, or other social circumstances that cause an individual to be anxious.

Social Relationships and CBT

- Recall the layers from the cognitive model. Using the CBT triangle, you have learned to look at cognition and behavior to help you understand emotions. Starting at the top, or the surface, there are automatic thoughts and beliefs, which are responses to an activating event.

- Below that we have rules or conditional assumptions, such as if-then statements. Beneath those rules we have core beliefs—those irrational, deeply held beliefs about ourselves, our world, and the people around us. And related to that are our values—what matters most and why.

- In terms of beliefs, we can often boil things down to lovability and achievement. The primary driver of avoidance is safety behaviors, which are in-the-moment behaviors that provide comfort but prevent the person from doing what he or she needs or wants to do.

- For anxiety, we can do somatic quieting, an ABCD exercise, and a thought record as well as talk about exposures. We can create a SUDS (subjective units of distress) hierarchy, in which the patient starts at the bottom of his or her hierarchy and works up. We can also target interfering factors—cognitions and behaviors. But having skills and tamping down anxiety isn't enough to create new relationships. How can we move the patient forward?

- In terms of personality, there are a number of conceptually sound measures of introversion and extroversion. The Myers-Briggs Type Indicator is probably the most common measure that looks at introversion and extroversion, among a number of other things. Introversion indicates a preference, not an ability, and it doesn't prevent an individual from having meaningful social relationships.

Social Support Networks

- Social support has been conceptualized in a number of different ways. In fact, it's a notoriously slippery concept to define and even more difficult to measure. The common definition of social support is that it is the perception that one is cared for, has assistance available from other people, and that one is part of a supportive social network.

- Research studies use the term "social support," but terms such as "social integration," "social connectedness," and "social support networks" are also used. Each is a slightly different angle on this complex and difficult-to-measure idea.

- A structural characteristic of an individual's social support network is its size. Other characteristics include the density and the distance. Are all your friends gathered locally in the same geographic area, or are they dispersed around the country or even the world? What is the diversity of individuals? Do they all have approximately the same age, same gender, and same background—or is there a wider range? Another characteristic is level of reciprocity. Does the individual always give support but receive less, or vice versa? Additionally, does the social support network go beyond an inner circle of familial relationships?

- We might also want to look at some of the functional characteristics of an individual's social support network. Does the individual receive emotional support? Does he or she receive informational support? Does the individual have friends that can give him or her advice or help him or her work through problems? Does an individual receive tangible or practical support? Does the person have someone who can help him or her with dinner, pay the mortgage, or drive him or her to a doctor's appointment? Does the person have someone who can provide companionship or belonging?

- Another key feature to keep in mind as you're doing a social support assessment is the idea of perceived versus actual. We can look at actual indicators of social support—such as density, shape, structure, and function—but it's really an individual's perception of his or her social support and the quality that he or she receives that is most important.

- We also want to look at whether the individual is giving or receiving support and whether that seems to be balanced. Sources of support might include significant others or family and friends. Even though you might see greater levels of intimacy in romantic relationships, this doesn't have to be the case. Emotional closeness is often about shared life experiences, so it could certainly be platonic.

- In a social support assessment exercise called a circle diagram, the patient fills in the names of his or her sister, brother, and friends. Then, he or she starts to think about how to rank or qualify the level of intimacy with each of those individuals.

- After the exercise, we might learn that the patient is not completely isolated and has been close to family and friends before, but it takes him or her a long time to feel comfortable with someone. The patient might not reach out to social supports or nurture those relationships, but he or she might want both more quality and quantity in his or her social support network.

- How do we address quantity, or adding new people to your social network? What is the right size for a social network? Does it really become difficult to form new relationships as you grow older?

- There is a recent phenomenon of online social networks and the use of platforms like Facebook in order to connect to other individuals. Could we consider this a source of social support? Do online social networks fill in the gaps, if we have gaps from our personal relationships?

The quality of social support recieved on social media websites is inferior to that of in-person relationships.

- A study done by Jonathon Cummings at Carnegie Mellon University looked at both bankers and college students that were using the Internet, the phone, and in-person meetings to connect with others and then compared the quality of those meetings and perceived social support. The study showed that even though people enjoy things like Facebook, the quality of social support the subjects received was inferior to that of in-person relationships.

- When we look at the types of support we receive, we want to ensure that an individual has adequate amounts of each type of support: informational, practical, emotional, and companionate support. It's the support needer's responsibility to know what kind of support he or she needs and then to go to the right person to ask for that support. Specify what you need, and speak up if you aren't getting what you want.

Growing One's Social Network

- How might a patient grow his or her network? First, he or she needs to identify a target. Is it someone who was already on the circle diagram and the patient just wants to pull him or her into an inner circle and improve intimacy? Or does the patient want to meet new people entirely? The patient probably wants to do a little bit of both.

- We want to set expectations, and we want the patient to have a system of how he or she can capture even tiny steps forward—this isn't something that changes overnight, or even over a few weeks. We want the patient to keep a success diary, because we can predict that he or she might get discouraged that the progress is not going quickly enough.

- Social support networks don't have to be composed just of humans. For example, a study conducted by Erika Friedmann and published in 1995 in the *American Journal of Cardiology* analyzed individuals who had suffered a myocardial infarction, or heart attack, and who owned a dog versus those who didn't own a dog. The study also analyzed those who had human social supports versus those who didn't. In both cases of dogs and humans, the social support was important and helped increase rates of survival.

Suggested Reading

Butler, *Overcoming Social Anxiety and Shyness*, p. 226–233.

Friedmann and Thomas, "Pet Ownership, Social Support, and One-Year Survival after Acute Myocardial Infarction in the Cardiac Arrhythmia Suppression Trial (CAST)."

Hendrix, *Getting the Love You Want*.

Langer and Rodin, "The Effects of Choice and Enhanced Personal Responsibility for the Aged."

Mitchell, Powell, Blumenthal, Norten, Ironson, Pitula, et al, "A Short Social Support Measure for Patients Recovering from Myocardial Infarction."

Shklovski, Kraut, and Cummings, "Keeping in Touch by Technology."

1. Complete the structural and functional social support exercise described in the lecture (using the concentric circles figure). Do you need to work on the quantity or quality of your network? If relevant, set some SMART goals.

2. Who do you support? What kind(s) of support are you best at providing? Consider at least one concrete way in which you can improve your role as a support provider.

Building and Deepening Relationships
Lecture 20—Transcript

PROFESSOR SATTERFIELD: Let's return to our case of Carol, a 30-year-old, smart, gainfully employed accountant who's socially anxious. Others see her as quiet, shy, maybe distant, but generally kind and pleasant. But Carol is very lonely, and she's very anxious. She tries to cover her feelings, and she tries to be invisible. She hates drawing attention to herself. Now, she did OK in college, and she does OK at work, but she regularly exerts a good deal of effort just finding the courage to speak to other people. She longs for closer friends, and she longs for a romantic partner. She wants to feel like she belongs. She wants to be happy.

Many have argued that we've evolved multilayered, complex social relationships in order to help us survive and thrive. And we've developed some rather complex and nuanced rules about how those relationships should work, rules that are always evolving and are only partly derived from biology.

Now, it's cliché to say that people need people, and this idea of love and attachment is, of course, the thing that music, art, literature, and movies are made of. But is it true? Can't being alone, or even totally isolated, be just fine? In the classic studies of Harry Harlow, he studied maternal separation and social isolation in infant monkeys taken from their mothers. He began to systematically tease apart what it was that made infants bond to their mother. He assumed it was food and survival.

He took infants away from their mothers and placed them in a variety of different conditions with fake mothers made of either wire or terry cloth, complete with a fake face that the infants came to recognize. The infants bonded to their mom. He then wanted to see if food was the key factor or if it was touch and sensation. He put two mothers in the cage, a wire one and a cloth one. Sometimes the wire mother had a bottle connected to the food, and sometimes it was the cloth mother. In both instances, regardless of where the food was located, the infants clung to the cloth mother. They received all of their nurturance and love from touch. It wasn't just about food.

But what about the widower that dies shortly after his wife, even though he seemed to be in OK health? What about the socially isolated elderly man who can't seem to bounce back after a relatively mild heart attack? What about the 35,000 suicides per year involving many people who are socially isolated and depressed?

While true that some people are more social than others—extroversion and introversion are real—we all need relationships. We don't have to be popular, but we need at least one key relationship to help us get by in life. Not having any relationships is bad both for your mental health and your physical health. So, what is it that gets in the way? If relationships are so critical, then why are there so many people who are lonely? Why does Carol long for attachment, but spend most of her time being alone and feeling terrified of other people? How do you assess both the quality and the quantity of relationships, and how can you explain a deficiency in either?

So what are some of the things that I would look for as a therapist? I want to look for impairments in social functioning, and they can come from a variety of places, namely two places that I like to look. First, I want to look at whether or not an individual has a skills deficit. Do they have those basic skills necessary for human interaction to reach out, connect, and have some sort of social reciprocity with another person? Now, I would derive this partly from self-report, but also from observation, and maybe from some in-session exercises.

The next place I would look is maybe they have sufficient skills, but there's something blocking their use of those skills. In this case, it might be social anxiety. Maybe Carol knows exactly what to do, but she's so anxious she forgets or she's not able to perform those particular skills. And, of course, we want to look for other diagnoses, such as depression, or maybe there are other circumstances that cause an individual to be anxious.

Let's move now to our first clip of Carol, where we're doing an assessment of her social skills and other possible interfering factors.

PROFESSOR SATTERFIELD: So Carol, we have your anxiety surveys. And you've been great about sharing a lot of information about yourself and your history and your family, all of which has helped us put together the formulation for you and to set some goals. And you did mention that one of your goals was having more friends and deepening the friendships that you do have. And ultimately, you would like to begin to romantically date and have a significant other.

So in thinking about those goals and the steps it'll take us to get there, one of the things we need to do is something called just a social skills assessment. So whenever someone is unsatisfied with their current social network, it could either be maybe they haven't yet learned the skills it takes to connect with other people or it might be they have the skills, but the anxiety gets in the way of using those skills. So we need to decide for you which is it or maybe it's a little bit of both.

And I'll tell you part of what I have been noting and part of the data that I'm using, whenever I first talked with a patient over the phone, you get a sense of how comfortable are they speaking. When they come in for a first visit, do they make eye contact or not? Do they send nonverbal signals like you're doing, with nodding your head and smiling? And so you've already shared a lot of data with me that you have those skills in place already.

The other thing I look at is whether or not you have existing friendships. And you mentioned that you have some good friends from college, you have your family members, you have your sister, you've dated in the past before. So to me, it says that there must have been some skills to be able to make those connections. And those connections, some of them have been maintained since college, so 10 years or more for those relationships. But there's a lot of different levels of social skills. So one of the ways we ask about social skills is to give hypothetical scenarios, social encounters, and then you tell me what you might do next.

CAROL: OK.

PROFESSOR SATTERFIELD: All right. And no right or wrong answer, it's just what do you believe is the best next move, not would you feel afraid or feel anxious. That's the emotion part. But what would be the appropriate social response, assuming there's no anxiety that's around. So we'll start with the easy one. Let's say that you are at work in the cafeteria. You're eating lunch. And someone comes over and sits down and says hello. What's the most appropriate social response?

CAROL: Saying hello back.

PROFESSOR SATTERFIELD: Right. And then what would you say?

CAROL: How are you?

PROFESSOR SATTERFIELD: All right, and they might say how are you back. So how are you?

CAROL: Good.

PROFESSOR SATTERFIELD: Then what?

CAROL: I don't know. Then I would probably just eat my lunch.

PROFESSOR SATTERFIELD: OK, so you probably feel a little bit of anxiety, so knowing an opener or a conversation extender or something maybe, assuming they wanted to continue talking. All right. Let's go to the next hypothetical scenario. Let's say you are standing on a busy street corner and a stranger comes up to you and says, hey, could you give me directions to 17th and Madison. You have no idea where that is. So what's the socially appropriate response?

CAROL: I would say I'm sorry, I don't know how to get there.

PROFESSOR SATTERFIELD: And what if they say, oh, come on, it looks like you're a local here. Can you tell me where 17th and Madison is?

CAROL: I'd say, no, sorry, I'm not local.

PROFESSOR SATTERFIELD: OK.

CAROL: Yeah. That's probably what would happen.

PROFESSOR SATTERFIELD: OK. All right. So let's go to another hypothetical scenario. Let's say that you are at a holiday event, a holiday party of some sort. And a guy comes over to you. He's about your age. You think he's kind of attractive. And he says, hey, how's it going? What do you say next?

CAROL: What should I say or what would I say?

PROFESSOR SATTERFIELD: What is the socially appropriate response at that point?

CAROL: I don't know. I guess now I'm all in a tizzy, because I don't know what I would do.

PROFESSOR SATTERFIELD: I can see those emotions coming up.

CAROL: I don't know. I mean, if he asked me how I was doing, I guess I'd say, good, how are you?

PROFESSOR SATTERFIELD: OK. All right, so you would respond and also give him a question so that you could volley the conversation back and forth.

CAROL: Yes, I would probably try not to hide under the table.

PROFESSOR SATTERFIELD: All right, all right. And let's say that your sister does something that hurts your feelings and you're pretty angry about it. Maybe she forgot your birthday or something. And this is like the third year in a row that she's done that. And you want to talk to her, but you don't really like conflict. So what do you do? What's the socially appropriate response?

CAROL: I guess maybe saying something like … I don't know. I wouldn't want to accuse her of forgetting my birthday, but that's what happened. So I guess it may be appropriate to say something like, hey, this really upset me. But again, it's like OK, I understand that maybe that's what should happen, but I still wouldn't want to. I would prefer to just avoid having that conversation altogether.

PROFESSOR SATTERFIELD: Right. So remember, we're trying to decide for you, as we want you to build more relationships: Is it a skills deficit or is it anxiety or emotions that are getting in the way? And to me, it sounds like it's more the anxiety and the emotions getting in the way. Does that sound right to you, or what do you think?

CAROL: I think that sounds right. I think in my head, I know what I should be doing, but I just can't do it.

PROFESSOR SATTERFIELD: Well, what I would like to do is to give you a few things to read about conversation. And I know it might sound funny of we all learn to talk and you don't have to be trained in how to talk. But the art of conversation is something that we often don't learn, like what's a good opener or what's a good conversation extender?

What's a good conversation closer? Sometimes people get stuck talking to someone and they would really like to move on to the next person at their cocktail party, but it's hard to do. So it's just a lot of little tips and suggestions and things that you can try out. And some of them will fit your style and some of them won't.

But I think that's the kind of thing that you can read on your own and you can try out as a behavioral experiment and see if it works for you. For me, it sounds like we're really needing to focus on the anxiety part. And if we can turn down the intensity of that anxiety, then you can start accessing and using those skills.

CAROL: OK.

[VIGNETTE END]

PROFESSOR SATTERFIELD: So, let's review Carol's assessment. As we might predict, she's overly modest, and she downplays here social skills. She doesn't have the social network she wants, so she deduces that she's no good at social activities or social interactions. Do you agree based on what you saw? What counter evidence did you see? What about her job, her family, her relationships, her past friendships? Recall her answers to the hypothetical scenarios. She knows the answer or what to do, but that doesn't mean she can actually do it. Notice her in-session behaviors. I immediately started gathering data from their first point of contact. She called me, and although nervous, she was totally appropriate and pleasant. And when she came to our first session, again, she demonstrated a mastery of those basic and expected social skills and social exchanges. So the bottom line with Carol is that, while some social skills practice couldn't hurt, a skills deficit is not the primary driver of her social isolation. We'll do a quick brush up on skills, but we'll focus more of our energy on managing her interfering emotions, cognitions, and behaviors, specifically her social anxiety. The obvious obstacle, her social anxiety, is what we'll tackle, but that only begs the question of why her anxiety is there.

I would ask you to recall the layers from the cognitive model. So you would first use the CVT triangle, and you've learned to look at cognition and behavior to help you understand emotions. We would start with cognition, and again, we start up at the top and we work our way down. So starting at the top or the surface, she shared a couple of different examples of being called on at work, of needing to talk to a coworker, of passing people on the street. That's the activating event. She then has beliefs. She's not liked. She doesn't know what to say. She's going to be rejected. That's on the surface, but below that we have rules or conditionally assumptions, like the if-then statements. So she might believe, or might say to herself, if I say hello, then people will be irritated. If I reach out to connect with another person, then they'll reject me.

Now, beneath those rules, those conditional assumptions, we have core beliefs, those irrational, deeply held beliefs about ourselves, our world, and the people around us, and related to that are our values, what matters most and why. What might you hypothesize her beliefs to be? Remember we can often boil things down to lovability and achievement.

Now, the primary driver of anxiety for Carol is avoidance and safety behaviors. Now Carol, for instance, at work, she oftentimes will time her arrival at a meeting so she's one or two minutes late because she doesn't want those unstructured few minutes where she'll have to interact with other people. When a meeting ends, she's the first one out the door, because, again, she doesn't want that unstructured interventions. Other things that she will do if she needs to talk in a meeting, she will not make eye contact and she will talk rapidly. If she has to engage someone in a conversation, she will ask them lots of questions so she doesn't need to disclose anything about herself. All of these would be considered her sort of safety behaviors. Of course, her behavior of preference is just to avoid social interactions at all. She feels safest when she's alone or when she's at home with her pets.

Now, recall from our anxiety lecture when we did some somatic quieting, we did an ABCD; we did a thought record; we talked about exposures. And with Carol, we created something called the SUDS Hierarchy, the Subjective Units of Distress, where she started at the bottom of her hierarchy and started working up. We're also targeting those interfering factors, cognitions, and behaviors, but we're pushing against that tendency towards avoidance, and we're pushing against those safety behaviors, which she likes to do.

But having skills and tamping down anxiety isn't enough to create new relationships. How can we move her forward? Now, of course, there's the issue of personality. She seems like more of an introvert to me. We know that introversion and extroversion is conceptually sound. There's a number of measures; the Myers Briggs probably being the most common that looks at introversion and extroversion among a number of other things. But remember that introversion indicates a preference, not an ability, and it doesn't prevent an individual from having meaningful social relationships.

So, what is social support, if this is what we're trying to give to Carol? Well, social support has been conceptualized in a number of different ways, and in fact, it's a notoriously slippery concept to define and even harder to measure. Now, the common definition of social support is that it is the perception that one is cared for, has assistance available from other people, and that one is part of a supportive social network. In research studies, you hear the term social support, but you also hear social integration, social connectedness, social support networks, and each has a slightly different angle on this complex and difficult-to-measure idea.

So, what are some of the characteristics? First, let's look at structural characteristics that might include the size of your social support network, the density, or the distance. Are all your friends gathered locally in the same geographic area, or maybe they are dispersed around the country or even the world? What is the diversity of individuals? Are they all approximately the same age, the same gender, the same background, or is there a wider range? What's the level of reciprocity? Does the individual always give support but receive less, or vice versa? And of course, we want to know whether or not it goes beyond that inter circle of familial relationships.

We might also want to look at some of the functional characteristics. Does an individual receive emotional support? Do they receive informational support? Do you have friends that can give you advice or help you work through problems? Does an individual receive tangible or practical support? Do they have someone that can help them with dinner, help them pay the mortgage, or drive them to a doctor's appointment? And of course, do they have someone that can provide companionship or belonging?

Now, other key features to keep in mind as you're doing a social support assessment is the idea of perceived versus actual. Now, we can look at actual indicators, the density, the shape, the structure, the function, but it's really an individual's perception of their social support and the quality that they receive which is most important.

We also want to look at is the individual giving or receiving support, and does that seem to be in balance? Now, sources of support might include significant others or family and friends, and even though you may see greater levels of intimacy and romantic relationships, it doesn't have to be the case. Emotional closeness is often about shared life experiences, so it could certainly be platonic.

Let's go on to look at our second clip where we're setting up a social support assessment exercise for Carol.

PROFESSOR SATTERFIELD: So Carol, let's continue our assessment of your social supports and social support network. And I thought we could do that by visually representing who's in your social support network and what kinds of support they can provide.

So let me explain the diagram that I've drawn up here just a little bit. So here, you get to be the center of the universe, so you're right in the middle there. And think of them as the rings of orbit, I guess. And what I want you to do is to put a person's name, anyone that you would consider a social support, somewhere in this universe.

And if they're close to you, they're going to be in your inner orbits. So they're going to be in your inner circle here. If they're a little further out, you place them a little further out on the circle. And if they're just somewhere sort of floating in space but they should be on the map somewhere, we'll write them out there.

And what we'll do from there is I will have a series of questions to talk about what kinds of support they might be able to provide. But for now, why don't we just get the names on the map. And we'll see who's in your network. So I'll let you write those up there. So who would you consider a social support?

CAROL: I guess my parents.

PROFESSOR SATTERFIELD: OK, so your mom and dad.

CAROL: Let's see.

PROFESSOR SATTERFIELD: OK, so mom and dad are in your inner circle. So you would consider them close supports.

CAROL: Yeah, well, I mean, I guess close. Closer than most people.

PROFESSOR SATTERFIELD: So the closest supports that you currently have. And are they about the same, or are you closer to one or the other?

CAROL: I think it's about the same, but in different ways. Does that make sense?

PROFESSOR SATTERFIELD: That makes sense. That makes perfect sense.

[VIGNETTE END]

PROFESSOR SATTERFIELD: So now you can see how we start the exercise. Carol then goes on to fill in the names of her sister, her brother, and her friends. Then she starts to think about how she could rank or qualify the level of intimacy with each of those individuals. Let's see how she does that in our next clip.

[VIGNETTE START]

PROFESSOR SATTERFIELD: So we have 1, 2, 3, 4, 5, 6 humans that are on there. And we have three that are in your inner circle and three on your outer circle. And when you look at this figure and the people that populate your social support network, what's the first thought you have? What reaction do you have?

CAROL: I feel like there should be more people on there.

PROFESSOR SATTERFIELD: You feel like there should be more people. OK, and why is that?

CAROL: It just looks kind of empty to me.

PROFESSOR SATTERFIELD: OK, it looks empty. And do you have a sense of what you think would be the right amount?

CAROL: Not really. I don't know. I think it was kind of hard deciding if anyone should even go on the inner circle for me, but if I had to call someone and ask for help, then those would be the people to do it.

PROFESSOR SATTERFIELD: You know, there's no right number or right quantity of social supports to have. It's really about are they high enough quality that your social support needs can be met, that you're having intimate, satisfying friendships, relationships, family connections with them or not? And one of the ways that we can see if you have the right balance or the right quality is looking at the kinds of support that the different people are able to provide. And we typically divide support up into these three categories.

We have practical support, so if you need a ride to the doctor or you need help paying your rent for the month or someone to cook you dinner, that's a very practical supportive thing to do. It might be emotional support, so this is the good listener, the shoulder to cry on. You don't really expect them to do anything to change the situation, but it's really nice to be listened to.

And the last one, we call it informational supporter. These are the folks that are good at giving advice. So let's say that you have to choose between job A or job B or college one or college two. Someone who's just really good at thinking out loud with you and can help turn things over.

So practical advice, emotional advice, or informational advice. Some people are good at just one. Some people are good at two or maybe all three of them. So what I want to do then is to visit each of these people on your social support network. And I want you to think about what kind of advice or what kind of support that they're good at. Is it practical, emotional, or informational? And we'll just start with your mom. So is she practical, emotional, informational, or all of the above?

CAROL: I think she would definitely be practical and emotional. Informational, I feel like she kind of just takes over the whole conversation. So it's not much. So practical and emotional.

PROFESSOR SATTERFIELD: OK, and do you feel emotionally supported if she's taking over the conversation? Or is that just when you're making a decision?

CAROL: I think it's, I mean, I don't know. Maybe it's a mom thing. But if it's me asking for advice, then she'll take it all over. But if it's me, if I'm upset about something, something's happened, then—

PROFESSOR SATTERFIELD: She'll listen.

CAROL: She'll usually listen.

PROFESSOR SATTERFIELD: OK, so let's just put a dash and p and e after her, so she's good at those two kinds of support. And how about dad? Is he a p, an e, or an i?

CAROL: I think he would be p and i.

PROFESSOR SATTERFIELD: OK, so let's put him as p and i. And how about Stephanie?

CAROL: Stephanie would be e and i.

PROFESSOR SATTERFIELD: E and i. And Alicia?

CAROL: I think Alicia is just an i.

PROFESSOR SATTERFIELD: Is an i. And we can stop there. It gives you an idea of where we're going with this. And again, it's not about the number of social supports. It's the kind of support they can provide. And we want you to have enough close support of all different varieties. And if we look at the folks in your inner circle, it looks like we have a couple of p's, we have a couple of e's, and we have a couple of i's.

So even if one person isn't available, there's a second person that you could go to. So this helps me feel a little bit better. We can still work on adding more people. We can still work on building intimacy. It tells me, in terms of social support, you have some that's there. You're not fully satisfied with it yet, and that's important and we can work on it. But you have most of your bases at least minimally covered.

Now the next step then would be to decide are you going to add brand new people or are you going to lasso those folks in outer space and pull them in closer. So are you going to pull Jacob in, are you going to pull Alicia in, are you going to pull Sarah in? But let me start with the first question. Are there new people that you'd like to add? Maybe people you've met once or twice. They're not even really acquaintances, but there was a little spark there or something, some kind of connection. You were in sync with someone. Anyone you can think of?

CAROL: Sure. There's another person at work who is in a different department, but, I mean, we have said hi a couple of times. But it's nothing.

PROFESSOR SATTERFIELD: OK, so he's a possibility. If you're going to set a goal to meet new people, he might be a good place to start.

CAROL: Yeah, he seems nice enough. And then I don't really know. I guess there's some people who I used to hang out with in college that maybe I can reach back out to. I mean, we were friends in college and just haven't really talked since then, because we got jobs.

PROFESSOR SATTERFIELD: People graduate and scatter all over. OK, and how would you find them? I guess Facebook's good for that, right?

CAROL: Probably, yeah. Some of them live close, so I just I haven't really made much of an effort.

PROFESSOR SATTERFIELD: So you have a pool of people from college and you have this other coworker. What about the possibility of becoming closer to Alicia or Jacob or Sarah? Is that a possibility that you're interested in?

CAROL: Yeah. I mean, I like them fine. And Alicia and I talk enough. I think we already have some interaction going. And Jacob, I'd be interested to pull him in. But I don't know, I think it might be a little weird, just because we never really talked a whole lot. But I mean, I don't know. I might be willing to give that a try.

PROFESSOR SATTERFIELD: OK. Well, I'll let you think about it a bit. So you have those two options. They're not mutually exclusive. I mean, you can work on adding new people at the same time that you're working on deepening current relationships.

You don't have to do it all at once. We don't want it to feel overwhelming. But we do want you to push yourself a little bit to decide how can I enrich the circle by adding more people or by pulling existing people in a little bit closer to the center. So I'll let you think about that, and then next time, we'll develop a much more concrete plan about the steps we'd like to take next.

CAROL: OK.

[VIGNETTE END]

PROFESSOR SATTERFIELD: So what did we learn with Carol? Well, we've learned she's not totally isolated. She's been close to family and friends before, but it takes her a very, very long time before starts to feel comfortable with someone. She doesn't reach out to her social supports or nurture those relationships as she could, and she wants both more quality and quantity in her social support network.

So, let's first talk about quantity or adding new people to your network, and what exactly is the right size, and does it get hard to form new relationships as you grow older. First, I wanted to address a recent phenomenon of social networks and the use of things like Facebook in order to connect to other individuals. Could we consider this a source of social support? Do social networks maybe fill in the gap, if we have gaps from our personal relationships? A study done by Jonathon Cummings at Carnegie Mellon looked at both bankers and college students that were using the Internet social networks, phone, and in-person meetings to connect with others and then compared the quality of those meetings, and again, perceived social support. As you might guess, even though people enjoy things like Facebook, the quality of social support that they've received was inferior to in-person relationships.

Speaking of quality, when we look at the types of support we receive, we want to ensure that an individual has adequate amounts of each type of support—informational support, practical support, emotional support, or companionate support. But we need to remember that it's Carol's or the support needer's responsibility to know what kind of support you need and then to go to the right person to ask them for that support. Specify what you need and speak up if you aren't getting what you want.

So how could Carol grow her network? First, she needs to identify her target. Is it someone that's already on the diagram and she just wants to pull them in to an inner circle and improve intimacy? Or does she want to meet new people entirely? She probably wants to do a little bit of both. We want to set expectations, and we want to have her have a system of how she can capture even tiny steps forward, because this isn't something that changes overnight or even over a couple of weeks. We want her to keep a success diary, because we can predict that she might get discouraged that it's not going quite quickly enough.

The last source of support I wanted to address is based on a question I often get from other individuals and that's, "Does my social support network have to be composed just of humans?" And this actually came up with Carol as well. An example by Erica Friedman published in a study published in 1995 in the American Journal of Cardiology looked at individuals who had suffered a myocardial infarction, or a heart attack. They looked at individuals who owned a dog versus those that don't own a dog. They looked at human social supports versus those who don't. And in both cases of dog and human, that social support was important and helped to increase rates of survival.

The last thing I would like to leave us with is a frequently asked question about how cognitions influence intimacy? Do they help or hurt? How? Well, of course, the answer is both. Remember that CBT isn't necessarily seeing the glass as half full or half empty, it's about balance. It's about interpretation, but I think it's most relevant to intimacy if we remember one of those habits of mind is mind reading, and I think just naturally, we try to guess or we make assumptions about another individual's motivations or what they might be thinking about you. Often, we don't check those assumptions; we just make them and we act accordingly. In order to resolve conflicts or improve intimacy, it's important, of course, to check out those cognitions and their accuracy and see if they're helping to relationships or hurtful.

Now, in our next lecture, we will continue along the lines of talking about CBT and conflict, and you're going to meet Michael's wife. Thank you.

Constructive Conflict and Fighting Fair
Lecture 21

U p to this point in the course, our CBT examples have been nearly all dyadic: one patient and one therapist as a pair. We "step outside" of the therapy office by having the patient do homework in the real world that involves other people. The patient then reports back the next session, and we do problem solving and make adjustments to our treatment plan if necessary. But if the issue resides within a couple or family, then everyone might need to be in the room. In this lecture, you will learn about couples CBT.

Couples CBT

- Couples CBT works on many of the same issues that any type of couples therapy most likely wants to address, including communication (especially miscommunication and its role in conflict), empathy (emotional understanding and respect for each member of the couple and why it sometimes waxes and wanes over time), intimacy (emotional closeness), and expressed affection (either directly or implicitly). Of course, some of the foundations of any relationship will be addressed, such as trust and acceptance or, if a transgression has occurred, forgiveness.

- There are some important differences between individual CBT and couples CBT. First, with couples CBT, the cognitions that you work on are "hot," meaning that therapy doesn't just involve doing an ABCD exercise about an event that happened out in the world—sometimes the activating event is the session itself, so those cognitions are happening in the room and coming out in the moment. It makes the cognitions a little more difficult and challenging to work with but possibly more fruitful.

- Couples CBT is also a little more difficult to predict. It's easier to make a formulation for one person than for two people, but with a couple, the whole is greater than the sum of the parts. It's not just two people together; it's also the chemistry between those two individuals. Therefore, the work becomes much more complex, and the conceptualizations can be a lot trickier.

- Furthermore, we'll still work on SMART goals, but it's not just the goals of one individual—it's the goals of two individuals. We would hope that those goals overlap a fair amount within a couple, but sometimes those goals might be diametrically opposed.

Assessing Relationship Dynamics

- When assessing relationship dynamics, think of relationships as a potent trigger for automatic thoughts and emotions. Just as we have habits of mind, we have so-called habits of the heart. We develop our own romantic, or emotional, or intimate style.

In couples CBT, sometimes the activating event is the session itself, so the cognitions that need to be worked on are happening in the room and coming out in the moment, making the cognitions more challenging to work with but possibly more fruitful.

- We know that some people, when angry or upset, will withdraw and become very quiet. Some people might have the opposite style. Others might have a tendency to feel rejected even when rejection wasn't the intent. Others, when angry, might become passive-aggressive. Others might become competitive or even aggressive.

- But it's about the chemistry—it's about the interaction of those two different kinds of habits of the heart that we will see in action when we're doing couples CBT.

- When assessing a couple, a therapist might already have a formulation for a husband, for example, but wants to see if it holds true when his wife is also around. How does he communicate with her? What are his nonverbals? What is her style? What is the level of tension that is between them, and what is the level of their emotional intimacy?

- How do you assess the couple? We've learned from individual CBT that there are a number of different assessment methodologies, including semi-structured interviews and questionnaires. We would want to have a similar process for the couple.

- In a clinical setting, when assessing two individuals, we usually want to look for something called triangulation, where we take multiple sources of data and see where they overlap or where they don't overlap.
  - First, we would give individual self-report surveys to each person to fill out independently, not to share with the other person. The self-reports would often include the perceptions of how things are going in the relationship now versus how they would like them to be.

  - Second, we would interview each member of the couple separately. Sometimes without the other person in the room, one person might feel that he or she has more freedom to express his or her feelings or desires and the challenges that they might be facing as a couple.

○ Third, we would bring the couple together and interview them together so that we can observe the chemistry between them and how they interact with one another. Regardless of whether or not the sources of data overlap or don't overlap, it's instructive either way. From the data, we can develop a working formulation of how to best help the couple.

- There are a few examples of assessment tools for couples that are freely available online. The first, called the Relationship Closeness Inventory, was created by Ellen Berscheid and measures interdependence with three scales: frequency of intimacy, diversity of connection, and strength of connection.

- Another commonly used instrument that is used in religious or non-secular counseling is called the PREPARE/ENRICH couples assessment tool. It is often used as a way to prepare individuals who are considering becoming married. It is an online assessment tool that looks at strengths, conflict, family or origin, etc. Then, the couple is paired with a counselor.

- The next tool is the Experiences in Close Relationships questionnaire, which is a 36-item self-report attachment measure developed by R. Chris Fraley, Niels G. Waller, and Kelly A. Brennan. It yields scores on two subscales: avoidance (discomfort with closeness and discomfort with depending on others—which is certainly important for intimacy, or lack thereof) and anxiety (fear of rejection and abandonment).

Communication and Miscommunication

- Before we get into negotiating conflict, therapists can use a positive psychology exercise in which each person shares what he or she likes about the other person. We can ask the couple to engage in a simple behavioral intervention to do positive activities together, tabling conflict and enjoying one another for a week, for example.

- We start with a simple behavioral intervention, and the attention shifts in the direction of positive emotion. We want to create a bit of a cushion before digging into the conflicts the couple has.

- Before moving into conflict, we might need to look at communication: What is the current state of the couple's communication style or communication chemistry with one another? We use the usual processes to evaluate communication, such as self-report surveys, individual interviews, conjoint interviews, reports from others, or even observations that we do in the therapy session.

- One of the most commonly used communication skills tests is the Interpersonal Communication Skills Test, which has a number of different scales that help us better understand our strengths and our weaknesses in communicating with others. These scales include the following.
    - Insightfulness: the ability to understand other people's words and intentions.

    - Verbal expression: the ability to express yourself in a way that is clear, concise, and effective.

    - Assertiveness: the ability to express your opinions and ideas.

    - Listening skills: the ability to take turns and listen appropriately to others during conversation.

    - Emotional management: the ability to control your own emotions in conversation and the ability to properly respond to others' emotions.

- This questionnaire has 25 items that are rated on a scale of 1 to 5. Some of these items are the following.
    - I manage to express my ideas clearly.

    - I find it easy to see things from someone else's point of view.

- o People don't get what I am saying.

- o I have difficulty putting my thoughts into words.

- o I tend to postpone or avoid discussing touchy subjects.

- Miscommunication occurs commonly, and often there might be a gender issue—there are dramatic differences in the way that men and women communicate. For example, men spend approximately two-thirds of social conversations talking about themselves. Men are less likely to pick up on emotional cues and are less likely to take turns or give "openings" to others. In conversation, men tend to report, and women tend to engage in rapport talk.

- These are just two different styles of communication. The point is not to harshly criticize men. But there are pros and cons to each style. And of course, different kinds of conflict might emerge from those styles.

Conflict Management

- The most common sources of conflict for couples are money, sex, kids, and religion. But, of course, couples might have conflicts about just about anything.

- In addition to the emotional and biological components (anger and resentment), we want to look at some of the cognitive elements. What memories are activated during conflict, and what are the other conflicts that are brought up? What is the subjective interpretation of the events? What are the beliefs about the relationship or conflict in general?

- There are also behavioral elements when it comes to conflict. Does one of the pair of people withdraw during or after conflict? Does one of them ruminate over the conflict?

- The DESC (describe, emote, specify, consequences) method is a simple structured approach to describing conflict and going on to resolve it. It is a straightforward method that seeks to improve marital satisfaction and decrease conflict.

- There have been a few exemplary studies that have studied cognitive behavioral marital therapy—one from 1995 by Ryan Dunn and Andrew Schwebel and a meta-analysis from 2005 by Nathan Wood and colleagues. These studies found that cognitive behavioral conflict resolution skills in the context of couples therapy are indeed effective. But when researchers tried to determine whether there was a specific type or subtype of CBT that was most effective, they didn't find a difference. Across the board, couples CBT seemed to be equally effective.

Suggested Reading

Brennan, Clark, and Shaver, "Self-Report Measurement of Adult Romantic Attachment."

Epstein and Baucom, *Enhanced Cognitive-Behavioral Therapy for Couples.*

Gottman and Silver, *The 7 Principles for Making Marriage Work.*

Hendrix, *Getting the Love You Want.*

Questions to Consider

1. Many claim that history repeats itself and that we are compelled to repeat the relationship patterns of our family of origin. Do you see a kernel of truth to this belief in your own relationship? Have you worked to make sure that you don't repeat your parents' "mistakes"?

2. Expressions of intimacy are often highly influenced by culture. Some cultures are very demonstrative while others are subtler. How do you express intimacy or a desire for more intimacy? How can you be sure that your signals are correctly interpreted?

Constructive Conflict and Fighting Fair
Lecture 21—Transcript

PROFESSOR SATTERFIELD: Up to this point, our CBT examples have been nearly all dyadic—one patient and one therapist as a pair. We step outside of the therapy office by having the patient do homework in the real world that involves other people. The patient then reports back the next session, and we do problem solving and adjusting to our treatment plan if necessary. But if the issue resides within a couple or family, then everyone might literally need to be in the room.

In today's lecture, we're going to return to Michael, but we're also going to meet his wife Stephanie and follow them in their work together. Now, couples CBT works on many of the same issues that any type of couple's therapy most likely will want to address. We'll look at communication, and we'll especially look at miscommunication and its role in conflict. We'll look at empathy or emotional understanding and respect for each member of the couple, and understand why that sometimes waxes and wanes over time. We'll look at intimacy or emotional closeness, at expressed affection, either directly or implicitly. And of course it's some of the foundations in any relationship, such as trust and acceptance, or if a transgression has occurred, we'll look at forgiveness.

Now, if you're interested in what a full program of cognitive behavioral couples therapy might look like, there is a couple of different sources I wanted to point you towards. The first is a book called *Enhanced Cognitive Behavioral Therapy for Couples, A Contextual Approach*, written in 2002 by Epstein and Baucom. And the other is a series of articles that are freely available online about Integrative Behavioral Couples Therapy or IBCT, by Christensen and Neil Jacobson.

Now, there are some important differences between individual CBT and couples CBT. First and probably foremost, is that the cognitions that you work on with couples are hot, meaning, it's not just doing an ABCD about an event that happens out there; sometimes the activating event is the session itself, so those cognitions are coming out right in the moment. It makes them a little more difficult and challenging to work with, but maybe more fruitful.

Couples CBT is also a little harder to predict. It's easier to make a formulation for one person than for two people, but remember, in a couple, the whole is greater than the sum of the parts. It's not just two people together; it's the chemistry between those two individuals. So the work becomes much more complex and the conceptualizations can be a lot more tricky. And lastly, we'll still work on smart goals, but remember it's not just the goals of one individual, it's the goals of two individuals. Now we would hope that those goals overlap a fair amount within a couple, but sometimes those goals might be diametrically opposed.

Of course, we're going to look at relationship dynamics, and I think you would want to imagine relationships as a potent trigger for automatic thoughts and emotions. Just as we have habits of mind, we have habits of the heart. We develop our own romantic, or emotional, or intimate style. We know that some people, when angry or upset, they will shut down and withdraw and become very quiet. Some people might have the opposite style. Others might have a tendency to feel rejected, even when rejection wasn't the intent. Others, when angry, may become passive-aggressive. Others might become quite competitive or even aggressive. But remember, it's about the chemistry. It's about the interaction of those two different kinds of habits of the heart that we'll see in action when we're doing couples CBT.

Let's move on, then, to look at our very first clip, where you're going to meet Stephanie, we'll lay the ground rules, and we'll set the stage for the work ahead.

[VIGNETTE START]

PROFESSOR SATTERFIELD: Stephanie, welcome. I'm so glad you're here. As you know, Michael has had several sessions before. And we've been working on issues around anger. And it was actually his idea that you come in today.

STEPHANIE: Yes. Thank you. It's my pleasure. I'm a little nervous. But I know this is Michael's deal, but it affects me too. So, he's always saying, Jason said this, Jason said that—and always really good. But I'm glad I could be here too.

PROFESSOR SATTERFIELD: And I'm glad you could come as well. And Michael, how are you feeling right now?

MICHAEL: I'm feeling good. I think that this will be a good opportunity for us to talk to each other in an environment where obviously it's different and maybe we'll both learn something.

PROFESSOR SATTERFIELD: OK, good. Well, let's start just by just laying some ground rules, just so we know how to proceed from here. There's always conflict in every single relationship. But I think what differentiates between successful and unsuccessful conflict is if there's respect, if there's an opportunity to both speak and to listen. And I'm wondering what other rules you guys would like to suggest as we work through maybe some of the conflicts you've had.

STEPHANIE: Well, I think maybe one of the things that often happens is judging up the past and letting that—holding grudges and letting things like that—

MICHAEL: Because you think I do that?

STEPHANIE: Well, sometimes you bring up things that have happened years ago that I don't necessarily think—

MICHAEL: I don't really think I do that.

STEPHANIE: Well—

PROFESSOR SATTERFIELD: OK, so why don't we push pause. We push pause there, and you have a good ground rule and that's to focus on the present. And how about if someone says something you disagree with? What's a good way to disagree that opens conversation instead of shutting it down?

MICHAEL: Well, you could be the referee.

PROFESSOR SATTERFIELD: OK, there's that. But you know I'm only here an hour a week. It's a lot of other hours, so it's something you guys probably want to be able to negotiate on your own. We have respect and we have both listening and speaking, focusing on the present.

MICHAEL: How about focus on what the other person says, perhaps. I suppose we could reserve judgment.

PROFESSOR SATTERFIELD: OK, reserving judgment, maybe agreeing to disagree if you don't see things eye to eye?

MICHAEL: That makes sense.

PROFESSOR SATTERFIELD: And I think maybe just remembering that if you didn't care about each other, you wouldn't be here. You've been married for what, almost 20 years now. That's a lot of time together.

MICHAEL: It is.

PROFESSOR SATTERFIELD: And you've been through a lot of life together. You have a son together. He's a teenager now. But you've been through a lot. And we're hoping that we can get you guys back to a place where you remember what it is that brought together in the first place.

So I was hoping that, rather than jump in about conflict, we can lay some ground rules. And if things get stirred up here, that's fine. But I'll remind you of those rules. And I'll actually write them down and give them to you and put them on the fridge. Put them wherever you need to put them at home.

[VIGNETTE END]

PROFESSOR SATTERFIELD: So what are some of the things I'm immediately looking for? Remember that we already have a formulation for Michael, but I want to see if it holds true for when his wife is also around. How does he communicate with her? What are his non-verbals? What is her style? What is the level of tension that's between them, and what is the level of their emotional intimacy? That, of course, raises the issue of how do you assess the couple, and we've learned from individual CBT that there's a number of different assessment methodologies, semi-structured interviews, questionnaires, and so on. We would want to have a similar process for the couple. So in a clinical setting, though, with two individuals, we usually want to look for something called triangulation, where you take multiple sources of data and you see where they overlap or where they don't overlap.

So first I would give individual self-report packets, surveys really, to each individual that they would fill out independently and they would not share with one another. These would often include the perceptions of how things are going in the relationship now versus how they wish or want them to be. Secondly, I would probably interview each member of the couple separately. Sometimes without the other person in the room, they feel that they have more freedom to express their feelings or desires and the challenges that they may be facing as a couple. And finally, I would want to bring them together and interview them together so that, again, we can see that chemistry and how they interact with one another. Now regardless of whether or not those sources of data overlap or don't overlap, it's instructive either way.

So, what would an inventory look like? So what sorts of assessment tools? And I'll just give you a couple of examples of ones that you can find freely available online. The first is by Ellen Berscheid; it's the Relationship Closeness Inventory. That measures interdependence, looking at frequencies of intimacy, diversities of connection, and the strength of connection. Another commonly used instrument is used in religious or non-secular counseling; it's called the Prepare/Enrich Assessment tool. It's often used as a way to prepare individuals who are considering joining and becoming married.

The next is the ECR, or the Experiences in Close Relationships survey. It's a 36-item self-report attachment measure developed by Fraley, Waller, and Brennan. It yields two sub scales: one scale on avoidance, it looks at discomfort with closeness and discomfort with depending on others, certainly important for intimacy or lack thereof. And the second scale is about anxiety, so it looks at things like fear of rejection and fear of abandonment. If you're interested in this instrument or others, I would, again, encourage you to look online for the ECR. You can probably most easily find it at yourpersonality.net.

Let's move on, then, to look at our second clip. And in this second clip, we're going to use a positive psychology exercise before we get to negotiating conflict.

[VIGNETTE START]

PROFESSOR SATTERFIELD: But maybe we could start with some of the positives and getting you back to some of the positives. And Stephanie, if it's OK, I wanted to ask you, what are some of the things that initially drew you to Michael? So Michael at his best—why'd you pick him? What was it?

STEPHANIE: Well, obviously he's very attractive and he's only gotten more attractive as we've gotten older. And he's really funny. And I really appreciate that about him. More than anything, he's got a wonderful sense of humor. He's always making me laugh. I don't want to say that maybe he's lost some of his sense of humor, but you get older and things get stressed out.

PROFESSOR SATTERFIELD: We'll stay with the positive. So we got sense of humor, and he's a looker.

STEPHANIE: And obviously, he's very smart. And that's something that I enjoy about him a lot. I think we have a lot of common interests. And I can express my opinions about something and he always has an interesting response to it.

PROFESSOR SATTERFIELD: And Michael, I'm going to ask you the same question. So what was it about Stephanie that drew you to her? Stephanie at her best—what are the things you really like or love about her?

MICHAEL: Well, I think I'd echo a lot of the things that she said. And I'd also—one thing that probably doesn't come out when you think of me, but certainly when I think of Stephanie, I think caring. From the very beginning, that's one of the things that I first really noticed, appreciated, and eventually came to love about Stephanie. She's really caring. She talked about humor and intelligence. And I feel that early on in our relationship, there was just a sense that we communicated very, very naturally, because we were on the same wavelength. We found the same things funny. We thought about things the same way. And when you have that sort of, I don't know, camaraderie, it's hard to beat. And I felt like that was there almost—maybe you disagree, but from the beginning.

STEPHANIE: No, I agree. I agree. And it makes things much easier to get through together when you have that sort of understanding already.

PROFESSOR SATTERFIELD: And another question, Stephanie, we'll go back to you. What are some things that the two of you used to do together that you really enjoy that maybe you haven't done in a while?

STEPHANIE: Well, we used to spend a lot of time outdoors, hiking. And we did a lot of canoeing and camping, especially when we were younger, before we had our son. We haven't done so much of that lately. He has some health issues that don't allow us to get out as much as we used to. And he just quite frankly doesn't like it.

PROFESSOR SATTERFIELD: OK. So camping and outdoors—

STEPHANIE: Yeah, and we used to be a lot more social, I think, than we are now. Especially I guess when we were younger, we had a larger group of friends. And as you get older, you move and people move and so you lose track of them. So we do enjoy our neighbors and things like that. But I think our close friends are not as accessible maybe as they used to be.

PROFESSOR SATTERFIELD: OK. And so I'm just going to create a list of activities. And you can probably see where this is going. And how about for you, Michael? What are some of the positive memories or activities that the two of you used to do in addition to what Stephanie shared?

MICHAEL: Yeah, there was that sense of what Stephanie was talking about, getting busy, getting distracted. There was that sense of freedom, wasn't there, that you really—I really miss, I really miss. And I think when we were young, that freedom meant that we could do things like go to movies. I really enjoyed you introducing me to movies that I'd never seen, and me introducing you to movies that maybe were a little weird, but you endured them.

STEPHANIE: I always enjoyed them—well, most of them.

MICHAEL: But going to the movies even if we didn't necessarily come out thinking the same thing about them. I've always enjoyed—and this is something I've definitely got away from—cooking. I enjoy cooking for just the two of us.

STEPHANIE: He's a great cook.

MICHAEL: That was always something that I would like to do on a weekend, just to say, you know, it's Saturday. We could go out, but maybe we could just make it an event, eating in. So those are a couple things in addition to the outdoorsy things we used to do that I would mention.

PROFESSOR SATTERFIELD: OK, and I have outdoors, socializing, movies, and cooking. So those are four great, and I think realistic and doable ideas, to a certain extent. I'm thinking about these not because we don't have work to do. We do. There's a lot of water under the bridge. There's this anger issue. I've heard about the recent incident around smoking on the deck. So it stirred up and it's clear there were a lot of probably years of resentments and things that can get released with a poke.

STEPHANIE: Definitely.

PROFESSOR SATTERFIELD: But I think what we don't want to lose sight of, is there's a foundation that's here. There are strengths that are here. And while we're mucking around in the stuff that we need to fix, I think it's important that we remember that there's a lot of positive things that have happened, too. And if we can keep adding to that list of positives, even in a very little way, it might remind you who it is that you're arguing with, and in the heat of the moment, hopefully take a little bit of that heat off.

[VIGNETTE END]

PROFESSOR SATTERFIELD: So you can see that we've started with a simple behavioral intervention and a bit of attention shifting in the positive emotion direction. We wanted to create a bit of a cushion, if you will, before digging into their conflicts. Now, before moving into conflict, we might need to look at communication and what the current state of affairs is in terms of their communication style or their communication chemistry with one another. We have the usual processes in order to evaluate communication; it might be self-report surveys, it might be individual interviews, it might be conjoint interviews, reports from others, or even observations that we do in session. One of the most commonly used communication skills test is the interpersonal communication skills test, where it has a number of different scales that help us to better understand our strengths and our weaknesses in communicating with others. These scales would include insightfulness, the ability to understand other people's words and intentions, verbal expression, assertiveness, and your listening skills and your emotional management skills.

This particular questionnaire has 25 items that are rated on a 1 to 5 scale. I'll give you just a couple of ideas of what some of these items might be like. For example, "I manage to express my ideas clearly." "I find it easy to see things from someone else's point of view." "People don't get what I am saying." "I have difficulty putting my thoughts into words." Or, "I tend to postpone or avoid discussing touchy subjects."

Now, miscommunication, we know, occurs commonly. And often there may be a gender issue in the way that men and women prefer, or are taught to communicate. For example, we know that men spend approximately two thirds of social conversations talking about themselves. Men are less likely to pick up on emotional cues, and they're less likely to take turns or give openings to others. Men in conversation tend to report, and women tend to engage in rapport talk. Now, these are just different styles, and it's not to harshly criticize men. But there are pros and cons, and of course, different sorts of conflict that might emerge from those styles.

Now the most common sources of conflict in couples, I think of them as the big four, are money, sex, kids, and religion. But of course, folks might have conflict about just about anything. Now we'll want to look at some of the cognitive elements. So what are the memories, what are the other conflicts that are brought up? What is subjective interpretation of events or the beliefs about the relationship? What we do in this next clip is we illustrate a very simple structured approach to describing conflict and going on to resolve it. Let's watch the next clip.

[VIGNETTE START]

PROFESSOR SATTERFIELD: The conflict I thought we'd go to is one that we've talked about a little bit before. It was around smoking. But before we do that, I wanted to outline a process that we can try out. We can test drive it, see how it works for you guys around this issue of smoking and the conflict you had about smoking. The method is called the DESC method, just D-E-S-C. And the D stands for describe. So you're just describing the situation and setting a stage. And we know that if each of you describe the situation, it will sound a little different—maybe a lot different. But just the first step is describe.

The second step is to emote. So describe the situation, and how you felt in that situation. The S is for specify. So that's when you say specifically what you would like the other person to do differently next time. It doesn't mean they're going to do it or they agree with you. But it's what you need from the other person so that they understand what you need.

And the C is the consequences, or really, why is this important to me? And if we don't work it out, what's going to happen? It's not a threat, but it's why does this matter. So it's D-E-S-C-. And just to make sure we're on the same page with that, so the D stands for—

STEPHANIE AND MICHAEL: Describe.

PROFESSOR SATTERFIELD: And the E stands for—

STEPHANIE AND MICHAEL: Emote.

PROFESSOR SATTERFIELD: And the S?

STEPHANIE AND MICHAEL: Specify.

PROFESSOR SATTERFIELD: And the C?

STEPHANIE AND MICHAEL: Consequences.

PROFESSOR SATTERFIELD: Perfect. All right. And so Michael, you're up with the DESC method to talk about the incident where you came home from work. You're stressed. You went out on the deck, and you smoked a cigarette. And Stephanie came out and saw you smoking. So why don't you describe—and we can keep it brief—the incident. Let us know how you felt, the E, specify, and consequences. And then we'll give you a chance to respond.

MICHAEL: With the description, I had been caught doing something I wasn't supposed to.

PROFESSOR SATTERFIELD: If I could just pause there and have you talk to each other, instead of to me. And I'm just here to observe. And you can just talk directly to Stephanie.

MICHAEL: Well, I was smoking. I recognized I shouldn't have been—I was sneaking a cigarette out on the deck. And you arrived and you immediately launched into what I thought was a tirade about all the negative consequences of smoking and the reasons I shouldn't be doing it. And that led to my reacting, which led to your reacting.

PROFESSOR SATTERFIELD: So let's pause there if I can interrupt. And since this is our test drive of a particular method, I might jump in a little more than I usually do. And I think in the D part, the describe part, we want you to pretend like you're a really, really boring attorney. And you're not trying to sway or persuade a jury. You've essentially lost all color and life in the description of the incident. So, trying to remove evaluations or emotion-laden words like "tirade." That's kind of a powerful word, "tirade." But you just say, I went out, I was smoking. You came out of the house. You saw that I was smoking, and we started to have an argument.

MICHAEL: That sounds like a good description.

PROFESSOR SATTERFIELD: That gets the event on the table. And so let's get to the E part, the emote part. So she saw you smoking. You guys had an exchange. And how did you feel during and after that?

MICHAEL: I felt angry, because I felt you didn't understand why I needed to have a cigarette, just one cigarette, at that point. I felt a little embarrassed that I had been found out. I felt that you were attacking me. And I felt defensive because of that.

PROFESSOR SATTERFIELD: And let's pause again there. And thank you for sharing that. So there's a few layers there. And Stephanie, you probably heard that there's the emotion—anger, embarrassment, defensiveness. But then there's some thoughts that were underneath and some interpretation underneath—some about him, some about your behavior.

So he felt angry and embarrassed and defensive and felt that he was being attacked. That was sort of his interpretation of your behavior is that it was an attack. And he was also thinking, man, I need this and I deserve this and it's been a really stressful day. And that was all part of his head space in the moment.

Now, how about the S part, the specify part?

MICHAEL: And by specify, I would want to express what specifically I would like her to do.

PROFESSOR SATTERFIELD: So if we were to rewind, you're smoking on the deck. She comes out and she sees you. What kind of response would you like from her?

MICHAEL: I think I said the last time we were here that one of the things that I always appreciated about you was the fact is you're caring. So I would specify by saying the first response, instead putting me on the defensive by taking the offensive, might be, "Michael, I see that you're having a cigarette. What's up?" Just having the response of caring and understanding would be great.

PROFESSOR SATTERFIELD: And if that doesn't happen, or if this sort of pattern continues, what's your worry? Why is this important?

MICHAEL: My worry is that in this particular case you're not appreciating where I live, and that's an indication that maybe we don't understand each other. And if we can't get to a space where we we're demonstrating that we understand one another, I guess ultimately one would be worried about the relationship itself. Why would two people who don't understand each other continue drifting through the world this way?

PROFESSOR SATTERFIELD: So let's pause there. And Stephanie, I want to check in with you about how you're feeling right now. You've been very good about not speaking up. And I can tell you're listening.

STEPHANIE: Yes. So do I start at the beginning, like to go through everything? Well, I guess to describe the situation, you were outside smoking. And I was coming upstairs through the laundry room and just saw you out there. And yes, I came out to the deck and was quite upset about you being out there smoking.

Emote? I was upset. I don't know that I was—I don't feel like I was angry as much as I was just sad and frustrated, because you've been working so hard not to smoke and I just felt like that was a big setback. And I don't want you to get lung cancer like your father and die. That's the real basis for my being upset, is that we watched your father die, and here you are doing the same thing. And it makes me very sad because I care about you and I love you and I don't want anything like that to happen to you.

PROFESSOR SATTERFIELD: So if we can pause there, I wanted to ask, is there's some fear there—fear for his health?

STEPHANIE: Absolutely, yes. Yes, I mean the death of Michael's father was awful. It's no way for anybody to die. And I don't know that I can do that again. I don't want to. And there's no reason why I should have to, because there's an opportunity to head that off.

PROFESSOR SATTERFIELD: So given that's the emotions that you had and that's what you were feeling in the space that you were in, he has put a request on the table, and that is to say, hey, Michael, what's going on? Is that a request you could comply with?

STEPHANIE: Yes, I can, absolutely, because that is where my anger is coming from, is because I care for you and I want you to know that. And I'm sorry that I reacted that way, but it is coming from a place of love and not from trying to be a bully or to make you feel embarrassed. It's because I care for you.

PROFESSOR SATTERFIELD: So there's one more piece to this, and I want to make sure we get to that. So in the event as it happened, he was wanting a particular response. He got a different response from you. And what happened is the situation escalated. So you heard something that you felt was attacking and unfair and unsupportive. And describe how you reacted to that.

MICHAEL: I think the way that I reacted was basically to get back at you. And the way that I got back at you was to dredge up a conversation that we've had in the past, and usually an elevated tones. And that is that I feel that I work very, very hard and I'm under a great deal of stress and I threw that back at you, as though you aren't. I think when I'm calm, I realize how much you do take on day to day. But the way that I threw it back at you was to say that you're just at home. How can you understand all that I'm going through? Because clearly at that moment, I felt you didn't.

STEPHANIE: Right.

PROFESSOR SATTERFIELD: And how did it feel to hear that?

STEPHANIE: Well it's something that happens more often when we do get angry. It kind of comes down to, I'm not working. I used to, but I'm not right now. And I take care of the house and our teenage son. But I don't know that Michael really appreciates all of that. And so he often throws that back in my face for any sort of argument.

PROFESSOR SATTERFIELD: So that sounds like a definite violation of our rules of conflict, where we focus on the issue at hand. And the issue at hand in that situation was Michael was smoking. You saw him smoke. You said something he thought was unsupportive. And then Michael, you pulled in this other issue, and it was pushing an old tape. You had had that argument a lot of times before, and then you guys were sort of off to the races with the latest argument. So it sounds like maybe, if I can do the Specify part for Michael, the request would be when you have an exchange that you're not happy with or hurts you or feels unsupported, we want you to have an alternate response. Rather than pulling out or dredging up something from a past argument, what could you do instead, or maybe Stephanie, we could hear from you. What would you like him to say instead of dredging something up?

STEPHANIE: Well, I think if you could tell me why you're stressed out and why it's causing you to smoke, instead of just trying to pull me into an argument, that would be more beneficial. Because then I would understand what you're going through, and I might be able to give suggestions about how you can decompress, rather than coming out on the deck and smoking. Because it's not helpful for you to get angry at me because I'm angry at you for smoking. And you're still carrying around the stress from your day. So I guess your anger is a way of expressing your stress, but that's not very helpful.

PROFESSOR SATTERFIELD: And we've talked about how anger can be empowering, but it also pushes other people away. It's hard to be around someone that's angry, and it's even harder to try to show support for them.

[VIGNETTE END]

PROFESSOR SATTERFIELD: So this was just a quick example of a fairly straightforward way to negotiate a conflict. Does it work? Do we have evidence that shows us it works? And of course, there are a number of different studies, and I'll just point out two that I think are exemplary. The first was from 1995, done by Dunn and Schwebel, and the next in 2005, a meta-analysis done by Wood in *The American Journal of Family Therapy*. They found, in both of those cases, that the preponderance of evidence shows us that cognitive behavioral conflict-resolution skills in the context of couples therapy is indeed effective. What they weren't able to show is which of those different subtypes of CBT for couples is most effective; they seemed equally effective across the board.

Now, in this lecture and in other lectures we've talked about the importance of both quantity and quality of relationships. We've talked about challenges of building intimacy and some of the basic or beginning skills of conflict management. In our next lecture we're going to move to talking about occupational context and address work-related stress and functioning. Thank you.

Thriving at Work through Behavioral Health
Lecture 22

The average American spends nearly 100,000 hours at work during his or her lifetime. U.S. workers currently put in around 1,800 hours per year, much more than our European counterparts. Professional burnout is at an all-time high, but no end is in sight. In this lecture, as we prepare to define, measure, and maybe even improve occupational functioning, it's important to recognize that many of the core ingredients—concentration, motivation, emotional management, communication, or even assertiveness—are relevant at both work and home and have close ties to CBT.

Self-Help for Success

- Over the past several decades, we've seen a big shift from manufacturing to white-collar service jobs, with particularly large growth in health care and technology. And while we've seen a lot of national economic growth, salary growth has been relatively flat for middle- and lower-class jobs, necessitating longer hours and sometimes second jobs.

- Some of the consequences include the fact that 30 percent of U.S. workers are often or always under stress at work. Work stress has increased nearly 300 percent since 1995. About 40 percent of missed work is due to stress, and about 80 percent of job accidents are stress related. Problems at work are more strongly associated with health complaints than are any other life stressor—more so than even financial problems or family problems.

- And yet we keep plugging along. In fact, some people, or many, find a way to be successful. What skills or abilities led to that success? That question has fueled a good chunk of the self-help industry for years, with the best example being Steven Covey's book *The 7 Habits of Highly Effective People*, published in 1989.

Hours Worked

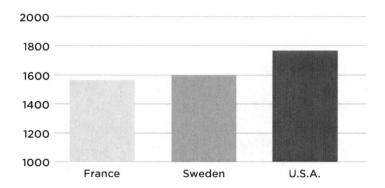

- The first three of the seven habits are related to a category Covey calls independence while the next three habits are related to interdependence and the last habit falls under the category of continuous improvements. The seven habits are as follows.

1. Be proactive: Realize that your decisions are the primary determining factor for effectiveness in your life. Take responsibility for your choices and the consequences.

2. Begin with the end in mind: Self-discover and clarify your deeply important character values and life goals. Envision the ideal characteristics for each of your various roles and relationships in life.

3. Put first things first: A manager must manage his or her own person. Managers should implement activities that aim to reach the second habit.

4. Think win-win: Have genuine feelings for mutually beneficial solutions or agreements in your relationships. Value and respect people by understanding that a "win" for all is ultimately a better long-term resolution.

5. Seek first to understand, then to be understood: Use empathic listening to be genuinely influenced by a person, which compels them to reciprocate the listening and take an open mind to being influenced by you. This creates an atmosphere of caring and positive problem solving.

6. Synergize: Combine the strengths of people through positive teamwork to achieve goals no one person could have done alone.

7. Sharpen the saw: Balance and renew your resources, energy, and health to create a sustainable, long-term, effective lifestyle. It primarily emphasizes exercise for physical renewal, prayer (meditation, yoga, etc.), and good reading for mental renewal. It also mentions service to society for spiritual renewal.

- Another book, written in 1936, is Dale Carnegie's classic *How to Win Friends and Influence People*, which has now sold more than 15 million copies. In the book, Carnegie gives us six ways to "make people like you." The six ways are as follows.

1. Become genuinely interested in other people.

2. Smile.

3. Remember that a person's name is, to that person, the sweetest and most important sound in any language.

4. Be a good listener. Encourage others to talk about themselves.

5. Talk in terms of the other person's interest.

6. Make the other person feel important—and do it sincerely.

Predictors of Success

- What are the predictors of success? Is it raw intelligence? Is it professional knowledge? Education? Income? Is it having connections, ambition, or drive? Is it just sort of rolling up your sleeves and working really hard?

- Before we can answer that question, we have to decide what success means. Is success money, advancement, prestige, status, growth, or satisfaction? It's a fairly personal issue with no correct answer. And there are some interesting findings from the business literature that shows us that objective measures of success—such as how much money you make and whether you get promoted—are often different from subjective measures of success, such as personal satisfaction with your career.

- Let's take a middle-of-the-road perspective and assume that success isn't about making millions of dollars or about being the CEO of a company but that it does include advancement, recognition, compensation, and constructive relationships with peers, bosses, and/or supervisors. And it includes a reasonable level of satisfaction and contentment. What do you need to get there?

- A 2006 study by Accenture of 251 executives in six countries concluded that while intelligence is important for career success, it's a matter of how you are smart. Interpersonal confidence, self-awareness, and social awareness—all elements of a broader construct of emotional intelligence—are better predictors of who will succeed and who won't.

- Social intelligence and emotional intelligence overlap. Social intelligence is defined as the capacity to effectively negotiate complex social relationships and environments. It includes skills in social perception, psychology, social dynamics, and behavioral skills—communication strategies, actions, and conflict resolution.

- Although this might seem like a new construct, Edward Thorndike was the first to coin the term "social intelligence" in the 1920s, and Howard Gardner's theory of multiple intelligences, which came out in 1983, also used the term.

- Can you cultivate social intelligence? Initial studies of children have been successful in teaching socioemotional skills—listening, asserting oneself, cooperating, or apologizing. These can be taught indirectly (on the playground, for example), or they can be integrated into curricula.

Socioemotional skills can be taught to children indirectly or integrated into curricula.

- But what about at work? What about for adults with decades of social habits that may or may not be so socially intelligent? There have been a number of different studies on this subject, and the findings are somewhat mixed when it comes to social intelligence as a global construct. It's more encouraging when you look at specific subskills, such as communication, conflict resolution, or time management.

Occupational Stress

- Just as people have core beliefs or conditional assumptions in the CBT sense, businesses have mission statements. They may articulate values. But even more important than what is written down is what is actually done. What are their business practices? How are the employees treated? How are problems solved?

- Just as we collect stories for a person to create a case formulation, a business consultant will collect stories about a business to create a formulation of that organization's culture. This would include the health of the organization but also the contributing or detracting factors.

- One of the biggest warning signs is occupational stress and professional burnout among employees. Occupational stress is defined as the experience of stress that is caused by work.

- Stress can include biological factors as well as emotional, behavioral, and cognitive ones. A stressor—in this case, an occupational stressor—can be anything real or imagined that sets off a whole chain of events. It's not just about the external situation; it's also about our primary and secondary appraisals.

- The National Institute for Occupational Safety and Health tells us that human health and social work employees are at greatest risk for occupational stress and burnout. Accountants and bookkeepers have extraordinarily high rates. Individuals who work the night shift, on weekends, or overtime also have very high rates.

- There are some common factors that are related to occupational stress across various jobs, including work demands, hostility, changes in expectations, and downsizing. In addition, occupational stress could result if an employee has a perceived lack of control with high job demand and high job strain coupled with low reward.

- Some of the protective factors are whether an individual has high perceived control, whether his or her level of reward is increased to match the level of demand (how hard he or she is working), whether there is a social status attached to the job, and whether he or she is able to derive a personal sense of meaning or purpose from it.

Measuring and Combating Occupational Stress

- How do you measure stress in the workplace? We can use the same kinds of processes that we use with individuals, such as interviews or online measures. We could also use objective data, such as staff turnover, satisfaction surveys of employees, financial indicators, or even human resources complaints.

- What are the ways to combat stress? We can make simple environmental changes to create a more comfortable workplace in terms of light, temperature, noise, space, or privacy. We can decrease ambiguity by being very clear about job descriptions and making things very predictable. We can move toward the direction of shared decision making so that the workplace doesn't feel dogmatic or autocratic. We can facilitate social relationships and offer rewards for good work.

The Top 10 Most Stressful Jobs

1. Enlisted soldier
2. Firefighter
3. Airline pilot
4. Air traffic controller
5. Police officer
6. Event coordinator
7. Inner-city school teacher
8. Taxi driver
9. Customer service operator
10. Emergency medical technician

- We might also use some CBT exercises. We could use cognitive skills to induce positive emotions. We could look at positive appraisals. We could also help people recalibrate their perspective and search for meaning.

- What are some of the ways to combat burnout, when the stress has become so chronic or severe that people feel that they can't necessarily recover? Probably the best intervention is to take a long vacation away from work. Other interventions include having a change in job description, experiencing a reengagement with sources of meaning (either at work or outside of work), and working on some stress-management skills to achieve a better work-life balance.

Suggested Reading

Carnegie, *How to Win Friends and Influence People.*

Covey, *The 7 Habits of Highly Effective People.*

Judge, Cable, Boudreau, and Bretz Jr., "An Empirical Investigation of the Predictors of Executive Career Success."

Maslach, *The Truth about Burnout.*

O'Boyle, Humphrey, Pollack, Hawver, and Story, "The Relation Between Emotional Intelligence and Job Performance."

Questions to Consider

1. Consider your model of social intelligence. What does it include? Can it be taught? Is it different from emotional intelligence? What do you think predicts high social intelligence?

2. How does the widening gap between rich and poor in the United States impact occupational stress? Is occupational stress also becoming unequally shared? What might we do about it?

Thriving at Work through Behavioral Health
Lecture 22—Transcript

PROFESSOR SATTERFIELD: The average American spends nearly 100,000 hours at work during their lifetime. U.S. workers currently put in around 1,800 hours per year, much more than our European counterparts. Unlike other countries, the U.S. does not require any paid vacation time off, although most of us get at least two weeks of vacation plus a few holidays. But nearly 60% of U.S. workers use less than half their vacation time each year.

Some say we're a nation of workaholics. We're ambitious, over-achieving, perfectionistic, either that, or just struggling to make ends meet in an increasingly polarized society of haves and have-nots. Professional burnout is at an all-time high, but no end is in sight. How did we get here? Of course, there are a lot of layers rooted in our national ethos. Pick yourself up by bootstraps, the early bird gets the worm, living the American dream. It's an ethos that has both religious or puritanical work ethic, and economic elements, our entrepreneurial spirit in the free market, capital competition.

It's also tied to technological advances, like the Industrial Revolution. We could work in factories year round and use artificial lighting to extend the workday. Of course, the modern-day equivalent would be e-mail and the ubiquitous smartphone. Even when you're not physically at work, you're still kind of at work. In fact, for many, they're potentially at work 24 hours a day, seven days a week, making it increasingly difficult to quantify what a work week really is.

But as we prepare to define, measure, and maybe even improve occupational functioning, it's important to see that many of the core ingredients, concentration, motivation, emotional management, communication, or even assertiveness, are relevant at both work and home and have obviously close ties to cognitive behavioral therapy.

But what does our workforce look like? Well, over the past several decades, we've seen a big shift from manufacturing to white-collar service jobs, with particularly large growth in health care and technology. And while we've seen a lot of national economic growth, salary growth has been relatively flat, at least for middle- and lower-class jobs, necessitating longer hours, and sometimes having a second job.

Some of the consequences include, 30% of U.S. workers, who are often or always under stress at work; work stress has increased nearly 300% since 1995; 40% of missed work is due to stress-related causes; and 80% of job accidents are stress related. Problems at work are more strongly associated with health complaints than are any other life stressors, more so than even financial problems or family problems. And yet, we keep plugging along, in fact, some, or many, find a way to be successful. What skills or abilities led to that success?

That question has fueled a good chunk of the self-help industry for years with a number of different books, and I want to illustrate just a couple of them. But when I mention these books, even though they may ring a bell, I want us to look at these books through a CBT lens. We're going to look at these well-known words of wisdom, but we're going to do a CBT analysis of some of their recommendations. We'll see what's old, we'll see what's similar, we'll see what might be new.

The first book I wanted to mention was Steven Covey's book, *The 7 Habits of Highly Effective People*, published in 1989. Now, the first three of those seven habits are related to a category he calls independence. Habit number one is to be proactive, to realize that your decisions are the primary determining factor for effectiveness in your life. You are to take responsibility for your choices and the consequences. Sounds good, but also sounds like patient empowerment. You have to see yourself as an active agent of change.

We know that many individuals who are anxious or depressed may not be able to be proactive, because they don't see themselves as powerful. We want to do a behavioral analysis. Where is their power? Can they be proactive? Can they make decisions? But we'll also want to look at cognitions that may interfere with their ability to be proactive.

Habit two: Begin with the end in mind. Here you're supposed to engage in self-discovery and clarify your deeply important character values and life goals. You should envision the ideal characteristics for each of your various roles and relationships in life. Now, I hope this very loudly rang a bell for you in terms of wave-three cognitive behavioral therapies, and specifically, the values clarification exercise we did as part of ACT, or acceptance and commitment to therapy. Very similar.

Habit number three: Put first things first. And here, really, they're talking about managers must manage his or her own person. In other words, take care of things at home or inside before you start reaching out and trying to manage other individuals. Now, this may have some similarities to couples CBT conflict resolution and communication, but is probably something that is a little outside of CBT and more in the business world.

The next three habits have to do with a category of interdependence, and habit number four is something called think win-win, and here they talk about genuine feelings for mutually beneficial solutions or agreements in relationships. You should value and respect people by understanding that a win for all is ultimately a better long-term resolution. Now, for this one, what I associate it to is not automatic thoughts so much from a CBT perspective, but really those conditional assumptions. Remember we have these rules for life that each of us have learned over time. So if your rule is a win for all means better long-term outcomes or resolution for everyone, then you're probably already in line with this habit number four.

Habit number five: Seek first to understand, then to be understood. Using empathic listening to genuinely be influenced by a person, which compels them to reciprocate the listening. Here it sounds like a lot of the couples therapy skills that we had mentioned before. Habit six is to synergize, to combine the strengths of people through positive teamwork so as to achieve goals that no one person could have done on their own. Again, probably more in the business world than in CBT, but interesting if you think about the chemistry of teams or co-workers, maybe in similar ways that you could think about and conceptualize the chemistry of a couple.

And the last habit falling under the category of continuous improvements is something that was called sharpen the saw. You need to balance and renew your resources, energy, and health to create a sustainable, long-term, effective lifestyle. It primarily emphasizes things like exercise for physical renewal, prayer, meditation, yoga, good reading for mental renewal. And it also mentions service to society or to communities as a way to encourage spiritual renewal. In here, I think we're squarely within the realm of cognitive behavioral therapy, stress management, somatic quieting, behavioral activation, connecting to our social supports.

The next example I wanted to show is much older, written in 1936. This was Dale Carnegie's classic How to Win Friends and Influence People, and has now sold over 15 million copies. He gives us six ways to "make people like you." Now, as a CBT person, whenever I hear that word, "make," I automatically associate to the cognitive model that tells us, it's not an activating event that makes you act a particular way, or makes you like or dislike another person. It's really that middle step, your interpretation. So I think what Dale Carnegie is telling us here is, here are some strategies to influence an individual's subjective interpretation so that the consequence is they will eventually like you. So what were those six ways? Becoming genuinely interested in other people. And here I think of a recommendation by William Carlos Williams, a physician that tells the medical student to always find the poem in every patient.

How else can we help influence people to make them like us? Number two is smile. Number three is to remember a person's name and to remember to that person, their name is the sweetest and most important sound in any language. Be a good listener. Encourage others to talk about themselves. Talk in terms of the other person's interest. And to make the other person feel important and to do it sincerely. And here, he's really pulling for the reciprocity element in interpersonal exchanges. If you look at individual CBT, it kind of focuses us on the individual and their own internal reactions. But here it moves into the realm of maybe couples therapy, or at least thinking about how to nurture our social supports.

So we have a lot of self-help books, some CBT influenced, some maybe not so much. But we, really, what we're interested in are what are the predictors of success? Is it raw intelligence? Is it professional knowledge? Education? Income? Is it having connections, ambition, drive? Is it just sort of rolling up your sleeves and working really hard. Well, I think before we can answer that question, we have to decide what success means. So, is success money? Is it advancement, prestige, status, growth, or satisfaction? It's a fairly personal issue with no correct answer, and there are some interesting findings from the business literature that show us that that objective measures of success, like how much money you make, and if you get promoted, are often different from subjective measures of success, such as personal satisfaction with your career.

So, let's take a sort of middle-of-the-road perspective, and let's assume that success isn't about making millions of dollars, and you don't have to be a CEO of a company, but it does include occasional advancement, recognition, reasonable compensation, constructive relationships with peers and bosses, and other supervisees, and it includes a reasonable level of satisfaction and contentment. That of course will wax and wane over time, but what do you need to get there?

Well, a 2006 study by Accenture of 251 executives in six countries concluded that while intelligence is importance for career success, it's a matter of how you are smart. Interpersonal confidence, self-awareness, social awareness, all elements of a broader construct of emotional intelligence, are better predictors of who will succeed and who won't. So if you are interested in digging a little bit deeper—Am I emotionally intelligent? In what ways am I smart?—there's a number of different exercises. We've demonstrated a few of them already. One was called Your Best Self/Your Worst Self, or Signature Strengths. You might also use the CBT Triangle and look at a number of different activating events that have occurred at the workplace, maybe outside of the workplace, and see where your weaknesses are and where your strengths might be.

There is also something called a 360 evaluation, or a multi-source evaluation. Our university actually requires all department chairs and division chiefs to do this. A questionnaire is sent out to everyone that you've worked with on all sorts of different levels. They all give anonymous and very detailed feedback about your strengths, about your weaknesses, and of course, you evaluate yourself. You then sit down with an executive coach, kind of a CBT therapist of sorts, that goes over all of this data with you and helps you to develop an individualized plan to improve your skills.

But let's go back to this idea of how you are smart, or how you are intelligent, and I specifically wanted to talk about a construct called social intelligence. Now, social intelligence and I think emotional intelligence definitely overlap. But social intelligence is more specifically defined as the capacity to effectively negotiate complex social relationship and environments. Now, although this might seem like a new construct, Edward Thorndike was the first to coin the term in the 1920s. And in Howard Gardner's theory of multiple intelligences that came out in 1983, he also used the term social intelligence. So it's not really that new. I think it's come back into public awareness after the surge in interest in emotional intelligence, and social intelligence just followed. Now, as I mentioned, this will include skills in social perception, psychology, social dynamics, and behavioral skills and communication strategies, actions, and conflict resolution, many of which we've talked about before.

But can you cultivate social intelligence? Well, initial studies of children have been successful in teaching what they called socio-emotional skills, things like listening, asserting yourself, cooperating, or apologizing. And these can be taught, of course, indirectly, say on the playground, or they can be integrated into curricula. But what about the workplace? What about for adults who may have decades of social habits that may or may not be so socially intelligent. Well, there's been a number of different studies, and honestly, the findings are somewhat mixed looking at social intelligence as a global construct. It seems to overlap and get a bit confused with personality and extroversion and introversion and other factors. It's more encouraging when you look at specific sub-skills, like teaching communication, conflict resolution, or time management. Let's go on to look at a clip, and here we'll see Michael. He's talking about an individual event that's occurred, but it's occurred in the workplace, and it may have ramifications for his health and wellness at his work.

[VIGNETTE START]

PROFESSOR SATTERFIELD: What was the first event?

MICHAEL: Well, the first event was actually—it's at work. And it involved a coworker. And there was a meeting coming up. This coworker was actually supposed to be taking the lead in the meeting. So I sent a reminder, an e-mail reminder to this guy. And I reminded him, you know, you're responsible for taking the lead here. So make sure you're prepared. And just let's be on time, because we don't want to look bad there. It wasn't a hugely important meeting, but I think it was important to have the right presentation. So he had that advance notice—be on time, be prepared.

PROFESSOR SATTERFIELD: And what happened?

MICHAEL: He arrived late, for starters, and he wasn't prepared. So what happened then is I kind of got very, very angry at him but not wanting to show that in the meeting. I suppose really the way it was coming across is I became pretty distracted. I was having a very difficult time even focusing on what was going on.

PROFESSOR SATTERFIELD: OK. So just to make sure I understand, the activating event was you had done some advance work to prepare, or make sure your coworker was prepared; he showed up late, not prepared. You felt angry but tried to keep your poker face on so that other people couldn't see how angry you were, but you felt it for sure.

MICHAEL: Yeah. And the interesting thing about that was I guess my poker face isn't so great because then during the meeting, people actually began to say, are you OK, Michael? Is anything up? Which actually didn't help things. It made me, if anything, more angry.

PROFESSOR SATTERFIELD: OK. And remember, one of the things we want to do is to rate the intensity of the emotion that is evoked by the thoughts you have. So on a scale of 0 to 100, 0 you're not angry all, 100 is you're angry as you could possibly imagine, where were you on that?

MICHAEL: I would say around 70%.

PROFESSOR SATTERFIELD: Around 70. OK.

MICHAEL: Yeah. That's how I rate myself.

PROFESSOR SATTERFIELD: What were the thoughts that were related to that anger?

MICHAEL: Well, some of the thoughts that I've written down, the automatic thoughts that I was having, was you are so immature. How could you do this to me? You had the reminder. You knew what you had to do. And you show up here late and unprepared. So one of the things that I wrote down was that's really immature and kind of how dare you.

PROFESSOR SATTERFIELD: So outrage.

MICHAEL: Outrage, outrage. And another automatic thought that I found myself having is it's not my job to do everybody else's job. My job is my job. And your job is your job. So that was one of the thoughts that I was having. And I also was feeling kind of connected with that. Do I have to carry everybody? So those were the thoughts.

PROFESSOR SATTERFIELD: So those sound like powerful thoughts. Do I have to carry everyone? It's not my job to do everyone else's job. But in a sense, here you are and here this is happening.

MICHAEL: Yeah. And I think that goes back to that emotion I was having of anger and frustration.

PROFESSOR SATTERFIELD: So anger, frustration—any other emotions?

MICHAEL: I also wrote down—maybe this is a good word, maybe not—but I wrote down indignant. I don't know if that fits here, but that kind of indignation. And that's you really should be doing something, and you're not doing it. I got indignant.

PROFESSOR SATTERFIELD: OK. Now, remember what we want to do is to take those thoughts—and thoughts aren't necessarily true or false. They're helpful or hurtful. So in terms of the outcome or the effect that those thoughts had on you, your feelings, your emotions, your behavior, your relationships, would you say those were helpful or those are something that you might want to nudge in a different direction?

MICHAEL: I would say I'd want to nudge those in a different direction. Definitely.

PROFESSOR SATTERFIELD: And the way to do that is to look for evidence that supports the thought and evidence that argues against the thought. So which one of those thoughts do you want to pick? Because there was a whole string of different thoughts.

MICHAEL: Well, I think the "how dare you" part of this that I was feeling. And what I wrote about that was that evidence supporting that thought was, well, in fact, you were late. And in fact, you didn't prepare. So that's evidence supporting this sense of indignation. I've told them in advance I did my job, so I think that that's all—for me, that's all evidence that the reaction wasn't entirely unreasonable. The reaction of being angry was not entirely unreasonable.

PROFESSOR SATTERFIELD: Now, let's back up a little bit, because I think a kind of thought like how dare you, there's beliefs that are nested underneath. So that sense of outrage or indignation is someone has violated what you see as a norm, of something they should have done. Any normal, hardworking, good, decent person should have done this, and that was violated. So you feel that "how dare you" moment. So what are the thoughts underneath the "how dare you?" And maybe I just said them. But what sorts of thoughts or expectations did you have for your coworker?

MICHAEL: I have the expectations that that coworker is going to do in those circumstances what I would do, and that is if I am going to be late or I have a reason to be late, I'm going to notify you in advance of this. I wasn't notified in advance. If I am asked to be prepared for a meeting, then I am going to prepare for the meeting. If for some reason I can't prepare for the meeting, I should have that conversation in advance. And this coworker did none of these things for me. So there's an expectation of professionalism, I guess.

PROFESSOR SATTERFIELD: So is it fair to say that when you saw his behavior, experienced his behavior, you thought he was being unprofessional, irresponsible?

MICHAEL: Exactly, exactly.

PROFESSOR SATTERFIELD: So let's look for evidence for his lack of professionalism, his irresponsibility. So what evidence—he showed up late. He wasn't prepared. OK, what else?

MICHAEL: Didn't really seem all that apologetic immediately. Now, later on he did apologize—but at the outset did not apologize, did not come into the meeting and say, I'm sorry, I'm late. Here's why. So I think that that would've been professional, and that was evidence of unprofessionalism.

PROFESSOR SATTERFIELD: And have there been meetings in the past when she showed up or didn't show up or prepared—

MICHAEL: I would not say that this particular person has a history of always being late. But yes, he's been late in the past on occasion. And I guess when I looked at someone coming in—anyone, whether it's this or anybody else coming in late—I would've expected some admission that this was not professional.

PROFESSOR SATTERFIELD: Sure. So we have again, if we're looking at evidence for and against—there have been at least a handful of episodes where he's been late. If we're looking at evidence against the idea that he's unprofessional, it sounds like that there are times when he has been on time and he was prepared.

MICHAEL: Perfectly fair to say that he's actually generally a good worker who rarely—he may be late sometimes, but rarely would he not deliver when he's asked to prepare. I certainly expected him to come to the meeting prepared, because that's generally what he does. So that would be evidence against, I suppose, the idea that he's unprofessional in the big sense.

PROFESSOR SATTERFIELD: OK. So generally prepared, wasn't this time. So it sounds like there's a belief, again, sort of nested down a little bit deeper, about one time is too much. Even if it's an exception, that it's too much.

MICHAEL: Yeah. And maybe that's going a little bit too far, perhaps.

PROFESSOR SATTERFIELD: Well, let me ask—and I know you're a very sort of diligent, conscientious guy. Have you been late to meetings before?

MICHAEL: It's happened.

PROFESSOR SATTERFIELD: Missed an e-mail or something like that?

MICHAEL: It's happened, and I have missed an e-mail before. And I think that that's actually one of the things that I jotted down as evidence that doesn't support this hot thought, is that nobody is perfect and you in fact have missed meetings or been late for meetings yourself.

PROFESSOR SATTERFIELD: So you're moving us now into the next column where you're rewriting the thoughts. And it's true. Something negative happened, and we don't know his reason. There could have been extenuating circumstances—maybe, maybe not. But can you say your thought again? It was—

MICHAEL: Well, the idea that I had for kind of rethinking this process was that I've been late to meetings before. We can't necessarily expect perfection. And I guess if I step back from it, I have to say there are times when I haven't been prepared, when I haven't been on time, when I maybe have missed an e-mail or just let it go right past me, blow right past me.

PROFESSOR SATTERFIELD: Sure. So we can hope for perfection but expect that most of the time, we're not going to be perfect, ourselves or our coworkers. So as you sort of think about it in a more balanced way and we maybe think about extenuating circumstances or your own experience of sometimes being late. If you were to re-rate how angry you are—you were at a 70 before, so where would your anger be now?

MICHAEL: I would say about a 30.

PROFESSOR SATTERFIELD: About a 30. So we dropped from a 70 to a 30.

MICHAEL: Dropped from a 70 to a 30. I think that probably the lingering sense of anger is that I did take the step myself to put the reminder out there and said very specifically, be on time and be prepared. But in the context of the fact that this wasn't the most important meeting in the world, not the end of the world, and all of the other things we've discussed, I feel backing away from it much less angry, annoyed, irritated.

PROFESSOR SATTERFIELD: And what do you think you might do differently next time? Because I guess there will be more meetings and more people who are late occasionally?

MICHAEL: I think it's a matter of stepping back. One of the things that we really didn't get into was that feeling as I was getting flustered, and people were asking about me and saying, OK, are you OK? And that was actually making me more angry. I think that that's probably the easiest part of this scenario for me to think how I'd do it differently in the future. Because really, as I was rewriting, my initial thought was, well, now the focus is all on me, and it's this guy that's getting off the hook. That's really, I think, what I should've been thinking—is they're just expressing concern. They're just expressing concern. So that part of the process, I think, is easier for me, to step back and say, if someone is asking how you are, don't take that as a further reason to get angry. See that as an opportunity to respond to somebody and understand that they're actually concerned about you.

PROFESSOR SATTERFIELD: And it's nice to see how your comfort and skill with the thought record has been growing. So you've just talked about an event nested within an event, and you've done a DTR about a DTR, which I don't know if you did that on purpose or not, but you did. So the event was about the worker. But then the secondary event was you were sitting in a meeting and people were asking if you're OK. And that triggered a different set of thoughts of, oh my gosh, why is the focus on me now and not on this guy? He's the one who screwed up, not me. But now you're rewriting thoughts about that secondary event. They're just concerned about me.

MICHAEL: And I hope it's not, but it's maybe a little bit of a copout because it's focusing on something that I feel like I can more easily deal with, but maybe that's part of the step. I do think if I imagine this happening again, I send an e-mail to someone and I say, be on time and be prepared, and they come in, and they're neither of those things. I'm not sure that I would not be very angry. But I think that all of these other things that we've talked about can help me at least step back from that moment initial response, that sort of instinctive gut response that gets angry to say, it's just a meeting. We've all been late. Nobody's perfect.

PROFESSOR SATTERFIELD: So I know you have two more thought records we want to make sure we get to. But as we've talked about before, there's often themes that come up—core beliefs or parts about your personality, your personal history. And we see them, so they sort of make these guest appearances in different events that come along. And the theme of perfectionism is one that's sort of been woven throughout a number of events. And the theme of personal responsibility and when is it your responsibility to police other people or to be the advocate for justice or not. And if you're in a supervisory role, sure. If you're not in a supervisory role, maybe you said—and one of your thoughts was it's not your job to do other people's jobs. So it's one of those themes we want to sort of keep our eye on and see if we can shift that over time.

MICHAEL: OK.

[VIGNETTE END]

PROFESSOR SATTERFIELD: In this example, we're really looking at the personal style of one employee, Michael, and a conflict that he has with one other person, but it's important to remember that these sort of events, if common, can contribute to an overall work culture, in part depending on the frequency, but also on the person doing it. So, is that person a leader, a supervisor? How influential are they in the workplace? And just as people have core beliefs or conditional assumptions in the CBT sense, businesses have mission statements. They may articulate values.

But even more important than what is written down is what is actually done. What are their business practices? How are the employees treated? And how are problems resolved? Just as we collect stories for a person to create a case formulation, a business consultant will collect stories about a business to create a formulation of that organization's culture. This would include the health of the organization, but also contributing or detracting factors. One of the biggest warning signs is occupational stress and professional burnout among the employees.

Occupational stress is defined simply as the experience of stress that is caused by work. Remember that stress can include biological factors, as well as emotional, behavioral, and cognitive, and remember that a stressor, and in this case, an occupational stressor, can be anything real, or it can be imagined, and these imagined events might also set off a whole chain of stressful events. Recall that it's not just about the external situation, but also about our primary and our secondary appraisals.

The National Institute for Occupational Safety and Health tells us that human, health, and social work employees are at greatest risk for occupational stress and burnout. We know that accountants and bookkeepers have extraordinarily high rates. Individuals who work the night shift, weekend work, or overtime also have very high rates. So if you wanted a top ten-list of the jobs that are most stressful, up at the top of the list, the enlisted soldier; followed by a firefighter; airline pilots; air traffic controllers; and police officers. Next up might be a surprise. Number six is event coordinators; seven, inner-city school teachers; followed by taxi drivers; customer service representatives; and then rounding out the list are emergency medical technicians or paramedics.

So, what factors, though, across these very different kinds of jobs, are related to occupational stress? Well, it's really about the level of work demands; it's about whether or not there's hostility in the climate of the workplace. If there are constant changes and expectations, if the individual, the employee, has a perceived lack of control with high job demand and high job strain, coupled with low reward.

What are some of the protective factors? Well, if an individual has high perceived control, if their level of reward is increased to match their level of demand or how hard they're working, if there's a certain amount of social status attached to their job, and if they're able to derive a personal sense of meaning or purpose, and I'll ask you to recall the lecture where we talked about how to construct meaning. So how do you go about measuring stress in the workplace? Again, we could use the same sort of processes through interviews or online measures. We could also use objective data, such as staff turnover, satisfaction surveys of the employees, financial indicators, or even HR compliance.

So, what are some of the ways to combat stress? Well, we can make simple environmental changes so it's a more comfortable workplace in terms of light, temperature, noise, and space, or privacy. We might want to decrease ambiguity by being very clear about job descriptions and making things very predictable. We want to move towards the direction of shared decision making so things don't feel quite so dogmatic or autocratic. We want to do things to facilitate social relationships, and of course, have rewards for good work.

Now, remember that we might also use some of our CBT exercises. We could use cognitive skills to induce positive emotions. We could look at positive appraisals. We could also help folks to recalibrate their perspective and, again, to search for meaning.

So what are some of the ways to combat burnout when the stress has gotten so chronic or severe that folks just feel that they can't necessarily recover? Well, probably the best intervention is to take a nice, long vacation away from work; have a possible change in your job description; maybe a reengagement with sources of meaning, either at work or outside of work; and working on some of our stress management skills to achieve a better work-life balance.

Now I wanted to end by moving to one of our frequently asked questions, and this question was, "What if you've done all you can, and you just have a toxic job or a toxic boss? How can CBT help then?" Now remember, if you think back to our treatment of depression, there were four stages. There was education, behavioral strategies, cognitive strategies, and the last was social and potentially occupational changes. So some of those strategies are being able to step back and take a very critical look at whether or not you need to find the courage to end a relationship or to end a job and to move on somewhere else. And if it doesn't make sense to end or to change, then using those skills for stress management to help you cope more effectively. Along those lines, in our next lecture we're going to talk about ways to promote flexibility and ultimately resilience.

Developing Emotional Flexibility
Lecture 23

I n this lecture, you will learn about the construct of resilience—which is succeeding, maybe even thriving, in the face of adversity—and the frequent companion of resilience, flexibility. You will discover what the literature tells us about these two constructs and explore how we might use CBT tools to promote both flexibility and resilience. You also will learn about the general factors that predict resilience, and you will be exposed to research on cognitive styles and positive emotion.

Resilience

- There are a few different definitions of resilience. Resilience is defined as when a powerful biologic and/or environmental diathesis or risk factors do not produce the expected negative outcome—high subjective well-being, even in the presence of adversity. Another definition of resilience is the ability to negotiate significant challenges to development yet consistently "snap back" in order to complete the most important developmental tasks that confront people as they grow.

- In a qualitative study done by Gina Higgins and published in her book *Resilient Adults*, she interviewed 40 adults who had been abused as children but had gone on to be successful and have a self-reported high quality of life as adults. She wanted to deduce from those interviews some of the common features that helped those individuals be so resilient.

- She found that these individuals used resilience as a developing phenomenon propelled by vision and stamina—a belief in control, freedom, and change. There was a focus on strength, ability, and pro-action. They were able to establish what she called a place of refuge. She saw that their resilience waxed and waned over time, and she encourages us not to "overlook the phoenix for the ashes."

- Other quantitative studies of resilience have found similar features. In terms of the environment, studies have shown that having enriched environments, a supportive adult or parental surrogate, or some place of refuge was important for resilience.

- In the category of cognitive or personality factors, some predictors of resilience include having an optimistic style, a flexible cognitive style, high affect or emotion regulation skills, and an affectionate or outgoing temperament (which is more effective in eliciting social support from other individuals).

- A primary factor in resilience is having positive relationships, either inside or outside one's family. In fact, it's probably the single most critical means of handling both ordinary and extraordinary levels of stress. These positive relationships include traits such as mutual trust, reciprocal support, and caring.

- There are also a number of CBT skills that might help an individual develop and sustain his or her resilience, including the ability to make realistic plans and follow through with them, having a positive self-concept, and confidence in one's strength and ability. It is also important to have communication and problem-solving skills, as well as the ability to manage strong impulses and feelings.

- Other elements of resilience fall into the cognitive and emotional styles category. The attributional or explanatory style is a cognitive style from the seminal work of Martin Seligman, who started with animal studies in the 1960s and 1970s and then moved on to human studies.

- The explanatory style essentially tells us that we have habits in how we explain why events occur. Seligman believed that the explanatory style has three key dimensions: internal, stable, and global. The explanatory style is particularly important in explaining achievement and also with its relationship to depression.

- Individuals who explain negative events with an internal, stable, and global style—it's my fault, it's never going to change, and it's going to affect all areas of my life—are the individuals who are less likely to pick themselves up and continue pushing forward. They are the ones who are more likely to become more depressed.

- An important outgrowth of the work of the explanatory style is the Penn Resilience Project, a CBT program to teach kids from inner-city Philadelphia schools how to have more optimistic explanatory styles. The goal was to make them more resilient to stressors in their home life as well as to prevent possible depression in the future.

- A meta-analysis of 17 Penn Resiliency Program studies showed that the interventions significantly reduced and prevented depressive symptoms over time. However, it's not clear if the Penn Resiliency Program has an enhanced effect among children who experience adversity (compared to peers who experience lower or no adversity). This would be a necessary criterion to support claims of promoting resilience, given definitions of resilience as doing well despite risk or adversity.

- Another cognitive style, or really emotional style, is positive emotion. While some research indicates that psychological resilience is a relatively stable personality trait, new research suggests that positive emotions are critical to the trait of resilience. This is not to say that positive emotions are merely a by-product of resilience but, rather, that feeling positive emotions during stressful experiences might have adaptive benefits in the coping process of the individual.

- Empirical evidence for this prediction arises from research on resilient individuals who have a propensity for coping strategies that concretely elicit positive emotions, such as benefit-finding and cognitive reappraisal, humor, optimism, and goal-directed problem-focused coping. Individuals who tend to approach problems with these methods of coping might strengthen their resistance to stress by allocating more access to these positive emotional resources.

- Judith Moskowitz studied individuals who were newly diagnosed with HIV and parents who were caring for sick children and found that if she was able to induce positive emotions, it essentially gave them more of a reservoir to cope with the stressful and negative times ahead.

- Barbara Fredrickson taught us that positive emotions are there to broaden and build. They help to broaden our cognitive repertoire and build important social relationships that will help us be more resilient in the future.

- A study by Anthony Ong and colleagues in 2006 looked at widows and positive emotion. They found that widows with high levels of resilience experienced more positive and negative emotions than those with lower levels of resilience. The former group shows high emotional complexity, which is the capacity to maintain the differentiation of positive and negative emotional states while undergoing stress. These researchers further suggested that the adaptive consequence of resilience is a function of an increase in emotional complexity while stress is present.

- By examining people's emotional responses to the September 11th attacks, Barbara Fredrickson and colleagues suggested in 2003 that positive emotions were critical elements in resilience and served as a mediator that buffered people from depression after the crisis. Moreover, they showed that highly resilient people were more likely to notice positive meanings within the problems they faced (for example, feeling grateful to be alive), endured fewer depressive symptoms, and experienced more positive emotions than people with low resilience.

Flexibility and Resilience
- Cognitive flexibility has been described as the mental ability to switch between thinking about two different concepts and to think about multiple concepts simultaneously. Despite some

disagreement in the literature about how to operationally define the term, one commonality is that cognitive flexibility is a component of executive functioning.

- Research on flexibility has primarily been conducted with children at the school age. However, individual differences in cognitive flexibility are apparent across the lifespan. Measures for cognitive flexibility include the A-not-B task, the dimensional change card-sorting task, the multiple classification card-sorting task, the Wisconsin card-sorting task, and the Stroop test.

- Cognitive flexibility also has implications both inside and outside of the classroom. A person's ability to switch between modes of thought and to simultaneously think about multiple concepts has been shown to be a vital component of learning and problem solving.

- There are many types and definitions of cognitive flexibility. Philip Tetlock developed a concept called integrative complexity, which is defined as the degree to which thinking and reasoning involve the recognition and integration of multiple perspectives and possibilities and their interrelated contingencies. Essentially, when an individual talks about a challenging or charged topic, is he or she able to see both sides of the coin and discuss the nuances of the topic?

- Attributional or explanatory flexibility is related to the explanatory style. The idea with the explanatory style is that a person has a habit of explaining things in a certain way, so it essentially looks at how strong the habit is. If you explain 10 different events, are they essentially the same kinds of explanations, or do you tend to move or flex depending on the situation?

- To measure attributional flexibility, the standard deviation of an individual's explanatory style scores is analyzed. The greater the standard deviation, the greater the person's attributional flexibility.

- A set of studies conducted by David Fresco and colleagues analyzed attributional flexibility in college students and found that students who were more flexible could be more resilient to stressful events that occurred and were less likely to get depressed.

CBT and Resilience
- CBT can be helpful for resilience in terms of generating positive emotions. It teaches us to reappraise attributions and, potentially, explanations. It gives us general cognitive restructuring skills and teaches us to be more cognitively flexible, or maybe more integratively complex.

- A recent report by the American Psychological Association offers the following 10 ways to build resilience.
  1. Maintain good relationships with close family members, friends, and others.

  2. Avoid seeing crises or stressful events as unbearable problems.

  3. Accept circumstances that cannot be changed.

  4. Develop realistic goals and move toward them.

  5. Take decisive actions in adverse situations.

  6. Look for opportunities of self-discovery after a struggle with loss.

  7. Develop self-confidence.

  8. Keep a long-term perspective and consider the stressful event in a broader context.

  9. Maintain a hopeful outlook, expecting good things and visualizing what is wished.

10. Take care of one's mind and body, exercising regularly, paying attention to one's own needs and feelings.

Suggested Reading

Bonanno, Galea, Bucciareli, and Vlahov, "What Predicts Psychological Resilience after Disaster?"

Brunwasser, Gillham, and Kim, "A Meta-Analytic Review of the Penn Resiliency Program's Effect on Depressive Symptoms."

Diener, Suh, Lucas, and Smith, "Subjective Well-Being."

Fredrickson, Tugade, Waugh, and Larkin, "A Prospective Study of Resilience and Emotions following the Terrorist Attacks on the United States on September 11th, 2001."

Fredrickson and Branigan, "Positive Emotions Broaden the Scope of Attention and Thought-Action Repertoires."

Fresco, Rytwinski, and Craighead, "Explanatory Flexibility and Negative Life Events Interact to Predict Depression Symptoms."

O'Connell Higgins, *Resilient Adults.*

Ong, Bergeman, Bisconti, and Wallace, "Psychological Resilience, Positive Emotions, and Successful Adaptation to Stress in Later Life."

Reivich and Shatte, *The Resilience Factor.*

Robertson, *Build Your Resilience.*

Seligman, *Learned Optimism.*

Singer and Ryff, "Hierarchies of Life Histories and Associated Health Risks."

Tugade and Fredrickson, "Resilient Individuals Use Positive Emotions to Bounce Back from Negative Emotional Experiences."

Waugh, Thompson, and Gotlib, "Flexible Emotional Responsiveness in Trait Resilience."

Werner, "The Value of Applied Research for Head Start."

1. Does developing a mental illness or psychological symptoms necessarily mean that you lack resilience or flexibility? Can you be resilient and flawed or ill?

2. Is there a way to promote resilience before an anticipated trauma occurs (for example, military combat, living in a violent neighborhood, etc.)? Would anticipation make the event more or less traumatic?

Developing Emotional Flexibility
Lecture 23—Transcript

PROFESSOR SATTERFIELD: Maya Angelou, renowned author and past poet laureate of the United States, was raped by her mother's boyfriend when she was only seven years old. She told her brother, and shortly thereafter, when her attacker got off scot-free, her uncles most likely killed the man. Seven-year-old traumatized Maya was horrified. She thought her words— her telling—had killed the man, so she decided to never speak again, and she didn't speak for almost five years.

She was sent to live with her maternal grandmother, and she met a teacher named Bertha Flowers. Bertha was very patient, and as you'll see, a bit of a cognitive behavioral therapist. She introduced Maya to great literature— Whitman, Poe, Dickens, Langston Hughes. And she found that Maya loved A Tale of Two Cities. She started Maya on what we would call a course of systematic desensitization to get her to talk again. She asked Maya to take out her book and just to read the first chapter to herself quietly. Step two was to move her lips while she was reading. Step three was to quietly whisper the very first word; then the first sentence; then the next sentence; then the first chapter. You can see step, by step, by step what was happening is that Maya was beginning to find her voice. Through the help of her maternal grandmother and through the help of her teacher, Maya learned that not only can words hurt, but words can heal. And she used that knowledge to go on to heal many others by becoming a poet.

In today's lecture, we're going to look at the construct of resilience and the frequent companion of resilience, flexibility. We'll look at what the literature shows us, then see how we might use our CBT tools to promote both flexibility and resilience. Now, first thing I wanted to share are a couple of different definitions of resilience, where the first is resilience defined as when a powerful biologic and/or environmental diathesis or risk factors do not produce the expected negative outcome; high subjective well-being, even in the presence of adversity. Or another definition, resilience defined as the ability to negotiate significant challenges to development, yet consistently snap back in order to complete the most important developmental tasks that confront people as they grow. So succeeding, maybe even thriving, in the face of adversity.

Now, in a qualitative study done by Gina Higgins and published in her book, Resilient Adults, she interviewed 40 adults who had been abused as children but gone on to be successful and to have a self-reported high quality of life as adults. She wanted to deduce from those interviews what were some of the common features that helped those individuals to be so resilient. She found that these individuals used resilience as a developing phenomenon over time, a phenomenon propelled by vision and stamina, a belief in control, freedom, and change. There was a focus on strength, ability, and proaction. They were able to establish what she called a place of refuge. She saw that their resilience with wax and wane over time, and she encourages us to don't overlook the phoenix for the ashes.

Other quantitative studies of resilience have found similar features. From the environment, they found that enriched environments, or finding a supportive adult or a parental surrogate, was important, or finding some place of refuge. I have a patient of mine who was able to survive a very abusive childhood because he spent most of his hours, when not in school, at the public library. That was his place of refuge, and his surrogates were the librarians.

The other category falls in the cognitive or personality factor category. And we know some of those predictors of resilience include having an optimistic style, having a flexible cognitive style, which we'll define in just a moment, and having high affect or emotion regulation skills and having an affectionate or outgoing temperament, which we know is more effective in eliciting social support from other individuals.

Now, a primary factor in resilience is having positive relationships, either inside or outside one's family. In fact, it's probably the single most critical means of handling both ordinary and extraordinary levels of stress. These positive relationships include traits such as mutual trust, reciprocal support, and caring. There are also a number of CBT skills which might help an individual develop and sustain a person's resilience. The ability to make realistic plans and being able to take steps necessary to follow through with them is an important skill. And here, you should think of our smart goals, and you should think of our suggestions on how to create an effective action plan, having a positive self-concept, and confidence in one's strengths and abilities. And here, we want to dig below those automatic thoughts and get to those conditional assumptions, and even more so, we're going to get to those core beliefs about your individual self-worth.

We want to work on communication and problem-solving skills, as we've talked about in the social support and the couple's conflict lectures, and of course, the ability to manage strong impulses. Many individuals with a history of trauma or history of abuse talk about the intense feelings that they have. We might not be able to change the intensity of those feelings, but we can teach people more effective skills and how to control those feelings and not act on impulses.

Now, with Maria, we saw a transformation over time, a sort of softening. She flexed, and she was willing to join a support group for caregivers. She flexed, and she was willing to hire more in-home help for her husband to give herself some respite. Let's look at this example of Maria adapting on the fly when one of her homework exercises in a social interaction didn't go quite so well.

[VIGNETTE START]

MARIA: Well, I had an opportunity this week to add a little to my social life.

PROFESSOR SATTERFIELD: Oh, good, good, good. How did that go?

MARIA: Not very well actually.

PROFESSOR SATTERFIELD: Oh.

MARIA: This lady from our church called up and said she heard my husband had been ill. And she had made a pie and wanted to bring it over. I guess a few weeks ago I just sort of told her not to come. But I said I was thinking about our agreement about having more social life, so I invited her to come over.

PROFESSOR SATTERFIELD: OK.

MARIA: And she came and brought her pie. And we were having a nice little chat. And then Jack wandered in, and he wasn't wearing a lot of clothes, sort of in his underwear and no shirt. And she was obviously feeling awkward and didn't know what to say. And he called her Betty, which was his sister's name and not her name, although we know her fairly well from church and all. And she left almost right after that. So I felt really bad about it and it didn't quite go the way I was hoping or imagining it might.

PROFESSOR SATTERFIELD: Sure, sure. Well, first let me say bravo for reaching out and trying. I know that that wasn't easy to do. But I also know that friendships and relationships are important to you. And you're trying to be true to those values. So you invited her over, we had an outcome that wasn't what you had wanted. And I think that's oftentimes a signal that it's time to take out the toolbox and to try something cognitive or behavioral to help you better understand the situation and what maybe to do differently next time. So we have our cognitive toolbox and we have our behavioral toolbox. Which would you like to start with?

MARIA: Let's start with the behavioral one.

PROFESSOR SATTERFIELD: OK, so behavioral one. So what's in our behavior toolbox? So one is scheduling things like social contacts. You did that.

MARIA: Yeah, but maybe I should have gotten Jack dressed ahead of time. That would be one thing I could do differently.

PROFESSOR SATTERFIELD: All right, so a little bit of preparation.

MARIA: Yeah, a little bit of preparation. And I think most people are just feeling awkward about when somebody is really sick. I mean, like they want to say the right thing, but there's no right thing you could say really. I mean, how can you say I hope you husband gets better? You can't.

PROFESSOR SATTERFIELD: Right.

MARIA: So they just don't know what to say. And I think she felt awkward about that. So maybe I just could have said something to her, just made her more at ease. I guess I was so anxious myself about it and sort of embarrassed about Jack; you know how that feels.

PROFESSOR SATTERFIELD: Sure.

MARIA: I don't like him to be exposed like that to someone's contempt or pity or whatever.

PROFESSOR SATTERFIELD: Right.

MARIA: So I don't know, I guess maybe I could have prepared her a little more and explained that he had Alzheimer's.

PROFESSOR SATTERFIELD: So you could prepare Jack and you could prepare her.

MARIA: That's right. I could have done a little more than I did. It's just I guess I was thinking too much about myself and how I was feeling. I could've been thinking more about what she was feeling and what he was up against.

PROFESSOR SATTERFIELD: And I think you raise an important point. When we think about social supports, we think about our relationship supporting us through a stressful time. But sometimes our social supports need direction; they need some instructions. And it happens often around illness where people don't know what to say, and they don't know what to do. And unfortunately, many of them avoid that awkwardness by avoidance. So they don't come over, they don't call.

MARIA: The truth is, they could say almost anything, just the support and comfort would be nice.

PROFESSOR SATTERFIELD: Just showing up.

MARIA: Yeah, just being there.

PROFESSOR SATTERFIELD: Just showing up. And she thought enough to bring the pie.

MARIA: She came. That was nice.

PROFESSOR SATTERFIELD: And to come over. So what could you say to her to make it less awkward or more comfortable for both of you? What ideas do you have? Just explain what the situation is, I guess. Ask her if she would be understanding about it. I think that would put her in a better position to feel magnanimous about it then. Something like that. Do you have any thoughts about it?

PROFESSOR SATTERFIELD: Well, you know, it probably depends on the relationship and depends on the person. Maybe having coffee with her first and saying, hey, thank you so much for reaching out that means a lot to me. I just wanted to let you know how Jack's doing and a little bit what to expect. And she may have had experiences on her own caring for a father or her spouse or a son or someone. So sometimes it's good to find that common ground and for both of you to realize, hey, this is tough, but we're both expressing a desire to be connected. She offered, and you accepted her invitation. So the two of you are, where it matters the most, you're agreement with each other.

MARIA: Maybe I could write her a little note and thank her for coming by and say some of those things that I couldn't think of saying.

PROFESSOR SATTERFIELD: Absolutely. It's not too late. So that's our behavioral box. How about the cognitive box? So what tools do we have in there?

MARIA: Well, disputing what you're thinking I guess. I was embarrassed.

PROFESSOR SATTERFIELD: So we have a thought record. Why don't we do one of those really quick? And I'll just sketch one out. So we have the activating situation and you did a great job.

MARIA: Jack in his underwear.

PROFESSOR SATTERFIELD: OK, Jack in his underwear. And we have the emotion is embarrassment.

MARIA: Yeah, embarrassment and feeling protective towards him, feeling sort of ashamed. And, of course, feeling bad for the woman who didn't know what to do with it.

PROFESSOR SATTERFIELD: OK. OK. And if we were to write the intensity zero to 100 of embarrassment?

MARIA: Oh, about 100 for all of them. I was feeling pretty bad.

PROFESSOR SATTERFIELD: OK. Those were all pretty strong. And what were some of those automatic thoughts you were having?

MARIA: How do I get rid of him? How do I get him out of here? I should have done something before. I should've realized this was going to happen or something bad would happen. I shouldn't have had her over. What am I going to say? How am I going to make it right?

PROFESSOR SATTERFIELD: That sounds like a lot of shoulds in there. Right? OK, all right. A lot of that 20/20 hindsight right?

MARIA: That's right.

PROFESSOR SATTERFIELD: Any other automatic thoughts?

MARIA: Let's see. I can't think of anything.

PROFESSOR SATTERFIELD: Any guesses about what she might have been thinking? Were you worried about what she might have been thinking?

MARIA: I was, of course, worried about what she was thinking. She looked pretty horrified, so that might be part of it.

PROFESSOR SATTERFIELD: OK, she's horrified.

MARIA: She was embarrassed too, of course. And she didn't know what was happening and she didn't know that he was sick in that way. She just knew that he was ill.

PROFESSOR SATTERFIELD: Right, right.

MARIA: And we weren't close friends with her so it wasn't something where if it was my friend I would just be able to explain or say something.

PROFESSOR SATTERFIELD: Sure. Well, let's look at these thoughts. And remember thoughts aren't true or false. They're opinions, they're interpretations of a situation. They often pop to mind uninvited. We can take a step back and see if there's a different way that we could see the same situation that might help you feel less embarrassed or ashamed or the other emotions. So rather than looking at evidence for or against, let's use some of those techniques we used in the ABCD of if this happened to someone else what might you say or the yes but technique or the whole list of strategies that we had. So if we were looking at some of these shoulds, I should have done something, I shouldn't have had her over, I should have prepared Jack, all these should, should, should, shoulds, what would you say to a friend that's beating herself up?

MARIA: Stop beating yourself up.

PROFESSOR SATTERFIELD: Right.

MARIA: You know, he's sick. This is a reality. This is the fact; this is what it's like. It's nothing to be ashamed of, its human.

PROFESSOR SATTERFIELD: Right.

MARIA: It's just the way it is.

PROFESSOR SATTERFIELD: Right. Trust in the integrity of your friend and their compassion that she might feel embarrassed, but would understand and not judge as a consequence. So in the moment, what thought could you have? Would those thoughts be helpful?

MARIA: Yes, that would be helpful indeed.

PROFESSOR SATTERFIELD: OK, so can you imagine having someone else over, he comes out in his underwear?

MARIA: Oh, please. He'll be dressed this time; it won't happen that way.

PROFESSOR SATTERFIELD: You'll have done the behavioral strategies and prepared him.

MARIA: Right, and I'll have prepared my guest. In fact, when she calls on the phone, I'll explain what the situation is and ask her if she's uncomfortable with it. And then, that will give her a chance to know ahead of time. I'll do it before she gets there, because you never know when Jack's going to come out.

PROFESSOR SATTERFIELD: OK. All right, so if he is loud or disruptive or calls her the wrong name or starts asking the same question over and over and over again—

MARIA: Which he does, yes.

PROFESSOR SATTERFIELD: He does. What can you think in that moment?

MARIA: What I'm thinking is maybe we should do this in a different place and not have people necessarily to the house. But if he did it, maybe I could just say, this happens, he asks me these questions all the time. And maybe I could just gently get him out of there. Something like that.

PROFESSOR SATTERFIELD: Sure. So any acknowledgement of what's going on? Maybe an explanation if it's needed. But saying to yourself also it's OK. You've done the precession, right? You've explained what it is going on and your friend understands. They know the situation they're in and the reason they're there is to support you, because they know what you're going through. So are you willing maybe at some point down the road to have another person over?

MARIA: Yeah, I think I might start with somebody that I know better.

PROFESSOR SATTERFIELD: A little better, OK.

MARIA: Maybe for other people, maybe I could find time to go out and just have a chat, a girl chat.

PROFESSOR SATTERFIELD: That sounds like a great idea too.

[VIGNETTE END]

PROFESSOR SATTERFIELD: So in this clip with Maria, she gives us a fairly straightforward example of something we would call planful problem solving. Even the best-laid plans sometimes go awry. She just wanted to have more increased positive social contacts. Things didn't go quite so well. But instead of becoming discouraged or defeated, she was able to step back, do a behavioral analysis of what was happening, and to think constructively of what she might do differently next time.

Other elements of resilience that we might want to think about and we might want to teach fall into the cognitive and emotional styles category. We'll talk about something called attributional or explanatory style. We'll go back to the notion of positive emotions and how they can serve as a reservoir or a recharge when we are in the face of stress, and we'll also talk about flexibility or adaptability.

Now, the cognitive style that I wanted to share, something called attributional or explanatory style, it was from the seminal work of Marty Seligman at the University of Pennsylvania, first starting with animal studies in the '60s and '70s, and then moving on to human studies. Now, explanatory style essentially tells us that we have habits and how we explain why events occur.

So here we're very much in the realm of subjective cognitions. As human beings, we almost have a compulsion to try to explain why things happen. Big things, small things, positive things, and especially negative things. Now, Marty Seligman believed that explanatory style has three key dimensions, which he called internal, stable, and global. Well, let's say a negative event happens to you. You have this compulsion to search for an explanation, and you probably have to make your best guess. Are you going to blame yourself, or is it the fault of something outside of you? That's the internal dimension. Is this cause, is it going to be there all the time now, even in the future? Or was it a one-time only? That's the stable dimension. And is this cause, maybe it's your intelligence; maybe it's you environment, whatever it might be, is it going to affect all areas of your life? And that's the global dimension. Internal, stable, and global.

Now, we know the explanatory style is particularly important in explaining achievement and also with its relationship to depression. Individuals who explain negative events with an internal, stable, and global style—it's my fault, it's never going to change, and it's going to affect me everywhere—those are the individuals who are less likely to pick themselves up and to continue pushing forward. Those are the individuals who are going to become more depressed.

An important outgrowth of the work of explanatory style is the Penn Resiliency Project. This was a CBT Program to teach kids from inner-city Philadelphia schools how to have a more optimistic explanatory style. And the goal was to make them more resilient to stressors in their home life, as well to prevent possible depression in the future. Much of this work was done by my fellow graduate students at the time, Karen Reivich, Jane Gillham, and Andrew Shatte.

Since then, there have been quite a few studies looking at the Penn Resiliency Program. I'll just mention a meta-analysis of 17 different studies looking at this program that showed that the interventions significantly reduced and prevented depressive symptoms over time in these children. However, it's not clear if the Penn Resiliency Program had an enhanced effect among children who were experiencing adversity. Now, that's important, because if we define resilience as someone who is able to withstand adversity, we want to see that it's more effective in individuals who are in that circumstance. Well, it worked for pretty much all of the kids, whether or not they were having stressors or not. I say, if it works, we should use it.

Now, the other cognitive style, or really, emotional style, I wanted to mention is to go back to positive emotion. And we've had a couple of lectures talking about how to induce positive emotions, how to find meaning, or how, really, to construct meaning. And while some research indicates that psychological resilience is a relatively stable personality trait, new research suggests that positive emotions are critical to the trait resilience. That's not to say that positive emotions are merely a byproduct of resilience, but rather, that feeling positive emotions during stressful experiences may have adaptive benefits in the coping process of the individual.

Empirical evidence for this prediction arises from research on resilient individuals who have a propensity for coping strategies that concretely elicit positive emotions, such as benefit finding, cognitive reappraisals, humor, optimism, and goal-directed or problem-focused coping. Individuals who tend to approach problems with these methods of coping may strengthen their resistance to stress by allocating more access to these positive emotional resources. And here I'd hope you could recall the work of Judy Moskowitz, where she looked at individuals newly diagnosed with HIV, she looked at parents who were caring for sick children, and found that if she was able to induce positive emotions, it essentially gave them more of a reservoir to cope with the stressful and negative times ahead.

I would also ask you to remember the work, or the theory, of Barbara Fredrickson, who taught us that positive emotions are there to broaden and build. They help to broaden our cognitive repertoire, and they help to build important social relationships that will help us to be more resilient in the future.

I'd like to share a few new studies, and the first by Ong and colleagues in 2006, which was looking at widows and positive emotion. Their group found that widows with high levels of resilience experienced more positive and negative emotions than those with lower levels of resilience. The former group shows high emotional complexity, which is the capacity to maintain the differentiation of positive and negative emotional states while undergoing stress. Their group further suggested that the adapted consequence of resilience is a function of an increase in emotional complexity while stress is present. So it's not just they have the rose-colored glasses on, they're feeling things fairly intensely, both positive and negative, but they're able to differentiate and to use both of those states constructively.

Barbara Fredrickson did a study looking at the way that individuals coped following the events of September the 11th, and published her work in 2003. Her work suggests that positive emotions were critical elements in resilience, and they served as a mediator that buffered people from depression after the crisis occurred. Moreover, she showed that high-resilient people were more likely to notice positive meanings within the problems that they faced, for example, feeling grateful to be alive. They endured fewer depressive symptoms, and they experienced more positive emotions than low-resilient people after the terrorist attacks.

So, we've talked about general factors predicting resilience, and we've expanded the work on cognitive styles and positive emotion. Now, let's look at flexibility and how it might relate to resilience. Now, cognitive flexibility has been described as the mental ability to switch between thinking about two different concepts and to think about multiple concepts simultaneously. Despite a good bit of disagreement in the literature about how to operationally define the term, one commonality is that cognitive flexibility is a component of executive functioning.

Now, a lot of the research on flexibility has been conducted with children at the school age. However, individual differences in cognitive flexibility are apparent throughout the lifespan. In fact, there are a number of different clinician-administered neuropsychological tests to measure flexibility, such as the A-not-B task, dimensional change card sorting, or the Wisconsin card sort, or the Stroop test, which we demonstrated in our last course, *Mind-Body Medicine*. Cognitive flexibility also has implications, both inside and outside the classroom. A person's ability to switch between modes of thought and to simultaneously think about multiple concepts has been shown to be a vital component of learning and of problem solving, and that includes social conflict.

I wanted to describe a different kind of cognitive flexibility, and it's also called cognitive complexity, and this was developed by Phil Tetlock. He's a psychologist, but I really think of him almost as a political scientist. He developed the concept called integrative complexity, which is defined as the degree to which thinking and reasoning involve the recognition and integration of multiple perspectives and possibilities and their interrelated contingencies. Now, that's a big mouthful of jargon, but essentially, what he's talking about is, when an individual talks about a challenging topic, are they able to see both sides of the coin? Are they able to verbalize to discuss the nuances of a particular charged topic. Not only are they able to see the different sides and the nuances of that topic, are they then able to balance them or play them off of one another and come up with some sort integrated perspective that takes all of that possibly disparate data into account.

Now, as I mentioned, he's partly a political scientist, because he uses this concept of integrated complexity to help us understand politicians and the political process. He's found that the electorate, the voters, they tend to prefer politicians who are low in integrative complexity, meaning someone that doesn't talk about both sides of the coin, someone who's more dogmatic, who only sees one side, but they sound very confident and very determined. Otherwise, they're wishy-washy. He would call that integrative complexity, and of course, there's pros and cons of both styles.

Now, the idea of different cognitive styles can be applied in many different situations; an example would be the dissertation that I did for my doctorate, where we used integrative complexity; we used something called pessimistic rumination; and we also used explanatory style in order to better understand the decisions made by the major players in World War II. And here we're talking about Hitler, Stalin, Churchill, and Roosevelt. Why were they aggressive at times? Why were they more or less tolerant of risk at particular times? We were able to do a content analysis of their diaries, of their letters, and of interview transcripts in order to better understand those decisions and their behaviors. Much to our surprise, and our delight, it worked.

The last type of flexibility I'll talk about is called attributional, or explanatory, flexibility. And this, of course, is related to explanatory style. Now remember the definition of explanatory style is that you have a habit of explaining things in a certain way. This looks at essentially how strong is that habit. If you explain 10 different events, are they are all essentially the same sorts of explanations, or do you tend to move or flex depending on the situation? Here, oftentimes, you'll look at the standard deviation of an individual's explanatory style scores. The greater the standard deviation, the greater their attributional flexibility. I'll mention just one set of studies that was done by Dave Fresco. He looked at attributional flexibility in college students, and found those students who were more flexible could be more resilient to stressful events that occurred, and they were less likely to get depressed.

So where does CBT fit in? Well, we know that CBT can be helpful in terms of generating positive emotions. We know that CBT teaches us to reappraise attributions, and potentially, explanations. It gives us general cognitive restructuring skills, and hopefully teaches us, through that process of looking at evidence for and evidence against, it teaches us to be more cognitively flexible, or maybe more integratively complex. I'll mention a recent report put out by the American Psychological Association that gives us 10 ways to build resilience. And again, I would encourage you to look at these through the lens of CBT. So first, telling us to maintain good relationships with close family members, friends, and others; we've talked about that skill set. Two, avoid seeing crises or stressful events as unbearable problems, and here we're talking about appraisals. Three, accept circumstances that cannot be changed, and we've talked about acceptance and constructing meaning and even forgiveness.

Four, to develop realistic goals and to move towards them, we've talked about smart goals and action plans, which brings us to number five, to take decisive actions in adverse situations. Six, to look for opportunities of self-discovery after a struggle with loss. To develop self-confidence, to keep a long term perspective, to maintain a hopeful outlook. And ten, to take care of one's mind and body exercising regularly and paying attention to one's own needs and feelings, as well as social relationships. If you're interested in other fully fleshed out CBT programs to build resilience, I would encourage you to look at a book by Robertson written in 2012 called *Build Your Resilience*.

So let's tie all of this back to our cases. Now, Carol who has anxiety, we really want to help her have more courage in the face of her anxiety and resilience to go out and build those social connections. Michael, we want to increase the need for flexibility. He has a very specific way of seeing the world and becomes very angry when that view is violated. Maria, we want to help her be more flexible in order to meet the chronic stress of caregiving and the upcoming death of her husband. I hope you'll join us in our next lecture, where we'll talk about case endings, finding treatment, and how to evaluate your progress. Thank you.

Finding the Best Help
Lecture 24

This final lecture will tackle the questions of when you or a loved one should seek help and how to go about it getting it. As you will learn, there are many levels of care and many pathways to finding help. There's no one right way. Nonetheless, finding help can still be overwhelming and confusing, so this lecture will review general guidelines and help you through the process of searching for and selecting a therapist for your mental health needs.

When and How to Seek Help

- Do you think that you or someone you love might need therapy? How can you decide? There's no clear-cut threshold or rule, but there are several guiding principles.

  - Are you suffering? Most people seek help when they're suffering the most. We look at intensity and duration. This doesn't have to be a mental illness, but maybe it's above and beyond what an individual is used to coping with.

  - Do you feel stuck? Have you made multiple attempts but failed to make the changes that you need to make in a high-stakes situation?

  - Has your level of social or occupational functioning been changed? Has it declined and you have not been able to pull it back up?

  - What is your quality of life? Is it not what you want it to be, or has it dropped suddenly or precipitously?

  - Are you trying to make a decision? Maybe you are wrestling with a big decision and have talked with friends and family, but it might be helpful to talk with an objective, emotionally uninvolved professional who could help you weigh the options.

- Are you trying to build some new skills and maybe you need a workspace or rehearsal space where you can work with an objective professional to build those new skills and get some direct feedback?

- There are other important reasons to seek therapy, such as having a psychiatric illness, but even then, it depends on the severity of symptoms. We're especially concerned about safety or issues of harm. Personal growth, insight, and evolving as a human being are all good reasons to seek therapy, but there are a number of important concerns that yield fairly typical and understandable ambivalence.

- Some of the practical considerations for therapy include the cost and the time involved in psychotherapy, the availability of quality service, privacy issues or concerns, concerns about the stigma of seeking out a psychotherapist, the potential for harm (fear of things getting worse) if you talk with a therapist, prior family or personal history of psychotherapy, denial, and readiness.

- There is a continuum of treatment modalities, where at one end you see a problem, have suffering, and need to make a decision, so you try to do it on your own. It's certainly more private and less expensive than therapy, but it might be difficult to find the motivation, and if you're stuck in a rut, you're probably going to see the same problem in the same way and not be able to bring in new perspectives.

- You might use basic self-help, so you might buy a self-help book or visit websites. In addition, there are online classes, seminars, and videos. There are technology-enhanced self-help programs. There are other physical and mental wellness programs, such as yoga, meditation, or exercise.

- Continuing along the continuum, you might reach out to some of your social supports (nonprofessionals). This is a little less private, but you're going to feel more connected to someone else, and you're going to get a different perspective and maybe some more motivation.

- Further along the continuum, you might reach out to other family and friends for their advice, problem-solving skills, and support.

- Past that are the peer-peer programs, such as 12-step programs or support groups. Although this does not involve a trained mental health professional, there are other people—maybe outside of your social support network—that will give you a richer and more diverse perspective.

- Furthermore, you might decide to take in-person classes or seminars.

- The other end of the continuum is seeking professional help. Even within this category, you might decide to first talk to a primary care provider, religious or spiritual counselor, or psychologist or psychiatrist. You need to make decisions about how long you're willing to invest in therapy as well as what modality—individual, couples, or family therapy—and what theoretical orientation— CBT, psychodynamics, or first-, second-, or third-wave therapies— would work best for you. In addition, medications might be available at any point, so that also would be part of your decision-making process.

- In reality, most people try something on their own first. Sometimes it works; sometimes it doesn't. People might try some self-help strategies, religious or spiritual counseling, or videos, the Internet, or television.

Self-Help
- There are many types of self-help, including books, videos, websites, and smartphone apps. Keep in mind that many of these are written with a for-profit motive, so be careful to avoid fads and programs that are not based on evidence.

- There are some quality indicators you want to look for. Don't focus on sales volume or press coverage. Look for academic affiliations and credentials of the author. You might want to look for awards, such as the Book of Merit Award, which is awarded by the Association for Behavioral and Cognitive Therapies. There is also a helpful series put out by Oxford University Press called *TreatmentsThatWork*.

- Adherence and motivation are usually the Achilles' heel of self-help, even if a quality resource is found. When you go to a therapist, there's more accountability and extrinsic motivation. Plus, you have an individual who asks probing questions to help you create a case formulation, develop SMART goals, and make course corrections over time if things aren't working out.

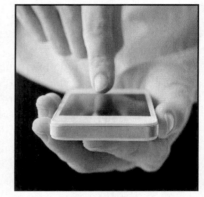

Some smartphone apps encourage adherence to self-help by issuing alerts and reminders.

- Some websites and smartphone apps try to mitigate the adherence issue by using automated reminders and text messages or by setting up incentives or penalties. They're getting better, but they're still somewhat all-or-none, one-size-fits-all systems.

Seeking Professional Help

- Maybe you've tried self-help and weren't happy with the results, or maybe you want to go straight to a professional for help. How should you begin your search? You want to go back to your reason for seeking help, but you need to get more concrete and specific.

- What symptoms do you find most troublesome—depression, anxiety, concentration, drinking too much, marital conflict? Narrowing your focus will help you search for evidence-based treatments, which is the most important starting point.

- How do you find a therapist? It's fairly straightforward. Google evidence-based psychotherapy for whatever your issue might be— depression, anxiety, or marital conflict, for example. A number of different websites as well as academic articles and books will come up that describe the evidence behind a particular kind of therapy for the disease or condition you're interested in.

- There are also a few general resource websites that have summaries about evidence-based practices, including the American Psychological Association, the Association for Behavioral and Cognitive Therapies, and the National Registry of Evidence-Based Practices and Programs (sponsored by the federal government's Substance Abuse and Mental Health Services Administration).

- Some of the therapies that you find might include CBT, CBT-I (for insomnia), and TF-CBT (trauma-focused CBT). Many of them will include such tools as cognitive restructuring (the ABCD exercise and dysfunctional thought records), behavioral activation, behavioral rehearsals, behavioral experiments, self-monitoring, goal setting, and action planning.

- You might learn more about some of the third-wave therapies and particularly about acceptance and commitment therapy (ACT) or mindfulness-based cognitive therapy (MBCT). There are also special therapies designed for treatment of substance use and support of families, including the community reinforcement approach (CRA) and the community reinforcement approach and family training (CRAFT).

- Most psychotherapies, regardless of their theoretical orientation, have nonspecific, or common, factors that can be healing, including a therapeutic alliance, empathy or unconditional positive regard, education or persuasion, a safe and healing setting, and the promotion of insight and emotional learning. All of these things are important, but you should also think about what a therapy gives you over and above those common factors.

Searching for and Selecting a Therapist

- Once you have picked the type of therapy, what modality will you choose? Do you want individual, couples, family, or group therapy? It depends on the nature of the problem and who else might be involved. What would give you the best results?

- Should you try medications first? Should you try them concurrently? Should you try them only if talk therapy fails? If you think you might be interested in medications, get a few opinions—one from a prescriber of medications and one from a non-prescriber—before you make that sort of decision.

- Once you have your focus, goals, and symptoms and an idea of what treatment is based on evidence, you can use these terms to filter your search for a therapist. Keep in mind other factors, such as insurance coverage, transportation, and accessibility.

- Try to see whether any friends or family in your social support network have recommendations for therapists. Find out whether your insurer has recommendations or limitations on who they will allow you to see. You also want to try some online search engines.

- Some of the better referral directories can be found at websites for the American Psychological Association (locator.apa.org), the Association for Behavioral and Cognitive Therapies (abct.org), and the Academy of Cognitive Therapy (academyofct.org).

- In addition, you can always go to your state psychological association, or you can use the Substance Abuse and Mental Health Services Administration treatment locator (findtreatment.samhsa.gov).

Suggested Reading

Campbell, Nunes, Matthews, Stitzer, Miele, Polsky, Turrigiano, Walters, McClure, Kyle, Wahle, Van Veldhuisen, Goldman, Babcock, Stabile, Winhusen, and Ghitza, "Internet-Delivered Treatment for Substance Abuse."

Carroll, Kiluk, Nich, Gordon, Portnoy, Martino, and Ball, "Computer-Assisted Delivery of Cognitive-Behavioral Therapy."

Carroll, Ball, Martino, Nich, Gordon, Portnoy, and Rounsaville, "Computer-Assisted Delivery of Cognitive Behavioral Therapy for Addiction."

Carroll, Ball, Martino, Nich, Babuscio, and Rounsaville, "Enduring Effects of a Computer-Assisted Training Program for Cognitive Behavioral Therapy."

Questions to Consider

1. Go to the Apple App Store or the Google Play Store (Android). Type in "health promotion" or "mental health." How can you choose between the hundreds of choices that pop up? How can you determine quality before you invest money and time?

2. Explore the ABCT website at www.abct.org. Select an illness or symptom/issue that has affected you or someone you know. Review the information sheet (if available). Use the referral tool to find a cognitive therapy provider in your geographic region. How many are there? If there are several, how might you go about selecting one?

Finding the Best Help
Lecture 24—Transcript

PROFESSOR SATTERFIELD: Let's go back in time to about six months ago when Maria was thinking about whether or not she'd like to go to therapy. She knew she was stressed. She knew she was not her regular self. Her daughter and her friend had mentioned maybe getting some counseling, but it seemed a bit extreme, not to mention confusing, when she looked at her insurance and the long list of possible therapists she could contact. So she waited and she waited, until finally she read an article online about cognitive behavioral therapy and how it could give her some practical tools.

After a good bit of soul searching and quite a few calls to her insurer, she found me. She found my number. She called. We did a brief interview over the phone, and we set up her first appointment. Welcome to our 24th and final lecture. In this lecture, we'll tackle the question of when someone or their loved one should seek out help, and how to go about it. As you'll see, there are many levels of care and many pathways to finding help, so there's no one, right way. Nonetheless, finding help can still be overwhelming and confusing, so we will review general guidelines.

From there, we'll look at how to make the most of your therapy once it has started, how to evaluate its progress, and when to end it or terminate your work together. We'll see how our three cases ended and wrap up by reviewing some very exciting changes coming to the field, mostly thanks to new technologies like smartphone apps and sensors.

So, do you think that you or someone you love might need therapy? Exactly how can you decide? Well, there's no clear-cut threshold or rule, but there's maybe several things to keep in mind. The first I think about is suffering. Most people seek out help when they're suffering the most. We look at intensity and duration. Now, this doesn't have to be a mental illness, but maybe above and beyond what an individual is usually used to coping with. Do you feel stuck? Have you made multiple attempts but failed to make the changes that you need to make in a high stakes situation? Has your level of social or occupational functioning been changed? Has it declined and you've not been able to pull it back up?

And what is your quality of life? Is it not what you want it to be, or has it dropped suddenly or precipitously? Are you trying to make a decision? Maybe you're wrestling with a big decision and you talked with friends and family, but it might be helpful to talk with an objective, emotionally uninvolved professional who would be helpful in weighing the options. Are you trying to build some new skills and maybe you need a work space or a rehearsal space where, again, you can work with an objective professional to build those new skills and get some direct feedback?

Of course, there are other important reasons to go, such as having a psychiatric illness. And remember that one in four people, or 25%, of the population will have a diagnosable mental illness at some point in their life. Of course, that's a reason to seek out psychotherapy, but even then, again, it depends on the severity of symptoms, and we're especially concerned about safety or issues of harm.

I don't want to downplay the use and the importance of psychotherapy in promoting personal growth or personal insight. And in fact, many years ago, most people would go to psychotherapy over an extended period of time because they wanted to better understand themselves or their relationships. For example, an individual maybe just experienced her third breakup, and she wants to know why she keeps picking the wrong sorts of guys, but she just can't seem to understand why. It's not about psychopathology. Maybe there is some suffering, maybe there is some decision making, but it's really about trying to understand a pattern and then take some steps forward to change it.

Now, these are all good reasons to seek out therapy, but there are a number of important concerns that yield fairly typical and understandable ambivalence. So some of the things you might think about is first of all the cost and the time involved in psychotherapy. Now, it's always surprised me that people might be willing to spend a fairly vast amount of money for plastic surgery, but they're reluctant to spend the time or money in order to improve their mental health.

What about the availability of quality service? There are great therapists out there, there's medium quality, and there's also fairly low quality. So you do have to be careful. There might be issues or concerns around privacy. There might be concerns about the stigma of seeking out a psychotherapist or someone labeling you with a mental illness. Is there potential for harm? If you open things up and talk with a therapist, are you afraid that things might actually get worse?

Do you have a prior family or personal history of psychotherapy? And often, when I finally connect with patients who've maybe been considering treatment for years, they'll talk about the horror stories of their mother or their brother, or maybe they saw a therapist that things didn't work quite so well, and it took them a while before they were ready to try it again.

Now, you want to think about the different treatment modalities, and I kind of placed them on a continuum, where, at one end, and this is where most people start, honestly, is, you see a problem, you have suffering, you need to make a decision, so you try to do it on your own. It's certainly more private; it's certainly less expensive; but it might be hard to find the motivation, and if you're stuck in a rut, you're probably going to see the same problem in the exact same way and not really be able to bring in new and genuinely different perspectives.

You might use basic self-help, so you might buy a self-help book, you might go to websites. There are online classes, seminars, videos. More recently, there are technology-enhanced self-help programs, where you will enroll in a program online, they might send you text messages or alerts to try to promote you or prompt you to continue going through their program, or there might be other physical and mental wellness programs, such as yoga, meditation, or exercises.

If we continue along that continuum, you might reach out to some of your friends or some of your social supports, and here we're really talking about non-mental-health professionals. It's a little less private, but you're going to feel more connected to someone else, and you're going to get that different perspective, and maybe a little bit more motivation.

Further along the continuum, you might reach out to other family and friends, again, to get their advice and their problem-solving skills, and support. Past that are the peer-peer programs, and here I'm thinking about things like 12-step programs or support groups. Again, there's not a trained mental health professional, but there are other people, maybe outside of your social support network, that will give you a richer and more different perspective.

You might decide to take in-person classes or seminars, or you might go to the other end of the continuum and seek out professional help. Now, even within that particular category, you might decide to first talk to a primary care provider. You might talk to a religious or spiritual counselor. You might seek out a psychologist, a psychiatrist. You need to make decisions about how long you're willing to invest; what modality, individual, couples, family; and what theoretical orientation, CBT, psychodynamic, first, second, or third wave, would work best for you. And of course, there might be medications that are available at any point in time, so that would be part of your decision process.

In reality, we know that most people try something on their own first. Sometimes it works, sometimes not. They'll try some of the self-help strategies I've mentioned, maybe spiritual or religious counseling. They might turn to video, internet, or TV. Do these things work? And how can you find the good stuff? Because it seems like there's an awful lot of material out there, some of it not quite so good.

Since people tend to try self-help first, then move on to professional help only when they have to, that's where I'm going to start. So let's review what's meant by self-help and how you can go about maximizing your chances for success. We've mentioned many of the kinds of self-help, the books, videos, websites, and now smartphone apps. But I think it's important to remember that many of these are written in a for-profit frame of mind, so there's often a lot of marketing. I was recently in a bookstore, and I saw a book that promised me that I could have self-esteem within 10 days if I just follow their program. Needless to say, I didn't buy the book. We don't want to go for fads. We don't want to go for empty promises. Again, we want to look for something that's evidence based.

So what are some of the quality indicators? Well, I wouldn't look for, necessarily, for the best sellers, although that sometimes means that it's a quality book, so it's not about sales volume or press coverage necessarily. You want to look for the academic affiliations, background, and training, really, the credentials of the author. You might want to look for awards, such as the Book of Merit Award that's awarded by the Association for Behavioral and Cognitive Therapists. There's also a really helpful series put out by Oxford University Press called *Treatments That Work*. They have about a dozen and a half books right now. They're very specialized on specific challenges or specific mental illnesses. But all of them go through a panel of experts that then give the thumbs up or the thumbs down on whether or not that's a good book and if it is teaching evidence-based psychotherapies.

Now, we've mentioned a number of different self-help books throughout this, so I hope that you are able to jot those down or look at those websites that we mentioned. Of course, this is not a complete list, and new books are coming out all the time, so I do encourage you to keep your eyes open.

Now, with self-help, adherence and motivation are usually the Achilles heel. You buy the book, it looks really interesting, and most self-help books sit on the shelf and they're not used. Or you might flip through them or read a chapter or two but don't really work through those exercises. When you go to see a therapist, a mental health professional, we know that there's more accountability. You have more extrinsic motivation. Plus, you're making an investment in yourself. You've put your nickel down and decided that you're going to commit to this particular course of action. You also have an individual there to ask those probing questions to help you create a case formulation, develop those smart goals, and make course corrections over time if things aren't working out. Some websites and smartphone apps try to mitigate the adherence issue by using automated reminders and text messages or setting up incentives or penalties. They're getting a little bit better, but they're still somewhat all or none, one size fits all.

So let's say you've tried self-help, and maybe you weren't happy with the results, or you just couldn't quite get yourself started, so what should you do in terms of seeking out professional help? Well, you want to go back to your reason for seeking help, but you need to get more concrete and specific. So what symptoms do you find most troublesome? Is it depression, anxiety, concentration, drinking too much, marital conflict? Narrowing your focus will help you search for evidence-based treatments, and that's the most important starting point.

So how would you go about finding it? Honestly, it's fairly straightforward. So you would go to Google, and you would type in "evidence-based psychotherapy for blank." That would be depression, anxiety, marital conflict, whatever the issue might be. You will see that there are a number of different websites, as well as academic articles and books that come up that describe the evidence behind a particular kind of therapy for the disease or condition you're interested in.

There's also a couple of other general-resource websites that have nice summaries about evidence-based practices. You might go to the American Psychological Association. You might go to the ABCT.org website; that's the Association for Behavioral and Cognitive Therapies. You might also look at something called NREPP, that's the National Registry of Evidence-Based Practices and Programs, and that's a site sponsored by the federal government, the Substance Abuse and Mental Health Services Administration. They list, literally, dozens and dozens of pages by many, many different conditions about what they believe works best.

So some of the therapies that you find might be things that we've talked about, such as CBT; CBTI for insomnia; or TFCBT, trauma-focused CBT for post-traumatic stress disorder. A lot of them will include those same tools in that toolbox that we've talked about throughout the course, the cognitive restructuring, the ABCD, the dysfunctional thought records. They might talk about behavioral activation, behavioral rehearsals, behavioral experiments, and of course, self-monitoring, goal setting, action planning, all these things which I hope you're quite familiar with by now.

You may hear more about some of the third-wave therapies, and particularly, about ACT, Acceptance and Commitment Therapy, or mindfulness-based cognitive therapy. And let's not forget those special therapies designed for treatment of substance use and support of families, the community reinforcement approach, and a community reinforcement for families. In general, when you do this sort of search, you're going to find more short-term, focused, manualized therapies, and in part, it's because those tend to be the things that are studied and are more amenable to research methods. But I also think, in part, because when we're looking at symptom-focused outcomes, those are the kinds of therapies that work.

Now, in your search, you may run across something called the Dodo bird verdict, or the idea that all psychotherapies are equal. The term was coined by Saul Rosenzweig in the 1930s, and it was taken from Alice in Wonderland, where the Dodo bird says, "Everybody has one, and all must have prizes." Well, it's true that most psychotherapies, regardless of their theoretical orientation, have what are called nonspecific or common factors that can be healing. So these would be things like forming a strong therapeutic supportive alliance. This would be the use of empathy or unconditional positive regard. This would be education, persuasion, providing a safe and healing setting, promoting insight and emotional learning. And all of these things are absolutely important.

But I would encourage you to also think about what does therapy give you over and above those common factors. I would encourage you to look at the evidence, and in fact, the Dodo bird verdict has been debunked, mostly from studies looking at cognitive behavioral therapy for anxiety and for depression. This category of research is called comparative effectiveness research, where they put two kinds of therapies side by side. And when we're looking at a specific therapy for a specific disorder, the Dodo bird verdict seems to be a myth.

So let's say that you've picked your type of therapy, but what modality? Do you want individual, couples, family, or group? And again, it depends on the nature of the problem, and it depends on who else might be involved. What would give you the best results? And that might be something that you would ask a clinician after you make that first call. But there's also the issue of medications. Should you try medications first? Should you try them concurrently? Should you try them only if talk therapy fails?

Now I think you do have to be aware of the phenomenon, if you have a hammer, then all the world is a nail. So if you go to someone that only prescribes, they're probably going to prescribe. But if you go to someone that only does psychotherapy, they're probably going to downplay medications.

So I encourage people, if you think you might be interested, to at least get a couple of opinions, one from a prescriber, maybe one from a non-prescriber, before you make that sort of decision.

Once you have your focus, your goals, the symptoms you're going to work in, and an idea of what treatment is evidence based, you can and use these terms to filter your search for an actual therapist. So keep in mind other factors like your insurance coverage, transportation, accessibility, all of that's going to be important. So first, you want to send out feelers to see if any friends or family in your social support network have recommendations. You want to see if your insurer has recommendations or limitations on who they will allow you to see or not, and of course, you want to try some online search engines.

Now, some of the better referral directories, again, can be found at the American Psychological Association. They have a site called locator.apa.org, where you enter in a number of different variables that you believe are of interest, and they start filtering down a list for you. You could also go, again, to abct.org, or you could go to the Academy of Cognitive Therapy, that's just the academyofct.org, and they, again, have a referral directory of people that have received high quality training in cognitive behavioral therapy.

Two other places I wanted to mention, you can always go to your state psychological association. For me, that would be the CPA or the California Psychological Association. Or, you can use the SAMHSA treatment locator, which is simply findtreatment.samhsa.gov.

So once you find a couple of names, and I would recommend you find at least three to five names, you'll make the first call. Usually you will get a voicemail or an answering service, and you want to keep it very short, you want to keep it very direct. You'll ask for a call back. So the first filter is whether or not they call you back. And honestly, many of them will not have case openings, and you won't get a call back. So those that do call you back, what questions should you ask? And what sort of response should you expect? So here are some sample questions. You might want to ask things like, are you a licensed mental health professional? How many years have you been practicing psychotherapy? Tell me your areas of expertise. What experience do you have in helping people with these types of problems? And then you might want to list what you are interested in. What kinds of treatments do you use, and have they been proven and effective? How do you measure progress? How do you measure satisfaction? Do you have any special experience with, and then if you have cultural, language, age, or other considerations, you might want to insert that there. What are your fees? And what types of insurances do you accept?

Let's move, then, to the first session. Let's say that you've found someone, and you should always remember that that first session is a two-way interview. You have a choice, and you should feel comfortable with your therapist. You want to look at whether or not the therapist is adept at establishing rapport and starting to build an alliance. You want to see if there is a clear and immediate discussion of goals and a treatment plan. You want to see whether or not the therapist seems to have a grasp of the content area that you're talking about and ask important clarifying questions.

What are some other quality indicators? Well, of course, I come from a CBT perspective, but I think it's important that we do talk about goals, that therapy should not be open ended, that it goes wherever it may go; you should have an end point in mind. You should have that star on the horizon at minimum. You want some baseline measurements. You want some assurance that there will be reassessments over time to track your progress. And of course, there are the, I think of them as intangibles, the comfort you have, the connection, how motivated you feel, and how responsive the therapist is.

Now how long should you wait before you start seeing results? Well, again, that depends. If you had a problem that has been present for a number of years, it's unrealistic to assume it's going to change in a few weeks. But you do want to have that conversation with a therapist about setting expectations and establishing a timeline.

Now, I do think it's important that we have realistic expectations, and as we've said many times, things don't work, and it's simply grist for the mill. So I think, even if it doesn't work the first time, doesn't work the second time, as long as the attitude is, we'll figure out what happened and we'll try something different, then maybe it's worth continuing. But how long should therapy last? When is someone cured? Well, again, that depends on the goals that you've set, and you should be reassessing those goals. Once you've reached those goals, then it might be time to talk about closure. It might even be time to talk about possible booster sessions.

So let's move to our final clip. This is a clip of Maria, where she's near the end of her treatment and we're assessing whether or not she's made adequate progress.

[VIGNETTE START]

MARIA: For our session today, I brought these questionnaires about my feelings and so forth, and I thought we might go over and see how my progress was.

PROFESSOR SATTERFIELD: Sure, sure, and this wonderful, as we mentioned, and when you first started back in session number two, I think it was, you brought in questionnaires about depression and anxiety and physical symptoms.

MARIA: Right, that's what this is.

PROFESSOR SATTERFIELD: OK, so you brought these again. We had looked at a midpoint refresh of those surveys, and it looked like there were some improvements, but there was still work to do. So this is a great time to check in again on your progress. According to the records that I have, you have two more approved visits after today. So this will be good data to use to decide if we're on track and two's OK, or if we need to try to extend that a little bit.

So let's see what you have. And the first one here is depression, and it covers cognitive, social, physical, even neurological symptoms related to depression. And in the beginning, I have that you had started at a 27, which was up at the moderate-severe range. You had dropped down a bit by midpoint, and it looks like you're at a 13. That's really good.

MARIA: And I do feel good, I feel so much better.

PROFESSOR SATTERFIELD: And the usual goal is we want to get people below 10, but that's just sort of an arbitrary cutoff. We got you from 27 and it's more than halved down to 13. I think there are still some very real stressors in your life, and there are some very real things to be sad about. But being sad and being depressed are different. It's OK if you're sad. Depression is what we're trying to get rid of.

MARIA: I'm beginning to see that now.

PROFESSOR SATTERFIELD: Well let's look at the anxiety, and see how you did here. So for anxiety there were the two categories, or the cognitive worry stuff, and then there were the physical symptoms, the tension and jitteriness that's often associated with anxiety. And you were in a moderate range at the beginning.

So it looks like from worry, there's still some worry here. I would say significant worry, probably not debilitating worry. And again, you have some very real things to worry about. What we want to do is to make sure that the worries that you're having are not only understandable, but the worry is used in a way that's constructive or productive. That worry is a way that our mind directs our attention to a problem that maybe can be turned over or looked at in a different way so you can cope with it more effectively.

In this column, with the physical sensations, it looks like you've dropped quite a bit. Any idea of why?

MARIA: Well, I'm sleeping a little better, and I think that helps a lot. And the relaxation techniques that you taught me have been very helpful, really. There are times when I do them, right after I do them, that I don't have any pain at all.

PROFESSOR SATTERFIELD: So the relaxation strategies—the somatic quieting, guided imagery, progressive muscle relaxation—those have really helped with the body aspect of anxiety. Great, so depression looks like terrific progress. Physical sensations of anxiety, terrific progress. With worry, there's still some worry that's there, but again, that's to be expected, probably.

PROFESSOR SATTERFIELD: In the last one, you had filled out the somatic symptoms questionnaire. And this focused on your own health, and you had talked about body pains. And part of them were emotionally driven, and part of them were physical: Your osteoarthritis, it seemed like it had been flaring up a little bit. And if we look at this, you're in a mild range. And before it wasn't severe; you're in the mild/moderate, so it's dropped a little bit, but maybe not as much as we want it to drop. So how do you interpret that?

MARIA: Well, I think I can bear it now. I felt before as if I just couldn't bear it. I think I can bear it. I might also try seeing my doctor again, and seeing if there's something physical that I can do about it, or some medication that I should be taking. I think exercising has helped some, and sleeping better has helped some, and just generally feeling better.

PROFESSOR SATTERFIELD: Now, it seems from the questionnaires that you've made great progress, and we're in a really good place, and there's still two visits left after today. But I wanted to talk about something that's a little harder to quantify on a questionnaire, and I know the star on the horizon was you wanted to be the best caregiver you could possibly be for your husband. And recognizing that all of the challenges inherent in that. And you just felt like you were working harder and harder, but not performing the way you wanted to. So if we were going to reassess your job, your performance, as a caregiver, how would you say you're doing?

MARIA: Well, I would say that I'm certainly doing better now than I was before, because I have a little more energy, and I have a few more resources, things that I can do when I'm not doing so well. But I think I've also given up the idea of being the perfect caregiver, and I realized that I need some help. Nobody can do it all the time. I tried, I really tried, and I couldn't do it. So it's been very helpful to have somebody come in and help out occasionally.

PROFESSOR SATTERFIELD: So let's talk about some of the lasting structural changes you've made that will continue, hopefully, to help you going forward. And one of them was bringing in more help, in terms of the home health worker, and she has more hours and comes in on more days now. Are there other changes you've made?

MARIA: You suggested getting together with that support group for caregivers, and I have done that. And it is very helpful. I've met a couple of women there that I really like and respect, and I think I'll try to continue that at least for a while.

PROFESSOR SATTERFIELD: OK. Any other changes that you want to make sure you hold onto, or some things you keep doing?

MARIA: Things I want to keep doing are seeing Judith, which we've started doing once a week, and it's really wonderful to be back with her, and spending a little more time with my grandchildren, and reading some. I still haven't been able to read like I used do, but I've read a little bit more. And getting some exercise. I think that's been a huge help for me. Not that I'm doing a lot, but some.

PROFESSOR SATTERFIELD: Well I wanted to remind you that part of the philosophy of cognitive behavioral therapy is that it's symptom focused. It tends to be shorter term, but it's shorter term because we want to teach other people the skill so that when you leave, even if there's not a therapist present, you've become your own therapist in a sense. You can, at any time, take out your toolbox, and you can do a thought record, you can do some activity scheduling, you can do some active problem solving or values clarification exercises, or what have you. So I wanted to ask you, does it feel like you have a toolbox, and if so what's in it?

MARIA: Well, one of the most important things I think is just disputing my ways of thinking about things. Sometimes the feelings are so strong that you think they are the only truth. But I think one thing I learned here was that strength of feelings doesn't mean truth of feelings, and that there are other ways of looking at things. So I think that's helped me a lot. And the guided imagery has helped me a lot, relaxation.

PROFESSOR SATTERFIELD: And I want to make sure that you have all of the forms, you have the websites, you have the resources and tools. And we'll leave it to you to essentially decide, hey, I'm having moment. I need to take out my toolbox and I need to practice one of these tools. And I think of it just like with physical fitness: Even if you've gotten to peak performance, you still need to exercise, right? Or you lose it. You use it or lose it.

It's the same for these cognitive behavioral therapy exercises. Even if you're feeling pretty good, practice some mood hygiene and do some of these exercises, and make sure that you're still on track.

MARIA: OK, I'll do that.

PROFESSOR SATTERFIELD: So what I would recommend, you have two visits left, and we've been going about every week. I think we rescheduled once in the middle there. But you have two more left, and I think it's often helpful for folks to go ahead and schedule those visits, maybe increase the time between visits.

MARIA: Could I save one for emergencies?

PROFESSOR SATTERFIELD: And you could save one for emergencies, you could. So what we want to do then is maybe our next one, it won't be in a week, but maybe in a month or so. Does that feel OK, in a month?

MARIA: I can always play your tape if I miss you.

PROFESSOR SATTERFIELD: And you have the tape, right, you have the tape and you can play the tape. That's absolutely yours.

MARIA: Thank you.

PROFESSOR SATTERFIELD: So when you come back in a month we'll have that; we can also discuss what to do with that final visit. And if you don't have to use it, you don't have to use it. I do recommend that folks, especially if you've had something like depression, that you come in for checkups periodically, and we can decide what frequency is best for you.

MARIA: Maybe I can just come back and thank you for saving my life. I really feel that way.

PROFESSOR SATTERFIELD: It was a collaborative effort, and you've worked really hard. And I'm so glad to see that you've gotten so much better.

MARIA: Thank you.

[VIGNETTE END]

PROFESSOR SATTERFIELD: But what about Carol? When Carol came in for her reassessments, when we were thinking about potentially wrapping up, we saw that she had substantial drops in her Beck anxiety inventory. We saw that she had a new and budding friendship at work, someone that she ate lunch with every day. She started taking an art class that she was enjoying, and she had begun having coffee afterwards with her classmates. She's still not dating. She's still a little anxious. But she's more hopeful. She smiles more. She started dressing differently. She has hope for her future.

What about Michael? Now, he and his wife are still together, and he has stopped smoking completely. He still has a short fuse, as he probably will for the rest of his life, but he feels better able to regulate his anger and to not act on his impulses. He is working less. He is enjoying more time with his family and friends, and he decided to join an ongoing mindfulness meditation group, and he uses his stress management smartphone app regularly.

Now, speaking of apps, we're on the cusp of some very exciting innovations and treatment delivery models and modalities. We may see less and less of the standard individual 50-minute therapy session and more tools or what are called clinician extenders, or technology tools, that help to expand the scope or the work that can be done inside and outside of therapy session. So examples of clinician extenders would be the use of video calls, the use of websites, smartphone apps, even interactive voice response calls; those are the robot calls that may call and administer a questionnaire to you in order to see how well you're doing.

Another program we're recently using at UCSF is we're sending text messages to patients who request them in order to remind them about their medications, about referrals, or about homework that they're supposed to be doing.

We've mentioned the Therapeutic Education System; these where the online CRA modules developed by Lisa Marsh. I wanted to point out one other online CBT program; it's called CBT4CBT. You can find that online. It is a computer-based training CBT for substance-use disorders. And she's published a number of studies in 2008, 2014 are just a few where she looked at treatment as usual, versus treatment as usual plus the computer and found that the computer was sufficient in order to decrease an individual's drug use. She also found that this was sufficient to help an individual prevent relapse over time if they continued to use the app.

Now, speaking of apps, I think we have to remember, it is let the buyer beware. We know that there are over 70,000 health apps for smartphones that are out. Health searches are actually the most common on the Internet right now. Unfortunately, the majority of apps are not tested, and they're not studied, and most are not evidence based. Nearly, 80% of folks that download an app won't even open it. And often the most motivated and successful people are the ones that use the apps, and they're not the folks that need it the most.

But if you are in the market and you're interested in some good apps, what are good apps for smoking cessation? Well, an example would be, and I'm partial, the UCSF San Francisco General Hospital Stop Smoking app, or QuitSTART is a second possibility. For depression and mood, we have the Depression CBT Self-Help Guide, or My Mood Monitor 3, or a recent find eCBT.

Now, there are other systems innovations such as the use of electronic health records, home health portals, where you can log in at home and potentially do some of your CBT work. That way, put it directly into your health record so that your provider can see it. We're also testing models where we're looking at health coaches and what we're calling near-peer counselors. Third-party payers, insurance companies, are also realizing how difficult it is for folks to find therapy, and they're developing more robust websites. An example is Optem's approach to teaching online CBT, which is available to their customers for free.

Now, the bottom line is that Internet and apps may be helpful, particularly, I think, for more mild and moderate cases and for individuals who are more motivated and able to stick with them. The models vary, and the evidence varies, the standalone models have the worst outcomes. In general, I think if you're going to use a technology tool, it's good to have a person, a professional, that's attached to it, so you have some sort of blended model. Now, a lot of these apps are more engaging than you might think. They're using something called gameification to pull you in, to excite you, and to pull you forward. These really are the new frontier, and I'm certain that you'll hear more about them.

So, we've covered a lot ground in this course, and I hope we've laid a firm foundation in cognitive behavioral therapy. I hope you have been able to put a number of different strategies or tools in your toolbox. And we've talked about enough applications so that you now have the facility to continue applying that lens and those tools to any new situation that may come up.

I want to thank you for joining me on this journey. May you be free, may you find peace, and may you have grace and courage. Thank you.

Crisis Resources

A psychiatric crisis—that is, a situation in which you are a danger to yourself or others as a consequence of mental illness—is no different from a medical crisis. It is appropriate to call 911 or to go directly to a hospital emergency room. Emergency medical technicians and 911 operators, as well as police and fire fighters, are trained in how to handle such issues, and they may be your best, fastest resources in the face of an immediate need.

Many specialty hotlines are also available, where counselors are trained to deal with specific needs. Most of these have both phone and online chat versions available. These resources are free and available 24 hours a day.

Some specific recommendations include the following:

National Suicide Prevention Lifeline

1-800-273-8255
www.suicidepreventionlifeline.org

National Council on Alcoholism and Drug Dependence Hopeline

1-800-622-2255
www.ncaad.org

National Domestic Violence/Child Abuse/Sexual Abuse Helpline

1-800-799-7233
http://www.thehotline.org/help/

Veterans Crisis Line

> 1-800-273-8255 ext. 1
> VeteransCrisisLine.net

National Center for Posttraumatic Stress Disorder

> 1-802-296-6300
> http://www.ptsd.va.gov/public/where-to-get-help.asp

RAINN National Sexual Assault Hotline

> 1-800-656-HOPE (4673)
> online.rainn.org

SAMHSA Disaster Distress National Helpline

> 1-800-662-HELP (4357)
> http://disasterdistress.samhsa.gov/

National Youth Crisis Hotline

> 1-800-442-HOPE (4673)
> www.hopeline.com

Compassionate Friends (for parents enduring the loss of a child)

> 1-630-990-0010
> www.compassionatefriends.org

Judi's House (for children dealing with the loss of a parent)

    1-720-941-0331
    www.judishouse.org

The Alzheimer's Association

    1-800-272-3900

Bibliography

Allemand, M., M. Steiner, and P. L. Hill. "Effects of a Forgiveness Intervention for Older Adults." *Journal of Counseling Psychology* 60, 2 (2013): 279–286. doi: 10.1037/a0031839. Epub 2013 Feb 25.

Allen, A. "Cognitive-Behavior Therapy and Other Psychosocial Interventions in the Treatment of Obsessive-Compulsive Disorder." *Psychiatric Annals* 36, 7 (2006): 474–479.

American Dietetic Association. *Complete Food and Nutrition Guide.* 3rd ed. Hoboken, NJ: Wiley Press, 2006.

Andrasik, F. "What Does the Evidence Show? Efficacy of Behavioural Treatments for Recurrent Headaches in Adults." *Neurological Sciences* 28, suppl. 2 (2007): S70–S77. doi: 10.1007/s10072-007-0754-8.

Antoni, M., G. Ironson, and N. Schneiderman. *Cognitive-Behavioral Stress Management.* New York: Oxford University Press, 2007.

Areán, P. A., P. Raue, R. S. Mackin, D. Kanellopoulos, C. McCulloch, and G. S. Alexopoulos. "Problem-Solving Therapy and Supportive Therapy in Older Adults with Major Depression and Executive Dysfunction." *The American Journal of Psychiatry* 167, 11 (2010): 1391–1398. doi: 10.1176/appi.ajp.2010.09091327.

Astin, J. A., W. Beckner, K. Soeken, M. C. Hochberg, and B. Berman. "Psychological Interventions for Rheumatoid Arthritis: A Metaanalysis of Randomized Controlled Trials." *Arthritis & Rheumatism* 47, 3 (2002): 291–302. doi: 10.1002/art.10416.

Babor, T. F., B. G. McRee, P. A. Kassebaum, P. L. Grimaldi, K. Ahmed, and J. Bray. "Screening, Brief Intervention, and Referral to Treatment (SBIRT): Toward a Public Health Approach to the Management of Substance Abuse." *Substance Abuse* 28 (2007): 7–30.

Babor, T. F., J. C. Higgins-Biddle, J. B. Saunders, and M. G. Monteiro. *AUDIT: The Alcohol Use Disorders Identification Test—Guidelines for Use in Primary Care.* 2nd ed. World Health Organization, Department of Mental Health and Substance Dependence, 2001. http://whqlibdoc.who.int/hq/2001/WHO_MSD_MSB_01.6a.pdf.

Bandelow, B., U. Seidler-Brandler, A. Becker, D. Wedekind, and E. Rüther. "Meta-Analysis of Randomized Controlled Comparisons of Psychopharmacological and Psychological Treatments for Anxiety Disorders." *World Journal of Biological Psychiatry* 8 (2007): 175–187.

Bandura, Albert. *Self-Efficacy: The Exercise of Control.* New York: Macmillan, 1997.

Barlow, D. H. *Clinical Handbook of Psychological Disorders.* 5th ed. New York: Guilford Press, 2014.

Barlow, J., C. Wright, J. Sheasby, A. Turner, and J. Hainsworth. "Self-Management Approaches for People with Chronic Conditions: A Review." *Patient Education and Counseling* 48, 2 (2002): 177–187.

Baron, R. M., and D. A. Kenny. "The Moderator-Mediator Variable Distinction in Social Psychological Research: Conceptual, Strategic, and Statistical Considerations." *Journal of Personality and Social Psychology* 51 (1986): 1173–1182.

Bath, J., G. Bohin, C. Jone, and E. Scarle. *Cardiac Rehabilitation: A Workbook for Group Programs.* New York: Wiley, 2009.

Beck, A. T. *Cognitive Therapy and the Emotional Disorders.* Harmondsworth, UK: Penguin, 1976.

———. *Prisoners of Hate: The Cognitive Basis of Anger, Hostility, and Violence.* New York: Harper Collins, 1999.

Beck, A. T., and G. Emery, with R. Greenberg. *Anxiety Disorders and Phobias: A Cognitive Perspective.* New York: Basic Books, 1985.

Beck, A. T., et al. *Cognitive Therapy of Depression*. New York: Guilford Press, 1979.

Beck, J. *Cognitive Therapy: Basics and Beyond*. New York: Guilford Press, 1995.

————. *The Beck Diet Solution: Train Your Brain to Think Like a Thin Person*. Birmingham, AL: Oxmoor House Publishing, 2008.

Beck, Richard, and Ephrem Fernandez. "Cognitive-Behavioral Therapy in the Treatment of Anger: A Meta-Analysis." *Cognitive Therapy and Research* 22, 1 (1998): 63–74.

Benson, H., and M. Z. Klipper. *The Relaxation Response*. New York: Harper Torch, 1976.

Bisson, J. I., A. Ehlers, R. Matthews, S. Pilling, D. Richards, and S. Turner. "Psychological Treatments for Chronic Post-Traumatic Stress Disorder: Systematic Review and Meta-Analysis." *British Journal of Psychiatry* 190 (2007): 97–104.

Bisson, J. I., N. P. Roberts, M. Andrew, R. Cooper, and C. Lewis. "Psychological Therapies for Chronic Post-Traumatic Stress Disorder (PTSD) in Adults." *Cochrane Database of Systematic Reviews* 12 (2013): CD003388. doi: 10.1002/14651858.CD003388.pub4.

Blazer, D., and L. Wu. "The Epidemiology of At-Risk and Binge Drinking among Middle-Aged and Elderly Community Adults: National Survey on Drug Use and Health." *The American Journal of Psychiatry* 166 (2009):1162–1169.

Bonanno, G. A., S. Galea, A. Bucciareli, and D. Vlahov. "What Predicts Psychological Resilience after Disaster? The Role of Demographics, Resources, and Life Stress." *Journal of Consulting and Clinical Psychology* 75, 5 (2007): 671–682. doi: 10.1037/0022-006X.75.5.671. PMID 17907849.

Bourne, E. J. *The Anxiety and Phobia Workbook.* 3rd ed. San Francisco, CA: New Harbinger Press, 2000.

Bowen, Sarah, Neha Chawla, and G. Alan Marlatt. *Mindfulness-Based Relapse Prevention for Addictive Behaviors: A Clinician's Guide.* New York: Guilford, 2010.

Brennan, K. A., C. L. Clark, and P. R. Shaver. "Self-Report Measurement of Adult Romantic Attachment: An Integrative Overview." In *Attachment Theory and Close Relationships,* edited by J. A. Simpson and W. S. Rholes, 46–76. New York: Guilford Press, 1998.

Brown, G. K., A. T. Beck, R. A. Steer, and J. R. Grisham. "Risk Factors for Suicide in Psychiatric Outpatients: A 20-Year Prospective Study." *Journal of Consulting and Clinical Psychololgy* 68, 3 (2000): 371–377.

Brunwasser, S. M., J. E. Gillham, and E. S. Kim. "A Meta-Analytic Review of the Penn Resiliency Program's Effect on Depressive Symptoms." *Journal of Consulting and Clinical Psychololgy* 77, 6 (2009): 1042–1054. doi: 10.1037/a0017671. PMID 19968381.

Burke, B. L., H. Arkowitz, and M. Menchola. "The Efficacy of Motivational Interviewing: A Meta-Analysis of Controlled Clinical Trials." *Journal of Consulting and Clinical Psychololgy* 71, 5 (2003): 843–861.

Butler, G. *Overcoming Social Anxiety and Shyness.* London: Robinson, 1999.

Butler, G., and T. Hope. *Manage Your Mind.* Oxford: Oxford University Press, 1995.

Cahill, K., and R. Perera. "Competitions and Incentives for Smoking Cessation." *Cochrane Database of Systematic Reviews* 4 (2011): CD004307. doi: 10.1002/14651858.CD004307.pub4.

Campbell, A. N., E. V. Nunes, A. G. Matthews, M. Stitzer, G. M. Miele, D. Polsky, E. Turrigiano, S. Walters, E. A. McClure, T. L. Kyle, A. Wahle, P. Van Veldhuisen, B. Goldman, D. Babcock, P. Q. Stabile, T. Winhusen, and U.

E. Ghitza. "Internet-Delivered Treatment for Substance Abuse: A Multisite Randomized Controlled Trial." *The American Journal of Psychiatry* 171, 6 (2014): 683–690. doi: 10.1176/appi.ajp.2014.13081055.

Carnegie, Dale. *How to Win Friends and Influence People.* New York: Simon & Schuster, 2009.

Carroll, K. M, B. D. Kiluk, C. Nich, M. A. Gordon, G. A. Portnoy, D. R. Martino, and S. A. Ball. "Computer-Assisted Delivery of Cognitive-Behavioral Therapy: Efficacy and Durability of CBT4CBT among Cocaine-Dependent Individuals Maintained on Methadone." *The American Journal of Psychiatry* 171 (2014): 436–444.

Carroll, K. M., S. A. Ball, S. Martino, C. Nich, M. A. Gordon, G. A. Portnoy, and B. J. Rounsaville. "Computer-Assisted Delivery of Cognitive Behavioral Therapy for Addiction: A Randomized Trial of CBT4CBT." *The American Journal of Psychiatry* 165, 7 (2008): 881–889. PMCID: PMC2562873.

Carroll, K. M., S. A. Ball, S. Martino, C. Nich, T. A. Babuscio, and B. J. Rounsaville. "Enduring Effects of a Computer-Assisted Training Program for Cognitive Behavioral Therapy: A Six-Month Follow-Up of CBT4CBT." *Drug and Alcohol Dependence* 100 (2009): 178–181. PMCID: PMC2742309.

Caudill, Margaret. *Managing Pain before It Manages You.* 3rd ed. New York: Guilford Press, 2009.

Chida, Y., and A. Steptoe. "The Association of Anger and Hostility with Future Coronary Heart Disease: A Meta-Analytic Review of Prospective Evidence." *Journal of the American College of Cardiology* 53, 11 (2009): 936–946. doi: 10.1016/j.jacc.2008.11.044.

Chodron, P. *When Things Fall Apart: Heart Advice for Difficult Times.* New ed. Boston, MA: Shambhala Publications Inc., 2000.

Choy, Y., A. J. Fyer, and J. D. Lipsitz. "Treatment of Specific Phobia in Adults." *Clinical Psychology Review* 27, 3 (2007): 266–286. Epub 2006 Nov 15.

Cipani, E., and K. M. Schock. *Functional Behavioral Assessment, Diagnosis, and Treatment: A Complete System for Education and Mental Health Settings*. 2nd ed. New York: Springer Publishing Company, 2010.

Covey, S. R. *The 7 Habits of Highly Effective People*. 15th ed. New York: Free Press, 2004.

Cuijpers, P., A. van Straten, and L. Warmerdam. "Problem Solving Therapies for Depression: A Meta-Analysis." *European Psychiatry* 22, 1 (2007): 9–15.

Danner, D. D., D. A. Snowdon, and W. V. Friesen. "Positive Emotions in Early Life and Longevity: Findings from the Nun Study." Journal Personality Social Psychology 80, 5 (2001): 804–813.

Davis, M., E. R. Eshelman, and M. McKay. *The Relaxation & Stress Reduction Workbook*. 6th ed. San Francisco, CA: New Harbinger, 2008.

DeRubeis, R. J., S. D. Hollon, J. D. Amsterdam, R. C. Shelton, P. R. Young, R. M. Salomon, J. P. O'Reardon, M. L. Lovett, M. M. Gladis, L. L. Brown, and R. Gallop. "Cognitive Therapy vs. Medications in the Treatment of Moderate to Severe Depression." *Archives of General Psychiatry* 62, 4 (2005): 409–416.

Diener, E., E. M. Suh, R. E. Lucas, and H. E. Smith. "Subjective Well-Being: Three Decades of Progress." *Psychological Bulletin* 125 (1999): 276–302.

Dimeff, Linda A., and Kelly Koerner. *Dialectical Behavior Therapy in Clinical Practice: Applications across Disorders and Settings*. New York: The Guilford Press, 2007.

Dobson, K. *Handbook of Cognitive-Behavioral Therapies*. 3rd ed. New York: Guilford Press, 2010.

Dowling, G. A., J. Merrilees, J. Mastick, V. Y. Chang, E. Hubbard, and J. T. Moskowitz. "Life Enhancing Activities for Family Caregivers of People with Frontotemporal Dementia." *Alzheimer Disease and Associated Disorders*. 28, 2 (2014): 175–181. doi: 10.1097/WAD.0b013e3182a6b905.

Duhigg, C. *The Power of Habit: Why We Do What We Do in Life and Business*. New York: Random House, 2012.

Emmons, R., and M. McCullough. "Counting Blessings versus Burdens: An Experimental Investigation of Gratitude and Subjective Well-Being in Daily Life." *Journal of Personality and Social Psychology* 84, 2 (2003): 377–389.

Enright, R. D. *Forgiveness Is a Choice: A Step-By-Step Process for Resolving Anger and Restoring Hope*. Washington, DC: American Psychological Association, 2001.

Epstein, N. B., and D. H. Baucom. *Enhanced Cognitive-Behavioral Therapy for Couples: A Contextual Approach*. Washington, DC: American Psychological Association, 2002.

Fanning, P., and J. T. O'Neill. *The Addiction Workbook*. San Francisco: New Harbinger Press, 1996.

Farronato, N. S., K. M. Dürsteler-Macfarland, G. A. Wiesbeck, and S. A. Petitjean. "A Systematic Review Comparing Cognitive-Behavioral Therapy and Contingency Management for Cocaine Dependence." *Journal of Addictive Diseases* 32, 3 (2013): 274–287. doi: 10.1080/10550887.2013.824328.

Fehr, R., M. J. Gelfand, and M. Nag. "The Road to Forgiveness: A Meta-Analytic Synthesis of Its Situational and Dispositional Correlates." *Psychological Bulletin* 136, 5 (2010): 894–914. doi: 10.1037/a0019993.

Feldman, M., J. Christensen, and J. M. Satterfield. *Behavioral Medicine: A Guide for Clinical Practice*. 4th ed. Stamford, CT: McGraw-Hill, 2014.

Flegal, Katherine M., Margaret D. Carroll, Cynthia L. Ogden, and Lester R. Curtin. "Prevalence and Trends in Obesity among U.S. Adults, 1999–2008." *The Journal of the American Medical Association* 303, 3 (2010): 235–241. doi:10.1001/jama.2009.2014.

Frankl, V. *Man's Search for Meaning: An Introduction to Logotherapy*. Boston, MA: Beacon Press, 1959.

Franz, M. J., J. J. VanWormer, A. L. Crain, J. L. Boucher, T. Histon, W. Caplan, J. D. Bowman, and N. P. Pronk. "Weight-Loss Outcomes: A Systematic Review and Meta-Analysis of Weight-Loss Clinical Trials with a Minimum 1-Year Follow-Up." *Journal of the American Dietetic Association* 107, 10 (2007): 1755–1767.

Fredrickson, B. L. *Love 2.0: Finding Happiness and Health in Moments of Connection.* New York: Plume, 2013.

Fredrickson, B. L., M. A. Cohn, K. A. Coffey, J. Pek, and S. M. Finkel. "Open Hearts Build Lives: Positive Emotions, Induced through Loving-Kindness Meditation, Build Consequential Personal Resources." *Journal of Personality and Social Psychology* 95, 5 (2008): 1045–1062. doi: 10.1037/a0013262.

Fredrickson, B. L., M. M. Tugade, C. E. Waugh, and G. R. Larkin. "A Prospective Study of Resilience and Emotions following the Terrorist Attacks on the United States on September 11th, 2001." *Journal of Personality and Social Psychology* 84, 2 (2003): 365–376.

Fredrickson, Barbara L., and Christine Branigan. "Positive Emotions Broaden the Scope of Attention and Thought-Action Repertoires." *Cognition & Emotion* 19, 3 (2005): 313–332.

Fredrickson, Barbara L., Karen M. Grewen, Kimberly A. Coffey, Sara B. Algoe, Ann M. Firestine, Jesusa M. G. Arevalo, Jeffrey Ma, and Steven W. Cole. "A Functional Genomic Perspective on Human Well-Being." *Proceedings of the National Academy of Sciences* 110, 33 (2013): 13684–13689. Published ahead of print 2013 July 29. doi: 10.1073/pnas.1305419110.

Fresco, David M., Nina K. Rytwinski, and Linda W. Craighead. "Explanatory Flexibility and Negative Life Events Interact to Predict Depression Symptoms." *Journal of Social and Clinical Psychology* 26, 5 (2007): 595–608.

Frewen, P. A., D. J. Dozois, and R. A. Lanius. "Neuroimaging Studies of Psychological Interventions for Mood and Anxiety Disorders: Empirical and Methodological Review." *Clinical Psychology Review* 28 (2008): 228–246.

Friedman, M., C. E. Thoresen, J. J. Gill, D. Ulmer, L. H. Powell, V. A. Price, B. Brown, L. Thompson, D. D. Rabin, W. S. Breall, et al. "Alteration of Type A Behavior and Its Effect on Cardiac Recurrences in Post Myocardial Infarction Patients: Summary Results of the Recurrent Coronary Prevention Project." *American Heart Journal* 112, 4 (1986): 653–665.

Friedmann, E., and S. A. Thomas. "Pet Ownership, Social Support, and One-Year Survival after Acute Myocardial Infarction in the Cardiac Arrhythmia Suppression Trial (CAST)." *American Journal of Cardiology* 76, 17 (1995): 1213–1217.

Gardner, C. D., A. Kiazand, S. Alhassan, S. Kim, R. S. Stafford, R. R. Balise, H. C. Kraemer, and A. C. King. "Comparison of the Atkins, Zone, Ornish, and LEARN Diets for Change in Weight and Related Risk Factors among Overweight Premenopausal Women: The A to Z Weight Loss Study—A Randomized Trial." *The Journal of the American Medical Association* 297, 9 (2007): 969–977.

Gawaine, S. *Creative Visualisation.* 2nd ed. New York: Bantam, 1997.

Glombiewski, J. A., A. T. Sawyer, J. Gutermann, K. Koenig, W. Rief, and S. G. Hofmann. "Psychological Treatments for Fibromyalgia: A Meta-Analysis." *Pain* 151, 2 (2010): 280–295. doi: 10.1016/j.pain.2010.06.011. Epub 2010 Aug 19.

Goldapple, K., et al. "Modulation of Cortical-Limbic Pathways in Major Depression: Treatment Specific Effects of CBT." *Archives of General Psychiatry* 61, 1 (2004): 34–41.

Goldapple, K., Z. Segal, C. Garson, et al. "Modulation of Cortical-Limbic Pathways in Major Depression: Treatment-Specific Effects of Cognitive Behavior Therapy." *Archives of General Psychiatry* 61 (2004): 34–41.

Goldman, D. B., and N. G. Wade. "Comparison of Forgiveness and Anger-Reduction Group Treatments: A Randomized Controlled Trial." *Psychotherapy Research* 22, 5 (2012): 604–620. doi: 10.1080/10503307.2012.692954. Epub 2012 Jun 12.

Gottman, J. M., and N. Silver. *The 7 Principles for Making Marriage Work.* New York: Three Rivers Press, 2000.

Greenberger, D., and C. A. Padesky. *Mind over Mood: A Cognitive Therapy Treatment Manual for Clients.* New York: Guilford, 1995.

Grossman, P., L. Niemann, S. Schmidt, and H. Walach. "Mindfulness-Based Stress Reduction and Health Benefits: A Meta-Analysis." *Journal of Psychosomatic Research* 57, 1 (2004): 35–43.

Groth-Marnat, G. *Handbook of Psychological Assessment.* 5th ed. New York: Wiley, 2009.

Gruber, A. J., H. G. Pope, J. I. Hudson, and D. Yurgelun-Todd. "Attributes of Long-Term Heavy Cannabis Users: A Case-Control Study." *Psychological Medicine* 33 (2003): 1415–1422.

Harris, A. H., F. Luskin, S. B. Norman, S. Standard, J. Bruning, S. Evans, and C. E. Thoresen. "Effects of a Group Forgiveness Intervention on Forgiveness, Perceived Stress, and Trait-Anger." *Journal of Clinical Psychology* 62, 6 (2006): 715–733.

Hayes, S. C. *Get Out of Your Mind and Into Your Life: The New Acceptance and Commitment Therapy.* Oakland, CA: New Harbinger Publications Inc., 2005.

Hendrix, H. *Getting the Love You Want: A Guide for Couples.* 20th ed. New York: Holt Paperbacks, 2008.

Henschke, N., R. W. Ostelo, M. W. van Tulder, J. W. Vlaeyen, S. Morley, W. J. Assendelft, and C. J. Main. "Behavioural Treatment for Chronic Low-Back Pain." *Cochrane Database of Systematic Reviews* 7 (2010): CD002014.

Hunot, V., R. Churchill, V. Teixeira, and M. Silva de Lima. "Psychological Therapies for Generalised Anxiety Disorder." *Cochrane Database of Systematic Reviews* 1 (2007): CD001848. doi: 10.1002/14651858. CD001848.pub4.

Hunot, V., T. H. M. Moore, D. M. Caldwell, T. A. Furukawa, P. Davies, H. Jones, M. Honyashiki, P. Chen, G. Lewis, and R. Churchill. "'Third Wave' Cognitive and Behavioural Therapies versus Other Psychological Therapies for Depression." *Cochrane Database of Systematic Reviews* 10 (2013): CD008704.

Ipser, J., S. Seedat, and D. J. Stein. "Pharmacotherapy for Post-Traumatic Stress Disorder: A Systematic Review and Meta-Analysis." *South African Medical Journal* 96, 10 (2006): 1088–1096.

Iribarren, C., S. Sidney, D. E. Bild, K. Liu, J. H. Markovitz, J. M. Roseman, and K. Matthews. "Association of Hostility with Coronary Artery Calcification in Young Adults: The CARDIA Study—Coronary Artery Risk Development in Young Adults." *The Journal of the American Medical Association* 283, 19 (2000): 2546–2551.

Jacobs, Eric J., Christina C. Newton, Yiting Wang, Alpa V. Patel, Marjorie L. McCullough, Peter T. Campbell, Michael J. Thun, and Susan M. Gapstur. "Waist Circumference and All-Cause Mortality in a Large U.S. Cohort." *Archives of Internal Medicine* 170, 15 (2010): 1293–1301. doi: 10.1001/archinternmed.2010.201.

Jacobs, G. D. *Say Goodnight to Insomnia*. New York: Holt, 1998.

Jacobs, G. D., E. F. Pace-Schott, R. Stickgold, and M. W. Otto. "Cognitive Behavior Therapy and Pharmacotherapy for Insomnia: A Randomized Controlled Trial and Direct Comparison." *Archives of Internal Medicine* 164, 17 (2004): 1888–1896.

Jacobson, N. S., and S. D. Hollon. "Cognitive-Behavior Therapy versus Pharmacotherapy: Now That the Jury's Returned Its Verdict, It's Time to Present the Rest of the Evidence." *Journal of Consulting and Clinical Psychology* 64, 1 (1996): 74–80.

Judge, T. A., D. M. Cable, J. W. Boudreau, and R. D. Bretz Jr. "An Empirical Investigation of the Predictors of Executive Career Success." CAHRS Working Paper #94-08. Ithaca, NY: Cornell University, 1994.

Kabat-Zinn, J. *Full Catastrophe Living: Using the Wisdom of Your Body and Mind to Face Stress, Pain, and Illness.* New York: Bantam Dell, 1990.

Kazdin, A. "Mediators and Mechanisms of Change in Psychotherapy Research." *Annual Review of Clinical Psychology* 3 (2007): 1–27.

Kenny, S. J, et al. "Survey of Physician Practice Behaviors Related to Diabetes Mellitus in the U.S.: Physician Adherence to Consensus Recommendations." *Diabetes Care* 16 (1993): 1507–1510.

Kersting, Annette, et al. "Brief Internet-Based Intervention Reduces Posttraumatic Stress and Prolonged Grief in Parents after the Loss of a Child during Pregnancy: A Randomized Controlled Trial." *Psychotherapy and Psychosomatics* 82 (2013): 372–381.

Kessler, David. *The End of Overeating: Taking Control of the Insatiable American Appetite.* Emmaus, PA: Rodale Books, 2010.

Knittle, K., S. Maes, and V. de Gucht. "Psychological Interventions for Rheumatoid Arthritis: Examining the Role of Self-Regulation with a Systematic Review and Meta-Analysis of Randomized Controlled Trials." *Arthritis Care and Research* 62, 10 (2010): 1460–1472. doi: 10.1002/acr.20251.

Koenig, H., D. King, and V. B. Carson. *Handbook of Religion and Health.* New York: Oxford University Press, 2012.

Lambert, N. M., T. F. Stillman, J. A. Hicks, S. Kamble, R. F. Baumeister, and F. D. Fincham. "To Belong Is to Matter: Sense of Belonging Enhances Meaning in Life." *Personality and Social Psychology Bulletin* 39, 11 (2013): 1418–1427. doi: 10.1177/0146167213499186. Epub 2013 Aug 15.

Landenberger, N. A., and M. W. Lipsey. "The Positive Effects of Cognitive-Behavioral Programs for Offenders: A Meta-Analysis of Factors Associated with Effective Treatment." *Journal of Experimental Criminology* 1 (2005): 451–476.

Langer, E. J., and J. Rodin. "The Effects of Choice and Enhanced Personal Responsibility for the Aged: A Field Experiment in an Institutional Setting." *Journal of Personality and Social Psychology* 34, 2 (1976): 191–198.

Layden, M. A., C. F. Newman, A. Freeman, and S. B. Morse. *Cognitive Therapy of Borderline Personality Disorder*. Boston, MA: Allyn & Bacon, 1993.

Lazarus, R. S., and S. Folkman. *Stress, Appraisal and Coping*. New York: Springer, 1984.

Lehrer, P. M., R. L. Woolfolk, and W. E. Sime. *Principles and Practice of Stress Management*. 3rd ed. New York: Guilford Press, 2007.

Levin, T. T., C. A. White, and D. W. Kissane. "A Review of Cognitive Therapy in Acute Medical Settings: Part I—Therapy Model and Assessment." *Palliative and Supportive Care* 11, 2 (2013): 141–153. doi: 10.1017/S147895151200082X. Epub 2012 Nov 22.

Linehan, M. M., H. E. Armstrong, A. Suarez, D. Allmon, and H. L. Heard. "Cognitive Behavioral Treatment of Chronically Parasuicidal Borderline Patients." *Archives of General Psychology* 48 (1991): 1060–1064.

Linehan, M. M., H. Schmidt III, L. A. Dimeff, J. C. Craft, J. Kanter, and K. A. Comtois. "Dialectical Behavior Therapy for Patients with Borderline Personality Disorder and Drug-Dependence." *The American Journal on Addictions* 8, 4 (1999): 279–292.

Lipsey, M. W., N. A. Landenberger, and S. J. Wilson. "Effects of Cognitive-Behavioral Programs for Criminal Offenders." *Campbell Systematic Reviews* 6 (2007): 1–27. doi: 10.4073/csr.2007.6.

Luskin, F. *Forgive for Good: A Proven Prescription for Health and Happiness*. New York: HarperOne, 2003.

Mackintosh, M. A., L. A. Morland, B. C. Frueh, C. J. Greene, and C. S. Rosen. "Peeking into the Black Box: Mechanisms of Action for Anger Management Treatment." *Journal of Anxiety Disorders* 28, 7 (2014): 687–695. doi: 10.1016/j.janxdis.2014.07.001.

Martin, Susan E. "The Epidemiology of Alcohol-Related Interpersonal Violence." *Alcohol Health & Research World* 16, 3 (1992): 230–237.

Maslach, C. *The Truth about Burnout: How Organizations Cause Personal Stress and What to Do about It.* San Francisco, CA: Jossey-Bass, 1997.

McGinnis, J. M., and W. H. Foege. "Actual Causes of Death in the United States." *The Journal of the American Medical Association* 270, 18 (1993): 2207–2212.

McGinnis, J. M., P. Williams-Russo, and J. R. Knickman. "The Case for More Active Policy Attention to Health Promotion." *Health Affairs* 21, 2 (2002): 78–93.

McGonigal, K. *The Willpower Instinct: How Self-Control Works, Why It Matters, and How You Can Get More of It.* New York: Penguin Books, 2012.

McKay, M., P. D. Rogers, and J. McKay. *When Anger Hurts: Quieting the Storm Within.* 2nd ed. San Francisco, CA: New Harbinger, 2003.

Mendoza, T. R., X. S. Wang, C. S. Cleeland, et al. "The Rapid Assessment of Fatigue Severity in Cancer Patients: Use of the Brief Fatigue Inventory." *Cancer* 85, 5 (1999): 1186–1196.

Miller, W., and S. Rollnick. *Motivational Interviewing: Helping People to Change.* 3rd ed. New York: Guilford Press, 2012.

Mitchell, M. D., P. Gehrman, M. Perlis, and C. A. Umscheid. "Comparative Effectiveness of Cognitive Behavioral Therapy for Insomnia: A Systematic Review." *BMC Family Practice* 13 (2012): 40. doi: 10.1186/1471-2296-13-40.

Mitchell, P. H., L. Powell, J. Blumenthal, J. Norten, G. Ironson, C. R. Pitula, et al. "A Short Social Support Measure for Patients Recovering from Myocardial Infarction: The ENRICHD Social Support Inventory." *Journal of Cardiopulmonary Rehabilitation and Prevention* 23 (2003): 398–403.

Mitte, K. "A Meta-Analysis of the Efficacy of Psycho- and Pharmacotherapy in Panic Disorder with and without Agoraphobia." *Journal of Affective Disorders* 88, 1 (2005): 27–45.

Mokdad, A. H., J. S. Marks, D. F. Stroup, and J. L. Gerberding. "Actual Causes of Death in the United States, 2000." *The Journal of the American Medical Association* 291, 10 (2004): 1238–1245.

Morin, C. M., C. Colecchi, J. Stone, R. Sood, and D. Brink. "Behavioral and Pharmacological Therapies for Late-Life Insomnia: A Randomized Controlled Trial." *The Journal of the American Medical Association* 281, 11 (1999): 991–999.

Moskowitz, J. T., D. Shmueli-Blumberg, M. Acree, and S. Folkman. "Positive Affect in the Midst of Distress: Implications for Role Functioning." *Journal of Community & Applied Social Psychology* 22, 6 (2012): 502–518.

Moskowitz, J. T., J. R. Hult, L. G. Duncan, M. A. Cohn, S. Maurer, C. Bussolari, and M. Acree. "A Positive Affect Intervention for People Experiencing Health-Related Stress: Development and Non-Randomized Pilot Test." *Journal of Health Psychology* 17, 5 (2012): 676–692. doi: 10.1177/1359105311425275. Epub 2011 Oct 21.

O'Boyle, E. H., R. H. Humphrey, J. M. Pollack, T. H. Hawver, and P. A. Story. "The Relation Between Emotional Intelligence and Job Performance: A Meta-Analysis." *Journal of Organizational Behavior* 32 (2011): 788–818. doi: 10.1002/job.714.

O'Connell Higgins, Gina. *Resilient Adults: Overcoming a Cruel Past.* New York: Wiley, 1996.

Ong, A. D., C. S. Bergeman, T. L. Bisconti, and K. A. Wallace. "Psychological Resilience, Positive Emotions, and Successful Adaptation to Stress in Later Life." *Journal of Personality and Social Psychology* 91, 4 (2006): 730.

Ost, Lars-Göran. "The Efficacy of Acceptance and Commitment Therapy: An Updated Systematic Review and Meta-Analysis." *Behaviour Research and Therapy* 61 (2014): 105–121. Epub 2014 Aug 19.

Papa, A., M. T. Sewell, C. Garrison-Diehn, and C. Rummel. "A Randomized Open Trial Assessing the Feasibility of Behavioral Activation for Pathological Grief Responding." *Behavior Therapy* 44, 4 (2013): 639–650. doi: 10.1016/j.beth.2013.04.009. Epub 2013 Apr 26.

Partnership for Solutions. "Chronic Conditions: Making the Case for Ongoing Care." September 2004 Update. Baltimore, MD: Johns Hopkins University for the Robert Wood Johnson Foundation, 2004.

Perrin, J. M., C. J. Homer, D. M. Berwick, A. D. Woolf, J. L. Freeman, and J. E. Wennberg. "Variations in Rates of Hospitalization of Children in Three Urban Communities." *New England Journal of Medicine* 320 (1989): 1183–1187.

Persons, J. *The Case Formulation Approach to Cognitive-Behavior Therapy.* New York: Guilford Press, 2008.

Piet, J., and E. Hougaard. "The Effect of Mindfulness-Based Cognitive Therapy for Prevention of Relapse in Recurrent Major Depressive Disorder: A Systematic Review and Meta-Analysis." *Clinical Psychology Review* 31, 6 (2011): 1032–1040.

Pimenta, Filipa, Isabel Leal, João Maroco, and Catarina Ramos. "Brief Cognitive-Behavioral Therapy for Weight Loss in Midlife Women: A Controlled Study with Follow-Up." *International Journal of Women's Health* 4 (2012): 559–567. Published online 2012 Oct 12. doi: 10.2147/IJWH.S35246.

Piper, B. F., S. L. Dibble, M. J. Dodd, et al. "The Revised Piper Fatigue Scale: Psychometric Evaluation in Women with Breast Cancer." *Oncology Nursing Forum* 25, 4 (1998): 677–684.

Pronk, T. M., J. C. Karremans, G. Overbeek, A. A. Vermulst, and D. H. J. Wigboldus. "What It Takes to Forgive: When and Why Executive Functioning Facilitates Forgiveness." *Journal of Personality and Social Psychology* 98 (2010): 119–131.

Reivich, K., and A. Shatte. *The Resilience Factor: 7 Keys to Finding Your Inner Strength and Overcoming Life's Hurdles*. New York: Broadway Publishing, 2002.

Robertson, Donald. *Build Your Resilience: How to Survive and Thrive in Any Situation*. New York: McGraw-Hill, 2012.

Rothbaum, B., E. Foa, and E. Hembree. *Reclaiming Your Life from a Traumatic Experience: A Prolonged Exposure Treatment Program Workbook*. New York: Oxford University Press, 2007.

Rye, M. S., K. I. Pargament, W. Pan, D. W. Yingling, K. A. Shogren, and M. Ito. "Can Group Interventions Facilitate Forgiveness of an Ex-Spouse? A Randomized Clinical Trial." *Journal of Consulting and Clinical Psychology* 73, 5 (2005): 880–892.

Salkovskis, P. "The Cognitive Approach to Anxiety: Threat Beliefs, Safety-Seeking Behaviours and the Special Case of Health Anxiety and Obsessions." In *The Frontiers of Cognitive Therapy*, edited by P. Salkovskis, 48–74. New York: Guilford Press, 1996.

Salzberg, S. *Loving-Kindness: The Revolutionary Art of Happiness.* Rev. ed. Boston, MA: Shambhala Publications Inc., 2002.

Sanders, D., and F. Wills. *Cognitive Therapy: An Introduction*. London: SAGE, 2005.

Sapolsky, R. *Why Zebras Don't Get Ulcers*. New York: Holt Paperbacks, 2004.

Satterfield, J. M. *A Cognitive-Behavioral Approach to the Beginning of the End of Life: Minding the Body*. New York: Oxford University Press, 2008.

———. *Minding the Body: Workbook*. New York: Oxford University Press, 2008.

Schnurr, Paula P., Matthew J. Friedman, Charles C. Engel, Edna B. Foa, M. Tracie Shea, Bruce K. Chow, Patricia A. Resick, Veronica Thurston, Susan M. Orsillo, Rodney Haug, Carole Turner, and Nancy Bernardy. "Cognitive Behavioral Therapy for Posttraumatic Stress Disorder in Women: A Randomized Controlled Trial." *The Journal of the American Medical Association* 297, 8 (2007): 820–830. doi: 10.1001/jama.297.8.820.

Segal, Z. V., M. G. Williams, and J. D. Teasdale. *Mindfulness-Based Cognitive Therapy for Depression: A New Approach to Preventing Relapse*. New York: Guilford Press, 2002.

Segal, Z., P. Vincent, and A. Levitt. "Efficacy of Combined, Sequential and Crossover Psychotherapy and Pharmacotherapy in Improving Outcomes in Depression." *Journal of Psychiatry and Neuroscience* 27, 4 (2002): 281–290.

Seligman, M. E. P. *Authentic Happiness: Using the New Positive Psychology to Realize Your Potential for Lasting Fulfillment*. New York: Free Press, 2004.

———. *Flourish: A Visionary New Understanding of Happiness and Well-Being*. New York: Free Press, 2012.

———. *Learned Optimism*. New York: Alfred Knopf, 1991.

Shapiro, F. *Eye Movement Desensitization and Reprocessing (EMDR): Basic Principles, Protocols and Procedures*. New York: Guilford Press, 2001.

Shklovski, Irina, Robert Kraut, and Jonathon Cummings. "Keeping in Touch by Technology: Maintaining Friendships after a Residential Move." *Proceedings of the Twenty-Sixth Annual SIGCHI Conference on Human Factors in Computing Systems* 978-1-60558-011-1 (2008). http://doi.acm.org/10.1145/1357054.1357182.

Singer, B., and C. D. Ryff. "Hierarchies of Life Histories and Associated Health Risks." *Annals of the New York Academy of Sciences* 896 (1999): 96–115.

Sivertsen, B., S. Omvik, S. Pallesen, B. Bjorvatn, O. E. Havik, G. Kvale, G. H. Nielsen, and I. H. Nordhus. "Cognitive Behavioral Therapy vs. Zopiclone for Treatment of Chronic Primary Insomnia in Older Adults: A Randomized Controlled Trial." *The Journal of the American Medical Association* 295, 24 (2006): 2851–2858.

Smith, M. T., M. L. Perlis, A. Park, M. S. Smith, J. Pennington, D. E. Giles, and D. J. Buysse. "Comparative Meta-Analysis of Pharmacotherapy and Behavior Therapy for Persistent Insomnia." *American Journal of Psychiatry* 159, 1 (2002): 5–11.

Smith, P. C., S. M. Schmidt, D. Allensworth-Davies, and R. Saitz. "Primary Care Validation of a Single-Question Alcohol Screening Test." *Journal of General Internal Medicine* 24, 7 (2009): 783–788.

Smyth, J. M., et al. "Effects of Writing about Stressful Experiences on Symptom Reduction in Patients with Asthma or Rheumatoid Arthritis: A Randomized Trial." *The Journal of the American Medical Association* 281, 14 (1999): 1304–1309.

Snyder, C. R. *Coping: The Psychology of What Works.* New York: Oxford University Press, 1999.

Stagl, J. M., M. H. Antoni, S. C. Lechner, L. C. Bouchard, B. B. Blomberg, S. Glück, R. P. Derhagopian, and C. S. Carver. "Randomized Controlled Trial of Cognitive Behavioral Stress Management in Breast Cancer: A Brief Report of Effects on 5-Year Depressive Symptoms." *Health Psychology* 34, 2 (2015): 176–180.

Stockwell, D. H., S. Madhavan, H. Cohen, G. Gibson, and M. H. Alderman. "The Determinants of Hypertension Awareness, Treatment, and Control in an Insured Population." *American Journal of Public Health* 84 (1994): 1768–1774.

Swain, J., K. Hancock, C. Hainsworth, and J. Bowman. "Acceptance and Commitment Therapy in the Treatment of Anxiety: A Systematic Review." *Clinical Psychology Review* 33, 8 (2013): 965–978. doi: 10.1016/j. cpr.2013.07.002. Epub 2013 Jul 16.

Teasdale, J. D., Z. V. Segal, J. M. G. Williams, V. A. Ridgeway, J. M. Soulsby, and M. A. Lau. "Prevention of Relapse/Recurrence in Major Depression by Mindfulness-Based Cognitive Therapy." *Journal of Consulting and Clinical Psychology* 68, 4 (2000): 615–623.

Toussaint, L., M. Barry, L. Bornfriend, and M. Markman. "Restore: The Journey toward Self-Forgiveness—A Randomized Trial of Patient Education on Self-Forgiveness in Cancer Patients and Caregivers." *Journal of Health Care Chaplaincy* 20, 2 (2014): 54–74.

Tugade, M. M., and B. L. Fredrickson. "Resilient Individuals Use Positive Emotions to Bounce Back from Negative Emotional Experiences." *Journal of Personality and Social Psychology* 86 (2004): 320–333.

Unützer, J., D. Powers, W. Katon, and C. Langston. "From Establishing an Evidence-Based Practice to Implementation in Real-World Settings: IMPACT as a Case Study." *Psychiatric Clinics of North America* 28, 4 (2005): 1079–1092.

Wagner, E. H. "Chronic Disease Management: What Will It Take to Improve Care for Chronic Illness?" *Effective Clinical Practice* 1 (1998): 2–4.

Wagner, E. H., B. T. Austin, C. Davis, M. Hindmarsh, J. Schaefer, and A. Bonomi. "Improving Chronic Illness Care: Translating Evidence into Action." *Health Affairs* 20 (2001): 64–78.

Watts, B. V., P. P. Schnurr, L. Mayo, Y. Young-Xu, W. B. Weeks, and M. J. Friedman. "Meta-Analysis of the Efficacy of Treatments for Posttraumatic Stress Disorder." *Journal of Clinical Psychiatry* 74, 6 (2013): 541–550. doi: 10.4088/JCP.12r08225.

Waugh, C. E., R. J. Thompson, and I. H. Gotlib. "Flexible Emotional Responsiveness in Trait Resilience." *Emotion* 11, 5 (2011): 1059–1067. doi: 10.1037/a0021786.

Wen, C. P., J. P. M. Wai, M. K. Tsai, Y. C. Yang, T. Y. D. Cheng, M. Lee, H. T. Chan, C. K. Tsao, S. P. Tsai, and X. Wu. "Minimum Amount of Physical Activity for Reduced Mortality and Extended Life Expectancy: A Prospective Cohort Study." *The Lancet* 378, 9798 (2011): 1244–1253.

Werner, E. E. "The Value of Applied Research for Head Start: A Cross-Cultural and Longitudinal Perspective." *National Head Start Association Research Quarterly* 1 (1997): 15–24.

Wildman, R. P., P. Muntner, K. Reynolds, A. P. McGinn, S. Rajpathak, J. Wylie-Rosett, and M. R. Sowers. "The Obese without Cardiometabolic Risk Factor Clustering and the Normal Weight with Cardiometabolic Risk Factor Clustering: Prevalence and Correlates of 2 Phenotypes among the U.S. Population (NHANES 1999–2004)." *Archives of Internal Medicine* 168 (2008): 1617–1624.

Wilfley, Denise E., Rachel P. Kolko, and Andrea E. Kass. "Cognitive Behavioral Therapy for Weight Management and Eating Disorders in Children and Adolescents." *Child & Adolescent Psychiatric Clinics of North America* 20, 2 (2011): 271–285.

Williams, A. C., C. Eccleston, and S. Morley. "Psychological Therapies for the Management of Chronic Pain (Excluding Headache) in Adults." *Cochrane Database of Systematic Reviews* 11 (2012): CD007407. doi: 10.1002/14651858.CD007407.pub3.

Williams, M. J. G., J. D. Teasdale, Z. V. Segal, and J. Kabat-Zinn. *The Mindful Way through Depression.* New York: Guilford Press, 2007. (With accompanying CD.)

Online Therapy Worksheets

Psychology Tools.

    http://psychology.tools/download-therapy-worksheets.html.

Internet Resources

American Pain Society.

    http://www.americanpainsociety.org.

American Psychological Association.

    http://www.apa.org/helpcenter/index.aspx.

Association for Behavioral and Cognitive Therapies.

    http://www.abct.org/home.

CBT4CBT: Computer-Based Training for Cognitive Behavioral Therapy.

    http://www.cbt4cbt.com.

The Drinker's Checkup.

    http://www.drinkerscheckup.com.

i4Health at Palo Alto University. Institute for International Internet Interventions for Health.

https://www.i4health-pau.org/.

i4Health at Palo Alto University. Institute for International Internet Interventions for Health. CBT Online Training Resources.

https://www.i4health-pau.org/cbt-online-training-resources/.

The Latino Mental Health Research Program of the University of California, San Francisco, and San Francisco General Hospital.

http://medschool2.ucsf.edu/latino/.

MyTOPCare.

http://mytopcare.org/patients/.

National Institute on Alcohol Abuse and Alcoholism (NIAAA).

http://pubs.niaaa.nih.gov/Publications/Practitioner/CliniciansGuide 2005/Guide_Slideshow.htm.

National Registry of Evidence-Based Practices and Programs (NREPP).

http://www.nrepp.samhsa.gov/Index.aspx.

Quantified Self: Guide to Self-Tracking Tools.

http://quantifiedself.com/guide/.

QuitNet.

www.quitnet.com.

Smokefree.gov.

http://smokefree.gov.

Substance Abuse and Mental Health Services Administration (SAMHSA).

http://www.samhsa.gov/sbirt.

Therapeutic Education System (TES).

http://sudtech.org/about/.

TreatmentsThatWork. Oxford University Press.

http://global.oup.com/us/companion.websites/umbrella/treatments/.

Image Credits

Notes